Measuring and Evaluating School Learning

LOU M. CAREY
UNIVERSITY OF SOUTH FLORIDA

Measuring and Evaluating School Learning

ALLYN AND BACON, INC.
BOSTON   LONDON   SYDNEY   TORONTO

Copyright © 1988 by Allyn and Bacon, Inc.
A Division of Simon & Schuster
7 Wells Avenue
Newton, Massachusetts 02159

Library of Congress Cataloging-in-Publication Data

Carey, Lou.
   Measuring and evaluating school learning.

   Includes bibliographies and index.
   1. Educational tests and measurements—United States.
I. Title.
LB3051.C36   1988   371.2'6'0973   87–17569
ISBN 0–205–11109–2

Series editor: Mylan Jaixen
Production administrator: Annette Joseph
Production coordinator: Helyn Pultz
Editorial-production services: Wordsworth Associates/Grace Sheldrick
Cover administrator: Linda K. Dickinson
Cover designer: Susan Slovinsky

Printed in the United States of America

10 9 8 7 6 5 4 3 2 1   92 91 90 89 88 87

BRIEF CONTENTS

COMPLETE CONTENTS

PREFACE

Measuring and Evaluating School Learning focuses on the information and skills teachers need to design, develop, analyze, and interpret tests; to use test results in planning, monitoring, and evaluating instruction; and to evaluate student progress. It is directed to undergraduate education students who are preparing to teach and to graduate students who want to improve their teaching and testing skills. It can also serve as a reference for educators in schools, universities, businesses, and government agencies.

The book assumes that readers have had little, if any, instruction in educational measurement, evaluation, or statistics. The practice exercises require readers to be familiar with the curriculum and skills in their field, with basic learning principles, and with the application of these principles to their discipline.

Some teachers believe they do not need the skills to design their own tests because textbook publishers provide tests to accompany their instructional materials. Teachers who adopt this position, however, will be poorly prepared to evaluate and adapt commercially prepared tests, supplement these tests with other tests, and develop tests when suitable ones are not available.

Testing is an integral part of the teaching and learning process, and it provides teachers with vital information. Teachers use readiness tests to determine whether students have the knowledge and skills necessary to begin a unit of instruction. Pretests help teachers identify skills that need to be emphasized during instruction. With practice tests, teachers can monitor skill development, identify instructional needs, and pace the instruction. Finally, posttests help teachers evaluate student progress and locate inadequacies in instruction.

Measuring and Evaluating School Learning presents the following three-part process for constructing and using tests: Part I, Planning for Instruction and Tests; Part II, Designing, Developing, and Using Classroom Tests; and Part III, Communicating Student Progress. Part I, Planning for Instruction and Tests, includes identifying and sequencing instructional goals, describing students' achievement characteristics, analyzing instructional goals, and writing behavioral objectives. Part II, Designing, Developing, and Using Classroom Tests, includes considering validity and reliability in designing tests, creating tables of test specifications, writing items, developing scoring procedures, and interpreting results. Test development is described for objective tests, essay tests, product development tests, and performance tests. Procedures for developing and using behavior observation forms are also included. Finally, the use of test results for evaluating tests, instruction, group performance, and individual performance is described. Part III, Communicating Student Progress, includes procedures for grading and reporting student progress and for interpreting students' performance on standardized tests.

Beginning with Chapter 2, each chapter includes a list of learning outcomes (objectives) to direct the reader's study. Applicable concepts, principles, and procedures are introduced for each phase, and accompanying examples refer to instructional goals taken from actual school curriculum guides. Each chapter after Chapter 1 concludes with a summary of key concepts and procedures, practice exercises, and a feedback section that provides answers and example solutions. Because readers' answers to many of the exercises will vary, the practice and feedback sections can serve as a basis for classroom discussions.

The book is intended for all students enrolled in an introductory measurement course for teachers. Such students typically are from a variety of disciplines, such as language arts, mathematics, science, social studies, physical education, business education, elementary education, and special education. Because these students have diverse backgrounds, they do not have the discipline expertise required to analyze correctly the instructional goals in secondary school curricula for disciplines other than their own. For example, students who are expert in American government, chemistry, or music can be expected to understand illustrations and apply skills in these disciplines. However, students lacking expertise in these areas would be at a disadvantage. Because similar problems surface, regardless of the discipline, areas chosen for illustrations and exercises were purposefully selected from common knowledge disciplines (e.g., analyzing goals related to reading maps, capitalization, and paragraph construction). All students, regardless of their majors, will be able to analyze such goals correctly, and they will find such analyses quite challenging.

Students must be able to look beyond the content of the goals in order to concentrate on the learning, measurement, and evaluation principles and procedures involved. After applying these skills using basic examples, they will be prepared to transfer them to their own disciplines for class projects or for their own work. Completing the activities prescribed in the enrichment section of the practice exercises for each chapter will also help students transfer the skills to their own disciplines.

These common knowledge examples also have an advantage for teachers of this course. Like students, our areas of expertise beyond measurement and evaluation are diverse. Using basic skills examples enables us to provide many illustrations, adequate guidance, and corrective feedback to students as they perform the tasks.

Many individuals participated in the formative evaluation of this book. I would like to acknowledge my colleagues, Roger Wilk and Constance Hines, who have field-tested versions of the text with their classes and have provided valuable criticism on content, organization, presentation, and effectiveness. Students in my classes also used field-test versions and provided valuable guidance. The following students deserve special mention: Sue Beck, elementary education; Mark Lange, English education; John Myrick, physics education; Allison Salisbury, biology education; and Katie Winterhalter, mathematics education. Working as a small field-test group, these individuals applied each chapter to their majors and substantially influenced the final version of the text. Their contributions have undoubtedly increased its relevance for other students who want to learn testing principles and procedures. I also wish to acknowledge Linda Laugin for her editorial assistance and Grace Sheldrick, Wordsworth Associates, for her editorial/production assistance.

Special thanks also are due to the following people who reviewed the manuscript of this book: Tony Allen, The University of Rhode Island; James Applefield, The University of North Carolina at Wilmington; Steve Dunbar, The University of Iowa; Richard Jaeger, The University of North Carolina at Charlotte; Don Mizokawa, University of Washington; Bruce Rogers, University of Northern Iowa; John Sanderston, University of Virginia; Landa Trentham, Auburn University; and Gaylen Wallace, University of Missouri – St. Louis.

Measuring and Evaluating School Learning

CHAPTER 1

Introduction

Teachers choose their careers in the classroom for a variety of reasons. Some enjoy a particular subject, some have been inspired by teachers they had when they were students, and others enjoy helping people learn. Few, if any, enter the profession because they want to design and develop tests or interpret test results. Testing, however, plays a vital role in teaching. It also can help you refine your teaching skills throughout your career.

Effective teachers must also be proficient in testing, and proficiency in testing requires the synthesis of many different skills. Teachers must know about their discipline; about the nature of learning; and about their students' language skills, interests, and experiences. They must be able to write clearly, summarize and analyze data, and make comparisons and inferences to interpret test results. In applying testing principles and procedures, they must use their professional judgment and make informed guesses about their methods and instruction. Because teaching is a decision-based activity, the quality of instruction will depend on teachers' ability to gather, interpret, and use relevant information.

This text discusses all aspects of test development, use, and interpretation. Each chapter begins with a list of objectives that should help direct your study. The objectives are followed by relevant concepts, principles, and procedures. Many tables and figures illustrate the concepts and procedures, and a summary section concludes each chapter. To help you develop your testing skills, each chapter ends with a comprehensive set of practice exercises. Many of these exercises require judgment and interpretation; thus, they should help you formulate questions you may want to ask during class discussions. Each set of practice exercises also includes suggestions for enrichment activities. These suggestions should help you transfer the skills to your discipline and classroom. As you read the text and complete the exercises,

FIGURE 1.1 Using Tests in the Classroom: Planning, Design, Development, Evaluation, and Communication

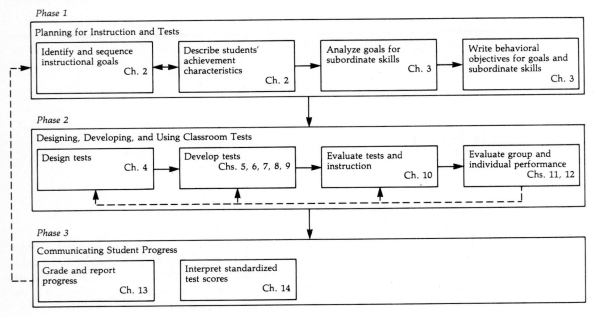

you will learn how to plan for new classes, create and use classroom tests, and report on students' overall progress.

The first phase, planning, consists of four activities: identifying and sequencing instructional goals, describing student achievement characteristics, analyzing instructional goals, and writing behavioral objectives. The information you gather and the decisions you make during this first phase become the basis for all subsequent activities. In the second phase of the process, you must design and develop tests and evaluate your students' performances. The information you gather during this phase will help you improve both your tests and your instruction. The last phase is communication. You will need to grade and report your students' progress and to interpret their performance on standardized tests. Figure 1.1 illustrates these three phases and indicates the chapters that describe each activity. The remaining sections of this chapter present an overview of each phase.

PLANNING FOR INSTRUCTION AND TESTS

The planning phase begins with two questions: What am I expected to teach in this course? and Whom am I expected to teach? To answer the first question, you will need to consult your curriculum guide, recommended lists of goals and objectives, and the manuals for standardized tests adopted by your district. After you have identified and compared instructional goals and objectives from these different sources, you will need to sort the goals by topic and then sequence the ones you will use. The list of sequenced instructional goals will guide your test design and development activities for each unit of instruction.

The best sources of information about your students' achievement characteristics are the students' permanent school records. These records contain standardized test scores, grades, and other pertinent information. After you decide which information you need, you can prepare a form on which you summarize the group's achievement characteristics. This group summary will help you design appropriate tests, establish minimum standards for performance, and interpret test results.

With the instructional goals in hand and the characteristics of students in mind, you are ready to analyze the goals to identify the skills students will need in order to demonstrate mastery of your instructional goals. You should separate each goal into subordinate tasks and then sequence the tasks in some logical order. This activity, which is called *goal analysis* or *task analysis*, produces a framework of tasks that becomes the foundation for both your lessons and tests.

Finally, you will need to develop a list of behavioral objectives that are based on each goal and its framework of skills. These objectives should specify the conditions or the circumstances under which the students will demonstrate their mastery of the skills. To create appropriate behavioral objectives, you will need to consider the achievement characteristics of the group, the task's content and specified behavior, the classroom environment, and available resources. In certain instances, you may also need to include criteria for judging the quality of a group's performance.

DESIGNING, DEVELOPING, AND USING CLASSROOM TESTS

The types of tests you design will depend on the kind of decisions you want to make. You may decide to use readiness tests and pretests, which will provide information about your students before you plan instruction. You may want to administer practice tests to enable students to rehearse the skills and to monitor their progress during instruction. Regardless of whether you use these types of tests, you will probably need to design posttests to evaluate both the students' progress and the quality of instruction. Your purpose and the decisions you wish to make should guide your design activities.

Test designs are called *tables of test specifications* or *test blueprints*. To develop a table of test specifications, you should consider not only the purpose for the test, but also the objectives for the unit, student characteristics, the classroom environment, resources available for testing and scoring, the time available for the test, and ways to produce valid and reliable scores. You can then use this information to select the specific objectives from the goal framework to be measured, prescribe the best test and item format, and determine the number of test items to include for each skill.

In prescribing the best test and item format for each objective, you need to consider the conditions, behavior, and content specified in the objective. Different objectives will require different test formats. Some objectives can best be measured using objective tests, some using essay tests, some using product development tests, and others using performance tests. Within the objective-test category, some objectives are best measured using completion questions and others are best measured using selected-response items. Some objectives can be measured adequately using one question; others may require a minimum of ten to fifteen items. Decisions about objectives selected, test formats, item formats, and the number of items required are recorded on the table of test specifications.

Developing Tests

With the table of test specifications complete, you are ready to develop tests. Factors to consider when writing test items include: (1) the conditions, behavior, and content specified in the selected objectives; (2) the achievement characteristics of the group, including the students' vocabulary and reading levels; (3) the contexts and situations familiar to group members; and (4) the clarity and accuracy of grammar and punctuation used to write the items. In addition to these major factors, you should consider recommendations for formatting objective and essay test items and for writing instructions for product development and performance tests.

When developing essay tests, product development tests, and performance tests, you will also need to develop checklists or rating scales that can be used to score students' work as objectively as possible, to analyze instructional quality and students' performance, and to provide students with informative feedback about the quality of their work.

In addition to measuring achievement, most teachers are expected to measure and evaluate students' attitudes and classroom conduct. To do this, you will need to know how to develop behavior observation forms and rate your students' behaviors.

Using Tests

Test results can be used to describe and evaluate the test, the instruction, the groups' overall performance, and individual student's test performance, in that order. To make judgments about quality, you will need some standard or criterion against which to compare results. These criteria are developed using your interpretation of the complexity of the skills measured and the achievement characteristics of the students tested. When measures indicate that students have performed as well as or better than anticipated, you can conclude that instruction and the test were effective. However, if students' performance falls short of anticipated levels, then you have evidence that the instruction, and perhaps the test, should be questioned.

When evaluating the quality of an objective test, the performance indicators used include each item's difficulty index and discrimination index. Items found questionable using these indices are reviewed further using a distractor analysis. Items judged defective following this review are eliminated, and test scores are adjusted accordingly before evaluating instruction, the group's performance, or an individual's performance.

When evaluating the quality of instruction, you will need to sort items by objective or goal and then compare difficulty and discrimination indices for sets of items. When students' performance does not meet anticipated levels for all or most items within a skill set, then instruction related to the skill is questioned.

Indicators you will use to evaluate a group's overall test performance include the shape and location of the raw score distribution; measures of central tendency, including the mean and median; and measures of variability, including the range and standard deviation. As before, the complexity of skills measured and the achievement characteristics of the group are used to set standards for performance. The actual measures are compared with the anticipated ones to determine the quality of the group's performance.

The fourth type of analysis involves evaluating each student's test performance. You will want to describe each student's performance by comparing it to the overall group's performance and by determining the number of skills mastered. Before you make your final judgment, you will want to compare each student's performance with her or his previous achievement to determine whether students have equaled or surpassed their previous records. By combining students' mastery performances into a group composite, you will be able to identify quickly the particular students who need enrichment and those who need review or remediation on specific skills. Finally, you can locate skill areas in which instruction was good, acceptable, and inadequate.

COMMUNICATING STUDENTS' PROGRESS

Grading and Reporting Progress

Your students' grades should accurately summarize and reflect their performances during each term, semester, and year. To ensure this accuracy, you will need to consider the instructional goals and objectives covered during a term; those measured by each posttest; each student's posttest scores; the district's grading policies; and the proportion each test will contribute to the final grade. In addition, you will need to synthesize individual scores into a composite score and either establish or locate standards for converting composite scores into term grades. You can design your gradebook to accommodate all of this information and aid your work.

Interpreting Standardized Test Performances

Every teacher should be able to interpret students' scores on standardized tests. The last chapter describes: (1) the nature, the purpose, and the construction of standardized tests; (2) the purpose for the norm group; (3) the normal distribution and its relationship to standardized test scores; (4) the relationship of the scores to each other; and (5) how each score on a student's profile is interpreted.

DOCUMENTING THE PROCESS

The documents related to planning, designing, developing, summarizing, analyzing, and evaluating tests presented in this text are closely related, and they build one on the other. Although each chapter provides many examples and illustrations, the book uses one instructional goal to illustrate how the decisions you make at any stage in the process influence your decisions at other stages. Thus, you will undoubtedly want to compare the documents developed at different stages. The primary documents for each phase of activity for the sample instructional goal are repeated in Appendixes A through K to help you avoid flipping through the chapters to make your comparisons. For example, if you want to compare the table of test specifications described in Chapter 4 (Table 4.1) with the documents on which it is based, turn to the Appendix. Appendix A contains the instructional goal framework (Figure 3.1), and Appendix B contains the behavioral objectives (Table 3.7) developed from the goal framework. If you want to see samples of tests developed from the table of specifications in Chapter 4, see Appendixes D through G. Appendixes I through K contain the analysis and evaluation documents from Chapters 10, 11, and 12 that are based on the planning, design, and development documents.

PART I

Planning for Instruction and Tests

CHAPTER 2

Planning for New Classes

OBJECTIVES

1. Identify sources of instructional goals for a course.
2. Determine the congruence among instructional goals found in various sources.
3. Describe how to sequence instructional goals for a course.
4. Describe how class groups are formed.
5. Define the terms *heterogeneous* and *homogeneous* and relate them to group achievement levels.
6. Determine which information to use in assessing the achievement characteristics of a class group.
7. Design a form for summarizing group achievement.
8. Use student achievement data to describe previous performance levels of newly assigned class groups.

Two of a teacher's first tasks at the beginning of a new school year are to determine what he or she is expected to teach and to whom. Although these tasks might at first appear to be unrelated to testing activities, they provide the foundation necessary for determining what skills to test and for interpreting the test scores obtained. This chapter describes these two planning activities. The first activity is to identify and sequence instructional goals for a course, and the second is to assess the achievement characteristics of assigned class groups.

IDENTIFYING INSTRUCTIONAL GOALS

Education is a highly complex system that requires curriculum planning and coordination. Curriculum plans are communicated through curriculum guides listing instructional goals that students in a given grade level and subject are expected to achieve. These guides are produced by a team that usually includes classroom teachers, curriculum specialists, and university-level content experts. Teams developing curriculum guides in vocational subjects commonly include experts from business and industry as well.

Curriculum guides serve as a foundation to plan and coordinate two main activities at the state, district, and school levels: instruction and testing. At the state level, the guides are used to coordinate instruction across school districts, to adopt the most relevant instructional texts, and to provide a foundation for statewide achievement tests. School administrators at the district level use the state guides as one resource for developing their own more comprehensive curriculum guides. The district guides are then used to coordinate instruction across schools and grade levels and to select instructional texts for each subject and grade. Related to testing, the guides are used to select the most appropriate standardized tests and to develop districtwide achievement tests. Classroom teachers use the district's curriculum guide to identify and sequence the instructional goals assigned for their subject and grade level, to plan instructional units and lessons, and to develop achievement tests that measure students' progress. Curriculum guides help ensure that important instructional goals are not inadvertently omitted, that unintended repetition is avoided, and that a direct match exists between the instruction provided and tests used to measure students' progress.

Most school districts publish curriculum guides, at least in the basic skills subjects; if one is provided for your subject, it will define your primary teaching responsibilities. Sometimes, however, guides either are not provided or are not as complete as you would like. If a curriculum guide is not provided for your subject, you should prepare one yourself. If the one provided is sketchy and incomplete, you will need to expand or clarify the instructional goals included. In either situation, you can turn to a variety of resources for help.

Sources of Instructional Goals

Instructional goals can be located in various places. As noted, some state departments of education provide curriculum guides for specific subjects, particularly subjects dealing with basic skills. These guides are one valuable source of instructional goals. The publications of professional associations that describe goals and standards for your discipline may be useful as well. You can also turn to textbooks and other instructional materials adopted for your subject. Scanning several adopted texts should give you an overview of the goals different authors consider important.

The teacher's and administrator's manuals for standardized achievement tests that will be administered to your students are another good source of instructional goals. These documents often describe not only goals, but related instructional objectives as well. For example, the CTB/McGraw-Hill

DMI Mathematics Systems Teacher's Management Guide lists all the goals measured on the California Achievement Test and the California Test of Basic Skills, and it describes the specific form of the test and the grade in which each objective is tested. Finally, it keys each objective to published instructional materials. Many test companies provide similar outlines of the instructional goals measured by their tests.

Elements of an Instructional Goal

The instructional goals listed in curriculum guides are broad statements of learning outcomes that indicate both the behavior and the instructional content students are to acquire. The behaviors included in an instructional goal should be observable and measurable. They describe overt student behaviors that demonstrate whether students acquired the desired knowledge or skill. Words typically used to describe overt behaviors include *list, select, define, recite, sequence, summarize, classify, predict, solve,* and *explain.* Terms like *understand, appreciate,* and *comprehend* are not used in instructional goals because they do not clearly indicate how students will demonstrate that they have acquired the desired skill or information. Although the underlying purpose of instruction is to produce understanding and comprehension, instructional goals are written to communicate how students will visibly demonstrate these internal processes.

The second part of an instructional goal identifies the content of the instruction. This content may be a topic, such as punctuation, capitalization, mixed fractions, or the Constitution. The content part of the goal identifies the topic and the particular portion of the topic to be studied.

The sample instructional goals listed in Tables 2.1, 2.2, and 2.3 were selected from elementary and secondary school curriculum guides in language arts, mathematics, and special education, respectively. Table 2.4 contains a sample of the instructional goals and objectives from the *DMI Mathematics Systems, Teacher's Management Guide.* The first column in Table 2.4 identifies the topic area; the second, the grade range and test form in which the goal is measured; and the third column lists three sample geometry goals and several related instructional objectives for each goal. Notice that regardless of the subject area considered or the source of the goals, each goal listed in the four tables includes both the desired student behavior and the instructional content to be learned. Note also that the behaviors included describe overt actions rather than such terms as *comprehends* and *understands.*

Comparing Instructional Goals from Different Sources

Comparing the instructional goals in the school district's curriculum guide with those found in other sources can often be useful. You may compare the guide with (1) the state guide, if one is available; (2) the text and instructional

TABLE 2.1 Sample Instructional Goals for Language Arts at Various Grade Levels

1. Sequence a group of four pictures.
2. Arrange four sentences into a meaningful paragraph.
3. Alphabetize any given list of words.
4. Use guide words to locate specified words in a dictionary.
5. Write a story using a logical organizational pattern.
6. Paraphrase a written passage.
7. Distinguish between fact and opinion.
8. Determine the cause and effect of an event or action.
9. Infer tone and mood from a written passage.
10. Use regular plural forms of nouns.
11. Capitalize proper nouns.
12. Capitalize appropriate words in titles.
13. Match nouns and pronouns.
14. Select the appropriate tense of regular verbs in context.
15. Make subjects and verbs agree.
16. Write declarative sentences.
17. Write interrogative sentences.
18. Write compound sentences using a comma, semicolon, and colon.
19. Use a comma to separate words in a series.
20. Use an apostrophe to form contractions.
21. Associate words that are the same or opposite in meaning.
22. Form derived words using prefixes and suffixes.
23. Determine the meaning of a word in context.
24. Identify metaphors and similes.

TABLE 2.2 Sample Instructional Goals for Mathematics at Various Grade Levels

1. Add whole numbers with regrouping.
2. Subtract whole numbers with regrouping.
3. Multiply whole numbers with regrouping.
4. Divide whole numbers with regrouping.
5. Add proper fractions having like denominators.
6. Subtract proper fractions having unlike denominators.
7. Multiply proper and improper fractions.
8. Read and write mixed decimal numbers through hundredths.
9. Add, subtract, multiply, and divide mixed decimal numbers.
10. Round a number having two decimal places to the nearest whole number.
11. Write equations to solve word problems.
12. Solve word problems involving money.
13. Solve word problems involving time.
14. Solve word problems involving temperature.
15. Solve word problems involving length.
16. Solve word problems involving liquid capacity.
17. Solve word problems involving mass.
18. Solve word problems involving percentages.
19. Calculate probabilities.
20. Calculate the mean.
21. Find the perimeter of given objects.
22. Find the area of given objects.
23. Read graphs including ordered pairs and coordinates.

TABLE 2.3 Sample Instructional Goals for Exceptional Students at Various Grade Levels

A. Educable Mentally Retarded Goals
   1. Match identical symbols (letters and numerals).
   2. Discriminate colors.
   3. Discriminate sounds.
   4. Copy upper-case and lower-case letters.
   5. Write own name and address.
   6. Compare objects by size, dimensions, quantity, position, or sequence.
   7. Write letters of the alphabet when named.
   8. Demonstrate self-care skills in personal hygiene.
   9. Demonstrate self-care skills in health and safety.
   10. Demonstrate appropriate peer group interactions.

B. Trainable Mentally Retarded Goals
   1. Distinguish basic sensory qualities (hot–cold, wet–dry, burning smell, hard–soft, spoiled–fresh).
   2. Name and locate body parts.
   3. Demonstrate self-help in safety situations.
   4. Demonstrate self-help in dressing.
   5. Demonstrate general work skills.
   6. Demonstrate appropriate work relations.

materials for the class; (3) recommended goal lists of professional associations; and (4) goals and objectives measured on mandated, standardized achievement tests. In making such an analysis, you may find some instructional goals recommended in all your resources. You may also discover that some goals in the curriculum guide are included in only a few, or none, of the other sources. The other documents may also recommend goals that the assigned curriculum guide does not. When the same instructional goal appears in multiple sources, it is undoubtedly one that content experts consider very important. When a goal appears only in the district's curriculum guide, it is one that local curriculum specialists and teachers consider important for the district. If the district's curriculum guide and the adopted text exclude goals appearing on mandated, standardized tests, you may want to insert these goals in your curriculum guide as an addendum.

If goals from various sources are worded differently but imply the same behavior and content, you may consider them the same. The language arts instructional goals for the fifth grade in Table 2.5 were taken from three different sources. Notice that, although the wording is different, their intent is the same. Because the goals prescribed in the state guide and the test manual are more complete than the one in the district guide, they could be used to clarify and expand the district's goal statement.

To help you remember the sources of similar goals, you can assign symbols to your sources and key them to your curriculum guide. When an instructional goal from another source matches one in the district guide, place the symbol for that source in the margin beside the goal. You may also want to edit the district's goal to include any clarifying information found in other

TABLE 2.4   Instructional Goals from the *DMI Mathematics Systems, Teacher's Management Guide* (1983) for the California Achievement Test (CAT), Levels C and D

CAT C and D Objective Category	CAT C and D Grade Range	DMI/MS Instructional Objective and Level
81 Geometry	2.6–3.9	55 Identify three-dimensional figures. Match cylinders, cones, cubes, pyramids, and spheres with their written names.
	6.6–9.9	57 Name lines, line segments, and intersections from labeled figures. Name line segments. Distinguish between figures for lines and line segments. Identify perpendicular, parallel, or intersecting lines and line segments.
	6.6–9.9	59 Find areas of polygons. Find the areas of triangles from figures marked off in unit squares. Calculate areas of rectangles from figures with lengths of sides labeled when a formula is not given. Calculate areas of triangles with lengths of base and height given when a formula is given.

From DMI Mathematics Systems, Teacher's Management Guide. Copyright 1983 by McGraw-Hill, Inc. Reproduced by permission of CTB/McGraw-Hill.

TABLE 2.5   Language Arts Instructional Goals

Goal Source	Goal
District curriculum guide	Uses context clues to supply the meaning of words
State level curriculum guide	Infer the meaning of words in context using: (a) example clues, (b) direct explanation clues, (c) synonym clues, and (d) compare and contrast clues
Teacher's manual for a standardized test	Selects the definition for multimeaning words in context and uses context clues to identify word meaning

sources. If you decide to add goals to the curriculum guide, you should note the source in the margin beside each one. Referencing other sources in your curriculum guide will help you evaluate the completeness of the curriculum guide, determine the guide's congruence with adopted instructional materials and standardized tests, and perhaps sequence goals for your new class.

Table 2.6 provides an example of the congruence between a school district's curriculum guide and three other goal sources. Goals similar to Goal 1, "Sequence a group of four pictures," appear on the standardized test and in the state curriculum guide. The adopted text does not include instruction for this goal. The second goal is included in the text, the standardized test manual, and the state curriculum guide. The third goal appears in the text and the state curriculum guide but not on the standardized test. A teacher reviewing this analysis should recognize that Goal 1 presents an instructional problem to be solved. Because the adopted text does not include instruction for this goal, the teacher will undoubtedly need to develop all instruction related to it.

TABLE 2.6   A Comparison of Instructional Goals from Different Sources

Goals in Curriculum Guide	Other Sources
1. Sequence a group of four pictures.	T(5), S
2. Arrange four sentences into a meaningful paragraph.	I, T(5), S
3. Write a friendly letter.	I, S

Note: T(5) = Standardized test (month usually administered)
  S = State curriculum guide
  I = Adopted instructional materials

Sequencing Instructional Goals

Once you have a list of instructional goals for the course, you should cluster them by topic and sequence them. This planning activity can help you decide where to begin your instruction and how to proceed during the year. When you have finished, your curriculum guide will have all your instructional goals ordered in the sequence you plan to present them. The guide can direct your instructional activities throughout the year and help you develop records to monitor students' mastery of your instructional goals.

The several strategies you can use to sequence instructional goals differ in importance. Three of the most important considerations in selecting a sequence are the relationships among the goals, the dates when standardized tests are administered, and the sequence of topics in the textbook. The most important consideration is the relationship among the goals. Some goals are hierarchically related, meaning that certain skills must be learned before others. For example, the goal "recognize nouns" is a prerequisite to the goal "differentiate between common nouns and proper nouns." In another hierarchical relationship, the goal "add without regrouping," must precede the goal "add with regrouping." The first sequencing strategy is to identify and sequence all goals in the guide that are hierarchically related.

Once goals are ordered according to their hierarchical relationships, the next important consideration is the timing of any standardized tests that all your students are required to take. Your goal sequence should permit you to teach the skills these tests measure before the tests are administered. The third consideration, text order, is one of convenience. To the degree possible, goals should be ordered to correspond to their presentation sequence in the textbook.

Even after sequencing goals in the curriculum guide using these three strategies, some goals may remain to be sequenced. These remaining goals can be sequenced using such factors as complexity, familiarity, chronology, or potential motivation. When you have completed your goal analysis and sequencing, you will be ready to consider the students who have been assigned to your class.

ASSESSING GROUP CHARACTERISTICS

Most teachers are assigned new class groups at the beginning of each school year. The achievement characteristics of the students in each group will affect all instructional activities, including the analysis of the instructional goals, lesson development, the selection of resource material, the delivery of instruction, the writing of test items, and the interpretation of test performance. Because each class will be different, you will want to assess the achievement levels of each group and tailor your instructional activities accordingly.

The Assignment of Class Groups

In forming class groups, school administrators consider several factors in addition to previous achievement. They usually try to balance the number of students in each class, the number of males and females in a group, and the cultural and racial mix at each grade level. They must also consider scheduling for such elective subjects as art, band, chorus, and special programs. All of these factors affect administrative decisions concerning class groups, but none of these factors is as important to the teacher as the students' previous achievement levels.

The school district's philosophy influences how classes are grouped. Some districts attempt to tailor instruction to the needs of students who are similar in previous achievement. Such districts form separate class groups of high, medium, or low achievers. In other districts each class group has a representative number of students from each achievement level. Some districts use a combination of the two methods depending on the subject and grade level. Given all the philosophical and practical trades that administrators made in forming your classes, it is important for you to identify the achievement characteristics of each group.

Homogeneous and Heterogeneous Groups

Information about a group's previous achievement will help you establish your expectations for group performance. As you observe your students' progress, you can compare these expectations with their actual performance and then refine your judgments about their work.

In analyzing student characteristics, you should first determine whether a group is homogeneous or heterogeneous in achievement. A homogeneous group contains students who are similar in a given characteristic. For example, a group that is homogeneous in previous achievement contains students with similar histories of either high, average, or low achievement. A heterogeneous group contains students who are dissimilar in a given characteristic. A group that is heterogeneous in achievement contains students with a wide range of previous performances.

Homogeneous and *heterogeneous* are not absolute descriptors. They are relative terms, much like such adjectives as *tall* and *average*. We might ask, How tall is tall, how average is average, and how homogeneous is homogeneous? A class group with only high-achieving students is easily classified as homogeneous. When compared to the first group, a class containing average and above-average students would be heterogeneous. On the other hand, this class would be more homogeneous than a group whose scores ranged from very low to very high.

Throughout the school year, teachers continuously ask themselves, How are my students doing? You can usually answer this question by comparing students' current achievement with their previous work. For example, if you have been assigned a group that is heterogeneous in previous work, you may expect a wide range of scores on your first test. For a homogeneous group of high achievers, you might anticipate a narrow range of high test scores, and for a homogeneous group of low achievers, a narrow range of lower test scores.

After you administer your first test, you can compare the students' scores with your expectations. If the two fall within the same range, you can tentatively conclude that the group is performing normally. If the students did not perform as expected, you should note the incongruity, seek reasons, and wait for more information on subsequent tests.

Class Summary Forms

The availability of computers for producing current records has enabled many school districts to provide teachers with a summary of each newly formed group's previous achievement. These performance summaries usually contain the grades each student in the class received on semester exams and final course grades in the same or closely related courses. They also frequently contain students' standardized test scores in such basic subjects as mathematics and language. These forms will help you determine whether each group is heterogeneous or homogeneous in previous achievement.

Although interpreting grades previously earned on semester exams and in courses is rather straightforward, some information about interpreting the commonly reported standardized test scores will be useful. The standardized test scores included on the permanent record indicate how well the student performed relative to a comparable norm group of students. Note the particular standardized test scores used to indicate the students' performance levels. Undoubtedly either stanine or percentile scores will be reported, and sometimes both scores are included in the record. If stanine scores are used, they can be interpreted as follows:

1. Stanines range from a low score of 1 to a high score of 9.
2. Stanines of 1, 2, and 3 reflect below-average achievement in the subject compared to the norm group.
3. Stanines 4, 5, and 6 reflect average level achievement compared to the norm group.
4. Stanines 7, 8, and 9 reflect above-average achievement compared to the norm group.

If percentile scores are reported, they can be interpreted as follows:

1. Percentile scores range from a low score of 1 to a high score of 99.
2. Any given score indicates that the student scored better on the test than that percentage of students in the norm group. For example, a percentile score of 86 means that the student who earned this score surpassed 86 percent of the students in the norm group.
3. Generally, percentile scores below 25 are considered to indicate below-average achievement compared to the norm group.
4. Percentile scores between 25 and 75 are considered to reflect average achievement.
5. Percentile scores above 75 are considered to signify above-average achievement compared to students in the norm group.

Using either the stanine or the percentile score, each student's performance can be classified as below average, average, or above average in the basic skills measured by the test.

Table 2.7 contains two abbreviated summary forms that a science teacher might have developed for two classes. A complete form would include data for many more students. In addition to science grades, the teacher summarized the students' English and math grades from the previous year, their

TABLE 2.7   Class Summary Forms

Group I

Students	Previous Grades			Standardized Achievement Test Stanine Scores[a]			Districtwide Semester Sci. Exams	
	Eng.	Math	Sci.	Lang. Mech.	Read.	Math	S1[b]	S2
Abrams	C	C	C	5	5	6	C	C
Brown	C	C	C	5	4	5	C	C
Crown	C	B	C	6	5	6	C	B
Davis	C	C	C	5	5	5	C	C
Evans	B	B	B	6	6	7	C	B
Flynn	C	B	C	6	6	6	B	C
Good	C	C	B	5	5	5	C	C
Hayes	B	C	C	5	6	5	C	C
Jones	C	C	C	4	5	5	C	D
Kelly	D	C	D	4	4	4	D	C

Group II

Students	Previous Grades			Standardized Achievement Test Stanine Scores[a]			Districtwide Semester Sci. Exams	
	Eng.	Math	Sci.	Lang. Mech.	Read.	Math	S1[b]	S2
Allen	A	B	B	9	9	7	B	A
Boyd	C	B	C	6	6	7	B	C
Carter	C	C	C	4	5	5	C	C
Doyle	A	A	A	9	9	9	A	A
Egan	B	A	B	6	7	8	B	B
Fowler	C	C	B	6	6	6	C	B
Graham	B	B	C	7	6	7	B	C
Howe	D	D	C	3	3	4	D	C
Johnson	F	D	D	2	3	3	F	D
Keller	C	B	B	7	7	6	B	B

[a] Stanine scores range from one to nine. Compared to norm group:
Scores 1, 2, and 3 indicate below-average achievement.
Scores 4, 5, and 6 indicate average achievement.
Scores 7, 8, and 9 indicate above-average achievement.
[b] S1 = Semester one of previous year; S2 = Semester two of previous year

most recent standardized test scores, and their grades on the previous year's semester exams in science.

Describing Class Groups

Given a summary form for a group of students, you are ready to interpret the information and describe the class. You will want to determine whether the class is heterogeneous or homogeneous, and if homogeneous, whether it is above average, average, or below average in previous achievement. You can then use this information to establish your initial expectations for the group's performance. Differences in assigned groups will influence how you analyze your instructional goals, plan lessons, and write test items.

In analyzing a class group, you should consider their performance levels in each category of data, such as previous grades, standardized test scores, and semester exam scores. Then, with their performance within a category described, you can compare their performance across categories to determine whether the information across categories is similar or incongruent. If the performance levels across all categories indicate the same range of performance, then you can be relatively sure you have an accurate description of the class. However, if you note incongruent performance across categories, you should consider this in establishing your initial expectations.

Consider how a science teacher might interpret the data in Table 2.7. The first clue about Group I's makeup comes from their grades in English, math, and science. Most students earned grades of C, along with an occasional B and D. This similarity of performance suggests a homogeneous, average group. The group's standardized test (stanine) scores range from 6 to 4 in language and reading, and all but one score in mathematics fall into the average range. Semester exam grades in science also indicate a homogeneous group of average performance. All three categories of performance reflect the same range of achievement for the group; thus, a teacher looking at these data may reasonably expect Group I to be a homogeneous class that will continue to achieve at an average level.

The data for Group II, however, indicate a different pattern of previous achievement. Grades range from A to F, stanine scores range from 9 to 2, and semester exam grades range from A to F. All three categories of performance reflect consistent, heterogeneous achievement for the group. The teacher might thus anticipate a wide range of achievement from this class group.

Unfortunately, in some school districts, the teacher is given only a list of students' names for each new class. It is very difficult to begin planning for a group without any information about the students' achievement characteristics. Should you find yourself in this situation, you will want to request that the school provide the necessary information. If your request is not honored, you may want to review your students' permanent records to obtain the background information. At a minimum, you will want to summarize the standardized achievement test scores in language and mathematics to determine whether the group is homogeneous or heterogeneous in these basic skills. Once you have decided on the information you want, find out where and how it is recorded on one student's record. Using this record as an example, you can design a form that will help you summarize and interpret the rest of your data.

In interpreting students' records, you should be careful not to develop inflexible expectations for the group. Previous performance is not a sure indicator of how individuals will perform in a new situation. A year's maturation, a new group of students, and a new teacher are all factors that can affect individual performances. In turn, these changes can produce different results for a portion, if not for all, of the class.

SUMMARY

Two planning activities can help a teacher prepare for new classes. The first is to establish the instructional goals for a course, and the second is to assess the achievement characteristics of assigned classes.

Instructional goals are general statements of intended learning outcomes that describe the behavior the student is to demonstrate and the content to be learned. Sources of instructional goals include the school district's curriculum guide, the state's curriculum guide, professional associations' recommended lists of instructional goals and objectives, adopted instructional texts, and the teacher's or administrator's manual for required, standardized achievement tests. A teacher should compare the instructional goals in all these sources and add goals and objectives from state guides and standardized tests that are not found in the district's curriculum guide. The teacher should then cluster the goals by topic, sequence them by logical order, and assign each goal to specific terms and semesters, depending on when students will be tested on each goal.

Knowing the previous achievement levels of a new class can help a teacher set initial expectations for class performance, analyze instructional goals, develop and pace lessons, write test items, and interpret group performance.

Many school districts provide teachers with class summary forms that can be used to describe the achievement characteristics of a new group. Using the data in these forms, you can determine whether each assigned group is homogeneous or heterogeneous in previous achievement. This determination will aid in planning instruction, designing tests, and interpreting students' performance. You should be cautious in forming opinions about new class groups, however, and should be willing to reinterpret students' progress depending on your own experiences with the group.

PRACTICE EXERCISES

A. Identifying Instructional Goals
   1. Who usually decides what skills will be taught in a given subject and grade level?

2. List the types of people usually included on a school district's curriculum team.
3. List potential resources you can use to identify the instructional goals for a course.
4. List three reasons for matching district curriculum guides with state guides, goals and objectives for standardized tests, and adopted textbooks.

B. Elements of an Instructional Goal
5. Name the two parts of an instructional goal and describe the function of each part.
6. Identify the behavior and content in the following instructional goals by underlining the behavior with two lines and the content with one line.
   a. Name synonyms for given words.
   b. Name antonyms for given words.
   c. Alphabetize any given list of words.
   d. Retell a story in own words.
   e. Recite a paragraph verbatim.
   f. Add three-digit numbers with regrouping.
   g. Solve story problems using addition.
   h. Name the capital city for each state.
7. Analyze the following instructional goals and revise those that need clarification or improvement. (There is no one correct way to revise these goals. Revised goals should include both observable behavior and content.)
   a. Understands currency of different denominations.
   b. Punctuate.
   c. Identify one-half, one-third, and one-fourth of a given area.
   d. Understand how to measure the length, width, and height of a given object.
   e. Identify the main idea in a paragraph.
   f. The mean and median.

C. Determining Congruence among Goals from Different Sources
8. The left column lists six mathematics goals taken from district curriculum guides. The right column lists mathematics goals from state curriculum guides. Although the state goals are worded differently, some match the goals in the district guides. Indicate matching goals by placing the number of the state goal in a space preceding the letter of the district goal.

Goals from District Guides	*Goals from State Guides*
a. Determine equivalent amounts of money.	1. Given a fraction, identify an equal decimal number.
b. Write fractions as decimal numbers.	2. Determine the correct change for a given purchase.
c. Calculate the lowest form of given fractions.	3. Multiply mixed fractions.
d. Add fractions.	4. Equate coins and dollar bills of different denominations.
e. Subtract fractions.	5. Reduce fractions.
f. Use multiplication to solve mixed-fraction problems.	6. Select the money required to equal a given amount.

D. Sequencing Goals
9. List four strategies for sequencing instructional goals.

10. Use the following procedure to cluster and sequence the set of instructional goals listed in Table 2.8.
    a. Divide the goals into three categories of similar goals and title each category.
    b. Write the names of the categories in the order you would present them to students.
    c. Sequence the goals within each category in the order you would present them to students.

TABLE 2.8   Exercise for Sequencing Instructional Goals

Goals
1. Locate the subject of a simple sentence.
2. Select verbs to show future tense.
3. Match singular subjects with singular verbs.
4. Locate the predicate of a simple sentence.
5. Match plural subjects with plural verbs.
6. Select verbs to show present tense.
7. Identify simple sentences.
8. Select verbs to show past tense.

Goal Categories (Topics)   *Goal Sequence (by Number)*

E. The Assignment of Class Groups
    11. List four factors that school administrators usually consider when they form class groups.
    12. Which of the four factors listed in item 11 (above) will have the most influence on teachers when they plan instruction and interpret student performance?
    13. What do the terms *heterogeneous* and *homogeneous* mean when applied to group achievement?
    14. List the four types of information that would help you determine if a class is heterogeneous or homogeneous in achievement.
    15. If you were designing a form to summarize a group's previous achievement, what would the rows and columns on your form indicate? Show how you might design your form.
    16. Table 2.9 presents achievement data for a newly formed English class. Use the information in the table to describe the class.
        a. Previous English grades
        b. Standardized achievement test in language skills
        c. Districtwide English exam
        d. Congruence among indicators

TABLE 2.9   Data Summary Form for an English Class

Students	Previous Year's English Grades	Standardized Achievement Test (Stanines[a])	Districtwide English Exam[b] (% Correct)
1. Allen, B.	C	3	72
2. Bonito, B.	C	2	60
3. Brown, L.	D	3	75
4. Carter, D.	C	3	78
5. Donovan, T.	D	1	43
6. Evans, R.	C	3	64
7. Fischer, A.	C	2	74
8. Garcia, J.	C	2	62
9. Good, T.	B	3	68
10. Graham, N.	B	3	76
11. Hanson, A.	C	3	75
12. Howe, R.	C	2	70
13. Kelley, N.	D	3	73
14. Miller, C.	C	2	64
15. Otto, J.	C	2	60
16. Potter, G.	D	1	53
17. Scott, H.	C	2	68
18. Smith, J.	C	2	72
19. Taylor, B.	B	3	78
20. Washburn, M.	D	1	46

Average
Score   = 67%

Range   =
78 − 43 = 35

[a] Stanine scores range from 1 to 9. Scores of 1, 2, and 3 are considered below average; 4, 5, and 6 average; and 7, 8, and 9 above average.
[b] The district has set a minimum passing score for the exam of 70 percent.

17. If you were the teacher for the class in Figure 2.9, how might you expect the group to perform during the coming year?

F. Enrichment

18. Obtain a school district curriculum guide for the subject and grade level you teach or plan to teach. Review the types and sequencing of instructional goals and the scope of the subject the goals define.

19. Ask teachers and administrators in a school how class groups are formed there.

20. If you can obtain permission to review a district's class summary form for a newly formed class in your subject, analyze the data provided on the form, describe the group in terms of its achievement characteristics, and predict the general level of achievement you would expect for the class.

FEEDBACK

A. Identifying Instructional Goals
  1. District curriculum teams write curriculum guides that describe the instructional goals and objectives for a given subject and grade level. When guides are not provided by the district, teachers create their own.
  2. Curriculum teams usually include classroom teachers, curriculum supervisors, university-level content experts, and representatives from business and industry.
  3. Resources include district curriculum guides, state curriculum guides, assigned textbooks and other instructional resources, professional societies' recommendations for instructional goals, and teachers' or administrators' manuals for mandated standardized tests.
  4. Matching goals in a school district's curriculum guide with other sources will permit you to:
      a. Identify matching goals and objectives.
      b. Identify goals and objectives that are unique to the district.
      c. Identify important goals and objectives not found in the district guide.
B. Elements of an Instructional Goal
  5. Instructional goals contain the desired student behavior and the content of the topic that students will learn.
  6. a. Name synonyms for given words.
     b. Name antonyms for given words.
     c. Alphabetize any given list of words.
     d. Retell a story in own words.
     e. Recite a paragraph verbatim.
     f. Add three-digit numbers with regrouping.
     g. Solve story problems using addition.
     h. Name the capital city for each state.
  7. The instructional goals may be clarified as follows:
      a. Equates coins and bills with their defined values.
      b. Some possible clarifications include:
         • Selects the correct punctuation to end a sentence.
         • Uses quotation marks, commas, and ending punctuation to punctuate direct quotations correctly.
         • Punctuates the greeting and closing of a letter.
         • Uses commas to separate items in a series.
      c. This goal includes both the behavior and content.
      d. Measures the length, width, and height of an object using metric and English scales.
      e. This goal includes both the behavior and content.
      f. Possible goals include:
         • Define the mean and median of a set of scores.
         • Calculate the mean and median of a set of scores.
         • Interpret the mean and median of a set of scores.
         • Plot the mean and median of a set of scores.
C. Determining Congruence among Goals from Different Sources
  8. The district and state curriculum guides contain these matching goals:

District Guide	State Guide
a	4
b	1
c	5
f	3

D. Sequencing Goals
   9. a. Group goals according to topics.
      b. Once you have grouped goals by topic, identify any hierarchical relationships among the goals in each set. If a hierarchy of goals exists, place prerequisite goals first.
      c. If the goals show no hierarchical relationship within a set, sequence each set according to either their order in the textbook or the dates the standardized tests will be administered.
      d. Other logical factors, such as chronology, complexity, concreteness, familiarity, or motivation potential, can be used to sequence goals not organized using the preceding strategies.

Goal Category	Goal Sequence
1. Identify complete sentences.	$1 \rightarrow 4 \rightarrow 7$
2. Match subjects and verbs.	$3 \rightarrow 5$
3. Select verb tense.*	$6 \rightarrow 8 \rightarrow 2$

10.

   * The goals in this category are not hierarchically related and may be presented in any order.

E. The Assignment of Class Groups
   11. Factors in class assignments include sexual balance, racial or cultural balance, the scheduling of elective subjects, and previous achievement levels.
   12. The previous achievement levels of students will have the most influence on teachers.
   13. Heterogeneous groups contain students who vary or are dissimilar in achievement. Homogeneous groups contain students who are similar in achievement.
   14. You might want to collect:
      a. Previously earned grades in the same subject.
      b. Previously earned grades in language and math skills if these subjects are important for the subject to be taught.
      c. The most recent standardized test scores.
      d. Grades on previous semester exams in the same subject.
   15. Your form should be tailored to the types of information you decide to collect. Your form should have a row for each student in the group and a column for each type of information you plan to record.
   16. The information in Table 2.9 shows that:
      a. Students' grades ranged from D to B, with most students receiving a C. Five students received a D, twelve students a C, and three students a B. Based on grades alone, the group appears to be relatively homogeneous and average in achievement.
      b. Students' scores on the standardized achievement test in language ranged from 1 to 3. Nine students received a score of 3, eight received a score of

2, and three a score of 1. Their performance was homogeneous and below average.

c. Students' scores on the districtwide English exam were low. The average score earned by the class was 67 percent; the scores ranged from 43 to 78 percent. Half the students passed the exam at a relatively low level, and half failed.

d. The three indicators of performance are relatively congruent, although the assigned grades appear to be somewhat higher than would be predicted by the test scores.

This information should lead you to conclude that the group is relatively homogeneous and below average in previous English achievement.

17. You might expect the group's test performances to be limited in range and toward the low end of the scale.

REFERENCE

Gessel, J. (1983). DMI mathematics systems, *teacher's management guide*. Monterey, Calif.: CTB/McGraw-Hill, pp. 99, 110.

CHAPTER 3

Relating Instructional Goals to Instruction and Tests

OBJECTIVES

1. Define the following six levels of learning commonly found in curriculum guides: knowledge, comprehension, application, analysis, synthesis, and evaluation.
2. Given a list of instructional goals, classify each goal by the level of learning required.
3. Define the following four types of learning commonly included in curriculum guides: intellectual skills, verbal information, motor skills, and attitudes.
4. Given a list of instructional goals, classify each goal by the type of learning required.
5. Given an instructional goal, identify the framework of subordinate skills required to perform the goal and sequence of skills.
6. Convert subordinate skills into behavioral objectives by adding performance conditions and, when needed, criteria for acceptable performance.

Chapter 2 presents procedures for identifying and sequencing instructional goals and suggests methods for describing assigned groups of students. This chapter reviews learning and goal analysis techniques that are essential prerequisites to effective instruction and evaluation. Goal analysis provides a foundation for developing and interpreting classroom achievement tests that should be directly related to the instructional goals for the course. Goal analysis identifies the type of learning involved, the subordinate skills required to achieve the goal, and the relationship among the subordinate skills. Such an analysis will help you relate the subordinate skills to your instruction and achievement tests. You can also use a goal framework to evaluate adopted textbooks and to select supplementary instructional materials. This chapter includes three sections. The first section summarizes the six levels of learning defined by Bloom, Madaus, and Hastings (1981). The second section presents the four types of learning Gagné (1985) describes and the instructional goal analysis procedures he recommends for each type. The third section suggests ways to write behavioral objectives for goals and their subordinate skills. If this is your first exposure to learning analysis, you may want to obtain the texts listed at the end of the chapter. They will provide more detailed information about the classification and analysis of instructional goals.

LEVELS OF LEARNING

Bloom, Madaus, and Hastings (1981) have identified six learning levels that educators often use in writing instructional goals and objectives. These levels help clarify the depth of skills students are to acquire and the kinds of responses that will demonstrate students' skills and knowledge. The six levels of learning appear in Table 3.1.

TABLE 3.1   Six Levels of Learning Defined by Bloom, Madaus, and Hastings

Level of Learning	Definition
Knowledge	Recalling or recognizing specific elements in a subject area
Comprehension	Translation: putting a concept or message into different words or changing from one symbolic system to another Interpretation: seeing the relationships among the separate parts of a communication Extrapolation: going beyond a literal communication and making inferences about consequences
Application	Using rules, principles, procedures, generalizations, and formulas to solve problems
Analysis	Separating a unit into its component parts so the relationship among the parts is made clear
Synthesis	Arranging and combining separate elements to form a whole
Evaluation	Using criteria and standards to make judgments about the value of ideas, products, and procedures

The first level, *knowledge,* involves the recall or recognition of information that has been learned. This level is sometimes referred to as rote memory or repetition. For example, a student who memorizes and repeats the statement, "In 1492 Columbus sailed the ocean blue," would be participating in a knowledge task. Other examples include memorizing and repeating poems or lines from a play; recalling dates and persons associated with important events; and recalling formulas, rules, procedures, facts, and definitions. No mental process other than remembering is involved.

The second level, *comprehension*, involves paraphrasing information or translating a given message into one's own words. Students participating in a comprehension task might explain the meaning of the sentence, "In 1492 Columbus sailed the ocean blue," with such statements as "Columbus began exploring in 1492," or "Columbus discovered America in 1492." Converting a story problem into a formula, converting a formula into words, inferring the main idea from a paragraph or story, and paraphrasing a definition are other comprehension tasks. Any translation, interpretation, or inference that demonstrates a student's understanding of a communication falls into this learning category.

At the *application* level, students solve problems by applying rules, principles, generalizations, or procedures. Using formulas to solve numerical problems, following rules of grammar and spelling, and constructing an object according to a plan are application tasks. At this level, students are expected to demonstrate their understanding of a rule, a principle, or a procedure by applying it to a task or problem.

The fourth level of learning, *analysis*, involves dividing a concept or unit into smaller parts so the parts and the relationship among them is clear. Dividing a story into the components of plot, characterization, and organization and then describing the relationship of these components is one example of analysis. Conducting a literature search for a term paper or a research project is another. In this chapter, you will learn how to divide an instructional goal into its subordinate skills and how to sequence the skills according to their relationship. These activities also represent the analysis level of learning.

At the fifth level, *synthesis*, the learner combines and integrates separate elements according to their relationship. This reassessment of components permits the learner to organize, summarize, and explain information and to make predictions. Assembling information for an essay or a position paper is one example of synthesis. The person writing the document must consider the ideas to be expressed, the interest and skills of the intended readers, the desired mood, and the appropriate writing style. The final product should reflect the writer's synthesis and interpretation of these elements. Original research also involves synthesis-level learning. The researcher analyzes the literature, identifies the variables, and synthesizes the relationships among the variables through statements of hypotheses. The procedures and instruments used to conduct the study constitute the researcher's interpretative summary of the context, the variables, and the relationships among the variables. The literature, the current hypotheses, the procedures used, and the research results are synthesized to make up the discussion and conclusions.

The sixth level of learning, *evaluation*, involves using criteria and standards to judge the quality and the value of ideas, products, or procedures. Criteria used to judge quality include such factors as accuracy, precision, economy, consistency, assumptions, evidence, and organization. In turn, these criteria become the basis for standards of work quality.

Teachers often expect students to judge the quality or worth of their own and others' work. Students can learn to evaluate many types of work including their own essays, papers, artwork, and term projects; other people's articles, artwork, and term projects; speeches, plays, books, and movies; commercial products; events they have planned or sponsored; and instruction and tests.

Teachers use the six levels of learning to clarify and interpret the behavior specified in instructional goals and to write their own goals and objectives. Considering the level of learning ensures that the desired behavior in the goal or objective clearly communicates the level of learning intended. The levels can also be used to ensure that achievement tests include items that measure student performance relevant to instructional goals.

TYPES OF LEARNING

Robert Gagné (1985) has identified four types of learning: intellectual skills, verbal information, motor skills, and attitudes. A summary and examples of each type of learning appear in Table 3.2. The following sections of the text explain each learning type and describe methods you can use to identify subordinate skills for instructional goals of each type. Many goals used as examples reflect basic skills because the content is obvious. Focus thus can be placed on definitions and procedures used in goal analysis. After reading about each type of learning, you should apply the procedures to goals in your own subject area.

Intellectual Skills

When we use symbols to interact with our environment, we are applying intellectual skills (Gagné 1985). To understand or make sense of phenomena we encounter, we *differentiate* among objects and ideas, generalize our learning by *classifying*, and *solve problems* that perplex us. Intellectual skills also enable us to *explain* why things happen and to *predict* what will happen under given circumstances. Our use of intellectual skills produces visible results, but the mental processes we use are not observable. Intellectual skills are also referred to as *procedural knowledge* or learning how to do something. The procedures involved, however, are mental rather than physical. Intellectual skills include the reading, language, and arithmetic goals commonly referred to as basic skills. They thus make up a large portion of school learning.

TABLE 3.2   Gagné's Four Types of Learning

Type of Learning	Definition	Examples
Intellectual Skills	The use of symbols to interact with the environment. Often called *procedural knowledge,* intellectual skills are used to interpret phenomena and solve problems.	
	Subcategories are: 1. Discriminations— Differentiating among objects as similar or different	1. Learning that rectangles are not the same as squares
	2. Concrete concepts— Using physical characteristics to classify objects into categories	2. Learning that an object is a square because it has four equal sides that are closed and form right angles
	3. Defined concepts—Using a definition to classify objects, events, or conditions into categories	3. Learning that the founder of an organization is the person primarily responsible for the existence of the organization
	4. Rules—Following a mental procedure to solve a problem or create a product	4. Learning to calculate the circumference of a circle, punctuate sentences, write a short story
	5. Principles—Combining two or more concepts and describing the relationships among them to explain observed phenomena or to predict an outcome	5. Explain erosion or predict the weather
Verbal Information	1. Associating objects, events, symbols, or conditions with their names	1. Learning that the symbol + means to add, the symbol 2 is two, a particular person is called John, and the word *fever* indicates an abnormally high body temperature
	2. Remembering facts and repeating or recounting information	2. Recalling that John had a fever on Saturday, the words to a popular song, and that given authors wrote fiction

(*continued on next page*)

TABLE 3.2 (*continued*)

Type of Learning	Definition	Examples
Motor Skills	Motor skills are physical procedures that require movement, precision, and timing, and they include simultaneous or sequential steps. Learning complex motor skills requires both knowledge of the steps and practice.	Playing the piano, riding a bicycle, operating machinery and equipment, tying knots and buttoning buttons, sewing, and painting
Attitudes	Attitudes are mental states that govern our choices and behavior. An attitude has three main elements: 1. Affective—a person's positive or negative feelings toward something 2. Behavioral—the way a person acts or behaves	Attitude: Respecting the property of others 1. Having a positive feeling about one-self and other people who show respect for the property of others 2. Obtaining permission to use another's property; exercising care and following directions when using borrowed property; returning property undamaged and quickly
	3. Cognitive—knowing about or how to do something. This component may include intellectual skills, verbal information, and motor skills. It usually includes information about cultural expectations, rewards, and consequences for behaving in a prescribed manner	3. Learning expectations for behavior with borrowed property; learning the rewards of and consequences for acceptable and unacceptable behavior; and learning how to use the borrowed property correctly

Intellectual skills are divided into four subcategories that form a hierarchy of simple to complex skills. The most basic skill is *discrimination* learning, which serves as a foundation for the development of *concrete concepts*. In turn, concrete concepts permit the formation of *defined concepts*, and both types of concepts are required for the development of *rules*. The following paragraphs explain each of these subcategories.

Discrimination   In discrimination learning, a student compares objects on the basis of their physical properties. At its simplest level, discrimination is the ability to recognize that two objects are the same or different. For example, a child learning to tell the difference between nickles and dimes must use the physical characteristics of the coins to determine whether they are the same or different. Being able to tell the difference between letters of the alphabet and between numbers are other examples of discrimination learning.

Concepts   Two types of concepts make up this category: concrete concepts and defined concepts. A concrete concept refers to objects whose physical properties permit us to recognize, classify, and generalize. Learning a concrete concept involves distinguishing the physical characteristics that make an object a member of a class. For example, children learn to classify neighborhood animals as dogs by first learning to recognize the distinguishing characteristics of dogs. Once they recognize these unique characteristics, they can correctly classify a dog when they see one. They learn to distinguish bottles, boxes, cans, and numerous other objects by their physical properties.

A defined concept includes more than physical properties in its definition. It may have physical characteristics as a component, but the definition will also describe a relationship between or among objects. For example, *teacher* and *father* are defined concepts. We cannot classify people as teachers or fathers if we know only their physical characteristics. We also need to know what they do and how they relate to other people. To determine whether someone fits into the category of teacher or father, we must know how these terms are defined.

Vase is another example of a defined concept. We can define a vase as an object that holds cut flowers or cut plants. This definition permits us to relate a vase to a class of objects (containers) and to discriminate cut flowers or cut plants from their growing counterparts. The word *holds* tells us what the vase does or is used for and thus describes the relationship between the objects. Using this definition, we can identify as vases all sorts of different containers, including tin cans, wine bottles, crystal containers, pitchers, and baskets. We can also discriminate between containers that are vases and those that are flower pots. For example, if we see a pitcher being used as a vase, we would not say to ourselves, "That is not a vase." Instead we would probably think, "That is an interesting vase." We recognize the pitcher's change in function because it now matches our definition of vase.

Other examples of defined concepts include *leader, honesty, fairness, principle,* and *dangerous*. To classify examples of these concepts, a person must know how each concept is defined. Some definitions will be brief and straightforward; others will be complex statements of related features, uses, relationships, and characteristics. The clearer and more precise a definition, the more accurately a person will be able to classify examples of the concept.

Rules   Rules are propositions that govern our behavior toward stimuli and cause us to respond in a given or expected way. We follow rules to perform skills correctly (Gagné 1985). Language and mathematics are two examples of rule-governed skills. If we want to use language correctly, we must follow rules of spelling, sentence construction, punctuation, subject and verb agreement, capitalization, and so forth. The rules for addition enable us to add numbers correctly, regardless of their nature, quantity, and size.

A rule may be brief, as in "Capitalize proper nouns," or it may be a long procedure, like the ones needed to do long division and to calculate a standard deviation. Rules are composed of two or more concepts. For example, the rule, "Capitalize proper nouns," is made up of three concepts: capitalize, proper nouns, and nouns. Before students can follow this rule, they must learn all three concepts. They must be able to follow the rules for capitalizing words, for classifying words as nouns, and for classifying the subset of nouns called *proper nouns*. To classify nouns and proper nouns correctly, students must know how these concepts are defined. Once they know the concepts involved, they are ready to learn and apply the rule for capitalizing proper nouns.

Principles are rules used to explain and interpret phenomena and to predict what will happen in given circumstances. They explain why events happen by combining two or more concepts and their relationships. The relationships of the concepts may be causal (one concept causes another concept) or correlational (one concept is positively or negatively related to another). "Poor eating habits usually result in digestive problems," exemplifies a commonly accepted principle that has a causal relationship between the named concepts. "Cigarette smoking is positively related to various health disorders," is an example of a correlational principle. We use these principles to predict what will happen if someone consistently overeats, eats the wrong foods, or smokes cigarettes. When individuals who have poor eating habits or who smoke cigarettes develop health problems, we then explain their condition using the commonly believed principles. Like rules, principles may be brief and straightforward or they may be lengthy with many concepts and their relationships. For example, you might use a principle to explain how a group of students performed on a test or to predict how one would perform. The concepts included in your principle might be (1) student's ability, (2) students' motivation and effort, (3) the quality of the instruction provided, and (4) the quality of the test administered. The principle might be expressed as follows:

$$\begin{matrix} \text{High Test} \\ \text{Achievement} \end{matrix} = \begin{matrix} \text{High} \\ \text{Student} \\ \text{Ability} \end{matrix} + \begin{matrix} \text{High} \\ \text{Motivation} \\ \text{and} \\ \text{Effort} \end{matrix} + \begin{matrix} \text{Quality} \\ \text{Instruction} \end{matrix} + \begin{matrix} \text{Quality} \\ \text{Measure of} \\ \text{Achievement} \end{matrix}$$

With this principle in mind, you would explain observed high test achievement as resulting from or as caused by the presence of this combination of factors. If you believed these factors to be present before administering an achievement test, you would undoubtedly predict high achievement on the test.

Analyzing Goals That Are Intellectual Skills

Intellectual skills are separated into learning hierarchies that show the rules, concepts, and discriminations that the goal requires. The subskills required to perform a goal are sometimes called subordinate skills. The goal, which is the most complex skill, appears at the top of the hierarchy, and the simplest skills are placed at the bottom. The relationships among the skills in the hierarchy are illustrated using task placement and directional arrows. In task placement, if one skill is hierarchically related to another, then the subordinate task is placed directly beneath the superordinate one, as illustrated here.

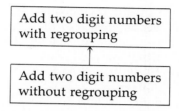

If two tasks are subordinate to another, yet they are not themselves hierarchically related, then they are placed side by side beneath the superordinate task. If one is considered less complex than the other, then it is placed on the left side of the diagram, as illustrated in the following example for proper nouns.

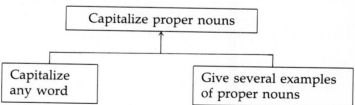

When tasks are related chronologically, they are placed side by side and connected using arrows that illustrate progression from task to task, as shown here.

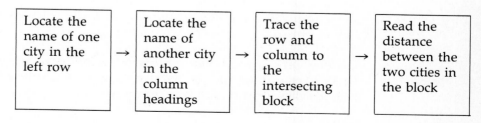

Constructing a diagram that specifies tasks and the relationships among them is the most appropriate way to analyze an instructional goal. The diagram is used to separate and sequence required skills and thus provides a visible and practical framework of subordinate skills for developing instruction and tests.

Although analyzing an intellectual skill instructional goal appears at first to be quite complex, it is relatively easy when you follow these three main steps:

1. Separate the rule or principle into its main rules, defined concepts, and/or concrete concepts and then sequence these main components or content elements.
2. Separate each of these main components (content elements) into its concepts and sequence them.
3. Combine each content element with behaviors to specify tasks that students will perform.

The following section describes and illustrates these main steps.

Identify and Sequence the Main Components in the Goal   The four initial steps in the procedure for analyzing an intellectual skill are to:

1. State the rule or principle clearly.
2. Separate the statement into its main components.
3. Identify the relationship among these components.
4. Sequence the main components according to their relationships.

The example in Figure 3.1 illustrates this process for the instructional goal, "Capitalize proper nouns."

Identify and Sequence the Elements in Each Main Component   Whether the elements you have identified consist of rules, defined concepts, or concrete concepts, the procedure in Figure 3.1 is repeated to identify and sequence the main elements in each. The examples in Figure 3.2 illustrate this process.

At this point in the analysis, you need to decide whether to continue breaking down the concepts. If you suspect that some members of your group cannot classify words that reference persons, places, things, or ideas, then these concepts should be further analyzed by listing the distinguishing characteristics of each. However, if you have identified concepts that you believe all members of your group can classify, then you are ready to begin the third step in constructing a learning hierarchy.

Combine Each Concept, Rule, or Principle with Behaviors to Specify Learning Tasks   Each concept in the framework must be combined with a behavior that specifies what students are to do with the concepts. Each concept can

FIGURE 3.1   Goal: Capitalize Proper Nouns

Steps	Example
1. State the rule or principle clearly.	Capitalize proper nouns.
2. Break the statement down into its main components.	<u>Capitalize</u> <u>proper nouns</u>
3. Identify the relationship among the main components.	1. The concepts *capitalize* and *proper nouns* are not hierarchically related.
	2. Proper nouns and nouns are hierarchically related: students must be able to classify nouns before they can classify proper nouns.
	3. Capitalize is less complex than either proper nouns or nouns, so it should be learned first.
4. Sequence the components based on their relationships.	

Capitalize   Proper Nouns
(1)   (3)
↑
Nouns
(2)

have several different behaviors that are themselves hierarchically related. For example, the concept *noun* can be combined with the following behaviors: (1) *state* the definition; (2) use the definition to *discriminate* between words that are nouns and words that are not nouns; and (3) use the definition to *generate examples* of words that are nouns. These behaviors have the following relationship:

Use definition or characteristics to *generate* other examples from memory.

↑

Use definition or characteristics to *discriminate* between given examples and nonexamples.

↑

State definition or *list* physical characteristics.

Figure 3.3 illustrates a learning hierarchy for this capitalization goal. Notice that there are two main strands of skills: capitalizing words and classifying proper nouns. No skills are listed below stating the rule for capitalizing words because it was judged that all students had mastered the alphabet, including both upper- and lower-case letters. Notice also the behaviors that are combined with each named concept or rule. The tasks are arranged so that the most basic or simple ones are located at the bottom; as they progress

FIGURE 3.2 Identify and Sequence Main Elements

Steps	Example
1. State the rule for capitalizing a word.	To capitalize a word, make the first letter upper case and all remaining letters lower case.
2. Separate the statement into its main components.	To <u>capitalize a word</u>, make the <u>first letter</u> <u>upper case</u> and <u>all remaining letters</u> <u>lower case.</u>
3. Identify the relationship among the main components.	1. Upper-case letters and lower-case letters are not hierarchically related. 2. First letter and all remaining letters are not hierarchically related to each other or to the elements in (1) above. 3. First letter is upper case. Must understand the elements in (1) and (2) above before this relationship makes sense. 4. All remaining letters are lower case. Must understand the elements in (1) and (2) above before this relationship makes sense. 5. Capitalize words. Must understand the elements in (3) and (4) above before this relationship makes sense.
4. Sequence the components according to their relationships.	capitalize words (7) first letter is upper case (5) all other letters are lower case (6) lower case letters (1) upper case letters (2) first letter of word (3) all remaining letters of word (4)

Steps	Example
1. State the definition clearly.	Proper nouns are nouns or words that refer to particular persons, places, things, and ideas.
2. Separate the definition into its main components.	<u>Proper nouns</u> are <u>nouns</u> or <u>words</u> that refer to <u>particular</u> <u>persons</u>, <u>places</u>, <u>things</u>, and <u>ideas.</u>

FIGURE 3.2   *(continued)*

Steps	Example
3. Identify the relationships among the main components.	1. The concepts *persons, places, things, ideas, words,* and *refer* are the most basic, and they are not hierarchically related to each other. 2. The elements in (1) above are all subordinate to the concept *noun.* 3. The concepts *noun* and *particular* are not hierarchically related. 4. The elements in (3) above are both subordinate to the concept *proper noun.*
4. Sequence the components according to their relationships.	

proper nouns
(9)

nouns   particular
(7)   (8)

persons   places   things   ideas   refer   words
(1)   (2)   (3)   (4)   (5)   (6)

toward the top of the diagram, they become more complex. The key to a carefully constructed learning hierarchy is to use (1) clear and comprehensive statements of principles, rules, and definitions, and (2) hierarchically related behaviors for each concept, rule, and principle included.

Verbal Information

Gagné (1985) identifies a second type of learning as verbal information. Verbal information involves learning names or labels, facts, and collections of information that are sometimes called bodies of knowledge. Unlike intellectual skills, which represent procedural knowledge, verbal information represents declarative knowledge. Much of what is taught in school is verbal information. When students learn to name the parts of the body, repeat historical facts, or memorize poems, they are learning verbal information.

Names and Labels   Learning the names for objects, events, ideas, and symbols involves consistently associating the name with a given object, event, idea, or symbol. For example, the symbol *9* is always called nine, the symbol + means to add, a particular teacher is Mr. Jones, the word *red* refers to a particular color, and $\overline{X}$ is the symbol for an average score. We often learn

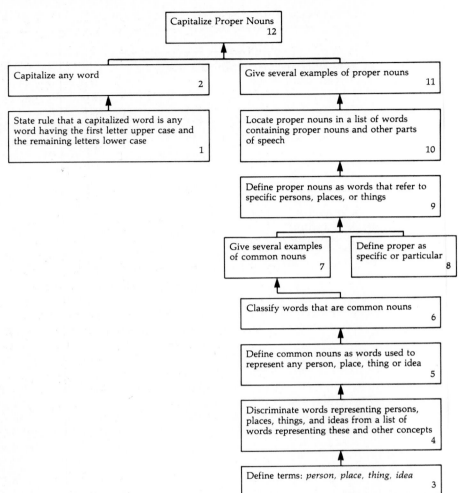

FIGURE 3.3
A Learning
Hierarchy for the
Instructional
Goal: Capitalize
Proper Nouns

the name for an object at the same time as we learn its distinguishing characteristics. A person who learns the name for an object, however, may not be able to generalize the properties of the object and to recognize other examples of the same concept. Thus, to name or label something, a person must simply remember the name of a given object, event, idea, or symbol when it is encountered.

Facts   Verbal information also includes facts, such as knowing that a particular building is the library, that the library is the newest building in town, that it contains more books than any other library in the state, and that it is open from eight o'clock in the morning until nine o'clock at night.

Verbal information and intellectual skills appear to work in a symbiotic way. Verbal information helps us communicate our intellectual skills, and intellectual skills help us organize and structure our verbal information. Although verbal information appears to be a simpler form of knowledge than do intellectual skills, it is not necessarily subordinate. For example, students could more easily communicate or verbalize the concrete concept *boat* if they knew the name of a floating vehicle that carries cargo or people. At the same time, they do not have to know the name *boat* to classify examples. Likewise, they can learn that the name of a particular object is *boat* without being able to classify other examples of the concept.

Analyzing Goals for Verbal Information

Students will learn and remember verbal information more easily if it is organized in a meaningful way and presented as interrelated or connected facts and names. Gagné recommends creating frameworks (*schemata*), which cluster similar facts and information, and providing a meaningful context for learning labels and names. For example, instead of presenting important historical figures in chronological order, a teacher might group them according to the nature of their accomplishments. Notable writers, inventors, politicians, and explorers could all be presented in their turn. In introducing new vocabulary, a teacher could present groups of related words, such as those associated with food and eating, work, recreation, and travel. Two schemata for presenting verbal information related to geography and biology appear in Table 3.3. Each diagram separates information into categories, and columns and rows provide space for related information and examples.

Motor Skills

Gagné (1985) describes *motor skills* as those skills requiring the coordination of muscular movement, such as walking, running, jumping, and lifting. We acquire some of these skills by watching other people perform them, trying them ourselves, and refining them through trial and error. Complex motor skills, such as driving a race car, forming a clay pot on a potter's wheel, and blowing glass into predesigned forms, require instruction and considerable practice. In school, students use motor skills to form printed and cursive letters, draw pictures, operate scientific equipment, perform in athletic events, use tools and machines, play musical instruments, and sing in a chorus.

Many motor skills can be separated into action steps, which may take place sequentially or simultaneously. These steps, often called *part skills*, make up the complete performance or total skill. Students may learn and practice part skills separately, but they must eventually integrate them into practice of the total skill (Gagné 1985).

TABLE 3.3   Schemata for Organizing Verbal Information Related to Geography and Biology

A. Geography

Countries Located in the Americas

	Name	Capital city	Size in sq. miles	Location on map	Population	Climate
Countries in North America						
Countries in Central America						
Countries in South America						

B. Biology

Human Body Systems

	Circulatory	Respiratory	Digestive	Nervous	Muscular	Skeletal
Function						
Structure						
Operation						

Analyzing Goals for Motor Skills

To analyze an instructional goal for a motor skill, you need to identify the total skill, the main part skills, and the proper sequence of the parts. Once the part skills are identified, each skill is further separated into required subskills.

Figure 3.4 contains a partial analysis of the goal, "Execute a golf swing." The statement for the total skill appears at the top. Five part skills are listed below: grip the club; address the ball; execute the backswing; execute the downswing; and execute the follow through. In this partial analysis, only the overlap grip is broken down into subskills, which appear in their proper sequence. In a complete analysis, each of the five part skills in the top row would be broken down into subskills. Although some of the part skills might be taught separately, a person learning how to execute a golf swing eventually would have to integrate and practice all of the skills in one smooth, continuous motion.

FIGURE 3.4 Partial Analysis of a Motor Skill Goal: Execute a Golf Swing

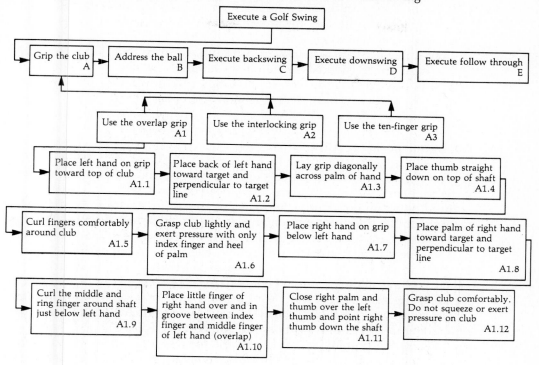

Attitudes

Gagné (1985) defines *attitudes*, a fourth type of learning, as internal states that influence an individual's choice of personal action. According to Gagné, an attitude consists of three elements:

1. An *affective* component that includes the positive and negative feelings a person has.
2. A *behavioral* component made up of behaviors or acts that result from a person's feelings and knowledge.
3. A *cognitive* component consisting of a person's knowledge about how to do something and the rewards or consequences for doing it.

Our feelings about people, things, events, and concepts affect our behavior. Learning theorists propose that human beings acquire many of their attitudes by watching and mimicking people they respect or want to emulate. In our society, teachers are expected to play an important role in developing their students' attitudes. For example, most teachers would encourage their students to demonstrate the following attitudes:

1. A negative attitude toward cheating
2. A positive attitude toward learning and toward participation
3. A positive attitude toward classroom and community rules for acceptable behavior
4. A negative attitude toward drug use, smoking, and other activities that are considered dangerous or harmful
5. A positive attitude toward thorough, careful work
6. A positive attitude toward responsible behavior

Analyzing Goals for Attitudes

As you develop instructional goals for your classes, you may want to include goals that address student attitudes. Once you have selected a goal for an attitude, you should identify the relevant factors for each of the three elements. For the affective component, list the positive and negative feelings that students are to acquire. For the behavioral component, identify the behaviors that will demonstrate a student's acquisition of the desired attitude. For the cognitive component, identify the skills and information students will need to behave in the prescribed way as well as the rewards or consequences for behaving in a certain way. Your attitude framework may contain intellectual skills, verbal information, motor skills, or a combination of these types of learning in addition to the positive and negative feelings.

Figure 3.5 presents a partial analysis for the goal, "Acquire a positive attitude toward cleanliness and personal grooming," taken from a curriculum guide for exceptional students. The goal statement appears at the top. The left column lists the positive feelings, which in this case are the same as the goal statement. The right column lists the behaviors that will demonstrate when students possess the desired attitudes. Notice that all of the behaviors listed are relevant and observable. Although the teacher will not actually witness some of these behaviors, physical indicators that they have occurred will be obvious. The bottom part of the table identifies the skills and information students must have in order to demonstrate one of the behaviors, "Wash hands."

Combination Goals

Some instructional goals do not fall into any single category of learning. For example, the instructional goal, "Serve a tennis ball," may appear to be only a motor skill. Certainly someone learning to serve a tennis ball must develop and combine several complex motor skills. At the same time, however, the person will need to know tennis serving rules and strategies. The person should also be able to identify parts of the playing court related to the serve.

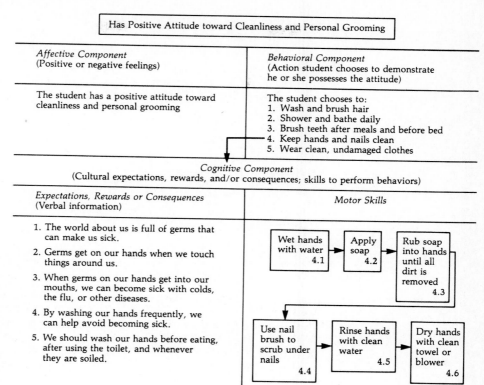

FIGURE 3.5
A Partial
Analysis of an
Attitude Goal:
Acquire a
Positive Attitude
toward
Cleanliness and
Personal
Grooming

Finally, the person will need to acquire positive attitudes about cooperation, fair play, consideration of other players, and practice. Because the goal includes motor skills, intellectual skills, verbal skills, and attitudes, it is considered a combination goal. This type of goal requires a combination of analysis procedures.

Figure 3.6 contains a partial analysis for the goal, "Serve a tennis ball." Section I contains a partial analysis of serving procedures. Only step B, "Toss ball," is broken down into subskills. Section II, Intellectual Skills, lists serving rules a player would need to know. The list also includes serving strategies. Section III, Verbal Information, includes the names of parts of the court used during the serve, and Section IV identifies desired attitudes.

Although the goal analysis procedure is time consuming, it is a necessary prerequisite to writing behavioral objectives, developing lesson plans, evaluating instructional materials, developing relevant tests, and diagnosing students' problems. If you have difficulty analyzing and sequencing subordinate skills for instructional goals, the skills probably have become automatic for you. This state of automatic performance enables you to perform efficiently with little conscious thought about what you are doing. Although automatic

Serve a Tennis Ball

I. Motor Skills

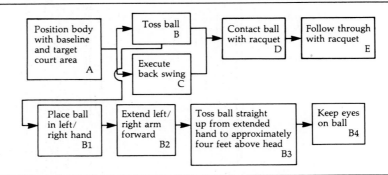

II. Intellectual Skills

Demonstrate the following rules related to designated tasks:

Task
A   When serving into the lefthand court, the player must stand between the center mark and the right sideline.

A   When serving into the righthand court, the player must stand between the center mark and the left sideline.

A   The player must keep both feet behind the baseline during each serve.

D   After the player contacts the ball with the racquet, the player's feet may touch the baseline.

Goal   When serving into either court, the ball must clear the net without touching it and land within the designated court area or on its boundary line.

Demonstrate the following strategies of serving:

1. Vary speed of ball.
2. Vary direction of ball.
3. Serve to opponent's demonstrated weak hand.

III. Verbal Information

1. Label court lines.
2. Label playing areas.
3. Label net.

IV. Attitudes

Affective Component	*Behavioral Component*
The player has positive attitudes toward skill development, fair play, and cooperation.	The player: 1. Practices serves when given the opportunity. 2. Accepts the umpire's and opponents' calls. 3. Does not verbally or physically abuse self, equipment, or other people.

FIGURE 3.6
A Partial
Analysis of a
Combination
Goal: Serve a
Tennis Ball

performance makes routine tasks easier, it also makes the analysis of subordinate skills for an instructional goal more difficult. New teachers often comment that they really had not understood their subject until they tried to teach it to someone else. This and similar comments indicate the automatic nature of the skills these teachers are trying to communicate. Before they can effectively convey these skills to other people, they must mentally relearn each skill by breaking it down into all of its component skills.

Table 3.4 summarizes goal analysis methods for each of the four types of learning. Notice in the table that the most complex intellectual skills (rules and principles) are listed at the top and the least complex (discriminations) at the bottom. This approach reflects the order in which you will usually need to work in analyzing the instructional goals in your curriculum guide. Because instructional goals are usually global statements of performance, they tend to be at the rules or principles level. To proceed in the analysis, you will need to separate the rule into its discrete concept components. With the concepts thus identified, you can then analyze each one and separate it into its subordinate elements. Working down from the most complex to the least complex task will help you maintain your focus on the skills embedded in the goal and avoid inserting superfluous tasks. After you have used one or more of these methods to analyze your instructional goals, you will be ready to convert the subordinate skills for each goal into behavioral objectives.

TABLE 3.4   Summary of Goal Analysis Methods for Each Type of Learning

Type of Learning	Goal Analysis Method
Intellectual Skills	
Rules and principles	1. State the rule or principle to be analyzed.
	2. Separate the rule into its main concrete concepts and/or defined concepts, and state the relationship among the component concepts.
	3. Sequence the component concepts according to their identified relationships.
Defined concepts	1. State the definition.
	2. Separate the concept into its main elements: concrete concepts and definitions that identify it as a member of the class.
	3. Identify the relationships between the concrete concepts and the definitions.
Concrete concepts	1. Separate the concept into the physical properties used to distinguish it as a member of a class of objects.
Discriminations	1. List relevant characteristics of the two or more concepts that differ.

(continued on next page)

TABLE 3.4 (*continued*)

Type of Learning	Goal Analysis Method
Verbal Information	
Names and labels	Place them in a meaningful context, such as the intellectual skill, motor skill, or attitudinal framework in close proximity to the concept it names.
Facts and information	1. Develop schemata that organize names, facts, and information in a meaningful way. 2. Arrange relevant topics in columns and rows. 3. Insert related facts or examples in appropriate intersection spaces.
Motor skills	1. Identify and sequence each main step in the physical procedure. 2. Separate each main step into smaller steps (part skills) and sequence these. 3. Separate smaller steps into the critical features of the step, such as timing, pressure, position, rules, or strategies that comprise efficient performance of the step.
Attitudes	
Affective component	State the positive and negative feelings related to the desired attitude.
Behavioral component	List the behaviors the student would choose to exhibit if he or she possessed each positive and negative attitude named.
Cognitive component	1. List relevant cultural expectations. 2. List the rewards one could expect for exhibiting the desired behaviors. 3. List the consequences one could expect for not exhibiting the desired behaviors. 4. Identify and analyze the intellectual skills and motor skills the student would need to behave in the specified manner.

WRITING BEHAVIORAL OBJECTIVES

A behavioral objective is a statement of intended learning outcomes that includes the subordinate skill, the conditions under which the skill will be performed, and the criteria for acceptable performance. The subordinate skills in the goal framework should already contain the behavior and content. Adding conditions helps define the nature and complexity of the task, and criteria specify the limits of an acceptable answer. Behavioral objectives (sometimes called *performance objectives* and *instructional objectives*) that include the conditions and criteria for performance are valuable guides for developing lessons and for writing test items that measure the intended performance.

Conditions

Conditions is a term used to indicate the information, tools, equipment, or other resources students will be given when they are asked to perform the skill. Conditions are used to prescribe the stimulus that will be provided for the task and to limit the task's scope and complexity so that it is reasonable for given students.

To prescribe the stimulus for a subordinate skill, you need to consider the behavior in the skill and what students will need in order to demonstrate that behavior. Consider how the conditions in the following examples prescribe the stimuli students will be given to perform the subordinate skills.

Conditions	*Subordinate Skills*
1. Given the name of a concrete concept, . . .	1. . . . list the distinguishing properties of the concept.
2. Given a prototype of a concrete concept, . . .	2. . . . list the distinguishing properties of the concept.
3. Given a list of the distinguishing properties of a concrete concept, . . .	3. . . . name the concept.
4. Given several examples and non-examples of a concept, . . .	4. . . . classify examples of the concept.
5. Given several examples of a concrete concept, . . .	5. . . . analyze the examples and list their common characteristics.

Although, at first glance, the stimuli appear to be obvious, this is not always the case. Notice, for example, that subordinate skills 1 and 2 are the same, yet the conditions are different. In example 1, students will be given the name as a stimulus, whereas in example 2, they will be given an actual object to work with. The differences in these stimuli will change the nature of the task. When given the name as a stimulus, students will need to search their memories to recall the distinguishing characteristics they have learned, with no clues provided. On the other hand, the actual object will provide clues, but it may also cause unskilled students to confuse "unique" characteristics with others not used to define the class. For example, birds, dogs, and fish all have two eyes. Being precise in prescribing the stimulus helps ensure that test items written measure the intended behavior.

In setting performance conditions, you should also consider the sophistication and achievement levels of students in the group. You can vary the conditions in a behavioral objective so that the required performance matches the skill level of your students. Consider the subordinate skill, "Locate specified places on a state map." The conditions you specify will determine the complexity of this task. Notice how the following three conditions affect the difficulty of the task:

Conditions	*Subordinate Skill*
1. Given a simplified state map with no more than ten identified points, . . .	. . . locate specified places on the map.
2. Given a simplified state map with 20 to 30 identified points, . . .	
3. Given a commercially prepared state map, . . .	

Notice that the basic stimulus remains the same: given a state map. However, qualifiers are added to each condition to limit the complexity of the stimulus and the behavior. The first condition would be most appropriate for lower elementary grades; the second for upper elementary grades; and the third for junior high, senior high, or adult students. Although the basic skill of locating specified places on a state map remains the same, the conditions have an important effect on the complexity of the task.

Performance Criteria

Behavioral objectives sometimes include performance criteria, which indicate how well the subordinate skill is to be performed. They should be added only when student responses are expected to vary. For example, you could expect a range of answers for a test question based on the behavioral objective, "Given no measurement tool, estimate the length of a specified object." By adding the criterion, "correct to within one foot," you could set the boundaries for an acceptable answer.

The behavioral objective, "Type, from handwritten copy, an average of fifty words per minute," specifies an acceptable speed for students' work. Adding another criterion, "with no more than two typing errors," establishes the number of acceptable errors. The speed and error criteria help communicate exactly what the student is expected to do.

If only one correct response is possible, criteria are not needed. Consider, for example, the behavioral objective, "Calculate the average score for a set of test scores." A criterion such as "correctly" or "80 percent of the time" is not necessary. If the student calculates the scores correctly, then only one answer is possible. For the criterion, "80 percent of the time," students would have to calculate average scores on five different test items. Although some teachers might require this, most would consider it impractical.

Table 3.5 lists three learning tasks and five related behavioral objectives.

TABLE 3.5   Behavioral Objectives for Three Learning Tasks

Task: Capitalize proper nouns

Conditions	*Performance*	*Criteria*
1. Given sentences without proper nouns capitalized, . . .	. . . locate and capitalize proper nouns.	
2. Given a list of words containing common and proper nouns, . . .	. . . locate and capitalize the proper nouns.	

Task: Estimate the distance between specified places on a map

Conditions	*Performance*	*Criteria*
1. Given a simplified map with 10 to 12 identified places, a ruler, and a scale with one inch equal to 10 miles, . . .	. . . estimate the distance between specified places, . . .	. . . with the distance accurate to within 2 miles.

Task: Add numbers

Conditions	*Performance*	*Criteria*
1. Given two whole numbers of two digits that do not require regrouping, . . .	. . . add the numbers.	
2. Given two whole numbers of two digits that require regrouping, . . .	. . . add the numbers.	

The two behavioral objectives for the task, "Capitalize proper nouns," specify different conditions. For the first objective, students are given sentences without proper nouns capitalized. For the second, they are given a list of words containing common nouns and proper nouns. The behavioral objectives do not include criteria because none are needed to judge the accuracy of students' work.

The behavioral objective for the second task, "Estimate the distance between specified places on a map," includes three conditions and the criterion for performance. The "givens" are a simplified map, a ruler, and a simplified mileage scale. To be considered accurate, the students' answers must be within 2 miles of the teacher's calculations.

The behavioral objectives for the third task, "Add numbers," has conditions that limit the digits in each number, the numbers in each problem, and whether regrouping is required. Criteria for judging answers are not needed because correct answers are not expected to vary.

SUMMARY

Instructional goals provide a focus for instruction and describe the learning outcomes for units and lessons. To develop lessons and tests, you should first clarify each instructional goal for a course according to the level of learning (Bloom, Madaus, and Hastings 1981) and the types of learning involved (Gagné 1985). Using the Bloom, Madaus, and Hastings classification strategy, cognitive goals can be identified as being either knowledge, comprehension, application, analysis, synthesis, or evaluation. Knowledge is the most basic level, and evaluation is the most complex. Using the Gagné classification strategy, goals can be classified as intellectual skills, verbal information, motor skills, or attitudes.

Gagné suggests procedures for analyzing each instructional goal based on its classification. Intellectual skill goals that are rules or principles should be separated into their discrete concepts and the relationships among the concepts. Defined concepts can be separated into their subordinate concepts and the relationships among them. Concrete concepts are separated into the unique physical properties that define the class. Dividing each intellectual skill into its subordinate tasks and sequencing the tasks according to their relationship result in a learning hierarchy, or task analysis, that can be used as a basis for writing behavioral objectives.

Gagné makes the following suggestions for analyzing verbal information:

1. Names and labels should be placed in a meaningful context.
2. Facts should be organized into bodies of knowledge or schemata of related facts using tables that help clarify the relationships among the facts.

His suggestion for organizing names and labels so they are placed in a meaningful context would result in placing these tasks, when possible, on the task analyses beside or near the named concepts. This means that verbal information will appear on the frameworks for intellectual skills, motor skills, and attitudes.

Analyzing motor skills requires separating the whole skill into its major part skills and then identifying the steps in the procedure required to perform each part skill. Part skills and their procedural steps should be arranged in chronological order.

Instructional goals that are attitudes should be analyzed by separating the attitude into three elements: the affective component, the behavioral component, and the cognitive component. In conducting the analysis, the desirable positive and negative feelings are listed for the affective component, and then behaviors that would reflect such feelings are described. Finally, information and skills needed to perform the behavior are identified and analyzed. Gagné suggests that information presented include cultural expectations for behavior and the rewards and consequences of behaving in prescribed ways.

The instructional goals and their subordinate skills, identified through task analysis, should be converted into behavioral objectives. Behavioral objectives include the subordinate skill, the conditions, and sometimes the criteria for acceptable performance. The stimulus required for the prescribed behavior and the skill level of target students help determine the conditions a teacher decides to include in behavioral objectives. When students' responses can vary, criteria are included to define an acceptable answer. Appropriately written behavioral objectives provide valuable guidelines for lesson planning and the development of test items.

PRACTICE EXERCISES

I. Levels of Learning. Match each task listed in Column 1 with the appropriate level of learning listed in Column 2. You may refer to Table 3.1 for definitions of each term in Column 2.

Column 1	Column 2
1. Calculate the average score for a set of test scores.	A. Knowledge
2. Break a rule or principle into its separate elements and describe the relationships among them.	B. Comprehension
3. Use specified criteria to judge the quality of a product.	C. Application
4. Use the relationships among a variety of elements to combine them into a whole.	D. Analysis
5. Paraphrase a fact, a definition, or a procedure.	E. Synthesis
6. Recall the verbatim definitions for a given list of concepts.	F. Evaluation
7. Write the formula for calculating a standard deviation.	
8. Write a technical report for a given target audience.	

II. Types of Learning

A. In your own words, define Gagné's four types of learning and write at least one instructional goal or behavioral objective from your content area that fits each type of learning: intellectual skills, verbal information, motor skills, attitudes.

B. Read the following list of instructional goals and classify the type of learning each represents as:

A. Intellectual skills
B. Verbal information
C. Motor Skills
D. Attitudes

1. Recite a short poem.
2. Choose to work independently on school assignments.
3. Name common traffic signs.
4. Choose to be punctual.
5. Bounce a ball.
6. Name the capital city for each state.
7. Write a paragraph containing a topic sentence, supporting facts, and a concluding sentence.
8. Button a shirt.
9. Alphabetize any given list of words.
10. Select the correct coins to make any given amount of money up to 99 cents.
11. On a map, name and locate all fifty states in the United States.
12. Interpret a state map.

C. Match each recommended goal analysis procedure in Column 1 with its associated type of learning listed in Column 2.

1. Identify and sequence all the part skills required to perform a physical task.	A. Intellectual skills
2. Develop schemata for organizing related facts required to achieve an instructional goal.	B. Verbal information
	C. Motor skills
3. Identify the affective, behavioral, and cognitive components required to achieve a goal.	D. Attitudes
4. Develop a learning hierarchy of all subordinate skills required to achieve a goal.	

III. Instructional Goal Analysis. Develop frameworks of subordinate skills for the following instructional goals. The feedback section provides sample analyses that you can compare with your own. Although your analyses can be expected to differ, there should be some similarity to those provided.

Note: Do not worry if your frameworks do not include enough detail or are different from those of other students. A sketchy framework is better than none at all, and your ability to analyze goals will improve with practice. Creating good frameworks takes time and experience. After developing and using a framework, you will want to make changes that reflect your classroom experiences with students.

A. Intellectual Skills

1. Choose any two of the skills in blocks (1), (2), (3.1), (3.2), and (3.3) in Figure 3.7, and identify the subordinate skills required to perform them. Draw arrows between the skills to identify their sequence and relationship.

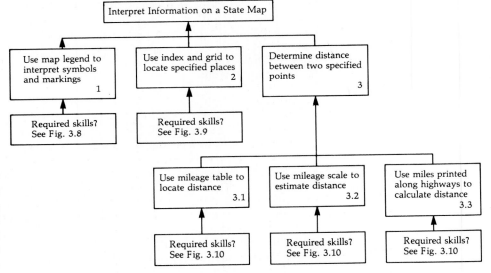

FIGURE 3.7
Subordinate Skills for the Instructional Goal: Interpret Information on a State Map.

2. Analyze the following instructional goal for an intellectual skill:

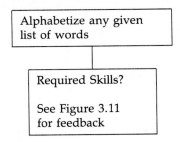

B. Verbal Information. Develop a table that includes information students will need to "Name common traffic signs." Your table should include sign colors, sign shapes, and sign names (See Table 3.6 for feedback).

    C. Motor Skills. Identify and sequence the steps students would need to achieve the goal, "Bounce a ball while standing still." See Figure 3.12 for feedback.

    D. Attitudes. For the attitude goal "Choose to be punctual" analyze the following (see Figure 3.13 for feedback):

       1. The positive feelings (affective component) a student is expected to possess.

       2. The overt behaviors that will indicate whether a student chooses to be punctual.

       3. The verbal information (cognitive component) a student should possess. The information should include cultural expectations, rewards, and consequences.

       4. A procedure for punctuality a student could follow.

IV. Behavioral Objectives. Choose Figure 3.3, 3.8, 3.9, or 3.10 and write behavioral objectives for each subordinate skill. Before you begin to write conditions, think about the behavior in each skill and the stimulus it would require. Also, select a target group of students with whom you are familiar. If you plan to work with junior high school through adult students, choose one of the map examples. If your target group is elementary students, select either the capitalization or the map framework. Then, write your behavioral objectives with the skill level of the target students in mind. Include criteria in the objectives only when they are needed.

    If you choose Figure 3.3, compare your objectives with those in Table 3.7. Feedback for Figures 3.8 and 3.9 is designed for average and above-average sixth grade students and is located in Tables 3.8 and 3.9. Feedback for Figure 3.10, also directed toward sixth graders, appears in Tables 3.10, 3.11, and 3.12.

V. Enrichment. Choose an instructional goal for a subject you know well. Identify the analysis procedure for the type of goal you choose and develop a framework of the subordinate skills required to achieve the goal. Ask another person who is familiar with the subject to critique your work. When you are satisfied that the framework is adequate, convert each subordinate skill into a behavioral objective by adding conditions and necessary criteria.

FEEDBACK

I. Levels of Learning

    1–C, 2–D, 3–F, 4–E, 5–B, 6–A, 7–A, 8–E

II. Types of Learning

    A. Definitions (If you are unsure about the appropriateness of your instructional goals or objectives, you may want to discuss your examples with classmates or with the professor.)

    Intellectual skills involve the use of symbols to interact with the environment. Intellectual skills are mental procedures used to interpret phenomena and solve problems. They include discrimination, concrete concepts, defined concepts, and rules.

    Verbal information, often called *declarative knowledge,* involves associating objects, symbols, events, or conditions with their names. It also includes remembering facts and repeating or recounting information.

Motor skills are physical tasks that require movement, precision, and timing. They often take the form of physical procedures having a series of steps to be performed either simultaneously or in a prescribed sequence.

Attitudes are mental states that govern our choices and behavior. Attitudes have three main components: affective, behavioral, and cognitive.

B. Classification

1. B	5. C	9. A
2. D	6. B	10. A
3. B	7. A	11. B
4. D	8. C	12. A

C. Analysis Procedures

    1. C, 2. B, 3. D, 4. A

III. Instructional Goal Analysis

  A. Intellectual Skills

    1. See Figures 3.8–3.10

    2. See Figure 3.11

  B. Verbal Information (see Table 3.6)

  C. Motor Skills (see Figure 3.12)

  D. Attitudes (see Figure 3.13)

IV. Behavioral Objectives (see Tables 3.7 through 3.12)

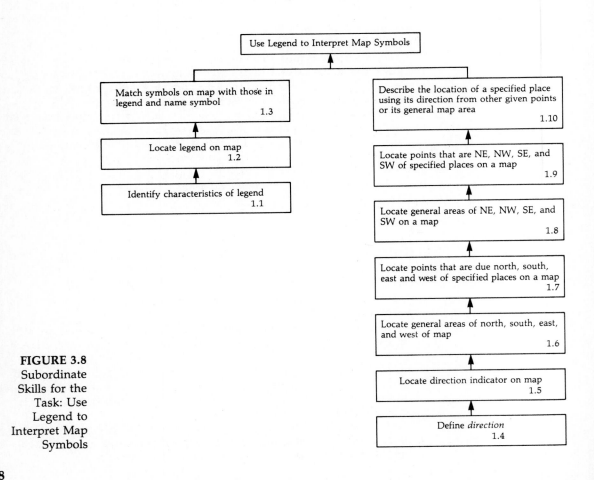

FIGURE 3.8
Subordinate Skills for the Task: Use Legend to Interpret Map Symbols

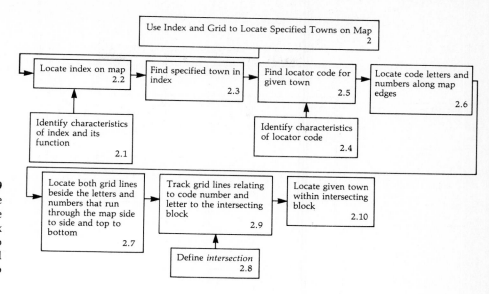

FIGURE 3.9
Subordinate
Skills for the
Task: Use Index
and Grid to
Locate Specified
Places on a Map

TABLE 3.6   Analysis of the Instructional Goal: Name Common Traffic Signs

Name of Sign	Shape of Sign	Colors of Sign
Stop	Octagon	Red with white
Yield	Triangle, tip down	
Do not enter	Circle within square	
Action prohibited		
Warning, road conditions	Diamond	Yellow with black
Warning, railroad	X within circle	
Warning, no passing	Triangle with tip pointing to right	
Warning, school zone	Triangle top, rectangle bottom	
Warning, construction	Diamond	Orange with black
Warning, maintenance		
Regulatory sign	Rectangle or square	White with black
Information sign		
Railroad crossing	Crossbuck	
Public recreation	Rectangle	Brown with white
Park signs		
Motorist service signs	Rectangle	Blue with white
Directional information	Rectangle	Green with white

FIGURE 3.10 Subordinate Skills for the Task: Determine Distance between Two Specified Points

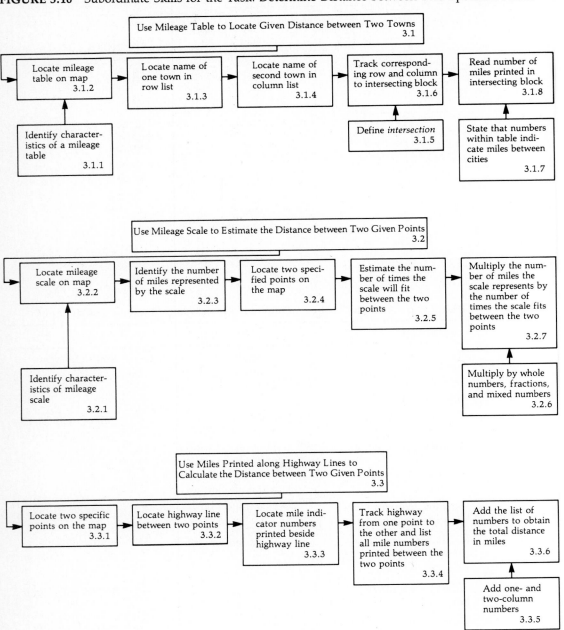

FIGURE 3.11 Subordinate Skills for the Instructional Goal: Alphabetize Any Given List of Words

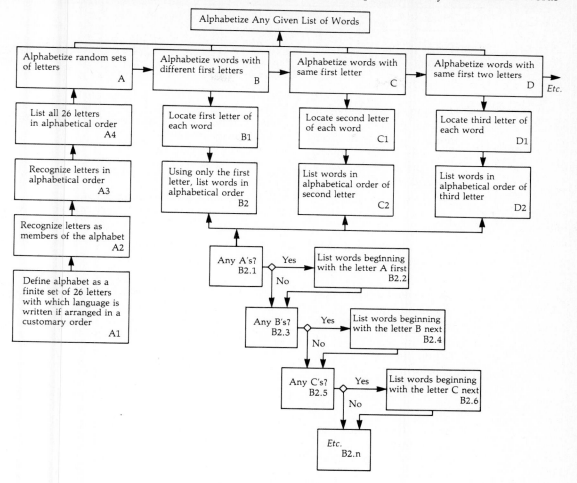

TABLE 3.7 Behavioral Objectives for the Instructional Goal: Capitalize Proper Nouns (Figure 3.3)

Subordinate Skills	Matching Behavioral Objectives
1. State the rule for capitalizing words	1.1 From memory, state the rule for capitalizing words.
	1.2 Select the rule for capitalizing words from a set of alternative rules.
2. Capitalize any word	2.1 Given a list of several words, select the letter in the words that should be capitalized.
	2.2 Given some words that are properly capitalized and some that are improperly capitalized, select those that are properly capitalized.

(continued on next page)

TABLE 3.7 *(continued)*

Subordinate Skills	Matching Behavioral Objectives
3. Define the terms *person, place, thing,* and *idea*	3.1 From memory, define the terms *person, place, thing,* and *idea.* 3.2 Match the terms *person, place, thing,* and *idea* with their definitions.
4. Discriminate words that represent persons, places, things, and ideas from lists of words containing these and other concepts	4.1 Given a list of words that contains persons, places, things, and ideas, classify each word into the appropriate category.
5. Define the term *noun*	5.1 From memory, define the term *noun.* 5.2 Given the definition for the term *noun,* identify it as such.
6. Classify words that are common nouns	6.1 Given a list of words containing common nouns and other parts of speech, select the common nouns.
7. Give several examples of common nouns	7.1 List several words that refer to persons. 7.2 List several words that refer to places. 7.3 List several words that refer to things. 7.4 List several words that refer to ideas.
8. Define the term *proper* as specific or particular	8.1 From memory, define the term *proper.* 8.2 Given several definitions, select the one for the word *proper.* 8.3 Given the definition of the word *proper,* identify it as such.
9. Define proper nouns as words that refer to specific persons, places, or things.	9.1 From memory, define proper nouns. 9.2 Given several definitions, select the one for proper nouns. 9.3 Given the definition for a proper noun, identify it as such.
10. Classify words as proper nouns	10.1 Given a list of words containing both proper and common nouns, with some proper nouns not capitalized and some common nouns capitalized, select the proper nouns.
11. Give several examples of proper nouns	11.1 Given the category, *persons,* list several proper nouns that name persons. 11.2 Given the category, *places,* list several proper nouns that name places. 11.3 Given the category, *things,* list several proper nouns that name things.
12. Capitalize proper nouns (goal)	12.1 Given sentences that include proper nouns that are not capitalized and common nouns that are capitalized, locate the capitalization errors. 12.2 Write sentences that include proper nouns and capitalize the proper nouns.

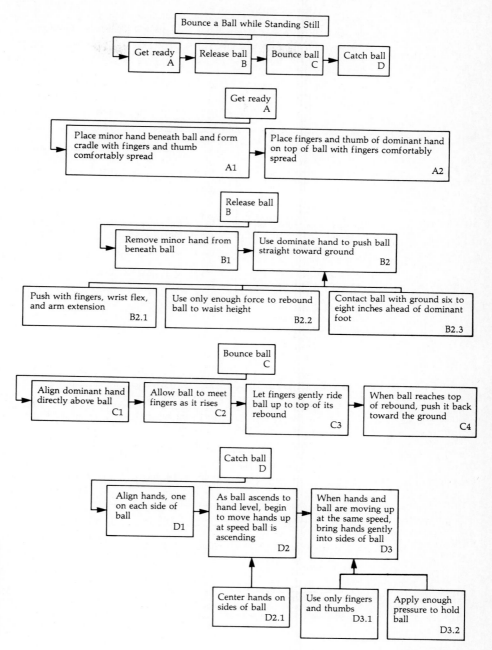

FIGURE 3.12
Subordinate
Skills for the
Instructional
Goal: Bounce a
Ball while
Standing Still

Choose to Be Punctual

Affective Component	*Behavioral Component*
The individual has a:	The individual chooses to:
1. positive attitude toward planning and self-discipline.	1. keep a calendar of appointments.
2. positive attitude toward being punctual.	2. plan activities to enable punctuality.
3. negative attitude toward inconveniencing others.	3. arrive shortly before the scheduled beginning time.
	4. begin scheduled activity on time.
	5. end activity on or before scheduled ending time.

Cognitive Component (Verbal information)

Cultural Expectations	*Rewards*	*Consequences of Habitual Lateness*
1. We live in a time-oriented culture.	The individual gains increased respect from others because he or she has demonstrated:	The individual looses the respect of other people for being discourteous and undisciplined.
2. Punctuality is considered to be an indicator of a person's ability to plan and exercise self-control.	1. good planning skills.	The individual causes other people to worry.
3. Other people expect a person to be punctual.	2. good self-control. 3. respect for other people's time.	The individual causes other people to become annoyed and angry.
4. Other people dislike waiting for people who are not on time.	4. respect for other people's opinions.	
5. Being late is considered discourteous because it causes worry for your safety and demonstrates lack of regard for the feelings of other people.	5. the ability to be dependable.	

Cognitive Component (Procedure)

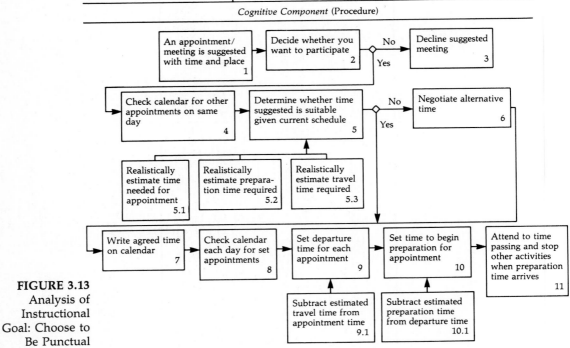

FIGURE 3.13
Analysis of
Instructional
Goal: Choose to
Be Punctual

TABLE 3.8   Behavioral Objectives for the Skill: Use Legend to Interpret Map Symbols (Figure 3.8)

Subordinate Skills	Matching Behavioral Objectives
1.1 Identify characteristics of legend	1.1.1 Describe the legend by appearance and function. 1.1.2 Given the characteristics and function of a legend, identify them as belonging to the legend. 1.1.3 Given a list of characteristics relating to map features, such as the grid, the index, and the legend, identify those related to the legend.
1.2 Locate legend on map	1.2.1 Given a map containing a legend, locate the legend.
1.3 Match symbols on map with those in legend and name symbol	1.3.1 Given a particular symbol on map, locate symbol and name in legend.
1.4 Define direction	1.4.1 From memory, define the term *direction*. 1.4.2 Select the definition for the term *direction* from a set of alternative definitions. 1.4.3 Given the definition for the term *direction*, identify it as such.
1.5 Locate direction indicator on map	1.5.1 Given a map containing a direction indicator, locate the direction indicator
1.6 Locate general areas of north, south, east, and west on map	1.6.1 Given a sample map, label map edges as north, south, east, and west. 1.6.2 Given a description of a map area and a sample map, identify the area described as either north, south, east, or west.
1.7 Locate points that are due north, south, east, and west of specified places on a map	1.7.1 Given a specified point on a map, name towns that are straight north, straight south, straight east, and straight west of the point.
1.8 Locate general areas of northeast, northwest, southeast, and southwest on a map	1.8.1 Given a sample map, label map edges as northeast, northwest, southeast, and southwest. 1.8.2 Given a description of a map area and a sample map, identify the area described as either northeast, northwest, southeast, or southwest.
1.9 Locate points that are northeast, northwest, southeast, and southwest of specified places on a map	1.9.1 Given a specified point on a map, name towns that are northeast, northwest, southeast, and southwest of the point.
1.10 Describe the location of a specified place using its direction from other given points or its general map area	1.10.1 Given a specified town on a map, describe its location using its direction from at least two other named towns on the map. 1.10.2 Given a specified town on a map, describe its location using the general map area in which it is located.

TABLE 3.9   Behavioral Objectives for the Skill: Use Index and Grid to Locate Specified Towns on a Map (Figure 3.9)

Subordinate Skills	Matching Behavioral Objectives
2.1 Identify characteristics of index and its function	2.1.1 Given the term *map index*, list the identifying characteristics of the index. 2.1.2 Given a statement of the purpose for an index, identify it as that for an index. 2.1.3 Given the characteristics of several map features, such as the legend, grid, and index, select the description for the index.
2.2 Locate index on map	2.2.1 Given a map containing an untitled index, locate index.
2.3 Find specified town in index	2.3.1 Given an index and a town name, locate town in index.
2.4 Identify characteristics of locator code	2.4.1 Given a code containing a letter and a number, identify it as a plausible locator code. 2.4.2 Given several codes containing a variety of symbols (2 letters, 2 numbers, direction symbols, and letter/number combinations), select those that are plausible locator codes.
2.5 Find locator code for a given town	2.5.1 Given an index and a town name, find locator code for town.
2.6 Locate code letters and numbers along map edges	2.6.1 Given any locator code, find the corresponding letters and numbers along all four map edges.
2.7 Locate both grid lines beside the letters and numbers that run through the map from side to side and top to bottom and that bound an area within the two lines.	2.7.1 Given a map and either a number or a letter, locate both grid lines that bound it, and follow the bounded map area completely through the map to the corresponding number or letter on the opposite edge.
2.8 Define the term *intersection*	2.8.1 Given the term *intersection*, state the definition. 2.8.2 From a given set of definitions, choose the one for the term *intersection*.
2.9 Track grid lines relating to a code number and letter to the intersecting block	2.9.1 Given any locator code, track within the grid lines for the number and letter to the intersecting block.
2.10 Locate a given town within intersecting block	2.10.1 Given a specified town, locator code, and corresponding intersecting block on map, locate town within block.

TABLE 3.10   Behavioral Objectives for the Skill: Use Mileage Table to Locate a Given Distance between Two Towns (Figure 3.10)

Subordinate Skills	Matching Behavioral Objectives
3.1.1 Identify characteristics of mileage table	3.1.1.1 Given the name *mileage table*, list identifying characteristics of table.
	3.1.1.2 Given several descriptions of map features, select the description of a mileage table.
3.1.2 Locate mileage table on map	3.1.2.1 Given a map containing a mileage table, locate mileage table.
	3.1.2.2 Given several map locations, select the location of the mileage table.
3.1.3 Locate name of one town in row list	3.1.3.1 Given a mileage table and a town name, locate town in row list of towns.
3.1.4 Locate name of second town in column list	3.1.4.1 Given a mileage table and a town name, locate town in column list.
3.1.5 Define the term *intersection*	3.1.5.1 Given the term *intersection*, state the definition.
	3.1.5.2 Given alternative definitions for the term *intersection*, select the best definition.
3.1.6 Track corresponding row and column to intersecting block	3.1.6.1 Given mileage table and the names of two towns, track corresponding row and column to intersecting block for two towns.
3.1.7 State that numbers within table indicate miles between cities	3.1.7.1 From memory, define meaning of numbers in table.
	3.1.7.2 Given several interpretations for numbers within table, select correct interpretation.
3.1.8 Read number of miles printed in intersecting block	3.1.8.1 Given mileage table and the names of two towns, locate miles between towns in mileage table.

TABLE 3.11   Behavioral Objectives for the Skill: Use Mileage Scale to Estimate the Distance between Two Given Points (Figure 3.10)

Subordinate Skills	Matching Behavioral Objectives
3.2.1 Identify characteristics of mileage scale	3.2.1.1 From memory, describe mileage scale. 3.2.1.2 Given several descriptions of map features, select description of mileage scale.
3.2.2 Locate mileage scale on map	3.2.2.1 Given map with mileage scale, locate mileage scale.
3.2.3 Identify number of miles represented by the scale	3.2.3.1 Given a map with a scale indicating 1 inch equal to 100 miles, identify the number of miles represented by scale.
3.2.4 Locate two specified points on the map	3.2.4.1 Given the map, index, grid, and names of two points, locate the points.
3.2.5 Estimate the number of times the scale will fit between the two points	3.2.5.1 Given the map, two specified points, and the scale, determine the number of times the scale fits between the two points.
3.2.6 Multiply by whole numbers, fractions, and mixed numbers	3.2.6.1 Given a mileage scale with 1 inch equal to 100 miles, identify the number of miles represented by: a. 1 inch c. $2\frac{1}{2}$ inches b. 2 inches d. $\frac{1}{2}$ inch
3.2.7 Multiply the number of miles the scale represents by the number of times the scale fits between the two points	3.2.7.1 Given two points on a map and a scale with 1 inch equal to 100 miles, multiply to find the number of miles between the two points, correct to within 10 miles.

TABLE 3.12 Behavioral Objectives for the Skill: Use Miles Printed Along Highway Lines to Calculate the Distance between Two Given Points (Figure 3.10)

Subordinate Skills	Matching Behavioral Objectives
3.3.1 Locate two specified points on the map	3.3.1.1 Given an index, a grid, and the names of two points, locate the two specified points.
3.3.2 Locate the highway line between the two points.	3.3.2.1 Given two specified points, locate the connecting highway line by indicating the route number.
3.3.3 Locate mile indicator numbers printed beside highway line	3.3.3.1 Given a map with clearly marked mile numbers along highway lines, locate printed numbers.
3.3.4 Track highway from one point to another and locate all mile numbers printed between the two points	3.3.4.1 Given specified points and a specified highway connecting the two points, list all mile numbers shown on the highway line between the two points.
3.3.5 Add one- and two-column numbers	3.3.5.1 Given a set of one-column numbers, add the numbers.
	3.3.5.2 Given a set of two-column numbers, add the numbers.
3.3.6 Add the list of numbers to obtain total distance in miles	3.3.6.1 Given two specified points and a specified highway connecting the two points, add all mile numbers shown on the highway line between the two points.

REFERENCES

Bloom, B. S.; Madaus, G. F.; and Hastings, J. T. (1981). *Evaluation to improve learning.* New York: McGraw-Hill Book Company.

Gagné, R. M. (1985). *The Conditions of learning and theory of instruction.* New York: Holt, Rinehart and Winston.

SUGGESTED READING

Dick, W., and Carey, L. M. (1985). *The systematic design of instruction.* Glenview, Ill.: Scott, Foresman.

Gronlund, N. E. (1985). *Measurement and evaluation in teaching.* New York: Macmillan Publishing Company, pp. 24–54, 513–29.

Mager, R. F. (1975). *Preparing instructional objectives.* Palo Alto, Calif.: Fearon Publishers.

Mehrens, W. A., and Lehmann, I. J. (1984). *Measurement and evaluation in education and psychology*. New York: CBS College Publishing, pp. 33–54.

Nitko, A. J. (1983). *Educational tests and measurement*. New York: Harcourt, Brace, Jovanovich, pp. 94–115.

Reigeluth, C. M., ed. (1983). *Instructional design theories and models: an overview of their current status*. Hillsdale, N.J.: Lawrence Erlbaum Associates.

PART II

Designing, Developing, and Using Classroom Tests

CHAPTER 4

Designing Test Specifications

OBJECTIVES

1. Define *measurement, test, evaluation,* and *criterion-referenced test*.
2. Define *test validity* and describe test design considerations that help ensure valid decisions based on test results.
3. Define *test reliability* and describe test design considerations that help ensure reliable test results.
4. Divide subordinate skills in the goal framework into prerequisite and enabling skills.
5. Define *entry behaviors test, pretest, practice test,* and *posttest* and describe how each type of test

provides information teachers need for their planning and evaluation decisions.
6. Define *table of test specifications* and describe how such a table is developed and used.
7. Develop a table of test specifications for all the behavioral objectives identified for an instructional goal.
8. From the table of test specifications, select objectives for an entry behaviors test, a pretest, a practice test, and a posttest.
9. Develop a table of test specifications for a comprehensive examination.

MEASUREMENT, TESTS, AND EVALUATION

Three terms frequently used in this text are *measurement, test,* and *evaluation.* Although these terms are related, there are important differences among them. The term *measurement* refers to quantifying or assigning a number to express the degree to which a characteristic is present. Some common characteristics measured for people include height, weight, and skill attainment. The number or measure used to express height is based on a scale of feet and inches; the measure for weight is expressed as pounds; and the measure of skill attainment is a score that reflects the number of items answered correctly or points earned on some type of achievement test. Using any of these measures, people can be ranked on scales that reflect the degree to which they possess the characteristic.

Measures of a characteristic are obtained using measuring instruments. A yardstick is the instrument used to obtain a measure of height; a weight scale is the instrument used to obtain a measure of weight; and an assigned set of tasks to be performed, called a test, is the instrument used to obtain a skill measure. The quality or stability of the instrument used to obtain a measure will influence the accuracy of the measure.

Evaluation is the procedure used to determine the quality of something. Decisions about quality require criteria or standards that can be applied to judge worth. Once you have a measure of some characteristic, you can compare the measure against established criteria or standards to determine whether it reflects an excellent, good, adequate, poor, or unacceptable level of the characteristic. Both the measures and the tests or instruments can be evaluated. For example, some criteria for evaluating a measure of height are based on group norms (e.g., he is quite tall compared to other boys his age); some on cultural expectations (e.g., he is too short to be considered handsome); and others on health (e.g., his growth rate and height reflect physiological problems). Standards for judging a measure of weight are also based on group comparisons, cultural expectations, and health. Likewise, standards for evaluating a skill measure are based on group comparisons (e.g., above average, average, or below average compared to other people with similar experience and training), or on a level set to reflect high accomplishment of the skill itself (e.g., typing sixty words a minute with no mistakes).

Instruments used to obtain measures are also evaluated. One criterion for judging the quality of an instrument is the consistency with which it produces the same measure under the same conditions. For example, a weight scale that produced three different weight measures for the same person at ten-minute intervals would be an inadequate instrument, whereas one that indicated the same weight each time would be considered good. Likewise, a skill test that resulted in very different scores for the same person on the same day would be judged an inadequate test.

A second criterion for evaluating a test or instrument is whether it actually measures the characteristic it is supposed to measure. A yardstick would be an inadequate instrument to measure weight, and a test focused on tennis rules would not provide an adequate measure of a student's ability to play the game. Other less important criteria used to evaluate a test include costs and practicality. Tests that consistently measure what they are supposed to measure, yet are either too expensive or too cumbersome for a given situation, would be judged inadequate for the circumstances.

Teachers use measures of student achievement to evaluate: (1) students' progress throughout a term or year, (2) the quality of their tests, and (3) the quality of their instruction. Schools use measures of students' achievement, behavior, and attitudes to evaluate the quality of the curriculum and the overall program. Because measures of an individual's performance are the building blocks of evaluation, accurate evaluation at the classroom, school, and district levels cannot be accomplished without accurate measures. Likewise, accurate measures cannot be obtained without quality tests. This chapter presents methods you can use to design tests most likely to produce accurate measures of students' achievement.

CRITERION-REFERENCED TESTS

Chapter 3 describes procedures you can use to analyze your instructional goals and to write behavioral objectives for the subordinate skills identified in the goal frameworks. A goal framework of subordinate skills, sometimes called a *domain*, provides the foundation you need to design both your instruction and your classroom tests. Three names are generally used for tests based on the carefully identified and sequenced set of skills in a goal framework: *criterion-referenced tests, domain-referenced tests*, and *objective-referenced tests*. The set of skills in the framework is the criterion or standard used to judge students' progress on an instructional goal. The term *criterion-referenced test* simply means that the items on the test are referenced to or drawn from a carefully specified set of subordinate skills that make up the goal. On a *domain-referenced test*, the test items are referenced to or drawn from a carefully delineated domain of tasks. Thus, students' performance on such tests is referenced to the criterion set of skills or domain. For *objective-referenced tests*, the subordinate skills in the goal framework are converted to measurable behavioral objectives before test construction.

Whether an objective-referenced test is also criterion-referenced depends on the foundation for the objectives used. Objective-referenced tests based on a loosely connected set of objectives are not criterion-referenced tests. They do not become true criterion-referenced tests by simply specifying a cut-off score or criterion for passing or by selecting the number of items that must be answered correctly for each objective measured. Because the objectives developed in Chapter 3 are based on carefully specified goal frameworks, objective-referenced tests based on those objectives would be criterion-referenced tests. Although these terms might be interchangeable under these circumstances, the terms *test* and *criterion-referenced test* are used for convenience in the following chapters on test design, development, and analysis.

Four major factors need to be considered in the test design process. The first factor is to design tests most likely to yield valid results for the decisions you need to make. The second is to design tests most likely to provide reliable, or consistent, results. The third factor is the main purpose for the test, and the fourth is the type of test that best suits the prescribed purpose. This chapter describes each factor and how it influences design considerations.

Decisions made during the design stage are recorded in matrices called *tables of test specifications*. These tables are used to record the sample of objectives to be included on each test, the best item format to use for each objective selected, and the number of items to be written for each objective. Procedures for developing tables of test specifications are described.

VALIDITY AND TEST DESIGN

The term *validity* refers to the appropriateness of inferences made from students' test results. If a test adequately measures the behavioral objectives it is intended to measure, the students' test scores should be valid for the inferences based on these scores. The tests you administer are more likely to result in valid decisions if you consider validity as you design the test. To help ensure that your tests provide valid measures of student progress, you need to consider the following five questions during the design process.

1. *How well do the behavioral objectives selected for the test represent the instructional goal framework?* Ensuring that the skills measured accurately reflect the goal framework or domain involves a particular form of validity called *content validity*. A goal framework usually includes behavioral objectives that represent different, but related, content areas and different levels of skill. For example, the instructional goal on capitalizing proper nouns includes objectives related to three content areas: capitalization, nouns, and proper nouns. Different levels of learning are also commonly found among the objectives in a goal framework. Some objectives require students to recall names, facts, characteristics, rules, or principles. Other objectives require students to apply this information in order to classify, analyze, synthesize, solve, or create something. For example, both recall and application level skills are included in the goal on capitalizing proper nouns. Students need to recall the rule for capitalizing words, the definition for words that are common nouns, and the definition for words that are proper nouns. They also need to be able to apply these rules and definitions for discriminating between nouns and other parts of speech, discriminating between common and proper nouns, and capitalizing proper nouns. In designing a test that will have good content validity, objectives should be selected to represent each main content area and level of learning included in the goal framework. Inferences made about students' achievement of an instructional goal that are based on an imbalanced test are likely to be invalid or incorrect.

2. *How will test results be used?* You are more likely to obtain valid test results if, during the design process, you consider the planning and evaluation decisions you need to make. Related to planning instruction, you may want to determine whether you will need to develop remedial instruction, whether you need to develop lessons for all the behavioral objectives in the

framework or only a subset of them, or whether you need to develop review or enrichment lessons for the unit. Evaluation decisions will be necessary regarding the appropriateness of the instructional goal for a given group of students, the quality of your lessons, or students' achievement in order to assign grades. Considering the use of test results during the design stage will help you select, for each test, the most appropriate objectives from the goal framework and the best item formats for each objective chosen.

3. *Which test item format will best measure achievement of each objective?* A variety of item formats can be selected, and some types measure the behaviors prescribed in objectives better than other types. The more closely students' responses match the behavior specified in the objectives, the more likely their scores will validly reflect their achievement of the objectives. Objective item formats that require students to select an answer from among a set of alternatives may be best for measuring student performance on some objectives. Other objectives in the goal framework may be measured best by requiring students to supply a missing word or complete a sentence. Still others may be measured best by essay questions, product development, or some type of active performance. In designing a test, the behavior specified in the objective should be considered carefully when selecting the most appropriate item format.

4. *How many test items will be required to measure performance adequately on each objective?* Objectives that require students to recall names, facts, characteristics, or definitions usually require only one item to determine whether the student can recall the required information. However, if students are to apply this information to classify examples or solve a problem, then several items will be needed for them to demonstrate their application skills. For example, only one item would be needed to test whether students can recall the definition for a common noun; several items would be needed to determine whether students can discriminate consistently between common nouns and other parts of speech. When designing tests, you should consider the complexity of each objective selected and then prescribe an adequate number of items to measure the objective.

5. *When and how will the test be administered?* Considering the purpose for the test will help you design a test schedule and administration procedure most likely to result in scores that are valid for the decisions to be made. Tests used for planning decisions, such as whether remedial instruction is needed for a group and which behavioral objectives need to be emphasized during a unit, should be scheduled and administered before planning lessons for the unit. These preliminary tests need not be announced in advance because students are not expected to prepare for them; they can be administered informally during a class session or as a homework exercise.

Tests used to provide students with an opportunity to practice skills after instruction, to evaluate the quality of lessons, or to determine whether review or enrichment is needed should be administered following initial instruction. They can be administered informally as a class exercise, small group activity, or as individual tests. They also can be administered either during a class period or as a homework assignment. Tests used to evaluate students' overall achievement and grade their progress should be administered following all instruction and review, and they should be announced in advance to enable students to prepare for them. They also should be administered during a class period, whenever possible, to ensure that each student's score reflects only his or her efforts. Tests used for the purpose of assigning students' grades that are administered unannounced, before the conclusion of instruction, or in an unsupervised setting may not accurately reflect students' achievement. Thus, decisions based on these scores may be invalid.

RELIABILITY AND TEST DESIGN

Reliability refers to the consistency or stability of the test scores obtained. For example, if a student received a low score on a test taken in the morning, the teacher should be able to expect similar results if the student were to take the same or an equivalent test in the afternoon. Similar test scores would suggest that the test was reliable. If the student received a substantially higher or lower score the second time, the test would be unreliable. Valid inferences about students' performance cannot be made when test scores are unreliable.

Because students' test performances are influenced by many factors, including variations in memory, motivation, attention, and fatigue, absolute reliability (i.e., obtaining the exact same score twice) is unlikely. Test scores should be stable enough, however, to permit accurate judgments about students' mastery of the objectives.

Although you will not be able to eliminate fluctuations in test scores, you can help ensure that your tests will produce the most reliable scores possible. When designing a test, you will want to take the following five steps.

1. *Select a representative sample of objectives from the goal framework.* The better your objectives represent the entire framework, the more reliable the scores will be. For example, a test covering a goal framework that has ten objectives ranging from easy to difficult should include test items that reflect each objective. If two different forms of the test are to be used, the second form should also contain items for every objective. The two test forms should produce relatively consistent scores because both cover the entire framework of objectives. On the other hand, one test containing items for the five easiest objectives and a second test reflecting the five most difficult objectives would produce very different scores. If time is available to measure only a subset of objectives from the framework, then objectives should be selected to represent both the easy and difficult objectives.

2. *Select enough items to represent adequately the skills required in each objective.* Enough test items should be included for an objective to cover all the possible situations implied in the objective. For example, if students are to select common nouns from among a list of words that includes nouns and other parts of speech, enough items should be prescribed to include all categories of nouns that students will encounter. One or two items that relate to only one category, such as persons, would not adequately measure students' mastery of the objective. A test that included only one or two items in one category of nouns and one that included several items from all four categories are likely to produce very different scores.

3. *Select item formats that reduce the likelihood of guessing.* Students who do not know an answer may guess. If they guess correctly on one form of a test and incorrectly on the second, their scores will not be stable. When guessing is possible, the reliability of test scores will be lower than if guessing were not possible.

4. *Prescribe only the number of items that students can complete in the time available.* Test scores will be more reliable when students are given enough time to complete the test. Students' emotional states during a test can influence their performance, and hurrying causes some students to become careless. To increase the reliability of scores, adjust the length of the test to match the time available for its completion.

5. *Determine ways to maintain positive student attitudes toward testing.* Students' attitudes about a test can affect their motivation and effort, and test planning should identify ways to ensure positive attitudes. For example, you should plan to inform students of a test's date and time, the purpose for the test, and how the results will be used. Never plan to use tests as a punishment or as a substitute for unplanned lessons. Such misuses produce poor motivation and may result in unreliable scores.

TYPES OF SUBORDINATE SKILLS

The subordinate skills in the instructional goal framework can be divided into two categories: skills students should have mastered during a previous unit or year and skills that should be the primary focus for current instruction. Subordinate skills in the goal framework that should have been previously mastered are commonly called *prerequisite skills*. Subordinate skills that constitute the primary focus for current instruction are called *enabling skills*.

Before beginning to design tests for a unit of instruction, divide the subordinate skills in the goal framework into prerequisite and enabling skills. This division is based on your best judgment about whether a particular skill or set of skills in the framework were mastered by students during previous instruction. For example, the subordinate skills for the goal "Capitalize proper nouns" can be divided into prerequisite and enabling skills in the following way: skills related to the rule for capitalizing words and for classifying common nouns can be considered prerequisite skills; and skills related to classifying and capitalizing proper nouns can be considered enabling skills. This division is logical because it is unlikely that students will encounter instruction on proper nouns before having studied common nouns in detail. Likewise, the skills related to capitalizing words are so basic that they undoubtedly were learned during a previous unit. Thus, these two areas of subordinate skills can be classified as prerequisite skills for the goal. Related to the goal "Interpret information on a state map," you probably would classify the skills related to addition and multiplication as prerequisite skills and those related to using map features, such as the mileage table and mileage scale, as enabling skills for the unit. The existence of prerequisite skills in a goal framework has implications for the type of achievement tests you design.

TYPES OF TESTS

Teachers develop and administer four types of achievement tests: entry behaviors tests, pretests, practice tests, and posttests. Each type is administered for a different purpose, and the purpose helps determine which subordinate skills will be selected for the test and when the test is administered.

Entry Behaviors Tests

Teachers use entry behaviors tests (also known as *readiness tests*) to determine whether students have mastered the prerequisite skills they need to begin a unit of instruction. The skills selected from the goal framework for an entry behaviors test include only those classified as prerequisite skills. Entry behaviors tests are administered before planning any unit lessons. Results from entry behaviors tests are used in three ways:

1. To determine whether the instructional goal is appropriate for a given group of students. If none or few of the students in a class have mastered the prerequisite skills, then the goal is probably too complex for the class.
2. To determine whether remedial instruction is necessary. If several students in the class have not mastered the prerequisite skills, then these students will need remedial instruction.
3. To group students in the class for instruction in the unit. Students can be grouped according to whether they have or have not mastered prerequisite skills. Thus, instruction can be tailored to students' needs.

It is not always necessary to design an entry behaviors test. If none of the subordinate skills in the goal framework are classified as prerequisites, or if you have recently taught the prerequisites and are familiar with students' mastery of them, then no entry behaviors test is needed. Additionally, if you have a homogeneous group of high-achieving students, you may safely assume that they have mastered the subordinate skills classified as prerequisite. However, if you have a heterogeneous group and are unfamiliar with their skills in the area, then consider designing an entry behaviors test to determine whether remedial instruction is warranted. Students may struggle with the enabling skills in a unit of instruction, not because the materials or instruction are poor, but because they do not possess essential prerequisite skills. Without testing the group on these skills before instruction begins, a teacher may not detect the real cause of students' problems until it is too late.

Pretests

Pretests are also administered before instruction, and results are used to plan lessons for the unit. When adequately designed they include all the subordinate skills classified as enabling skills in the goal framework and thus provide an overview of students' skills for the entire unit. The teacher can use this information to plan review for any skills previously mastered and to develop lessons emphasizing skills that remain to be learned. Pretest data can also be used to group students who already have mastered most of the enabling skills and students who have not.

Pretests are not always necessary. If the enabling skills in a goal framework are not likely to have been encountered during previous instruction at school or at home, then it is reasonable to assume that instruction should be developed for each skill. However, if students are likely to have encountered previous instruction on any of the enabling skills, then a pretest will help you identify these skills and develop efficient instruction by focusing lessons on skills that remain to be learned. Sometimes students benefit from a pretest even if the teacher does not. Pretests can help students identify important skills to be learned, guide their study, and help them review for posttests.

If you decide that both an entry behaviors test and a pretest would be useful for a particular unit, you can combine them into one test because both need to be administered before planning instruction. However, items for each test should be scored separately because each serves a different purpose. A total score on the entire test will not help you determine who is ready for the instruction or how the lessons should be designed.

Practice Tests

Teachers often administer informal practice tests immediately following instruction on a limited set of enabling skills. These tests are completed either in class or as homework. Data from these tests can be used in at least four ways. First, the teacher can determine the effectiveness of the instruction, identify skills that most students have not mastered, and seek new ways to present additional instruction. Second, students can be regrouped according to their mastery of the objectives. Third, the data can help the teacher diagnose misconceptions and problems that students may have developed during instruction. Fourth, practice test results can be used for developing review materials and posttests. Students can also use these tests to determine whether they have learned required skills, to help them formulate questions, and to guide their study for exams.

To make adequate judgments, both teachers and students need detailed information; thus, practice tests should be designed to cover only a limited number of the enabling skills and their corresponding behavioral objectives. Because these tests are meant to provide practice for students and to help teachers plan, they should not be used to determine course grades.

Posttests

Posttests are given after instruction is completed; they help a teacher determine the effectiveness of instruction, evaluate student progress, and assign grades. The teacher can use posttest data to identify ineffective elements of the instruction and to improve the lessons for subsequent classes.

Any test used to assign term grades, whether a short quiz, an exam covering an entire unit, or a comprehensive exam over several units, is a posttest. Quizzes usually include the enabling skills for one or two lessons; unit exams cover a representative sample of all the enabling skills in a unit; and comprehensive exams contain a few of the most important enabling skills for each of several units. The enabling skills selected for a comprehensive exam are usually at the highest level of learning for each unit and should encompass all other enabling skills in the goal frameworks.

Because posttests are used to assign term grades, they should represent students' best efforts. The teacher should inform students of test dates and content to be covered. Unannounced tests, including pop quizzes, are inappropriate because they may not be valid reflections of students' learning. Unannounced quizzes fall into the category of practice tests.

DEVELOPING TABLES OF TEST SPECIFICATIONS FOR INDIVIDUAL UNITS

Once you have determined the types of tests you will administer, you need to write a prescription for each type. Developing tables of test specifications will help you construct tests most likely to produce reliable scores valid for the decisions to be made. The process involves the following six steps:

1. Group all the subordinate skills in the goal framework according to their major skill areas and learning level.
2. Classify each subordinate skill as either a prerequisite or an enabling skill.
3. Identify the test item format that best measures students' mastery of each behavioral objective. Consider both the behavior and the conditions specified in the objective when selecting an item format.
4. Determine the number of test items needed to measure adequately students' accomplishment of each objective. In selecting an adequate number of items, consider the complexity of the content in the objective and the different kinds of instances the student is likely to encounter.
5. Review the types of planning and evaluation decisions you wish to make and decide on the appropriate types of tests.
6. From the table, select the subordinate skills and behavioral objectives to be included on each test.

The following sections describe the procedures just outlined. The unit on capitalizing proper nouns, which appeared in Chapter 3, will be used as an example. Although many units of instruction consist of more goals, subordinate skills, and objectives, this smaller unit adequately illustrates the procedures for developing test specifications. You may wish to refer to the framework of subordinate skills for the unit in Figure 3.3 and the behavioral objectives in Table 3.7.

Group Subordinate Skills and Objectives by Major Skill Area and Learning Level

In Table 4.1, the subordinate skills and behavioral objectives for the unit on capitalizing proper nouns are grouped according to major skill areas and learning levels. There are three major skill areas: capitalize words, common nouns, and proper nouns. The subordinate skills and objectives from the goal framework are organized according to skill area. For this particular instructional goal, two different levels of learning will suffice: (1) *recall/comprehension*, which includes recalling and describing verbal information, concepts, or rules; and (2) *application*, which involves actually *using* the information, concepts, or rules to classify examples, solve problems, or explain phenomena. You might choose to use alternative categories to classify objectives according to learning level to make finer distinctions among levels. However, you should at least differentiate between very basic objectives that require recalling and describing and more complex ones that require skill use. Using at least these two categories helps ensure that your tests have the desired balance between remembering and performing. Subordinate skills and behavioral objectives from Table 3.7 are inserted in the appropriate column according to the major skill area and learning level. Organizing the subordinate skills and related

TABLE 4.1 Table of Specifications for Unit on Capitalizing Proper Nouns

| | Recall (Knowledge and Comprehension) | | *Learning* | |
| | | | | |
Major Skill Groups	*Subordinate Skills*	*Behavioral Objectives*	*Item Format[a]*	*Number of Items*
Capitalize words (prerequisite skill)	1. State the rule for capitalizing words	1.1 From memory state the rule for capitalizing words.	W	1
		1.2 Select the rule for capitalizing words from a set of alternative rules.	S	1
Common nouns (prerequisite skills)	3. Define terms *person, place, thing,* and *idea*	3.1 From memory, define the terms *person, place, thing,* and *idea*.	W	4
		3.2 Match the terms *person, place, thing,* and *idea* with their definitions.	S	4
	5. Define the term *noun*	5.1 From memory, define the term *noun*.	W	1
		5.2 Given the definition for the term *noun*, identify it as such.	W/S	1
Proper nouns (enabling skills)	8. Define the term *proper* as specific or particular	8.1 From memory, define the term *proper*.	W	1
		8.2 Given several definitions, select the one for the word *proper*.	S	1
		8.3 Given the definition of the word *proper*, identify it as such.	W/S	1
	9. Define proper nouns as words that refer to specific persons, places, or things	9.1 From memory, define proper nouns.	W	1
		9.2 Given several definitions, select the one for proper nouns.	S	1
		9.3 Given the definition for a proper noun, identify it as such.	W/S	1

[a] Item format codes: W = Write response from memory; S = Select response from among alternatives; W/S = Either write or select response.

Application

Subordinate Skills	Behavioral Objectives	Item Format	Number of Items
2. Capitalize any word	2.1 Given a list of several words, select the letter in the words that should be capitalized.	S	5
	2.2 Given some words that are properly capitalized and some that are improperly capitalized, select those that are properly capitalized.	S	5
4. Discriminate words that represent persons, places, things, and ideas from lists of words containing these and other concepts	4.1 Given a list of words that contains persons, places, things, and ideas, classify each word into the appropriate category.	S	12
6. Classify words that are common nouns	6.1 Given a list of words containing common nouns and other parts of speech, select the common nouns.	S	15
7. Give several examples of common nouns	7.1 List several words that refer to persons.	W	2
	7.2 List several words that refer to places.	W	2
	7.3 List several words that refer to things.	W	2
	7.4 List several words that refer to ideas.	W	2
10. Classify words as proper nouns	10.1 Given a list of words containing both proper and common nouns, with some proper nouns not capitalized and some common nouns capitalized, select the proper nouns.	S	16
11. Give several examples of proper nouns	11.1 Given the category, *persons*, list several proper nouns that name persons.	W	2
	11.2 Given the category, *places*, list several proper nouns that name places.	W	2
	11.3 Given the category, *things*, list several proper nouns that name things.	W	2
12. Capitalize proper nouns (goal)	12.1 Given sentences that include proper nouns that are not capitalized and common nouns that are capitalized, locate the capitalization errors.	S	5
	12.2 Write sentences that include proper nouns and capitalize the proper nouns.	W	3

objectives into a table helps ensure that the objectives selected for tests represent all content and learning levels in the goal framework.

Although recopying all the enabling skills and behavioral objectives from the goal framework would constitute unnecessary busy-work for a teacher, it is done in Table 4.1 for illustration purposes. After becoming familiar with the congruence between enabling skills, objectives, and the design of tests, many teachers choose to use the abbreviated method illustrated in Table 4.2 for convenience. In this table, only the identifying numbers of subordinate skills and behavioral objectives are inserted in each column. Using the goal framework in Figure 3.3 and the behavioral objectives list in Table 3.7 along with an abbreviated table serves the same design purpose and saves time.

TABLE 4.2   Abbreviated Table of Specifications for Unit on Capitalizing Proper Nouns

| | *Learning Levels* | | | | | | | |
| | Recall/Comprehension | | | | Application (Classify, Solve, Explain) | | | |
Major Skill Groups	*Subor. Skill #*	*Behav. Obj. #*	*Item Format*[a]	*Number of Items*	*Subor. Skill #*	*Behav. Obj. #*	*Item Format*	*Number of Items*
Capitalize words (Prerequisite skills)	1	1.1	W	1	2	2.1	S	5
		1.2	S	1		2.2	S	5
Common nouns (Prerequisite skills)	3	3.1	W	4	4	4.1	S	12
		3.2	S	4				
	5	5.1	W	1	6	6.1	S	15
		5.2	W/S	1	7	7.1	W	2
						7.2	W	2
						7.3	W	2
						7.4	W	2
Proper nouns (Enabling skills)	8	8.1	W	1	10	10.1	S	16
		8.2	S	1				
		8.3	W/S	1				
	9	9.1	W	1	11	11.1	W	2
		9.2	S	1		11.2	W	2
		9.3	W/S	1		11.3	W	2
					12	12.1	S	5
						12.2	W	3

Note: The numbers in the Subordinate Skill column correspond to the subordinate skills in Figure 3.3. The numbers in the Behavioral Objective column correspond to the objectives in Table 3.7.

[a] Item format codes: W = Write response from memory; S = Select response from among alternatives; W/S = Either write or select response.

Classify Each Subordinate Skill as Prerequisite or Enabling

Remember that prerequisite skills are subordinate skills that should have been mastered before entering the unit, and enabling skills are the main focus for the unit. Table 4.1 illustrates that the teacher classified all subordinate skills related to capitalizing words and common nouns as prerequisite skills for the unit. Only subordinate skills 8 through 12, or those related to proper nouns, are classified as enabling skills. This division of skills is recorded in the far left-hand column of the table.

Identify the Test Item Format for Each Objective

The best item format for a behavioral objective permits students to respond as the objective specifies. Table 4.1 lists test item formats for each objective in the unit. All objectives require students to write a short definition or rule or to select the correct response from a set of alternatives. Three objectives, 5.2, 8.3, and 9.3, indicate that either a written or selected response item would be appropriate.

Determine the Number of Items for Each Objective

The number of test items prescribed for each objective appears beside each item format. A test should include enough items for each objective to ensure that the behavior and content in the objective are adequately measured. In choosing the number of items needed to measure students' performance, you must use your own judgment. Some objectives will require only one item; others will require several. The number of items depends on the complexity of the behavior and on the content. For example, objective 5.2 in Table 4.1, "Given the definition for the term *noun*, identify it as such," has only one item prescribed. Only one item was judged necessary to demonstrate this skill because it is a straightforward, recall-level skill. On the other hand, objective 6.1, "Given a list of words containing common nouns and other parts of speech, select the common nouns," has fifteen items prescribed. The teacher realizes that the list needs to contain words that represent persons, places, things, and ideas as well as other parts of speech, such as adverbs, adjectives, verbs, and conjunctions, to measure adequately this objective. A list that contained at least two of each noun category plus six inappropriate words would include fourteen words. Each word in the list is considered as a separate test item because the students need to judge each word individually. Objectives 7.1 through 7.4 and 11.1 through 11.3 each have two items prescribed. If students can name two examples of each type of noun, you can infer that they can list more if asked to do so. Generating two examples or generating ten requires the same skill.

Decide on the Appropriate Types of Tests

Table 4.1 provides the information a teacher would need to design tests for the unit on capitalizing proper nouns. For example, objectives can now be

selected for a combination entry behaviors test and pretest, practice tests, and
a posttest.

A Combined Entry Behaviors Test and Pretest   The entry behaviors portion
of the test should contain a representative sample of objectives for all the
prerequisite skills. The pretest portion should contain a representative sample
of objectives for all the enabling skills listed in the table. Because the test is
intended to identify problems, rapid scoring is desirable. Thus, the teacher
might reasonably choose objectives that require students to select a response.
Objectives suited to this purpose are as follow (see Table 4.1 and the example
entry behaviors test and pretest in Appendixes D and E):

Entry Behaviors

Test Objectives:	1.2	2.1	3.2	4.1	5.2	6.1	7.1	7.2	7.3	7.4	Total Items
Number of Items:	1	5	4	12	1	15	2	2	2	2	46

Pretest

Objectives:	8.2	9.2	10.1	11.1	11.2	11.3	12.1	Total Items
Number of Items:	1	1	16	2	2	2	5	29

Practice Tests   Practice tests serve three main purposes: (1) they permit students to practice the enabling skills; (2) they permit the teacher to diagnose
any misconceptions or problems students are having with the skills; and (3)
they provide information on the quality of instruction. Several practice tests
may be required to provide for adequate practice and evaluation before administering the posttest. Practice tests might be designed as follows (see Table
4.1 and the example practice tests in Appendix F):

Practice Test 1

Objectives:	8.1	9.1	10.1	Total Items
Number of Items:	1	1	16	18

Practice Test 2

Objectives:	8.3	9.3	10.1	11.1	11.2	11.3	Total Items
Number of Items:	1	1	16	2	2	2	24

Practice Test 3

Objectives:	11.1	11.2	11.3	12.1	12.2	Total Items
Number of Items:	2	2	2	5	5	16

The Posttest   The posttest should contain a representative sample of all the enabling skills for the unit (thus it resembles the pretest). To make administration and scoring easier, the teacher will want to choose a selected response format whenever feasible. The objectives selected for a posttest on capitalizing proper nouns might include the following (see Table 4.1 and the example posttest in Appendix G):

Posttest Objectives:	8.2	9.2	10.1	11.1	11.2	11.3	12.1	12.2	Total Items
Number of Items:	1	1	16	2	2	2	5	3	32

This section describes ways to design tests for one instructional goal. The following section discusses procedures for designing a comprehensive test covering several instructional goals and their related units of instruction.

DEVELOPING A TABLE OF SPECIFICATIONS FOR A COMPREHENSIVE POSTTEST

Teachers frequently want to measure students' progress on several instructional units. Such comprehensive tests should be balanced by content areas and learning levels. Because several different frameworks of skills will be tested, prescribing test items that represent all of the enabling skills is not feasible. A table of specifications can help you manage the process of test development and design a test that best represents all the units covered.

Although skipping the development of a table of specifications for a comprehensive exam may save time, it is not recommended. Using items from previous unit tests will not ensure that the comprehensive posttest is balanced according to content, learning levels, and representative behavioral objectives. A posttest developed without appropriate prescriptions may produce scores of limited use and interpretation, thus compromising the entire project.

As you develop a table of specifications for a comprehensive posttest, you should consider the following six elements: (1) balance among the goals selected for the exam; (2) balance among the levels of learning; (3) the test format; (4) the total number of items; (5) the number of test items for each goal and level of learning; and (6) the enabling skills to be selected from each goal framework. A table of specifications incorporating these factors will help ensure a comprehensive posttest that represents each unit and is balanced by goals and levels of learning.

In constructing the table you should first consider the balance among the goals to be represented on the exam. Study the goals and their respective frameworks and determine the relative complexity of the goals. The more complex a goal, the more emphasis it may need. For example, if ten goals of approximately equal complexity are represented, the items for each goal may account for 10 percent of the total test. If five goals are more complex than the others, test items for these goals may take up a larger proportion of the test, with the five less complex goals represented by a smaller percentage of items. Regardless of the rationale you use to determine percentages, you should record the proportion of items for each goal in your table of specifications.

Once the appropriate balance among goals is established, turn to the second important element, balance among the levels of learning within each goal. When allocating the proportion assigned for a goal among the levels of learning, remember that recall-level skills are often subsumed within application level skills. Additionally, recall-level skills are less complex than application skills and thus can be measured using fewer items. Therefore, you will usually want to assign a greater portion of the items allocated for each goal to application-level skills. A caution is in order, however. If only application level skills are included on a test, and students fail to answer these items correctly, you may have difficulty interpreting their scores. You will not be able to detect whether they missed the items because they did not know the rule or definition or because they knew it but had trouble generalizing it.

Table 4.3 contains three tables of test specifications that balance ten goals differently by goal and by level of learning. The specifications for Test A indicate equal emphasis among the ten goals; however, 80 percent of the items require application-level skills. The prescription for Test B emphasizes five of the ten goals and indicates that 75 percent of the items test application-level skills. The chart for Test C specifies uneven percentages for the ten goals and requires that 100 percent of the items test application-level skills. The different balances in goals and levels of learning in Tests A, B, and C will potentially result in different student scores for the three tests and different inferences about students' performance. The most appropriate balance among goals and levels of learning can best be determined by studying the relative complexity of the goals to be measured and assigning a portion of the test to each goal accordingly. Then, with each goal assigned a portion of the test, you can select the proportion for each level of learning within the goal.

Once you have weighted all the goals and learning levels to be covered, you need to select a test format. Depending on the instructional goals to be measured, you may decide on an objective test, an essay exam, a product development project, an active performance measure, or some combination of these formats. In making your decision, you need to review the behaviors specified in the instructional goals to be measured and the item formats prescribed in the tables of test specifications for each unit.

You are now ready to prescribe the total number of items to be included on the exam and the number of items allocated for each goal. In selecting the total number of test items, consider two factors: the time available for testing and the required level of performance.

The time available for testing depends on the length of the class period and on students' attention spans. Students should be able to complete the test within the class period and before they become fatigued.

TABLE 4.3   Partial Tables of Test Specifications for Three Comprehensive Posttests, Weighted by Goal and Learning Level

Goal	Percentage of Items	Percentage Recall[a]	Percentage Application[b]
Test A			
1	10	2	8
2	10	2	8
3	10	2	8
4	10	2	8
5	10	2	8
6	10	2	8
7	10	2	8
8	10	2	8
9	10	2	8
10	10	2	8
Total	100%	20%	80%
Test B			
1	14	3	11
2	6	2	4
3	14	3	11
4	6	2	4
5	14	3	11
6	6	2	4
7	14	3	11
8	6	2	4
9	14	3	11
10	6	2	4
Total	100%	25%	75%
Test C			
1	14		14
2	6		6
3	10		10
4	8		8
5	12		12
6	8		8
7	16		16
8	6		6
9	14		14
10	6		6
Total	100%	0%	100%

[a] The Recall category prescribes remembering and comprehension items.
[b] The Application category prescribes classification, problem-solving, explanation, and prediction items.

The required level of performance will also help determine the total number of questions on the exam. Recall-level items require less time than application-level items, whatever the test format. Items that ask students to solve problems, analyze or synthesize information, or evaluate examples all require more time than do items that require students to remember a term, fact, definition, rule, or principle. Essay questions require more time than either selected-response or short-answer items.

Suppose, for example, that your class period is fifty minutes long. Of this time, approximately ten minutes will be needed to distribute the tests, give instructions, and collect the tests. Forty minutes remain. If you estimate that students can answer an average of one short-answer question per minute, then your test can include a maximum of 40 short-answer items. If you plan to administer an essay test, and predict that each question will require approximately twelve minutes to answer, then you can include only three essay items. A test that contains a combination of short-answer and essay questions should allow enough time for each type of question.

After you have determined the total number of test items, you can determine the number of items for each goal. For example, if each of ten goals is to represent 10 percent of the test, and you have a total of forty questions on the test, then the total number of items can be multiplied by the allocated proportion to determine the appropriate number of items ($.10 \times 40 = 4$). Each goal would be represented on the test by four items.

The number of items allocated for each goal can then be divided between recall and application items. If you choose to measure only application-level skills for one goal, then all four of the assigned items would be designated for application-level skills. If you choose to emphasize application-level items, but also want to include some recall items for another one of the goals, then you probably would assign three of the available items to application-level skills and one to recall.

Table 4.4 illustrates a partially completed table of test specifications that prescribes the total number of test items, the percentage and number of items for each of ten goals, and the distribution of items according to learning level. For this comprehensive exam, 25 percent of the items measure recall-level skills and 75 percent measure application-level skills.

The final step in developing a table of specifications is the selection of enabling skills from each goal framework. Because the number of items for each goal must be limited, you should select the enabling skills and behavioral objectives that best represent each goal. For example, the test specifications in Table 4.4 limits the number of recall-level objectives for each goal to one. Only three items for each goal can be included at the application level. In selecting application-level objectives, you have three options: develop three items for one objective; write one item for one objective and two items for another; or write one item for each of three objectives. Try to choose the option that will result in the best measurement of student performance on the goal. Next, place the identifying numbers for the objectives beside the number of items selected for each objective on the table of specifications.

TABLE 4.4   Partial Table of Test Specifications Prescribing Percentage and Number of Items for Each Goal and Level of Learning

| Goals | Levels of Learning | | Total No. | Percentage of Total Items |
	Recall[a] No. of Items	Application[b] No. of Items		
1	1	3	4	10
2	1	3	4	10
3	1	3	4	10
4	1	3	4	10
5	1	3	4	10
6	1	3	4	10
7	1	3	4	10
8	1	3	4	10
9	1	3	4	10
10	1	3	4	
Total	10	30	40	
Percentage of total items	25%	75%		100%

[a] The Recall category prescribes remembering and comprehension items.
[b] The Application category prescribes classification, problem-solving, explanation, and prediction items.

Table 4.5 contains a table of test specifications for a comprehensive post-test on capitalization rules. The first column lists the instructional goals to be represented on the exam. The framework for each goal contains two levels of learning, recall and application, so both are included in the table. Below each level of learning appear the number of test items for that level and the identifying number of each objective. The last two columns record the percentage and the number of items for each goal on the test. Notice that the ten instructional goals do not receive the same number of test items. Some goals are more complex than others, and thus require more test items. For example, three items are specified for goal one. This number of items should be adequate to measure students' ability to capitalize consistently the first word of a sentence. Goal three is more complex, however, and six items are allocated to measure students' ability to capitalize proper nouns.

Once you have decided on the number of items for each goal, you can select the enabling skills and objectives to be tested. If you were using Table 4.5 to prepare a test, you could include six items from the unit on proper nouns. One item should represent the recall-level objectives and five items should be application. The most representative recall-level objective is 9.2 (see Table 3.7 for a list of the proper noun objectives and Table 4.1 for the organization of these objectives by learning levels). Objective 12.1 best represents the goal at the application level for a selected-response test. (If a written-response test were to be developed, then objective 12.2 would be

TABLE 4.5 Partial Table of Test Specifications for Comprehensive Posttest Covering Several Units of Capitalization Instruction

| | Levels of Learning | | | | | |
| | Recall[a] | | Application[b] | | | |
Instructional Goals	Number of Items	Objectives	Number of Items	Objectives	Percentage of Test Items	Item Total by Goal
1. Capitalize the first word of each sentence	1		2		7.5	3
2. Capitalize the pronoun *I*	1		2		7.5	3
3. Capitalize proper nouns	1	9.2	5	12.1	15	6
4. Capitalize proper adjectives	1		3		10	4
5. Capitalize days and months	1		3		10	4
6. Capitalize regions of the country	1		3		10	4
7. Capitalize words that show family relationship	1		3		10	4
8. Capitalize titles of persons	1		3		10	4
9. Capitalize words in titles of artistic works	1		3		10	4
10. Capitalize the first word in quotations	1		3		10	4
Total test items:	10		30			40
Percentage of total items:	25%		75%		100%	

[a] The Recall category prescribes remembering and comprehension items.
[b] The Application category prescribes classification and application of rules.

specified instead because it more closely matches the behavior in the goal.) Thus, objective 12.1 will be represented by five items. You would select the objectives for the other units in the same manner using the prescribed number of items and the representativeness of the objectives as a guide.

Once you have completed your table of specifications, you are ready to develop your test. The following five chapters describe procedures for constructing tests and test items that correspond to the specifications in your tables.

SUMMARY

Carefully designed classroom tests can help you make correct decisions about the quality of your instruction and student progress. Test results can be used to tailor instruction and review for a particular group of students, evaluate the quality of instruction, and identify portions of your lessons that need improvement. Test results are also used to determine whether a group or individuals within a group have the prerequisite skills to begin a unit of instruction; provide students with practice during instruction; evaluate student progress; and determine students' mastery of instructional objectives.

During the design of classroom tests, you need to be concerned with the validity and reliability of test scores. Validity refers to the appropriateness of inferences made from test scores. Reliability refers to the consistency or stability of scores obtained from a test. If the scores are unreliable, decisions or inferences based on them are dubious. Tests must be designed carefully to yield reliable and valid scores.

Factors related to ensuring the content validity of a test include how scores will be used; how well the behavioral objectives selected represent the goal framework; the test item formats that would best measure students' achievement of each objective; and the number of items required to measure achievement of each objective.

To help ensure reliable test scores, you should take five steps during the design stage: (1) select a representative sample of objectives from the goal framework; (2) select enough items to represent adequately the skills required in the objective; (3) select item formats that reduce the likelihood of guessing; (4) prescribe only the number of items students can complete in the time available; and (5) determine ways to maintain positive student attitudes toward testing. The subordinate skills in an instructional goal framework should be divided into prerequisite skills (skills students should have mastered before entering a unit of instruction) and enabling skills (skills that comprise the main focus of instruction for a unit).

Teachers typically design four types of tests to help them with planning and evaluation activities. Entry behaviors tests help determine whether students possess the prerequisite skills needed for a unit of instruction. Pretests provide data useful in developing lesson plans. Entry behaviors tests and pretests are often combined and administered before instruction is planned. Practice tests are usually informal instruments administered during instruction. The data from practice tests permit a

teacher to evaluate students' progress, assess the quality of instruction, and provide corrective feedback to students. Posttests are administered after instruction, and the data used to evaluate student progress, assign grades, and refine the instruction.

Careful planning and the development of tables of specifications substantially increase the likelihood of valid and reliable test scores. The steps in developing test specifications for one unit of instruction are as follow:

1. Develop a table of test specifications.
   a. Group all the subordinate skills and behavioral objectives in the goal framework according to their major skill areas and learning levels.
   b. Determine whether any of the subordinate skills are prerequisites for the instruction.
   c. Identify the test item format that best measures students' mastery of each behavioral objective.
   d. Determine the number of items needed to measure adequately students' accomplishment of each objective.
2. Select the appropriate objectives from the table for each type of test to be administered.
   a. Review the types of planning and evaluation decisions you will be making and decide on the appropriate types of tests for the unit.
   b. Consider the purpose for each test and the time available for its administration and scoring, and then select the overall test format.
   c. From the table of test specifications, select the subordinate skills and behavioral objectives to be included on each type of test.

Teachers who want to test students on their mastery of goals from several units of instruction should design test specifications for a comprehensive posttest. The seven steps in this procedure are:

1. Construct a matrix that lists all instructional goals to be measured.
2. Review the goal framework, behavioral objectives, and tables of specifications for

each goal listed and insert the appropriate levels of learning across the top of the matrix.

3. Determine the overall portion of the test to be devoted to each goal and to each level of learning and record this information in the matrix.

4. Review the table of test specifications for each goal, note the item formats prescribed in each table, and select the best test format(s).

5. Use the selected test format, the time available for administering the test, and the skills of the students to determine the total number of test items.

6. Determine the number of items for each goal and for each level of learning and record this decision in the table.

7. Select the behavioral objectives to be measured and insert their identifying numbers in the table beside the number of items to be written for each.

PRACTICE EXERCISES

1. Test scores that accurately reflect students' mastery of instructional goals and lead to appropriate inferences about students' achievement are called _____ test scores.

2. Test scores that are consistent and that provide a stable indication of students' performance are called _____ test scores.

3. List four factors that affect the validity of test scores and that should be considered during test design activities.

4. List five steps a teacher can take during test planning to help ensure reliable test scores.

5. The subordinate skills in the goal framework that students should have mastered prior to beginning a unit are called _____ skills.

6. The subordinate skills in the goal framework that will be the main focus of instruction during a unit are called _____ skills.

7. List five ways teachers use test results to help plan instruction.

8. List four ways teachers use test results ot help monitor student progress.

9. Figure 4.1 includes a column for each of the four types of tests described in the chapter. The left-hand column contains statements that describe one or more tests. Match the descriptions with the appropriate type of test by checking the correct test columns.

10. Develop a table of test specifications for the unit on map reading described in Chapter 3. Use the subordinate skills and behavioral objectives in Tables 3.8, 3.9, 3.10, 3.11, and 3.12 as a basis for your work. In your table, include columns for the following:

    1. Major skill areas and levels of learning
    2. Subordinate skills
    3. Behavioral objectives
    4. Item format to be used to measure each objective
    5. Number of items to be written for each objective

FIGURE 4.1 Types of Tests and Their Descriptions

Descriptions	Entry Behaviors Test	Pretest	Practice Test	Posttest

A. Main purpose for test
  1. Plan instruction
  2. Evaluate instruction
  3. Revise instruction
  4. Monitor student progress
  5. Grade student performance				

B. When test is administered
  1. Before planning lessons
  2. During instruction
  3. After instruction is completed				

C. Objectives included on a test
  1. Only objectives for prerequisite skills
  2. A representative sample of objectives for enabling skills from the goal framework				

A sample table (Table 4.6) using these headings appears in the Feedback section. If you need help in designing your table, review the example but do not study information in the table until you have developed one yourself. Remember: there is no one way to design the table. Note differences between Table 4.6 and the table you create and explain the reasons for your decisions.

11. Review the behavioral objectives in Table 4.6 and locate those you believe would be prerequisite skills learned during previous lessons. Identify those skills you believe are prerequisite to this unit by placing an asterisk beside the objective in your table.

12. From your table of test specifications for the map unit, which objectives would you select to include on an entry behaviors test?

13. Select a representative set of enabling skills for a pretest on the map interpretation unit. (Use Table 4.6 to select the skills.) For each enabling skill selected, choose the most representative behavioral objective for each. Finally, choose the item format and the number of items to include for each objective from Table 4.6. See Table 4.7 to compare your work.

14. Select a set of enabling skills and corresponding behavioral objectives for a practice test on using a mileage scale to estimate the distance between two given points. For each objective selected, record the desired item format and number of items for each objective. (See Table 4.6.)

15. Choose a representative set of enabling skills and corresponding behavioral objectives for a posttest covering the entire map unit. Indicate the item format and the number of items you will include. (See Table 4.6.)

16. Assume you wanted to design a comprehensive posttest that could include only forty-five items. Also assume that only 20 percent of the test would be devoted to the map unit.
    a. How many items on the test would relate to map skills?
    b. Given that you are limited to this number of items, select the major skill areas and objectives you would include, the item format you would use, and the number of items you would include for each objective.

17. Enrichment. For the goal analysis framework and behavioral objectives you have developed in your own content area, construct a table of test specifications that includes the main content areas and levels of learning; the identifying objective number; the item format for each objective; and the number of items for each objective. Then:
    a. Using the item formats specified in the table, choose the overall test format(s).
    b. Decide whether an entry behaviors test will be necessary and, if so, select the objectives to be included.
    c. Select representative objectives for a pretest.
    d. Select representative objectives for practice tests.
    e. Select representative objectives for a unit posttest.

FEEDBACK

1. Valid
2. Reliable
3. Factors related to validity include:
   a. The purpose for the test and how the results will be used.
   b. How well the behavioral objectives selected represent the goal framework.
   c. The match between the behavior described in the objective and the test item format.
   d. The adequacy of the number of items used to measure performance on each objective.
4. The five steps for reliability are to:
   a. Select a representative sample of subordinate skills from the goal framework.
   b. Select items that adequately represent the skills required in each objective.
   c. Select item formats that reduce the likelihood of guessing.
   d. Include only the number of items that students can comfortably complete.
   e. Determine ways to maintain positive student attitudes toward testing.
5. Prerequisite skills
6. Enabling skills
7. Teachers use test results to help them:
   a. Determine whether prescribed instructional goals are at the appropriate level for students.

b. Separate the enabling skills that have been previously mastered from those that must be learned.
c. Plan remedial, enrichment, and review activities.
d. Evaluate the quality of the instruction.
e. Revise instruction.

8. In monitoring students' progress, teachers use test scores to help them:
a. Determine who is ready to begin a unit of instruction and who should receive remedial instruction prior to beginning a unit.
b. Identify subgroups of students to receive remedial or enrichment activities.
c. Identify students who have mastered the enabling skills for a unit.
d. Assign grades.

9. **FIGURE 4.1(F)**

Descriptions	Entry Behaviors Test	Pretest	Practice Test	Posttest
A. Main purpose for test				
1. Plan instruction	X	X		
2. Evaluate instruction			X	X
3. Revise instruction			X	X
4. Monitor student progress			X	X
5. Grade student performance				X
B. When test is administered				
1. Before planning lessons	X	X		
2. During instruction			X	
3. After instruction is completed				X
C. Objectives included on a test				
1. Only objectives for prerequisite skills	X			
2. A representative sample of objectives for enabling skills from the goal framework		X	X	X

10. See Table 4.6 for a sample of test specifications
11. See objectives that have asterisks(*) beside them in Table 4.6.
12. Objectives for an entry behaviors test drawn from Table 4.6 would include 3.2.6.1, 3.3.5.1, and 3.3.5.2

TABLE 4.6 Specifications for the Goal: Interpret Information on State Map

Major Skill Groups	Recall (Knowledge and Comprehension)		Learning	
	Subordinate Skills	Behavioral Objectives	Item Format[a]	Number of Items
Use legend to interpret map symbols	1.1 Identify characteristics of legend	1.1.1 Describe the legend by appearance and function.	W	1
		1.1.2 Given the characteristics and function of a legend, identify them as belonging to the legend.	S	1
		1.1.3 Given a list of characteristics relating to map features, such as the grid, index, and legend, identify those related to the legend.	S	1
	1.4 Define term *direction*	1.4.1 From memory, define the term *direction*.	W	1
		1.4.2 Select the definition for the term *direction* from a set of alternative definitions.	S	1
		1.4.3 Given the definition for the term *direction*, identify it as such.	W/S	1

Levels

	Application		
Subordinate Skills	*Behavioral Objectives*	*Item Format*	*Number of Items*
1.2 Locate legend on map	1.2.1 Given a map containing a legend, locate the legend.	S	1
1.3 Match symbols on map with those in legend and name symbol	1.3.1 Given a particular symbol on map, locate symbol and name in legend.	S	3
1.5 Locate direction indicator on map	1.5.1 Given a map containing a direction indicator, locate the direction indicator.	S	1
1.6 Locate general areas of north, south, east, and west on map	1.6.1 Given a sample map, label map edges as north, south, east, and west.	W	4
	1.6.2 Given a description of a map area and a sample map, identify the area described as either north, south, east, or west.	W/S	4
1.7 Locate points that are due north, south, east, and west of specified places on map	1.7.1 Given a specified point on a map, name towns that are straight north, straight south, straight east, and straight west of the point.	W/S	4
1.8 Locate general areas of northeast, northwest, southeast, and southwest on map	1.8.1 Given a sample map, label map edges as northeast, northwest, southeast, and southwest.	W	4
	1.8.2 Given a description of a map area and a sample map, identify the area described as either northeast, northwest, southeast, or southwest.	W/S	4
1.9 Locate points that are northeast, northwest, southeast, and southwest of specified places on map	1.9.1 Given a specified point on a map, name towns that are northeast, northwest, southeast, and southwest of the point.	W/S	4

(continued on next page)

TABLE 4.6 (*continued*)

| Major Skill Groups | Recall (Knowledge and Comprehension) | | Learning | |
	Subordinate Skills	Behavioral Objectives	Item Format[a]	Number of Items
Use index and grid to locate specified places	2.1 Identify characteristics of index and its function	2.1.1 Given the term *map index*, list the identifying characteristics of the index.	W	1
		2.1.2 Given a statement of the purpose for an index, identify it as that for an index.	W/S	1
		2.1.3 Given the characteristics of several map features, such as the legend, grid, and index, select the description for the index.	S	1
	2.4 Identify characteristics of locator code	2.4.1 Given a code containing a letter and a number, identify it as a plausible locator code.	S	2
		2.4.2 Given several codes containing a variety of symbols (2 letters, 2 numbers, direction symbols, and letter/ number combinations), select those that are plausible locator codes.	S	2

Application

Subordinate Skills	Behavioral Objectives	Item Format	Number of Items
1.10 Describe the location of a specified place using its direction from other given points or its general map area	1.10.1 Given a specified town on a map, describe its location using its direction from at least two other named towns on the map.	W/S	4
	1.10.2 Given a specified town on a map, describe its location using the general map area in which it is located.	W/S	4
2.2 Locate index on map	2.2.1 Given a map containing an untitled index, locate index.	S	1
2.3 Find specified town in index	2.3.1 Given an index and a town name, locate town in index.	S	2
2.5 Find locator code for a given town	2.5.1 Given an index and a town name, find locator code for town.	S	2
2.6 Locate code letters and numbers along map edges	2.6.1 Given any locator code, find the corresponding letters and numbers along all four map edges.	W/S	2
2.7 Locate both grid lines beside the letters and numbers that run through the map side to side and top to bottom and that bound an area within the two lines	2.7.1 Given a map and either a number or a letter, locate both grid lines that bound it, and follow the bounded map area completely through the map to the corresponding number or letter on the opposite edge.	W/S	2

(continued on next page)

TABLE 4.6 (*continued*)

			Learning	
		Recall (Knowledge and Comprehension)		
Major Skill Groups	*Subordinate Skills*	*Behavioral Objectives*	*Item Format^a*	*Number of Items*
	2.8 Define term, *intersection*	2.8.1 Given the term *intersection*, state the definition.	W	1
		2.8.2 From a given set of definitions, choose the one for the term intersection.	S	1
Use mileage table to locate given distance between specified towns	3.1.1 Identify characteristics of mileage table	3.1.1.1 Given the name *mileage table*, list identifying characteristics of table.	W	1
		3.1.1.2 Given several descriptions of map features, select the description for a mileage table.	S	1
	3.1.5* Define term *intersection*	3.1.5.1 Given the term *intersection*, state the definition.	W	1
		3.1.5.2 Given alternative definitions for the term *intersection*, select best definition.	S	1
	3.1.7 State that numbers within table tell miles between cities	3.1.7.1 From memory, define meaning of numbers in table.		
		3.1.7.2 Given several interpretations for numbers within table, select correct interpretation.	S	1
Use mileage scale to estimate the distance between two given points	3.2.1 Identify characteristics of mileage scale	3.2.1.1 From memory, describe mileage scale.	W	1
		3.2.1.2 Given several descriptions of map features, select description of mileage scale.	S	1

Application

Subordinate Skills	Behavioral Objectives	Item Format	Number of Items
2.9 Track grid lines relating to a code number and letter to the intersecting block	2.9.1 Given any locator code, track within the grid lines for the number and letter to the intersecting block.	S	2
2.10 Locate given town within intersecting block	2.10.1 Given a specified town, locator code, and corresponding intersecting block on map, locate town within block.	S	2
3.1.2 Locate mileage table on map	3.1.2.1 Given a map containing a mileage table, locate mileage table.	S	1
	3.1.2.2 Given several map locations, select the location of the mileage table.	S	1
3.1.3 Locate name of one town in row list	3.1.3.1 Given a mileage table and a town name, locate town in row list of towns.	S	2
3.1.4 Locate name of second town in column list	3.1.4.1 Given a mileage table and a town name, locate town in column list.	S	2
3.1.6 Track corresponding row and column to intersecting block	3.1.6.1 Given mileage table and the names of two towns, track corresponding row and column to intersecting block for two towns.	S	2
3.1.8 Read number of miles printed in intersecting block	3.1.8.1 Given mileage table and the names of two towns, locate miles between towns in mileage table.	S	2
3.2.2 Locate mileage scale on map	3.2.2.1 Given map with mileage scale, locate mileage scale.	S	1
3.2.3 Identify number of miles represented by the scale	3.2.3.1 Given a map with a scale indicating one inch equal to 100 miles, identify the number of miles represented by scale.	W/S	1
3.2.4* Locate two specified points on the map	3.2.4.1 Given the map, index, grid, and names of two points, locate the points.	W	1

(continued on next page)

TABLE 4.6 (*continued*)

| | Recall (Knowledge and Comprehension) | | | *Learning* |
Major Skill Groups	*Subordinate Skills*	*Behavioral Objectives*	*Item Format[a]*	*Number of Items*
Use miles printed along highways to determine mileage between specified places				

* Prerequisite Skills
[a] Item format code: W = Write response from memory; S = Select response from among alternatives; W/S = Either write or select response

106

Application

Subordinate Skills	Behavioral Objectives	Item Format	Number of Items
3.2.5 Estimate the number of times the scale will fit between the two points	3.2.5.1 Given the map, two specified points, and the scale, determine the number of times the scale fits between the two points.	W/S	3
3.2.6* Multiply by whole, fraction, and mixed numbers	3.2.6.1 Given a mileage scale with one inch equal to 100 miles, identify the number of miles represented by: a. 1 inch c. $2\frac{1}{2}$ inches b. 2 inches d. $\frac{1}{2}$ inch	W/S	4
3.2.7 Multiply the number of miles the scale represents by the number of times the scale fits between the two points	3.2.7.1 Given two points on a map and a scale with one inch equal to 100 miles, multiply to find the number of miles between the two points, correct to within 10 miles.	W/S	3
3.3.1* Locate two specified points on the map	3.3.1.1 Given an index, a grid, and the names of two points, locate the two specified points.	W	1
3.3.2* Locate the highway line between the two points	3.3.2.1 Given two specified points, locate the connecting highway line by indicating the route number.	W/S	2
3.3.3 Locate mile indicator numbers printed beside highway line	3.3.3.1 Given a map with clearly marked mile numbers along highway lines, locate printed numbers.	W/S	2
3.3.4 Track highway from one point to another and locate all mile numbers printed between the two points	3.3.4.1 Given specified points and a specified highway connecting the two points, list all mile numbers shown on the highway line between the two points.	W/S	2
3.3.5* Add one- and two-column numbers	3.3.5.1* Given a set of one-column numbers, add the numbers.	W/S	2
	3.3.5.2* Given a set of two-column numbers, add the numbers.	W/S	2
3.3.6 Add the list of numbers to obtain total distance in miles	3.3.6.1 Given two specified points and a specified highway connecting the two points, add all mile numbers shown on the highway line between the two points.	W/S	2

13. Specifications for a pretest on map interpretation are included in Table 4.7. The table of specifications in Table 4.6 indicates that either a written or selected response would suffice for several objectives. A selected response format was chosen to make administration and scoring easier.

TABLE 4.7   Specifications for Pretest on Map Interpretation Unit

Main Skill Areas	Enabling Skills from Table 4.6	Behavioral Objectives from Table 4.6	Item Format from Table 4.6[a]	Number of Items from Table 4.6
1. Use legend to interpret map symbols	1.1	1.1.3	S	1
	1.3	1.3.1	S	3
	1.5	1.5.1	S	1
	1.7	1.7.1	S	4
	1.9	1.9.1	S	4
2. Use index and grid	2.2	2.2.1	S	1
	2.7	2.7.1	S	2
	2.10	2.10.1	S	2
3.1 Use mileage table	3.1.1	3.1.1.2	S	1
	3.1.8	3.1.8.1	S	2
3.2 Use mileage scale	3.2.3	3.2.3.1	S	1
	3.2.6	3.2.6.1	S	4
	3.2.7	3.2.7.1	S	3
3.3 Use miles along highways	3.3.2	3.3.2.1	S	2
	3.3.6	3.3.6.1	S	2
				Total 33

[a] Item format code: S = Selected response

14. The subordinate skills and behavioral objectives for a practice test on using a mileage scale include:

Enabling Skill	Behavioral Objective	Item Format	Number of Items
3.2.1	3.2.1.1	W	1
3.2.2	3.2.2.1	S	1
3.2.3	3.2.3.1	W	1
3.2.4	3.2.4.1	W	1
3.2.5	3.2.5.1	W	3
3.2.6	3.2.6.1	W	4
3.2.7	3.2.7.1	W	3
			Total: 14

15. The specifications for a unit posttest are:

Major Skill Areas	Enabling Skills	Behavioral Objectives	Item Format	Number of Items
1. Use legend	1.3	1.3.1	S	3
	1.10	1.10.1	S	4
2. Use index and grid	2.10	2.10.1	S	2
3.1 Use mileage table	3.1.8	3.1.8.1	S	2
3.2 Use mileage scale	3.2.7	3.2.7.1	S	3
3.3 Use miles along highway	3.3.6	3.3.6.1	S	2
				Total: 16

16. a. 9 items (20 percent of 45 items)
    b. Skill areas and objectives selected are:

Major Skill Areas	Objectives	Item Format	Number of Items
1.	1.3.1	S	1
	1.10.1	S	1
2.	2.10.1	S	1
3.1	3.1.8.1	S	2
3.2	3.2.7.1	S	2
3.3	3.3.6.1	S	2
			Total: 9

SUGGESTED READING

Crocker, L., and Algina, J. (1986). *Introduction to classical and modern test theory.* New York: CBS College Publishing, pp. 66–75, 218–29.

Ebel, R. L., and Frisbie, D. A. (1986). *Essentials of educational measurement.* Englewood Cliffs, N.J.: Prentice-Hall, pp. 70–125.

Gronlund, N. E. (1985). *Measurement and evaluation in teaching.* New York: Macmillan Publishing Company, pp. 55–132.

Hills, J. R. (1981). *Measurement and evaluation in the classroom.* Columbus, Ohio: Charles E. Merrill Publishing Company, pp. 3–24, 95–118.

Mehrens, W. A., and Lehmann, I. J. (1984). *Measurement and evaluation in education and psychology.* New York: CBS College Publishing, pp. 16–29, 55–83, 266–309.

Nitko, A. J. (1983). *Educational tests and measurement.* New York: Harcourt, Brace, Jovanovich, pp. 117–35, 387–408, 411–40.

Popham, W. J. (1981). *Modern educational measurement.* Englewood Cliffs, N.J.: Prentice-Hall, pp. 24–41, 45–65, 98–134, 203–34.

CHAPTER 5

Writing Test Items to Help Ensure the Validity and Reliability of Test Scores

OBJECTIVES

1. List four criteria that can be used in writing test items to help ensure the validity and reliability of test scores.
2. For each criterion, list steps that can be taken in writing items to help ensure valid test scores.
3. For each criterion, list steps that can be taken in writing items to help ensure reliable test scores.
4. Describe formative evaluation procedures for reviewing items.
5. Evaluate items for their congruence with behavioral objectives.

Chapter 4 describes steps in test design most likely to yield valid and reliable scores. With the behavioral objectives selected for each test and the number of items prescribed, the next step is to write the items. This chapter presents four major criteria that you can use to guide item writing activities and, within each criterion, steps you can take to help ensure the validity and reliability of the test results. The four criteria that guide item construction are:

1. Congruence of items with the conditions, behavior, and content specified in the behavioral objectives.
2. Congruence of items with the characteristics of students to be tested.
3. Clarity of items.
4. Accuracy of measures.

CONGRUENCE OF ITEMS WITH OBJECTIVES

Congruence between items and objectives helps ensure that test scores are valid. When writing items, you should pay careful attention to the behavior, content, and conditions prescribed in the objectives.

Behavior

The response format selected should match the behavior prescribed in the objective. It is important to note whether the student needs to define, list, select, solve, construct, perform, or evaluate. As you write each item consider alternative ways the student might respond to demonstrate the behavior, and then write the items to solicit the prescribed behavior.

Content

The content subsumed in each objective may be simple or quite complex. Instances of content selected for test items should clearly reflect all facets of the content students are likely to encounter. For example, if you were selecting instances of proper nouns, you would need to select some related to persons, places, and things. Writing items related to only one or two areas of content would be insufficient.

In writing test items, be careful not to confound the rules or principles measured. Items that measure two or more skills at once will be difficult to interpret because the student may select the correct answer for the wrong reason. For example, when measuring students' ability to capitalize a proper noun, the word used to measure this skill should not be placed first in a sentence. Students may respond correctly using the rule for capitalizing sentences rather than the one for capitalizing proper nouns.

Finally, you need to ensure that the instances of content you select for items are precise and relate only to the content measured. Using nouns again as an illustration, words that have multimeanings, such as *park, season,* and *field,* can be either nouns or verbs. Students will respond to multimeaning words depending on how they define them. If multimeaning words are used, they should always be placed in a context in which their meaning is precise.

Conditions

Many intellectual and motor skills can be measured only in a situation that allows students to demonstrate their skill. In order to perform, operate, analyze, synthesize, or evaluate, students must be given appropriate resources. Test items that require supplementary resources are called *context-dependent* or *interpretative* items.

For most teacher-made tests, the conditions specified in the objective can be matched closely or realistically simulated. The conditions of behavioral objectives, which describe what students are to be given, can specify a variety of resource materials. They may require that students be provided with such materials as short stories, pictures, charts, diagrams, data tables, models, slides, specimens, or particular products. They may also specify such equipment as computers, saws, dissecting tools, sewing machines, weighing instruments, or automobiles. In addition, conditions sometimes include facilities, such as the school library or a learning resource center. The resource materials provided to students during testing must be congruent with the conditions specified in the objective. These materials are just as critical to valid measurement as is the nature of the items.

CONGRUENCE OF ITEMS WITH TARGET STUDENTS' CHARACTERISTICS

In order to create tests that result in valid and reliable scores, the items must be congruent with the characteristics of target students. Factors that can influence the validity of a test are students' reading levels, vocabulary, and experience. Students of any age who are poor readers will have difficulty responding to items that require a lot of reading, and their answers may reflect their reading skills more than their achievement of the objective. Therefore, vocabulary used in either written or oral items should be familiar to students to ensure that their response reflects their achievement of the objective and not their vocabulary. For example, if you are selecting words to use in measuring students' ability to classify nouns, each word used to measure the skill should be one that all students in the group can define. Students' experience and age should also be used to create the context for an item. The word *context* refers to the situation posed to test the objective. For example, if you want students to punctuate sentences or analyze a short story, the sentences and story used should be about topics and situations familiar to them. Avoid using contextual material that may unnecessarily arouse students' sensitivities. Contextual references to such topics as religion or church, political affiliations, or sexual behaviors are not appropriate in items unless the *content* of the instructional goal specifies religion, politics, or sexual behavior. Consider the following item intended to measure verb choice:

1. Fritz _____ to church last Sunday.
    A. go
    B. gone
    C. went

The religious context used in this item is inappropriate and may arouse the sensitivities of students who do not attend church or who do so on different days.

Two factors related to students' characteristics can affect the reliability of a test. One is bias and the other is students' familiarity with the response format and test medium. Test items and resources should be free of stereo-typing and of cultural, racial, and sexual biases. People described in the items and resources should positively reflect the cultural, racial, and sexual char-acteristics of students in the group. The contexts and problem situations used should also be appropriate for males and females and for the cultural groups represented in the class. Students who are offended by items or unfamiliar with cultural-dependent contexts used may be less able to answer correctly, thus reducing the reliability of the scores. Careful editing of the items with potential bias in mind should eliminate unconscious stereotyping and biases.

The second factor that can influence reliability is students' familiarity with the item format and test medium. Their first experience with an essay, multiple-choice, matching, oral, or public performance exam should not be on a posttest. Likewise, testing procedures that require students to respond using such resources as a machine-scored answer sheet or a computer should not be introduced on a posttest. Students should practice using unfamiliar item formats and responding resources in a nongraded situation, such as a pretest or practice test, to avoid creating unnecessary confusion and anxiety during a posttest.

CLARITY OF ITEMS

The clarity of items also affects the validity and reliability of a test. To ensure valid measures, items should be carefully constructed to avoid ambiguity and unintended complexity. Clearly written items allow students to focus their attention on the actual skill being measured. The language should be clear and precise; grammar, sentence structure, and punctuation should be correct. Each item should pose only one question. Questions that contain multiple ideas or that address several issues will confuse students of any age. Irrelevant or extraneous materials should be avoided. Instructions for responding should be clear, explaining how students are to respond as well as how re-source materials are to be used.

To help ensure reliability, items should have only one correct or clearly best answer. Including more than one correct answer confuses students and can result in inconsistent answers, scoring, analysis, and interpretation.

ACCURACY OF MEASURES

Some items may measure students' skills more accurately than others. Factors related to the accuracy of measures are the novelty of items, susceptibility to guessing, and susceptibility to cheating.

The novelty of items and resources used on a test can influence test validity. Test items should not simply duplicate those previously used in classroom instruction or on earlier tests. Whenever feasible, novel items should be used each time an objective is measured. Otherwise, students may answer the questions correctly by remembering the correct answer from a previous unit test, practice test, or pretest. To ensure that students can perform the skill and are not simply recalling a previous instance, novel items should be used. The duplication of test items can lead to incorrect inferences about students' achievement levels.

Novelty of resource material and equipment is a different matter. Resources, such as charts, stories, pictures, and data tables, should contain novel information, but the organization and kinds of information as well as the degree of complexity and detail included should remain the same as that used during instruction. Such resources as computers, saws, sewing machines, and dissecting tools should not be changed for tests. Students should be tested using the same equipment they used to practice, particularly if changing equipment might increase the complexity of the task.

Guessing behavior tends to affect the reliability of test scores. While writing items, you should consider the probability of students' answering the question by guessing correctly. Test items that require students to select an answer are most susceptible to this problem. For example, students who do not know the answer to a two-choice item still have a 50 percent chance of answering correctly. Items containing three, four, or five choices reduce the probability of guessing correctly, but guessing remains a factor nevertheless. Items that require students to write rather than select answers also reduce the likelihood of guessing correctly.

Inadvertent clues in the item directions, or resources, also increase the probability that students will correctly guess an answer. For example, it is relatively easy for students to classify proper nouns in a list of words where all proper nouns are capitalized and all common nouns are not. Some students may use the capital letter rather than the meaning of the word to select correct examples of proper nouns. To avoid clues in this instance, capitalize all words in the list, capitalize no words in the list, or capitalize only some proper nouns and some common nouns. Removing potential clues from items will increase the reliability of students' scores.

A second factor that affects score reliability is the ease with which students can cheat on a test. When students are seated close together and their responses are brief, they can easily copy answers from other students' tests. When writing items that are susceptible to cheating, you should use strategies to reduce the likelihood of its occurrence. One such strategy is to create multiple forms of the test that contain the same questions but use a different item sequence on each form. With answers reordered, students' ability to locate corresponding answers at a glance will be eliminated.

FORMATIVE EVALUATION OF ITEMS

Even though items are written carefully, the first draft of a test may contain many errors. Before administering any posttest, a draft copy should be evaluated to locate and remove potential problems. Some errors in item construction are more critical than others. The primary consideration in evaluating an item is its congruence with the objective it measures. Without this congruence, the appropriateness of the item for target students, the clarity of item wording, and the accuracy of measures are irrelevant. The second most important consideration is the congruence of the item with the characteristics of target students. Once you are sure items meet these two criteria, next consider the clarity of each item. Finally, check to see whether the items are likely to result in accurate measures.

In addition to the criteria and their order of importance, consider who would be the best judge of each criterion. Table 5.1 lists each criterion and the individuals who can judge it. Like the criteria, the evaluators are listed in their order of importance because some may be better judges than others for each factor.

TABLE 5.1   Criteria and Evaluators for Test Items

Criteria in Order of Importance	*Evaluators in Order of Importance*
1. Congruence between the item and the objective	1. Colleagues 2. Author
2. Congruence between items and target students' characteristics	1. Target students 2. Author 3. Colleagues
3. Clarity of items	1. Colleagues 2. Author 3. Target students
4. Accuracy of measures	1. Author 2. Target students 3. Colleagues

Congruence between Items and Objectives

The primary consideration in evaluating a test item is its congruence with its behavioral objective. Colleagues are recommended as the primary evaluators of this criterion; authors are recommended as secondary reviewers because they will tend to see both what they intended to include in the item and what they actually included. This tendency may cause them to overlook important problems whereas colleagues, unaware of authors' intentions, can judge only what is present. Whether the item is being evaluated by colleagues or by the author, the following procedure is recommended for judging the congruence between items and objectives.

1. Place the objective and item side by side.

2. Break down both the objective and the item into their separate elements.
3. Relate comparable elements in the objective and item.
4. Judge whether comparable elements are congruent.

Figure 5.1 illustrates the first two steps in the procedure. The objective contains three elements: conditions, behavior, and content. The item also contains three elements: response directions, content, and stimulus material.

The third step is to relate comparable elements in the behavioral objective and the item. The conditions in the objective should be compared with the stimulus material in the item; the behavior in the objective should be compared with the response direction; and the content in the objective should be compared with the content specified in the directions and in the stimulus material.

The fourth step is to judge whether comparable elements are congruent. Stimulus material in the item should match the material prescribed in the conditions. For example, if the conditions prescribe that students be given a paragraph with the topic, supporting, and concluding sentences out of order, then the stimulus material in the item should be an unorganized paragraph. The behavior in the response directions should be compatible with the behavior in the objective. For instance, if the objective behavior prescribed sequencing the sentences in a paragraph, then the response directions should include comparable behaviors, such as reorder, reorganize, rearrange, or even

FIGURE 5.1   Objective and Items Separated into Elements

Objective	Item
Given a list of words containing nouns and other parts of speech, select words that are nouns.	Directions: Locate the nouns in the following list, and place a check beside each one. _____ 1. board _____ 5. library _____ 2. run _____ 6. religion _____ 3. boy _____ 7. flower _____ 4. happy _____ 8. smooth

Objective Elements	Item Elements
Conditions: Given a list of words containing nouns and other parts of speech, Behavior: select Content: words that are nouns.	Response directions: Locate place a check beside Content: nouns Stimulus materials: _____ 1. board _____ 5. library _____ 2. run _____ 6. religion _____ 3. boy _____ 7. flower _____ 4. happy _____ 8. smooth

sequence. The content in the objective should match the content in both the directions and the stimulus material. If the content in the objective specified a chronological sequence, then the directions should specify chronological order and the sentences included in the paragraph should have a clear chronological relationship.

The elements for the objective and items on discriminating between nouns and other words are compared in Table 5.2. The objective elements

TABLE 5.2 Comparison of Elements in Behavioral Objectives and Test Items

Objective Elements	Item Elements	Congruent?
Conditions	Stimulus Material	Yes
Given a list of words containing nouns and other parts of speech	1. board 2. run 3. boy 4. happy 5. library 6. religion 7. flower 8. smooth	1. A list of words is provided. 2. The list contains five words that are clearly nouns. 3. The list contains three words that clearly are not nouns.
Behavior	Directions for Responding	Yes
select	Locate	1. Students must discriminate between nouns and other words.
	Place a check beside	2. They can demonstrate their selections by checking the nouns.
Content	Directions	Yes
words that are nouns.	nouns	1. The content in the objective and item directions is the same.
	Stimulus Material	Yes
	1. board 2. run 3. boy 4. happy 5. library 6. religion 7. flower 8. smooth	1. Nouns included in the list refer to persons, places, things, and ideas; thus, they are representative of the content.

are included in the first column; the item elements are included in the second column; and the judgments about congruence are included in the last column. Based on these comparisons, these items and their objective would be judged congruent.

Now consider the objective and sample items in Table 5.3. The first column contains the objective with its elements separated. The second column contains items that are not congruent with the objective, and the last column contains items that are congruent. Consider first the incongruent items. Notice that the conditions specified in the objective do not match the stimulus material. The conditions specify that the sets of simple sentences be complete with proper capitalization and punctuation. However, the items in the stimulus material are already combined into compound sentences. The stimulus material in the items in the third column are congruent: two separate simple sentences are presented.

TABLE 5.3   An Example Behavioral Objective with Incongruent and Congruent Test Items

Objective	Incongruent Item	Congruent Item
1. Given sets of two simple sentences complete with their first words capitalized and their ending punctuation, rewrite them as compound sentences.	Directions: Punctuate the following compound sentences. 1. John is taller than Paul but Bill is taller than John. 2. Jill really enjoys the animals at the zoo, but she likes the elephants best.	Directions: Rewrite the following sets of simple sentences to form compound sentences. A. John is taller than Paul. B. Bill is taller than John. 1. _____ _____ A. Jill really enjoys the animals at the zoo. B. She likes the elephants best. 2. _____ _____

Consider next the behavior specified in the objective and that included in the directions. The objective specifies that students rewrite the sentences, whereas the item directions in column two tell students to punctuate only. Rewriting would require students to punctuate; select a coordinating conjunction, if needed; omit the ending punctuation in the first sentence; and omit the beginning capital letter in the second sentence. Obviously, rewriting the sentences is more complex than punctuating given compound sentences that already have these modifications. Thus, the behaviors in the objective and items are not congruent. The rewrite response specified in the third column is congruent with the objective.

Last, compare the content in the objective with that included in the items. The objective names compound sentences; the directions for the items in the second column specify compound sentences; and the stimulus material in the second column contains compound sentences. Thus, these items and the objective are congruent in content even though they are not congruent in conditions and behavior. The items in the third column also contain content congruent with that in the objective.

Congruence between Items and Students' Characteristics

After ensuring that items and objectives are congruent, you should next evaluate the appropriateness of items for given students. For this review you will need from one to three students typical of the target population. If you have a homogeneous group, the judgments of one student should suffice. However, if you have a heterogeneous group, you might want one student who is above average, one who is average, and one who is below average in achievement to review the items.

Ask the student reviewers to read the directions, to underline all words they do not understand, and to inquire about any instructions that are unclear. They should then read and respond to each item. Again they should underline any words that are unfamiliar and inquire about questions that confuse them. Based on their inquiries and on their responses to items, you can locate unfamiliar, ambiguous, or awkward material and rephrase it as needed. Although it is not important for these students to know the correct answers to items, it is important for them to understand what they are to do (directions) and the meaning of the questions. If these students can respond as you intend, then you can assume that the items are appropriate for similar students in your classes. You might also ask these student reviewers to show you answer clues that they find in either the directions or the items because students can often find clues that escape teachers.

If you have no student reviewers available, review the items for their appropriateness yourself since you are the one most familiar with the characteristics of students in your classes. In addition, colleagues who teach similar students can be asked to evaluate the appropriateness of the language and examples for their students.

Clarity of Items

The third criterion is the clarity of items. The most appropriate evaluators are your colleagues because the items may appear clear and grammatically correct to you. Colleagues can independently judge what you actually wrote instead of what you intended to write. These evaluations are especially tricky because many reviewers do not simply indicate errors in items; instead, they often rephrase the items to suit themselves. This problem usually can be avoided by providing reviewers with the following instructions: (1) first, mark *errors* in grammar and punctuation; (2) second, eliminate unnecessary words or phrases; and (3) third, only rephrase items that remain unclear after the first and second steps are complete.

The best colleagues to use for this review are those who judged the congruence between your items and objectives. This preliminary exercise helps clarify your intentions and helps critics avoid rewriting items so they are no longer congruent with the objective.

If colleagues are not available to assist with this review, evaluate the items for clarity yourself. This is best done after enough time has passed for you to forget what you intended to express.

Accuracy of Measures

You are the best person to judge the potential of your items for producing accurate measures. You are the only one who knows whether an item is novel or repeated; you know as well as anyone whether particular item formats are amenable to guessing behaviors; and you know the seating arrangements in your class and whether students can readily obtain answers from other students.

Item Formatting Criteria

Besides these four main criteria, there are several recommendations for formatting each type of item, including objective items, essay items, product development tests, and performance tests. Chapters 6, 7, 8, and 9 describe these recommendations. Following the formatting suggestions in these chapters while writing items helps ensure each item's clarity and potential for producing accurate measures. In addition to providing helpful guidelines for producing items, these suggestions provide criteria for formatively evaluating your items in each format. The only individuals who can judge whether your items are correctly formatted are people familiar with the suggestions for writing each type of item. People unfamiliar with item formatting rules will tend to focus on the general clarity of your items rather than on their structure.

SUMMARY

Table 5.4 summarizes questions you should consider when writing test items and developing or selecting resources to be used during the test. Although the questions are listed either under validity or reliability concerns, some will influence both areas. For example, ambiguous directions for an item and overly complex items will affect validity. At the same time, they will tend to increase guessing behavior, which will decrease the test's reliability.

Before administering any test used to determine students' grades, a draft copy of the test

TABLE 5.4   Criteria for Writing and Evaluating Test Items

Criteria	Validity Concerns	Reliability Concerns

Congruence between the item and the behavioral objective	1. Does the response required by the item match the behavior specified in the objective?
	
	2. Does the content in the item match that specified in the objective?
	  a. Do the items reflect an adequate, balanced sample of the content in each objective?
	  b. Do the items confound the concepts, rules, or principles?
	  c. Are instances of content used precise examples or nonexamples of the content?
	
	3. Do the resources provided match the conditions, behavior, and content prescribed in the objective?	

Congruence between the item and the characteristics of target students	4. Is the amount of reading required appropriate for the group? 5. Is the vocabulary used appropriate for the group? 6. Is the context used appropriate for students' experience?	1. Are the items free of cultural, racial, and sexual bias? 2. Is the group familiar with the item format and the test medium?
Clarity of items	7. Are the meanings of words precise? 8. Are grammar, sentence structure, and punctuation correct? 9. Is there only one question per item? 10. Is extraneous material excluded? 11. Are directions clear?	3. Is there only one correct or best answer?
Accuracy of measure	12. Are the items novel or different than those used during instruction and on previous tests?	4. Can students readily guess the correct answer? 5. Can students cheat easily?

should be formatively evaluated to detect errors or weaknesses. In judging the congruence between items and objectives, you should compare the objective's conditions with the item's stimulus materials; the objective's behavior with the item's response directions; and the objective's content with the item's directions and stimulus material. Colleagues and authors are the best judges of this criterion. In judging the congruence between an item's language and examples and the characteristics of target students, one to three students should work through the test indicating problems they encounter. Colleagues are the best judges of item clarity, and you are the best judge of whether a congruent, clear item is likely to produce accurate measures. Information gathered through these evaluations can be used to refine tests before they are administered to a class.

PRACTICE EXERCISES

I. Writing Test Items. Four criteria can be used while writing test items to help ensure that the items result in valid and reliable measures of students' achievement. In the following exercise, match each recommendation to its criterion.

Criteria
A. Congruence between items and behavioral objectives
B. Congruence between items and characteristics of target students
C. Clarity of items
D. Accuracy of measures

Recommendations
1. Include only one question in each item.
2. Use a response format for items that is appropriate for the prescribed behavior.
3. Exclude extraneous material from the item.
4. Construct items to minimize guessing correctly.
5. Use a familiar context.
6. Select or develop resources that accurately reflect the conditions.
7. Select instances of content that are clearly examples and nonexamples.
8. Use vocabulary that is readily understood.
9. Include instances that cover the scope of content that students are likely to encounter.
10. Select an item format that is familiar.
11. Use correct grammar and punctuation.
12. Construct items to reduce the probability of guessing the correct answer.
13. Use contexts that are free from cultural, racial, and sexual bias.

II. Formatively Evaluating a Draft of the Test. Match the evaluator with the criteria for quality test items that each evaluator can best judge. More than one type of judge may be appropriate, but when you list more than one, list them in their order of importance.

Evaluators
A. Students
B. Colleagues
C. The test author

Judgments
1. Congruence between items and behavioral objectives.
2. Congruence between items and characteristics of target students.

3. Clarity of items.

4. Accuracy of measures.

For the next four examples, evaluate the congruence between the objectives and test items. Use the responses below to indicate your judgments. You may use more than one response for each item.

A. The objective and item(s) *are* congruent.

B. The objective *conditions* and item *stimulus material* are *not* congruent.

C. The objective *behavior* and item *response directions* are *not* congruent.

D. The objective *content* and item *directions* and/or *stimulus material* are *not* congruent.

Objectives	*Items*
5. Given a list of words containing common and proper nouns with all words capitalized. identify the <u>proper nouns</u>.	*Directions:* Place a check (√) in the space before the <u>proper nouns</u> in the following list. _____ 1. french fries _____ 2. Burger King _____ 3. Whopper _____ 4. Big Mac _____ 5. hamburger _____ 6. McDonalds
6. Given a specified liquid capacity amount, state an <u>equivalent amount of liquid</u> in the specified unit.	*Directions:* For each of the liquid measures named in column A, identify an equivalent amount for the unit of measure specified in column B.

	A		B
1.	16 tablespoons	= _____	cups(s)
2.	3 cups	= _____	quart(s)
3.	2 quarts	= _____	gallon(s)
4.	8 quarts	= _____	gallon(s)

Objectives	*Items*
7. Given a lower case letter, write the <u>corresponding upper case letter</u> from memory.	Say, "For each of the letters I write on the board, circle the capital letter that matches it on your paper."

Letters on Board	*Responses on Answer sheet*				
f	B	G	E	F	C
a	B	C	P	T	A
l	I	L	J	T	M

Objectives	Items
8. Given simple sentences without proper nouns capitalized, locate the proper nouns.	*Directions:* Underline the words in the following sentences that <u>should be capitalized</u>. 1. he arrived early at school with his father. 2. they all enjoyed the picnic. 3. Barney went to the game with Mary and Fred. 4. seattle is located in the northwest.

FEEDBACK

I. Writing Test Items

1. C	5. B	9. A	13. B
2. A	6. A	10. B	
3. C	7. A	11. C	
4. D	8. B	12. D	

II. Evaluating a Draft of the Test. (The items in number 8 confound the following capitalization rules: proper nouns, first word of a sentence, geographic regions, and family relationships. The first two items contain no proper nouns.)
1. B, C
2. A, C, B
3. B, A, C
4. C, B, A
5. B
6. A
7. B, C
8. B, D

SUGGESTED READING

Crocker, L., and Algina, J. (1986). *Introduction to classical and modern test theory.* New York: CBS College Publishing, pp. 75–86.

Ebel, R. L., and Frisbie, D. A. (1986). *Essentials of educational measurement.* Englewood Cliffs, N.J.: Prentice-Hall, pp. 121–25.

Gronlund, N. E. (1985). *Measurement and evaluation in teaching.* New York: Macmillan Publishing Company, pp. 132–43.

Merrill, M. D. (1983). *Component display theory*. In C. M. Reigeluth, ed., *Instructional design theories and models*. Hillsdale, N.J.: Lawrence Erlbaum Associates, pp. 279–333.

Mehrens, W. A., and Lehmann, I. J. (1984). *Measurement and evaluation in education and psychology*. New York: CBS College Publishing, pp. 84–91.

Nitko, A. J. (1983). *Educational tests and measurement*. New York: Harcourt, Brace, Jovanovich, pp. 140–41, 215–41.

Popham, W. J. (1981). *Modern educational measurement*. Englewood Cliffs, N.J.: Prentice-Hall, pp. 286–93.

CHAPTER 6

Writing Objective Test Items

OBJECTIVES

1. Describe the following test item formats: completion, short-answer, alternative-response, matching, and keyed.
2. List suggestions for constructing items using each format.
3. Evaluate items written in each format by using the criteria for validity and reliability described in Chapter 5, as well as the specific criteria for each format.
4. Write written-response items and selected-response items using the criteria for validity and reliability and also using the suggestions for constructing items in each of the five formats discussed.
5. Develop group and individually administered tests for nonreaders.

Objective test items require students to write or select a correct or best answer. These items are called *objective* because they can be *scored* more objectively than any other type of item used to measure students' performance. Written-response items include sentence completion and short-answer questions. Selected-response items include alternative-response, matching, keyed, and multiple-choice items. This chapter suggests ways to construct test items for each of these formats except multiple-choice, which is discussed in Chapter 7.

Objective test items are popular with classroom teachers for several reasons. First, a teacher can use them to measure many types of learning, from verbal information to the use of rules and principles, and many levels of learning, from knowledge through evaluation. Second, a wide range of content can be measured because the items can be answered relatively quickly. Third, objective tests are easier to administer, score, and analyze than are other types of tests. Fourth, they can often be adapted for use with computers and can be scored and analyzed by machine. Finally, fewer scoring errors are likely to be made, yielding scores generally more reliable than those from other types of tests.

Despite their positive features, objective tests cannot be used to measure many of the skills found in curriculum guides. For example, objective test items cannot measure students' ability to write a report, deliver a speech, construct a mobile, operate equipment, paint a picture, or play the piano. Although objective items can measure certain aspects of these skills (e.g., related terminology, rules, or procedures), actual performance is a more valid measure of these skills.

In developing objective tests, you must consider the validity and reliability of test items. As described in Chapter 5, objective items must (1) be congruent with behavioral objectives, (2) be congruent with the characteristics of target students, (3) be clearly written, and (4) provide accurate measures. As you write objective items, these primary criteria should be kept in mind. The following sections describe a variety of objective item formats and suggestions for writing items using each format.

DEVELOPING WRITTEN-RESPONSE TEST ITEMS

Written-response test items require students to recall information from memory or to apply a skill before they write the answer. These items have several positive features. Because no alternatives are provided from which students can select an answer, students are less likely to guess correctly. By analyzing students' original responses, you can identify actual misconceptions and problems students have. The ability to identify actual misconceptions will help you tailor review materials to real problems and write plausible distractors for subsequent selected-response test items. Written-response items are very versatile because they can be constructed in a variety of formats and used to measure both verbal information and intellectual skills. The following list of possible uses is not exhaustive, but it illustrates the versatility of these items:

1. Students can be given a definition and asked to write the name of the concept defined.
2. Students can be given the name of a concept and asked to write a brief definition for it.
3. Students can be given the name of a concept and asked to list its unique characteristics.

4. Students can be asked to supply a missing word or words in a given definition, rule, or principle.
5. Students can be given a resource paragraph and asked to recall specific details from the paragraph, supply correct punctuation, reorder information, or edit it.
6. Students can be given a written passage to analyze and then asked to list the main ideas and the relationship among them.
7. Students can be given an incomplete paragraph and asked to write an introductory or concluding sentence for it.
8. Students can be given a product and asked to list its qualities and inadequacies.
9. Students can be asked to view materials, such as slides or specimens set up at different test stations, and then to write short answers for questions posed about each exhibit.

Despite their versatility, written-response items have their limitations. First, the item must be clearly written to produce the anticipated answer. More than one logical answer to an item will cause scoring problems and may reduce reliability. You must decide whether to accept logical, yet unanticipated, answers, whether to reduce credit for misspelled answers, and how much credit to allow for incomplete answers. Second, written answers cannot be machine scored. Scoring items, synthesizing answers by objectives, and analyzing individual and group responses all take time. Even though written-response items are time consuming and more difficult to score reliably, they should be the item format of choice when the behavior in the objective requires a written response.

Completion Items

Completion items require students to write in a key word or words that have been left out of a statement. The following are suggestions for writing clear, effective items in this format.

1. *Remove only key words from the statement.* A statement containing too many blanks does not adequately communicate the desired answer. For example, the item, "_____ _____ are words that refer to particular _____ , _____ , or _____ ," would be quite confusing to students. This ambiguity can be corrected in either of the following ways:

a. Proper nouns are words that refer to particular _____ , _____ , or _____ .

b. Words that refer to particular persons, places, or things are called

_____ .

2. *Place blanks for key words near or at the end of the statement.* Students should be able to anticipate the correct missing word before they encounter the blank. Placing the blank near or at the end of a statement does not change the meaning of the sentence, but students may find the item easier to read and answer.

The following suggestions will help you structure a completion item. First, write the complete statement. Second, select the key word or words you wish to eliminate. Third, if the key word is not located toward the end of the statement, rewrite the statement so the key word comes toward the end and replace it with a blank. Finally, read the statement with the words removed to ensure that enough information remains to guide students to the desired answer. The following series of statements illustrates these steps:

a. Write statement: Nouns are words that refer to persons, places, things, or ideas.
b. Select key word: *Nouns* are words that refer to persons, places, things, or ideas.
c. Rewrite statement: Words that refer to persons, places, things, or ideas are called _____ .

3. *Eliminate the possibility of several plausible answers.* Often, incomplete sentences can logically be completed using several different words. For example, the item, "Proper nouns are words that refer to _____ persons, places, or things," would likely produce a variety of responses. Students might insert the words *particular, specific, given, proper,* or *some.* When there are several plausible answers to an item, replace the word that was taken out and remove another instead. A much superior item would be, "Words that refer to particular persons, places, or things are called _____ .

4. *Eliminate clues to the correct answer.* Students will find clues to answers in blanks that are the length of desired words, in a blank preceded by *a* or *an,* and in the use of singular or plural verbs. You can eliminate these clues by making all the blanks the same length; by using *a(an)* instead of either *a* or *an;* and by avoiding singular or plural verbs that may suggest a correct response.

5. *Paraphrase statements taken from instructional materials.* Test items that consist of verbatim statements taken from text promote rote memorization and tend to reduce students' need to read for comprehension. A much better test item would paraphrase key ideas in the text.

6. *Reduce scoring time by using answer sheets or other devices that simplify scoring.* Scoring completion items is time consuming, but there are several

ways to make the task easier. Many teachers have students use a separate answer sheet with blanks numbered to correspond with those on the test. Another method is to make a column of blanks in either side margin of the test itself. Both techniques shorten the time required to score students' responses.

Short-Answer Items

One type of short-answer item is a complete statement or question that requires students to insert a word, a phrase, or a sentence. Examples include:

1. Briefly define the term *proper noun*. _____
2. What are words that refer to *particular* persons, places, or things called? _____
3. John had $5.00. He bought a model kit for $2.56 and glue for $1.29. He paid 5% sales tax on his purchase. How much money did he have left? $_____

A second type of short-answer item frequently appears on mathematics tests. A group of items appears with one set of directions. See Figure 6.1 for example.

A third type of short-answer format is association items that require students to associate a given stimulus with a response. Students are asked to associate a word, a symbol, or a picture with something else. The directions explain what the association should be. The examples in Figures 6.2–6.5 illustrate this format.

FIGURE 6.1   Test Items with One Set of Directions

Directions: Use the sign in each problem to find the answer.

(1) 56	(2) 78	(3) 56	(4) 80	(5) 24	(6) 52
+43	+25	−43	−45	×12	×46

FIGURE 6.2   Association Items: Stimulus and Response

Directions: Write a matching capital letter for each letter given.

a _____   m _____
e _____   q _____
i _____   u _____

FIGURE 6.3 Association Items: Stimulus and Response

Directions: The names of several traffic signs appear below. <u>Draw the sign</u> that matches each name in the blank provided.

    1. Stop _____
    2. Yield _____
    3. Do not enter _____
    4. Railroad crossing _____
    5. School zone _____

The following three suggestions will help you prepare good short-answer items.

1. *Provide a blank for each item that suggests whether the response should be one word or several (i.e., a phrase or sentence).* If you expect a one-word answer, the blank should be the length of one word. To avoid providing clues, make all word-sized blanks the same length. If the answer is a phrase or sentence, the blank or space should not permit students to write more than that. Some students will feel compelled to fill whatever space is allowed and will write an essay when a short answer is asked for.

2. *Specify the units required in the answer.* If the answer is to be in inches, dollars, or some other unit, specify the unit both in the question and beside the blank. Otherwise some students may use alternative or inappropriate units in their answers. Clearly indicated units help ensure that an incorrect answer was not the result of misreading or misunderstanding the question.

3. *Ensure that the directions for a cluster of items are appropriate for all items in the set.* If one set of directions is used for a set of items, ensure that all items included are compatible with the directions. When a set of associations is to be made, state the basis for the association and the type of response sought. Include only homogeneous stimuli in the set.

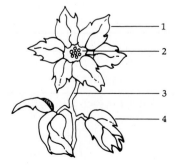

FIGURE 6.4 Association Items: Stimulus and Response

Directions: For each arrow in the diagram (1–4), write the <u>name</u> of the part indicated by the arrow.

    1.
    2.
    3.
    4.

FIGURE 6.5 Association Items: Stimulus and Response

Directions: Write the <u>time</u> each clock indicates: minutes after the hour; minutes before the hour.

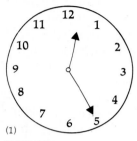

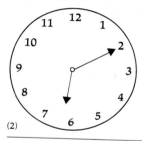

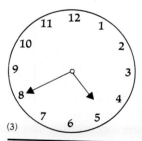

(1)

1. _____ minutes after _____ o'clock

2. _____ minutes before _____ o'clock

(2)

3. _____ minutes after _____ o'clock

4. _____ minutes before _____ o'clock

(3)

5. _____ minutes after _____ o'clock

6. _____ minutes before _____ o'clock

DEVELOPING SELECTED-RESPONSE TEST ITEMS

Selected-response items require students to choose an answer from a given set of plausible, alternative choices. Because each item must include one or more incorrect alternatives, selected-response items can be difficult to construct. Incorrect alternatives, sometimes called *distractors* or *foils*, should not be tricky or obscure and should not contain material unfamiliar to the students. Instead, they should represent plausible misconceptions that students may have developed. Because the correct answer appears in each item, students have a better chance of guessing correctly than they would with written-response items, and their potential for guessing correctly is increased when distractors do not appear reasonable.

Despite these drawbacks, using selected-response items has several advantages. First, each item requires students to choose among alternative responses that they may not have considered otherwise. These items can require students to make fine distinctions between or among several plausible answers. Therefore, teachers can use them to test aspects of students' skills that cannot be tested with other item formats. Second, students can answer more selected-response items than written-response items in the same period of time. Thus, a selected-response test can measure a wider range of skills than can a writt   equal. Third, ation, or scor- ifferent types velopment.

s. Each item ay ask stu- lse, correct desirable rning. For example,

1. To test students' ability to recall information. Students can be asked to determine whether a definition, a rule, or a principle is stated correctly.
2. To determine whether students can use a definition to classify examples and nonexamples of a concept.
3. To determine whether students can judge the correctness of given analyses or syntheses material.
4. To assess students' ability to evaluate material. For example, after reviewing selected materials, students can be asked whether they agree or disagree with given evaluations of the materials.
5. To apply principles in order to judge the accuracy of statements of causality or correlation.

In spite of its versatility, students have a 50 percent chance of guessing the correct answer to an alternative-response item. To reduce the potential for guessing correctly, some teachers modify the format by asking students to change an underlined word or words in an item if they believe the item is incorrect as stated. The students are directed to write the correct information either above the underlined word or in a blank provided beside the item. The following example illustrates a traditional and a modified true–false item.

Traditional:

T   F   1. A served tennis ball that strikes the net and lands in the appropriate area is called a net ball.

Modified:

T   F   <u>let</u>   1. A served tennis ball that strikes the net and lands in the appropriate area is called a <u>net</u> ball.

Because it reduces the probability of guessing, the modified alternative-response item results in more valid and reliable test scores than does the traditional item. Students may recognize that the statement in a traditional item is incorrect, but they still may not know the correct answer or the reasons they thought the statement was wrong. With the modified format, students must first recognize that the statement is false and then supply the correct information. Although this modification reduces the probability of guessing correctly, it also increases scoring time. It can no longer be totally machine scored unless the test is administered by computer. The desirability of this modification will depend on the time and resources available for scoring.

The following suggestions for developing alternative-response items deal primarily with the directions for items and with the statements students are asked to judge.

1. *Explain judgments to be made in the directions.* Alternative-response items can be used to have students make a variety of judgments, such as true–false, yes–no, correct–incorrect, and fact–opinion. The nature of the required judgment should be clearly described.

2. *Ensure that answer choices logically match the necessary judgments.* For example, if students are to determine whether statements are true or false, the best answer choices are *true* and *false*. If a statement logically requires a *yes* or *no* answer, the item should offer students these two choices. If students are to determine whether a statement reflects fact or opinion, the two answer choices should be *fact* and *opinion*.

3. *Explain in the directions how students are to record their answers.* Without explicit instructions, students are likely to respond in a variety of ways. Directions should indicate whether students are to circle letters or words, fill in circles or spaces on a machine-scored answer sheet, or write words in blanks beside the items.

4. *Include only one idea to be judged in each statement.* Statements that include several ideas or that are only partially true will confuse students and affect their answer choices. A simple sentence with clear, precise wording at an appropriate vocabulary level is most appropriate. One exception to this rule is an item intended to check students' ability to detect causality or correlation.

5. *Word statements in a positive manner*. Negatively stated items are more complex and difficult to interpret than are positive statements. Negative words, such as *no* and *not*, add confusion that can reduce both the validity and reliability of students' responses. In effect, such items may be measuring the students' ability to read carefully rather than their objective-based skills. For example, students attempting to respond to the statement, "The word *boy* is not a noun," would have to recall the definition for nouns and then determine whether the word *boy* fit the definition. If they decided that the word was a noun, they would then need to note the word *not* and select false as the correct response. Some students may know that the word *boy* is a noun, miss the word *not* in the statement, and incorrectly mark the statement as true. If there is a legitimate reason for including negative words in a statement, they should be underlined or written in all capital letters to attract students' attention.

6. *Avoid designing questions to trick students*. Teachers who intentionally create items meant to trick students may also be tricking themselves. Such items not only confuse students, but may also make the students' scores uninterpretable. A teacher using trick items would not be able to determine whether the instruction was effective or whether students were ready to begin the next lesson.

7. *Avoid providing clues to the correct answer*. Unintended clues help students guess the correct answer to test items. Any type of pattern, either in the directions, items, or responses, will guide students toward the right responses. An obvious example is the use of statements that are either all true or all false. Some students will quickly detect and accept this pattern whereas other students will distrust the pattern of their answers and change some of them to the alternative. Less obvious, but still detectable, patterns can affect test results. Such patterns include the consistent use of true and false statements of different lengths, the obvious preference for one answer type, and the alternate placement of true and false items. For example, students will quickly recognize a pattern in which true statements are always longer than false ones. To avoid providing these types of clues, you should make statements of both types approximately the same length, review the list of statements to ensure that one type is not dominant, and review the sequence of responses to ensure that no pattern exists.

A final type of clue is the use of determiners or qualifiers, such as *always*, *never*, and *absolutely*. A statement that includes these and similar words strongly suggests an answer of false or no. This type of clue is one of the easiest to avoid.

Table 6.1 contains poor and improved examples of test items for the objective, "Given the definition of a noun, identify it as such." The behavioral objective appears at the top of the table. The suggestions discussed in this section are listed on the left. The second column provides examples of items that do not incorporte these suggestions, and the third column shows revisions of the same items.

TABLE 6.1   Alternative-Response Test Items for the Behavioral Objective "Given the Definition of a Noun, Identify It as Such"

Suggestion	Item	Improved Item
Ensure that answer choices logically match the judgments to be made	**1 2** 1. Nouns are words that refer to people, places, things, and ideas.	**T F** 1. Nouns are words that refer to people, places, things, and ideas.
Include only one idea in each statement	**T F** 1. Nouns are words that refer to people, actions, places, conjunctions, things, and modifiers.	**T F** 1. Nouns are words that refer to people, places, things and ideas. **T F** 2. Nouns are words that refer to actions, conjunctions, and modifiers.
Use clear, precise wording	**T F** 1. Words used in the English language to reference persons we are speaking or writing about are called nouns.	**T F** 1. Words that refer to people are called nouns.
Statements should clearly relate to one of the alternatives	**T F** 1. Words that refer to any physical object are sometimes called nouns.	**T F** 1. Words that refer to physical objects are nouns.
Make the wording of statements positive	**T F** 1. Nouns are not words that refer to action.	**T F** 1. Nouns are words that refer to action.
Make both correct and incorrect statements about the same length	**T F** 1. Nouns are words that refer to persons, places, things, and ideas. **T F** 2. Nouns are words that refer to actions. **T F** 3. Nouns are words that refer to conjunctions.	**T F** 1. Nouns are words that refer to persons, places, things, and ideas. **T F** 2. Nouns are words that refer to actions, conjunctions, and adjectives.
Avoid specific determiners, such as always and never	**T F** 1. Nouns are words that always refer to people.	**T F** 1. Nouns are words that refer to people.

A useful modification in the alternative-response item is called the clustered alternative-response format. The purposes for this format are to eliminate redundancy in items and reduce reading time. These items include a common set of directions and short items of only one or a few words. For example, the following set of repetitive items could easily be clustered.

T F 1. The word *house* is a noun.

T F 2. The word *happy* is a noun.

T F   3. The word *bird* is a noun.

T F   4. The word *ran* is a noun.

To reduce the redundancy, you might redesign the items to appear as follows:

Directions: For each of the following words, circle <u>YES</u> if the word <u>is</u> a noun and <u>NO</u> if the word <u>is not</u> a noun.

Yes No   1. house
Yes No   2. happy
Yes No   3. bird
Yes No   4. ran

The following suggestions will help you write good clustered alternative-response items:

1. Ensure that every item in the cluster is congruent with the response directions.
2. Ensure that only one of the two response options can be correct for each item.
3. Ensure that the instances included adequately sample the content in the objective.
4. Ensure that no clues are provided through patterns of answers or the number of items included in each category.

Table 6.2 contains twelve clustered alternative-response items for the objective "Given a list of words containing nouns and other parts of speech, select words that are nouns." Using the suggestions as a guide, review the directions and cluster of items in Table 6.2 to see whether you can locate potential problems.

Initially, it appears that all the items in the set are congruent with the directions (suggestion 1). However, each word in the list cannot be answered correctly with only one of the options (suggestion 2). Of the words chosen for the list, both *farm* and *park* fail to meet this criterion because they can be either nouns or verbs. Some students may visualize *park* as a place whereas others may interpret it as an action. Some may visualize farm as a place whereas others may define it as what a farmer does to obtain crops. This means that both responses could be correct for these terms, thus creating scoring problems.

According to the third suggestion, the words in the cluster should adequately sample the content of the objective. Two items, *man* and *aunt*, refer to persons. *Farm, library,* and *park* refer to places, and *mouse* and *book* refer to things. There are no examples included to represent the idea category of nouns. Therefore, the list does not adequately cover the content.

TABLE 6.2 Clustered Alternative-Response Test Items for the Behavioral Objective "Given a List of Words Containing Nouns and Other Parts of Speech, Select Words That Are Nouns"

Directions: Each of the following words is either a noun or some other part of speech. If the word is a noun, circle <u>yes</u>. If the word is not a noun, circle <u>no</u>.

Words	Noun	Not a Noun
1. farm	yes	no
2. mouse	yes	no
3. library	yes	no
4. happy	yes	no
5. swiftly	yes	no
6. man	yes	no
7. tall	yes	no
8. aunt	yes	no
9. park	yes	no
10. book	yes	no
11. took	yes	no
12. where	yes	no

Finally, you should look for potential clues in the cluster. Clues might be found in the order of items in the list, in the number of instances included in each content category, and in the number of nonexamples. In Table 6.2, nouns related to persons, places, and things are dispersed throughout the list, and nonexamples are interspersed as well, so no clue is provided there. The number of instances for each category is varied—two words relate to persons, three to places, two to things, and five to nonexamples. Therefore, no clues related to the number of items in each category are provided.

Several adaptations could be made to the directions for responding to the clustered items in Table 6.2 to simplify responding and scoring. One would be to instruct students simply to place a check (√) in the blanks before words that are nouns and to make no mark in the blanks before words that are not nouns. Another set of directions could be used to adapt these items for machine scoring. Students could be instructed to darken response one on the answer sheet for items that are nouns and to darken response two for items that are not nouns. If answer sheets are to be used, it is a good idea to modify the cluster of items as well to help students remember which space on the answer sheet corresponds to the response they wish to make. The list of words could be modified for machine scoring as illustrated in Figure 6.6.

Matching Items

Matching items are another popular selected-response format. These items require students to match information in two columns. Items in the left-hand

FIGURE 6.6   Word List Modified for Machine Scoring

Directions: Each of the following words is either a noun or some other part of speech. If the word is a noun, darken ① on your answer sheet beside the item number. If the word is not a noun, darken ② on your answer sheet beside the item number.

Word	Ncun	Not a Noun
1. farm	①	②
2. mouse	①	②
3. library	①	②

column are called *premises*, and those in the right-hand column are called *responses*. Students are required to locate the correct response for each premise.

Although this format cannot be used to measure all levels and types of learning, matching exercises permit a teacher to measure many related facts, associations, and relationships quickly. It is an excellent way to measure students' ability to associate terms with their definitions, associate symbols with their names, name parts of an illustration, relate dates with names or events, match individuals with their accomplishments, and classify examples of concepts. Additionally, this item format is easily adapted for machine scoring. The one difficulty teachers have with the matching format is identifying multiple, plausible responses for each premise in the set. The following suggestions for writing matching items address the directions, the premises, and the responses.

1. *Provide clear, informative directions.* The directions should describe the types of items in each column and the basis for matching them. The directions should also indicate how and where responses are to be made and whether a response can be used more than once.

2. *Ensure that a set of premises is homogeneous and includes the more difficult reading material.* A set of premises should contain items that present the same kind of information (e.g., either authors, inventors, explorers, or politicians). Information on a variety of topics should not be included. If long phrases or sentences are to be used, they should be placed in the premise rather than the response column. For example, if definitions and symbols are to be matched, the premise should be the definition and the shorter symbol the response. The set should be limited to four to six items to help avoid irrelevant complexity.

3. *Ensure that responses are homogeneous, brief, and logically ordered.* Like the set of premises, the set of responses should be homogeneous; unrelated information is not likely to function well as distractors. The set of responses

should contain more than one plausible response for each premise to avoid students guessing the correct answer through the process of elimination. Because students will reread the responses several times while matching items in the set, the responses should be as brief as possible. The responses should be arranged in chronological, alphabetical, or numerical order to help students locate their chosen answers and to help avoid pattern clues.

4. *Avoid one-to-one correspondence between premises and responses (Table 6.3).* A different number of premises and responses should be included in a set.

TABLE 6.3   Matching Items for the Instructional Goal "Name Common Traffic Signs"

Directions: Column A contains the names of common traffic signs. Column B contains the shapes of traffic signs. For each sign named in Column A, select the matching shape in Column B. Place the letter of the matching shape in the blank before the name of each sign. A response may be used more than once or not at all.

Sign Names Column A	Sign Shapes Column B
_____ 1. Stop	
_____ 2. Yield	A.
_____ 3. Do Not Enter	
_____ 4. Warning: No Passing	
_____ 5. Warning: Construction	B.
_____ 6. Regulation	
_____ 7. Warning: Railroad	C.
_____ 8. Directional Information	
	D.
	E.
	F.
	G.
	H.

For example, if there are only four of each included, when three of the four items are matched, the answer to the fourth becomes automatic. This problem can be avoided in one of two ways. First, the set can be designed so that one response is correct for two or more of the premises. Second, more responses than premises can be included in the set. Either solution helps avoid the problem. The directions should always indicate whether a response can be used more than once.

Table 6.3 contains a set of matching items for the instructional goal "Name common traffic signs." The set, which measures students' ability to associate traffic sign names with their shapes, applies the suggestions just outlined. The directions describe the types of information in the columns, the basis for matching items, and how to mark responses. Both the premise and response columns contain homogeneous material. Notice that sign colors have not been included in the response list. Mixing colors and shapes would break the homogeneity of the list and substantially and unnecessarily increase the complexity of the item. There are more response choices than there are premises to avoid clues. The matching format is an efficient way to measure the verbal information skills in this goal.

Keyed Items

Keyed items combine the matching and alternative-response formats. Like matching items, they include a set of responses for several different questions. They resemble the alternative-response format because they include one statement or question. The suggestions for writing alternative-response and matching items also apply to keyed items. Table 6.4 provides an example of

---

TABLE 6.4 Keyed Items That Measure Knowledge of Bloom's Levels of Learning

---

Directions: The following items contain descriptions of Bloom's levels of learning. The responses name the levels of learning. Place the letter for the correct learning level in the blank before each description.

Responses
A. Knowledge
B. Comprehension
C. Application
D. Analysis
E. Synthesis
F. Evaluation

_____ 1. Divide a communication into its component parts and describe the relationship among the parts.
_____ 2. Use prescribed criteria to judge the quality of a product.
_____ 3. Recall the exact definition of a term.
_____ 4. Use rules and principles to solve a problem.
_____ 5. Paraphrase a given idea.

---

this format. The homogeneous set of responses appears above the item statements. Each item asks for the name of a learning level, and to avoid clues, there are more responses than items.

DEVELOPING AND ADMINISTERING TESTS FOR NONREADERS

Many students in the early elementary grades and some special education students throughout the grades are nonreaders. Although the preceding suggestions for designing and developing tests might seem irrelevant for teachers of nonreaders, this is not the case. These teachers do encounter some distinct technical problems; however, the suggestions for designing tests for readers also apply to designing tests for nonreaders. For example, teachers of nonreaders need to analyze instructional goals to create a framework of subordinate skills; write behavioral objectives; and create tables of specifications and sample objectives to design readiness tests, pretests, practice tests, and posttests. At the point of test development, these teachers must make some significant departures. Rather than writing directions and questions for students to read, they need to write direction and item scripts that they read to students. Instead of writing responses for students to read, they must create other ways for students to demonstrate that they can recall a fact or perform a skill. They must also use different methods for administering their tests and for recording students' responses. The following sections contain recommendations for testing nonreaders in groups and individually.

Group Testing Nonreaders

Testing an entire class at once requires less time than administering the same test individually to each student in a class. Testing nonreaders simultaneously, however, requires care because following oral instructions is difficult for students. Without clear directions, the group becomes baffled and frustrated, their responses become meaningless, and you become convinced that group testing is not feasible for your class. Most classes can successfully take group tests when the tests are carefully developed and administered. Developing such tests requires writing a script for yourself, creating a response form for students, and using special techniques during test administration.

Writing the Introduction Script   Good tests for readers contain introductory remarks and instructions for completing the test; nonreaders need the same information. Because they cannot read the instructions themselves, you need to provide them orally. Your introductory remarks should include what the test is about and an explanation and accompanying demonstration of what students are to do. To help ensure that you have their attention, this information should be provided before response forms are distributed. Table 6.5 provides an example introductory script for a test. Notice that the objective measured is written at the top and that the script includes (1) a general statement of the skill to be performed; (2) a demonstration of the skill that shows what students will find on their response forms and how they are to respond; and (3) a call for questions from the group.

Before using such instructions with an entire class, you should field-test them with one or two students. Pay careful attention to the clarifying questions they ask and revise your instructions as needed. This trial will reduce the number of questions asked during the test, which will decrease the amount of time required for the test and help avoid frustrating the students.

Writing the Questions Script You need to write a script for each question on the test. Students cannot reread a question they do not initially understand. Therefore, carefully ordering the directions, pausing to allow students time to perform a step, and repeating key information will help students perform the tasks with a minimum amount of confusion. Directions should be ordered in the following manner:

1. Tell students how to locate their place (e.g., "Find the star on your paper.").
2. Tell them what kinds of objects they will find in that location (e.g., "See the boxes beside the star?").
3. Describe the skill measured (e.g., "Find the box beside the star with four marbles in it.").
4. Tell them how to show that they can perform the skill (e.g., "Put an X on the box that has four marbles in it.").

This question script, with the recommended pauses and repetition inserted, appears in Table 6.5.

Initially, you might think that creating such scripts constitutes busy-work. However, writing a script has four benefits. First, it helps you avoid omitting important information needed for smooth test administration. Second, the script can be evaluated and refined to avoid the same problems in future test administrations. Third, it enables you to use teacher's aides to help with testing. Using your script, they can administer the test (1) to the class, freeing you to circulate among students and provide additional assistance when needed; (2) to individual students who were absent during the group test; and (3) to small groups or individuals who need to retake the test following additional instruction. Fourth, the script will be available when you need to measure the same skill for a new class.

Developing the Response Form As you write the questions scripts, you should develop the corresponding "paper and pencil" response form. Space

TABLE 6.5 Teacher's Script and Students' Response Form for a Nonreader Group Test

Introduction and Directions

Objective B.2: Given multiple sets of objects that contain up to ten objects, select the set that contains a specified number of objects.

Introduction: "Today I want you to show me that you can count the number of marbles in a box. On the paper I will give you, you will see a picture of something that will help you find the right boxes. (Draw a typical locator symbol on the chalkboard.) Beside the cat you will find three boxes of marbles." (Draw three boxes of marbles on the chalkboard beside the object.)

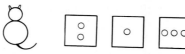

"See, one box contains two marbles (point to correct box), one box contains one marble (point to correct box), and one box contains three marbles (point to box). Only one of the boxes beside the cat will contain the number of marbles that I say. If I asked you to find the box with one marble in it, you would find this box (point to box) because it is the only one *beside the cat* that has one marble in it. I want you to put an *x* on this box (put large X on box) to show me that you can find the box with one marble in it. Do you have any questions?"

Distribute response forms

"Do you have any questions about your paper? Let's begin. I will read the questions, and you will mark your answers with an X."

Teacher's Question Script (Obj. B.2)	*Students' Response Form (Obj. B.2)*

Name _____ Date _____

Score _____

1. "Find the star on your paper. Do you see the star? (pause) See the boxes beside the star? (pause) Find the box that has four marbles in it. Find the box that has four marbles in it. (pause) Place an X on the box that has four marbles in it." (pause)

2. "Find the sailboat on your paper. Do you see the sailboat? (pause) See the boxes beside the sailboat? (pause) Find the box that has five marbles in it. Find the box that has five marbles in it. (pause) Put an X on the box that has five marbles in it." (pause)

3. "Find the apple on your paper. Do you see the apple? (pause) See the boxes beside the apple? (pause) Find the box that has seven marbles in it. Find the box that has seven marbles in it. (pause) Put an X on the box that has seven marbles in it." (pause)

145

for the student's name, the date, and the score should be included at the top. The illustrations on the form must match the information in the introduction and question scripts. The symbols used to help students locate their place should be familiar to the class. If they are familiar with numerals or letters, use them. If not, use such symbols as a star, ball, dog, cat, moon, bike, or sailboat. The responses in each set should be clearly separated and easy for children to distinguish. Similar to other selected-response tests, they should contain one clearly correct answer and one to three distractors that represent plausible misconceptions or errors. A sample response form is included in Table 6.5.

Administering the Test   Once the scripts and response form are developed, you are ready to administer the test. If you have a teacher's aide or parent volunteer available, he or she can provide valuable assistance with this challenging task. The person who reads the script should watch the group closely for clues about pacing and needed repetition. Having a second person who can circulate among students and provide additional attention (e.g., pointing to the correct location) will make the procedure progress more smoothly. If you have no help, seat those students you predict will need assistance close by you. The pauses built into the questions script enable you to scan the entire group for potential problems.

Individually Testing Nonreaders

It is not always feasible to test a group; thus, individual tests need to be given. This situation is common for special education teachers who provide individualized instruction and have each student in the class studying a different lesson. Developing individually administered tests for nonreaders requires a question script, sometimes objects that students manipulate, and a student response record. Keeping the required materials together in a test packet or kit will save time because you will need the same materials each time the test is administered. These kits can be labeled to identify the objectives measured and the material enclosed. They can be filed in sequence with other test kits that measure subordinate skills related to the same instructional goal.

Developing the Script and Response Form   Unlike group-administered tests, the script for individually administered tests is usually included on the same form as the student response record. They can be included on the same form because the teacher both reads the script and records the student's responses. The form should contain space for recording the student's name, the date the test is administered, the objective measured, the script used to introduce the test, the directions/questions script, and space for recording the student's responses. Consider the example test form in Table 6.6. The objective measured and introduction script are included at the top; the directions/questions script is included on the left side; and spaces to record the student's responses are in the right-hand columns. Notice the space to record each response the student makes and spaces for repeating the test if necessary.

TABLE 6.6   Teacher's Script and Student's Response Record for an Individualized Nonreader Test

Name _____

Objective A.4: Given a set of ten objects, count out two sets of objects containing a specified number and sum the total number of objects removed.

Introduction: "See the pile of <u>beans</u> I have given you? Today I want you to count the number of beans I say and take them from the pile. (Demonstrate with one bean and two beans). Then I want you to tell me how many beans you have taken from the pile altogether." (Demonstrate 1 + 2 = 3). "Are you ready?"

	Student's Responses	
Directions/Questions Script	Dates Tested	
	9–12	9–30
1. "Take three beans from the pile and place them here."	3	3
2. "Take two beans from the pile and place them there."	2	2
3. "How many beans have you taken from the pile altogether?"	5	5
"Put the beans back in the big pile."		
4. "Take four beans from the pile and place them here."	4	4
5. "Take four beans from the pile and place them there."	4	4
6. "How many beans have you taken from the pile altogether?"	8	8
"Put the beans back in the big pile."		
7. "Take five beans from the pile and place them here."	⨉4	5
8. "Take four beans from the pile and place them there."	4	4
9. "How many beans have you taken from the pile altogether?"	⨉8	9
Total Correct Responses	7	9

Manner of Responding   Because these tests are administered individually, a student can respond orally to your questions or can manipulate given objects to demonstrate skill. For example, a student can choose a specified picture from a set; sequence a set of pictures, numbers, or letters; count a specified number of objects; choose a particular shape, letter, number, or color from a set; or classify similar objects in a set. Objects needed for a test should be kept in the test kit along with the script and response record.

Administering the Test   To begin the test, introduce the skill to be measured and answer any questions the student might have about what you want her or him to do. When there are objects to be manipulated, you will find that demonstrating the skill using a simple example is helpful. As with group tests, such a demonstration will help ensure that the student's errors relate to skill rather than to understanding your directions. Watch the student carefully and pace your test according to his or her ability to follow your directions.

As the student responds to each question, you should record *all* the responses. Recording only incorrect or correct responses will affect a student's attitude and may influence performance on subsequent items. For the same reason, incorrect answers should be marked or identified only after the test is completed.

In addition to how you record responses, the way you behave during the test is important; the student will watch you closely to detect your reactions to responses. You should remain pleasant and patient regardless of whether the student makes an incorrect response or asks to have information repeated a third or fourth time. Coaching, rewarding (e.g., "Great, Johnny"), or criticizing behaviors will influence the validity of the measure.

Providing Corrective Feedback   You should provide feedback to the student immediately following an individual test, if time permits. You can review errors the student made, explain or show why the response was incorrect, and demonstrate how the task is performed correctly. After this additional instruction, you might give the student an opportunity to perform the skill correctly and include the amount of verbal guidance or coaching the student appears to need. However a correct response after coaching should not be counted as a correct answer on the test. The student's ability to perform the skill should be checked on another day to see whether the skill was remembered over time.

Summarizing and Analyzing Students' Responses

The suggestions for organizing, summarizing, and analyzing students' responses presented in Chapters 10, 11, and 12 are appropriate for both individual and group tests. You summarize and analyze the data you recorded on students' records during individual tests or the data students created using their own response forms on group tests. From these group summaries you can evaluate the quality of both your tests and your instruction.

SUMMARY

Objective tests typically consist of written-response and selected-response items. Written-response formats include completion and short-answer items; selected-response formats include alternative-response, matching, and keyed items. Several features of these items make them desirable for classroom tests. First, they can be used to measure several types and levels of learning. Second, a wide range of content can be tested in a relatively short period. Third, each format has several variations for flexibility. Finally, objective tests can be scored more reliably and quickly than can other types of tests.

In writing objective items, your primary concerns should be the validity and reliability of the resulting scores. Important factors in achieving these qualities are the congruence between the item and the behavioral objectives and characteristics of target students; the clarity of language used; and the accuracy of the measure. In addition to these primary considerations there are several suggestions for writing items using each format.

Written-response items can be used to measure a variety of types and levels of learning, minimize the probability of students guessing correctly, and help teachers analyze misconceptions and problems that students have. These items can either be single statements and questions that require an answer or clusters of items with one set of common directions. Clustered items usually have words, phrases, pictures, or symbols that act as stimuli. Two drawbacks of written-response items are lengthy scoring time and the difficulty of scoring items objectively. Suggestions for writing and scoring items in this format include:

Completion Items
1. Remove only key words from a statement.
2. Place blanks for key words at or near the end of the statement.
3. Eliminate the possibility of several reasonable answers.
4. Eliminate clues to the correct answers.
5. Paraphrase key statements taken from instructional materials.

6. Reduce scoring time by using answer sheets or other devices that simplify scoring.

Short-Answer Items
1. Provide a blank for each response that suggests how long it should be.
2. Specify the units required in an answer.
3. Ensure that directions for a cluster of items are appropriate for all items in the set.

Selected-response items require students to select an answer from a given set of alternatives. They are versatile and can be used to measure several types and levels of learning. One unique feature is that a well-constructed selected-response item can measure students' abilities to see different facets of a problem and to make fine discriminations. These items can be administered quickly, and a wide range of material can be tested. In addition, they can be hand scored quickly, adapted for computer administration, or adapted for machine scoring. Formats include the alternative-response item that requires students to select one correct answer from two alternatives; the matching item in which students match a set of premises and responses; and the keyed item that requires students to use the same set of responses for a group of items. Suggestions for writing selected-response items include:

Alternative-Response Items
1. Explain the judgments to be made in the directions.
2. Ensure that answer choices logically match the judgments to be made.
3. Explain in the directions how students are to record their answers.
4. Include only one idea to be judged in each statement.
5. Word statements in a positive manner.
6. Avoid designing questions to trick students.
7. Avoid providing clues to the correct answer.

Clustered Alternative-Response Items
1. Ensure that every item in the cluster is congruent with the response directions.
2. Ensure that only one of the two options can be correct for each item.
3. Ensure that the instances included adequately sample the content of the objective.
4. Ensure that no clues are provided through patterns of answers or the number of items included in each category.

Matching Items
1. Provide clear, informative directions.
2. Ensure that sets of premises are homogeneous and include the more difficult reading material.
3. Ensure that responses are homogeneous, brief, and logically ordered.

Nonreaders can be tested in groups or individually. Group tests require you to write scripts for directions and questions, develop a student response form, and administer the test carefully. Suggestions for developing and administering these tests include:

Directions Script
1. Describe the skill to be measured.
2. Write a script for demonstrating the skill.
3. Ask for clarifying questions.

Questions Script
1. Sequence instructions in the following order:
   a. Tell students how to find the correct location on the response form.
   b. Describe what they will find in that location.
   c. Describe the skill to be performed.
   d. Tell students how to mark their response.
2. Include pauses between instructions that enable students to perform the specified task.
3. Repeat key information (e.g., the skill to be performed).

Response Form
1. Include familiar symbols that students can use to locate the correct response set.

2. Clearly separate the responses within and across sets.

Administration
1. Seat students you predict will need extra help close by you.
2. Read the directions script.
3. Demonstrate the skill to be performed.
4. Ask for clarifying questions.
5. Distribute the response form.
6. Call for questions.
7. Read the questions script.
8. Observe the group during pauses to identify potential problems.
9. Repeat any instructions as needed.

Individual tests for nonreaders require a form that includes a script for directions and questions, space to mark a student's responses, objects to manipulate (sometimes), and special administration techniques. The procedures for developing the script are the same as those described for group tests. Procedures for creating the response form and administering the test are:

Response Form
1. Include space to record the student's response to each task.
2. Include space for administering the test several times.

Administration
1. Read the directions script.
2. Demonstrate the skill to be performed.
3. Ask for clarifying questions.
4. Read the questions script, pausing and repeating information as needed.
5. Record all responses.
6. Remain pleasant and patient throughout the test.
7. Avoid using coaching, rewarding, or criticizing behaviors.
8. Mark incorrect responses only after the test is completed.
9. Provide students with corrective feedback immediately following the test, if time permits.

PRACTICE EXERCISES

I. Using Figure 6.7, evaluate the congruence between test items and their objectives.

FIGURE 6.7

Directions: The left column contains objective test items and the right column contains corresponding behavioral objectives. Judge whether items and objectives are congruent. Use the responses at the top of the table, and record your answers in the margin beside each item.

Responses:
A. The behavior in the item and objective is *not* congruent.
B. The content in the item and objective is *not* congruent.
C. The item does *not* meet the conditions in the objective.
D. The item matches the behavior, content, and conditions in the objective.

Items	*Objectives*
1. *Directions:* Write a matching capital letter for each of the letters below.	Given lower case letters, write corresponding capital letters.

    1. a _____   4. p _____
    2. f _____   5. u _____
    3. k _____   6. z _____

2. *Directions:* Circle the matching capital letter for each of the letters below
    1. a: A E M P
    2. f: B E F Z
    3. k: D K R Y

3. *Directions:* Place a check (√) beside the proper nouns in the following list.	Given a list of common and proper nouns that refer to persons, locate the proper nouns.

    _____1. Boy   _____5. Teacher
    _____2. Harold   _____6. Mr. Smith
    _____3. Man   _____7. Girl
    _____4. Sarah   _____8. Lady

4. *Directions:* Some of the words in the following list are proper nouns. For each proper noun, place the letter or letters that should be capitalized in the space before the word.	Given sentences that include proper nouns without capital letters, identify the proper nouns and capitalize the first letter.

    _____1. fido   _____5. mr. brown
    _____2. boy   _____6. dog
    _____3. house   _____7. raccoon
    _____4. yellow-   _____8. sally
           stone
           park

(continued on next page)

FIGURE 6.7   (*continued*)

Responses:
A. The behavior in the item and objective is *not* congruent.
B. The content in the item and objective is *not* congruent.
C. The item does *not* meet the conditions in the objective.
D. The item matches the behavior, content, and conditions in the objective.

Items	*Objectives*
5. *Directions:* Place a check (√) in front of proper nouns in the following list. Do not use capital letters as clues.	Given a list of nouns that refer to persons, places, and things, locate the proper nouns.

     _____1. Town   _____5. state
     _____2. Country _____6. Smith Park
     _____3. United _____7. Library
             States   _____8. new york
     _____4. School

II. Using Figure 6.8, evaluate objective items.

FIGURE 6.8

Directions: The following exercise contains completion, alternative-response, matching, and keyed items. Evaluate whether each item is written using the suggestions for each item format. Write any problems you identify on a separate sheet.

A. Completion Items
   Directions: Complete each statement by writing the missing word or words in the blanks provided.
   1. The top of the map is traditionally _____ .
   2. The _____ contains the names of symbols used on a map.
   3. The _____ is used to locate towns on a map.
   4. The _____ of town names is included in an _____ .

B. Short-Answer Items
   Directions: Use the map in Figure A to answer the following questions. Write your answer in the blank before each question. (Assume that the map is appropriate for target students.)
       _____ miles 1. Use the mileage scale and your ruler to estimate the number of miles between Carter and Doyle.
       _____ miles 2. How far is it from Hyatt to Bryne?
       _____ 3. What is the name of the city to the north of Jackson?

C. Alternative-Response Items
   Directions: Circle T̲ if the statement is true and F̲ if it is false.
   T F 1. A map legend identifies symbols used in a map and can be used to locate particular cities.
   T F 2. The direction arrow on a map does not usually point north.
   T F 3. The map legend always contains the direction indicator and the mileage scale.

(*continued on next page*)

FIGURE 6.8 (*continued*)

D. Matching Items
   Directions: Place the letter from Column B in the space before the matching item in Column A.

   _____1. Legend
   _____2. Grid
   _____3. Index
   _____4. Globe
   _____5. AAA Automobile Club

   A. A sphere that contains map of the earth
   B. An alphabetical list of places contained on a map
   C. A key or legend used to identify symbols on a map
   D. An organization that provides maps
   E. A matrix of lines running through the map top to bottom and side to side

E. Keyed Items
   Directions: The following items describe aids that can be used to interpret maps. Identify the aid that each item describes. You may use each of the following responses more than once or not at all.
   A. Legend
   B. Grid
   C. Index
   D. Mileage scale
   E. Mileage table
   _____1. An alphabetical list of cities and towns
   _____2. Lines that divide the face of the map into blocks
   _____3. A key that contains map symbols and their names
   _____4. A table that contains the names of major cities and the distances between them
   _____5. A line marked off in miles
   _____6. An aid used to locate specified towns
   _____7. An aid used to estimate distance between small towns
   _____8. An aid used to locate types of highways

III. Write items to match objectives.
    Directions: Table 6.7 contains objectives and item specifications for the enabling skill "Use mileage scale to estimate the distance between two given points." (The goal framework for this skill is included in Table 3.11 and the table of specifications is included in Table 4.6). Using Table 6.7, write test items for each objective, and use the item format specified in the table. Table 6.8 in the Feedback section shows one possible test item for each objective. Expect your items to be different—any number of appropriate items can be written.

IV. Enrichment. Using the behavioral objectives and the corresponding table of specifications you have developed from your own content area, complete the following activities:
    A. Write appropriate objective test items and create either a pretest, a practice test, or a posttest.

TABLE 6.7 Test Specifications for the Enabling Skill "Use Mileage Scale to Estimate the Distance between Two Given Points" (See Tables 3.11 and 4.6)

Objectives		Item Format	Number of Items
3.2.1.1	From memory, describe a mileage scale	Write short answer	1
3.2.2.1	Given a map with a mileage scale, locate the mileage scale	Select answer	1
3.2.3.1	Given a map with a scale indicating 1 inch equal to 100 miles, identify the number of miles represented by the scale	Write short answer	1
3.2.4.1	Given the map, index and grid, and names of two points, locate the two points	Select answer	2
3.2.5.1	Given the map, two specified points, and the scale, determine the number of times the scale fits between the two points	Write short answer	2
3.2.6.1	Given a mileage scale indicating 1 inch equal to 100 miles, identify the number of miles represented by: a. 1 inch c. $2\frac{1}{2}$ inches b. 2 inches d. $\frac{1}{2}$ inch	Write short answer	3
3.2.7.1	Given two points on a map and a scale with 1 inch equal to 100 miles, multiply to find the number of miles between the two points, correct to within 10 miles	Write short answer	2
		Total	12

B. Evaluate your test items for:
   1. Congruence with the behavioral objectives
   2. Congruence with the characteristics of your target students. Be sure to look for bias of any kind.
   3. Clarity (grammar, punctuation, precision)
   4. Accuracy of measure (novelty, clues)
   5. Formatting suggestions
C. Ask a colleague to evaluate your items and directions and suggest revisions. Have the evaluator compare the items with your objectives and table of specifications.
D. Have any available target students read the items and mark any directions and items that they do not understand. Additionally, have them circle any words that they cannot define. Should your group be nonreaders, read your script to one or two students and have them respond according to instructions.
E. Use your colleague's suggestions and students' remarks to revise the directions and items.

FEEDBACK

I. Evaluate the congruence between test items and their objectives.
1. D
2. A   Students are instructed to select rather than write the letter.
3. D   Notice that all words are capitalized in the list to avoid providing clues to proper nouns.
4. C   Students are to be given sentences to read rather than single words.
5. C   Because the list of words includes only places, the items do not adequately meet the conditions specified in the objective.

II. Evaluate objective items. The sample items reflect the following problems:

A. Completion Items
1. The item is vague and many answers are possible.
2. The blank is at the beginning of the item.
3. The blank is at the beginning of the item, and there are two correct answers (index, grid).
4. The first blank is placed toward the beginning of the item and does not require a key term. Additionally, the word *an* preceding the second blank suggests that the response begins with a vowel.

B. Short-Answer Items
1. This item contains no major problems.
2. This item does not indicate how students are to determine the mileage. Instructions about whether they should use a mileage table, mileage scale, or miles printed along the highway should be added.
3. This item should be clarified as several towns are likely to be north of the one specified. Adding such information as "the first town north of Jackson" would help clarify the item.

C. Alternative-Response Items
1. The statement includes more than one idea.
2. The item contains an unnecessary negative word.
3. The item contains the determiner *always* and two ideas.

D. Matching Items. These items contain many problems.
1. The directions:
   a. do not explain the contents of the premise or response list.
   b. do not describe the basis for matching the items.
   c. refer to columns that are not titled.
   d. do not specify if a response can be used more than once.
2. The premises:
   a. are shorter than the responses.
   b. do not all have more than one plausible answer.
   c. are not homogeneous. Although both premises and responses are all related to maps, the sets are not homogeneous.

E. Keyed Items. The examples have several weaknesses:
1. The questions and the answers are placed in the same order.
2. Item four contains the word *table*, which matches the word *table* in the answer, thus providing a clue to the answer.
3. Items are not homogeneous. Some describe the aids (items 1–5) and others refer to how the aids are used (items 6–8).

III. Write items to match objectives. The items in Table 6.8 were written to match the objectives and specifications in Table 6.7. Assume that the figure referred to would be appropriate for the questions.

TABLE 6.8   Objectives and Test Items for the Enabling Skill "Use Mileage Scale to Estimate the Distance between Two Given Points"

Objectives	Items
	Directions: The following questions relate to the map provided in Figure A. To answer some of the questions you will need to circle information on the map. For others, write your answer in the blank provided.
3.2.1.1	1. Describe the mileage scale on the map. _____
3.2.2.1	2. Draw a circle around the mileage scale on the map.
3.2.3.1	3. The whole mileage scale equals how many miles? _____ miles
3.2.6.1	How many miles does each of the following represent? _____ miles 4. 2 lengths of the scale _____ miles 5. $2\frac{1}{2}$ lengths of the scale _____ miles 6. $\frac{1}{2}$ of the length of the scale
3.2.4.1	7. Draw a circle around Baker on the map.
	8. Draw a circle around Wyatt on the map.
3.2.5.1	9. How many lengths of the mileage scale fit between Baker and Wyatt? _____ lengths
3.2.7.1	10. How many miles is it from Baker to Wyatt? _____ miles
3.2.5.1	11. How many lengths of the mileage scale fit between Allen and Carter? _____ lengths
3.2.7.1	12. How many miles is it from Allen to Carter? _____ miles

SUGGESTED READING

Ebel, R. L., and Frisbie, D. A. (1986). *Essentials of educational measurement.* Englewood Cliffs, N.J.: Prentice-Hall, pp. 138–50, 191–201.

Gronlund, N. E. (1985). *Measurement and evaluation in teaching.* New York: Macmillan Publishing Company, pp. 146–68.

Mehrens, W. A., and Lehmann, I. J.

(1984). *Measurement and evaluation in education and psychology.* New York: CBS College Publishing, pp. 125–49.

Nitko, A. J. (1983). *Educational tests and measurement.* New York: Harcourt, Brace, Jovanovich, pp. 157–86.

Popham, W. J. (1981). *Modern educational measurement.* Englewood Cliffs, N.J.: Prentice-Hall, pp. 241–64, 266–84.

CHAPTER 7

Writing Multiple-Choice Items and Creating Item Banks for Objective Items

OBJECTIVES

1. Describe a multiple-choice item.
2. List positive features of multiple-choice items.
3. Describe the limitations of multiple-choice items.
4. Describe the characteristics of a good stem.
5. Describe the characteristics of a good set of responses.
6. Evaluate and revise given multiple-choice items.
7. Given instructional objectives, write multiple-choice items.
8. Describe item banks for objective items.
9. Describe a coding system for storing items and retrieving them from an item bank.

Chapter 6 describes suggestions for writing several types of objective items, including completion, short-answer, alternative-response, matching, and keyed formats. This chapter contains recommendations for developing multiple-choice items, which are also classified as objective items. In addition, it describes the development and use of item banks for objective items. Using item banks, you can increase your efficiency in developing multiple test forms to measure the same objectives, enabling skills, and goals.

WRITING MULTIPLE-CHOICE ITEMS

The most popular format for selected-response test items is the multiple-choice item. It commonly appears on classroom tests in all grade levels and subjects and is used almost exclusively on standardized tests. Although multiple-choice items can be formatted in several ways, these items have certain common characteristics: an initial stem that introduces a problem or asks a question and a list of three or more alternative responses following the stem. The list of responses includes a correct answer and several incorrect answers.

The versatility of multiple-choice items has caused teachers to select this item format more than any other. A test made of such items can be an excellent diagnostic tool with the following advantages:

1. Multiple-choice items can measure both verbal information and intellectual skills. Within the intellectual skill category, they can measure all levels, from knowledge through evaluation.
2. These items can be used to focus students' attention on particular aspects of a problem.
3. By providing multiple responses, these items can force students to choose among alternatives that they may not have otherwise considered.
4. By instructing students to select the best answer, these items can measure students' ability to make fine discriminations.
5. Multiple-choice items permit the use of more than one correct alternative in a set of responses (Both A and B are correct).
6. They enable measurement of a wide range of content in a relatively short time period.
7. They can be reliably scored.
8. They are easily adapted for machine scoring and for computer administration and scoring.
9. Multiple-choice items are easily compiled into item banks.

At the same time, multiple-choice items have their limitations. First, like other objective items, they cannot directly measure attitudes or motor skills that require demonstration and active performance. However they can measure the intellectual skills and verbal information that support attitudes and motor skills. Second, students who do not know the correct answer to a multiple-choice question can often guess correctly. Third, teachers usually have difficulty in thinking of plausible incorrect answers that reflect students' actual misconceptions and problems. Incorrect alternatives that are illogical to students diminish the diagnostic value of these items as well as the validity of the test results.

Before writing multiple-choice items, you should review the criteria related to validity and reliability. Like other objective item formats, multiple-choice items must be congruent with the conditions, behavior, and content specified in the behavioral objective. The vocabulary, complexity, and context of the items should be appropriate for target students, and wording should be clear and precise. In addition, items should be different from those students have already encountered. The following suggestions for writing multiple-choice items relate to the stem, the responses, and the placement of items.

The Stem

The stem of a multiple-choice item poses a problem or asks a question; it can be formatted in several ways. The most common format is a complete sentence or question. Using this format, the stem resembles the short-answer item except that students select rather than write their answers. A second popular format is the incomplete statement that students complete by selecting one of the responses. This stem format closely resembles the completion item. A third widely used format embeds the stem in the directions. The stem in this case poses a single problem for a series of items that contain only responses. This format avoids repeating the same problem numerous times. Table 7.1 contains an example of each of these stem formats.

TABLE 7.1 Common Formats for the Stem of a Multiple-Choice Item

1. *Complete Question*	What is the name of a word that refers to a person, place, thing, or idea? A. Adjective B. Adverb C. Conjunction D. Noun
2. *Incomplete Statement*	A word that refers to a person, place, thing, or idea is called a (an) A. Adjective B. Noun C. Subject D. Topic

3. *Common Stem Embedded in Directions*	Locate the nouns in the following sentences. Place the letter of the words that are nouns in the blank before the sentence.
	
	_____ 1. The plump squirrels ran up and down.
	          A B C D
	_____ 2. The band was energetic and noisy, if not
	          A B C
	          melodious.
	          D

Many teachers prefer stems that are complete questions or statements, such as those in examples 1 and 3, to the incomplete statement format illustrated in example 2. Complete questions and statements provide all the information students need to answer the question before they consider the response choices. Students may need to read an incomplete statement several times before they understand what is being asked. The complete question or statement is usually less confusing to them and, therefore, more efficient.

Regardless of the format used for stems, the suggestions for writing them are the same as those for writing other objective items. The wording should be clear and precise, and the punctuation should be accurate. If negative words are necessary, they should be underlined or highlighted to ensure that they will not be overlooked. When embedding the stem in directions, the stem or problem should precede the directions for marking responses.

Responses

The responses for a multiple-choice answer consist of a correct answer and two or more incorrect answers, which are called *distractors* or *foils*. The responses can be designed using a variety of formats. They may be symbols, words, phrases, or sentences that are listed vertically beneath the stem (the traditional format). However, responses can also be embedded in contextual material, such as sentences, paragraphs, or articles. They can be the labeled parts of pictures, illustrations, or data tables. When testing young children or nonreaders, responses may be a series of pictures or illustrations. They may also consist of a set of real objects, such as rocks, tools, equipment, slides of specimens, or beakers of liquid. In addition, an object can have its parts labeled as responses. Examples of these response formats appear in Table 7.2.

TABLE 7.2 Response Formats for Multiple-Choice Items

Type of Response	Test Items
1. Vertical list of symbols, words, phrases, or sentences following a stem	What is the name of a word that refers to a person, a place, or a thing? A. A noun B. A pronoun C. An adjective D. An adverb
2. Set of pictures or illustrations	Teacher says, "Color the square." □ △ □ ○

(continued on next page)

TABLE 7.2 *(continued)*

Type of Response	Test Items

3. Labeled parts of an illustration or picture

_____ 1. Which edge is north?

_____ 2. Which edge is west?

_____ 3. Which edge is south?

_____ 4. Which edges bound the northeast?

Directions: Locate direction in a map. The map in Figure 1 has its edges labeled A, B, C, and D. Choose the edge that answers questions 1 through 4.

Figure 1

```
            A
       ┌─────────┐
    D  │         │  B
       └─────────┘
            C
```

4. Labeled objects

At station 1 you will find a set of four leaves. Each leaf is labeled either A, B, C, or D. Which leaf was taken from a *deciduous* tree? (Assume four different leaves are labeled and placed at station 1.)

5. Embedded in sentences

Directions: Find the *verbs* in the following sentences. Write the letter under the verb in the space before the item number.

_____ 1. Beth ran swiftly down the path.
           A   B   C   D   E

_____ 2. John felt superb after the award.
           A   B   C   D   E

6. Embedded in paragraphs, stories, or articles

Read the following paragraph and decide whether you think all the sentences in it relate to the topic. If you find a sentence that does *not* fit the topic, underline it.

I can see so many things on a hike in my neighborhood. The trees, bushes, and flowers in my neighbors' yards are always interesting because they change with the seasons. Sometimes I can even see people in their yards mowing the grass, pruning the bushes, or weeding the flower beds. I enjoy planting flowers. Once I saw workmen sawing down a large oak tree and loading it into a big truck. I decided to sit down and watch them work. It was interesting to see how the appearance of the yard and house changed as more and more of the tree was removed. I see something different every time I take a walk.

Correct Responses   Good correct responses should be brief, clear, grammatically consistent with the stem, and clearly labeled with a number or letter. Information taken from the text should be paraphrased. Key words from the stem should not be repeated in the correct answer as this will provide a clue. When it is necessary to repeat a key word in the correct response, then the same word should be included in at least one of the distractors. An item should contain only one best answer, even when two or more of the options are correct. A single-answer choice can be used to combine multiple correct options into a best answer, for example, "Both A and B are correct" or "All of the above are correct." Although multiple correct answers add to the versatility of the multiple-choice item, do not use them simply because you cannot think of good distractors for the item.

Distractors   Ideally, an item should enable you to differentiate between students who know the correct answer and those who do not. Quality distractors that reflect common misconceptions and problems are more likely to help you make this differentiation. If unskilled students can immediately eliminate incorrect responses, the item is not functioning as it should.

Quality distractors are much more difficult to write than is the correct response. One problem is the difficulty of identifying misconceptions and problems students are likely to have. Plausible distractors can be found in the content of other enabling skills in the same or related lessons, in questions students ask in class about your presentations or their homework, and in students' written responses on pretests and practice exercises. If you analyze the nature of their questions and errors you will be able to construct quality distractors that help detect persistent problems.

Even though you may have identified actual misconceptions to use as distractors, several factors can reduce their attractiveness to unskilled students. The use of unfamiliar words or ideas unrelated to the lessons, the lack of homogeneity in the list of responses, and grammatical incompatibility between the distractor and stem can cause students to avoid otherwise attractive distractors. One strategy for increasing the attractiveness of a distractor to students who are guessing is to repeat a key word from the stem in a distractor. Students who are using key words as clues to the correct answer will be drawn to this option.

Machine-Scored Responses   When machine-scored answer sheets are used, students can become confused and mark the wrong space. Marking errors affect both the validity and reliability of the scores. Labeling the test responses so that they correspond to the response letters and numbers on the answer sheet will reduce the probability of marking errors. For example, answer sheets are designed so that either letters or numbers can be used to identify responses. One type of response will appear at the top of the column, and the other type will appear within the circles, parentheses, or brackets beside the item number. The following example illustrates such an arrangement.

		Responses			
Item	A	B	C	D	E
1.	①	②	③	④	⑤
2.	①	②	③	④	⑤
3.	①	②	③	④	⑤

As students continue down the answer sheet, they will have more and more difficulty using the response codes across the top of the column (in this example, A, B, C, D, and E). Thus, using the response codes beside the items on the answer sheet when constructing your items is a better method. One caution should be made. If the options beside the item number are numbers (as illustrated), and the answer to the question is also a number between one and five, then students are likely to confuse the answer number with the response code number. The following example illustrates this problem:

Question: 1. 2 + 0 = _____

1. 0	Correctly coded: 1. 1 2 ③ 4 5
2. 1	
3. 2	Misplaced: 1. 1 ② 3 4 5
4. 3	
5. 4	

When numbers are used to code the responses, students will often darken the numbered space that matches the numeric answer rather than the correct answer code. For such items you should use the letter codes across the top of the column or match the answer code and response numbers if possible. Other types of items on the same test can require students to use the more convenient numbered responses.

Editing Items

Once the stem, correct response, and distractors are written, you should evaluate the entire item. Words repeated in each response should be removed and placed in the stem to avoid unnecessary redundancies. The set of responses should be sequenced logically using an alphabetical, chronological, numerical, or procedural order whenever possible. Additionally, you should check to see whether clues to the correct answer have been provided. The following mistakes are common in writing multiple-choice items that provide clues:

1. Only the correct response repeats a key word from the stem.
2. Distractors are consistently longer or shorter than the correct answer.
3. The correct answer is more technical and detailed than the distractors.
4. Answer options that indicate multiple responses, such as "Both B and D are correct," appear only when these options are the correct answers. If other test items do not include these options as distractors, students will quickly identify the pattern.
5. The correct response frequently appears in the same position in the set. Some teachers consider the first and last positions too obvious, and they tend to place the correct answer in the middle. Using a

logical sequencing strategy for the responses, such as alphabetical or numerical, will help you avoid such detectable patterns.

Item Format and Placement

Practice in writing multiple-choice items will help you gain the skill necessary to write good, diagnostic items. The following suggestions for item format and placement can help you develop multiple-choice tests that are easy for students to use.

1. List single sentence, phrase, or word responses vertically beneath the stem and begin each response on a separate line.
2. Underline and code responses embedded in a sentence.
3. Provide clear instructions for selecting a correct sentence that is embedded in a paragraph. This may be done by having students underline the sentence of their choice. Other more traditional formatting suggestions include underlining each sentence and placing a response code beneath it or placing a response code and the first word of each sentence in a vertical list beneath the paragraph. The latter two options are well suited to machine scoring.
4. Place the stem and all responses on the same page.
5. Place resource materials that cannot be included on the same page on a separate, unattached page for easy reference.
6. Label resource materials with titles, such as Figure 1 or Table 1, so they can be clearly identified in the directions.
7. Place directions for locating and using resource materials before the resource materials.
8. Place resource materials included on the same page before the related items.
9. For items requiring the use of real objects, set up work stations with numbers that correspond to related items on the test.
   a. Sequence work stations to match the order of items on the test.
   b. Label each object or part of an object to match a response code on the test paper.

DEVELOPING ITEM BANKS FOR OBJECTIVE ITEMS

For most units of instruction, teachers need a number of different items to measure the same objectives. They require enough items to use novel ones for pretests, practice tests, unit posttests, and comprehensive exams. To maintain test security, a teacher with several classes of the same subject needs a considerable number of items. Invariably, teachers also need alternative tests for students who were unable to take the exam on the scheduled day or who need to retake a test for some reason. Organizing all of these objective items is a substantial task that requires some sort of management system. Developing an item bank is one way to reduce the time a teacher must spend in producing multiple tests.

Item Banks

Item banks (also called *item pools* and *item files*) are files of objective test items that are classified by behavioral objective, subordinate skill, and instructional goal. To develop an item bank, a teacher classifies and stores items as they are written. With the conditions, the behavior, and the content for an objective in mind, you should be able to write several items to measure the skill almost as easily as one. This approach is more economical than writing similar items as they are needed over the course of the unit or term. With the assistance of an item bank, you can develop several forms of a test that address the same objectives. Teachers who must test several classes on the same enabling skills will find item banks particularly helpful. In fact, they can be a very useful tool for any teacher whose test development time is limited.

The item bank structure in section A of Table 7.3 contains a matrix of eight objectives with five corresponding test items for each objective. Imagine that each numbered cell contains an item that matches the conditions, behavior, and content specified in the row objective. Sections B and C illustrate how the items in the bank can be chosen to create many different test forms using the same forty items. The columns in section B list six possible item

TABLE 7.3 Hypothetical Item Bank and Examples of Alternative Test Forms Developed Using the Bank

A. Hypothetical Item Bank						B. Six different test forms that include one item per objective						C. Three different test forms that include several items per objective		
Objectives	Corresponding Test Items					Test 1	Test 2	Test 3	Test 4	Test 5	Test 6	Test 1	Test 2	Test 3
1	1[a]	2	3	4	5	1	2	1	3	4	3	1	2	3
2	6	7	8	9	10	6	7	7	8	9	9	6,7	8, 9	10, 6
3	11	12	13	14	15	11	12	11	13	14	13	11, 12, 13	13, 14, 15	15, 11, 12
4	16	17	18	19	20	16	17	17	18	19	19	16, 17	18, 19	20, 16
5	21	22	23	24	25	21	22	21	23	24	23	21, 22, 23	23, 24, 25	25, 21, 22
6	26	27	28	29	30	26	27	27	28	29	29	26, 27	28, 29	30, 26
7	31	32	33	34	35	31	32	31	33	34	33	31, 32	33, 34	35, 31
8	36	37	38	39	40	36	37	37	38	39	39	36, 37	38, 39	40, 36

[a] A number representing a specific item contained in an item bank.

combinations for tests that require one item per objective; in fact, many more combinations are possible. The columns in section C contain three tests that meet the following test specifications: objective 1—one item; objective 2—two items; objective 3—three items; objective 4—two items; objective 5—three items; objective 6—two items; objective 7—two items; and objective 8—two items. Many more possibilities exist for creating test forms from the bank according to these prescriptions.

Initially, your item bank will probably contain only a few items for each objective. Over a period of years, you can enlarge and refine this pool by adding new items as you reteach the units and by revising or deleting items that prove ineffective.

Item Codes

Item codes key test items to their behavioral objectives, enabling skills, and instructional goals. The code helps you store and retrieve items and relate student performances to the enabling skills and objectives in the goal framework. An item code should include the following locator information:

1. The instructional goal category
2. The identifying instructional goal number from the curriculum guide
3. The identifying number of the enabling skill from the goal framework
4. The identifying number of the objective measured
5. The identifying item number in the pool

In addition to this locator information, codes can be used to identify the item format, the level of learning measured by the item, and perhaps the type of test for which it is intended.

Suppose you want to develop a coding system for the ten instructional goals on capitalization that appear in Table 4.5. First, your code might separate this category of goals from others in the curriculum guide. If the curriculum guide has already assigned a code to this set of skills, you should use that. In this case, let us assign the code number 4 to the set of capitalization goals. Thus, the item code will begin with 4. Next, you need to assign a number to each goal in the set. You might logically decide to use the numbers 1 through 10 that appear in Table 4.5. Thus, the code 4–1 would identify the first goal in the set, "Capitalize the first word of each sentence," 4–2 would identify the second goal, and so on. Next, you should assign appropriate code numbers to the enabling skills in each goal framework. For example, the goal framework for goal 4–3, "Capitalize proper nouns," has eleven enabling skills (see Figure 3.3). The numbers that you use to identify the enabling skills should be those from the framework. Thus, the code 4–3–10 would identify the enabling skill, "Locate proper nouns in a list of words containing proper nouns and other parts of speech."

Next, you need to assign a number to objectives for each enabling skill. Enabling skill 4–3–10 has one behavioral objective. The code 4–3–10–1 would identify it. As you write items for this and other objectives, you can continue the code by assigning a number to each item you add to the bank. For example, the code 4–3–10–1–1 would refer to the first item for this objective, 4–3–10–1–2 would refer to the second item, and so on.

You may also want to record each item's format and perhaps the level of learning involved. For example: 1 could indicate a completion item, 2 a short-answer item, 3 an alternative-response item, 4 a multiple-choice item, and so forth. This code will help you select items from the bank to match a particular test format. Related to learning levels, the following codes might be helpful: 1 could indicate a knowledge level item, 2 a comprehension item, 3 an application item, 4 an analysis item, 5 a synthesis item, and 6 an evaluation item.

Your code now has seven numbers, each representing different information about the item. To facilitate interpretations of each item code, you need to develop a legend that tells you what your numbers mean. For consistency, you should use the same coding format for each item bank you create. Figure 7.1 illustrates your legend for the numbering system just described. Using this type of code for storing items in the bank, you can quickly retrieve items for a particular test to measure the desired goal, enabling skill, objective, and learning level. You can also select items that match the format of other items you choose for the test. Such coding also enables you to analyze students' performance on the items relative to the particular enabling skills and goals measured.

Resources for Item Banks

You can set up your item bank in one of three ways, depending on the resources available. One method, which requires no special resources, is to write each item and its code on an index card and then file the cards according to the coding system. You can pull cards from the file for a particular table of test specifications and then arrange the cards in the order items will appear on the test. Once you have written the directions, your test is ready to be typed.

FIGURE 7.1 Code Legend

First Number	Second Number	Third Number	Fourth Number	Fifth Number	Sixth Number	Seventh Number
Goal Category 4	Goal Number 3	Enabling Skill 10	Objective 1	Item 1	Item Format 3	Learning Level 3

After you have administered and scored the test, you can write student performance information for each item on the back of the card. You can then revise or eliminate ineffective items and refile items you plan to use again. Using this system, you can easily update your item bank as new instructional goals are added to the curriculum.

A more efficient method of developing and maintaining an item bank is to use a computer with a word-processing or spread-sheet program. Instead of card files, computer disks are used to store coded items. This method substantially reduces typing time and typing errors. As a consequence, the time needed to produce tests and to proofread items will also be reduced. After administering and scoring tests, the items in the file can be edited as needed before they are used again. These many timesaving features make computers a valuable resource for item bank development and test production.

The most sophisticated method of developing an item bank requires a computer and specialized programs. Several commercially available programs help you write items, select items for tests, and administer the tests using the computer. Students take the tests at computer terminals, and their scores are produced by the computer on printouts that describe individual and group performance by item, objective, enabling skill, and goal.

Some computerized testing programs can also select the next test item for a student, depending on her or his response to a previous item. This capability provides an efficient way to measure intellectual skills in a hierarchy. A student beginning a test answers several items related to the most difficult skill in the hierarchy. If the answers are correct, the student does not receive items related to subordinate skills. If the answers are incorrect, the next items received are related to the enabling skill immediately below the one missed in the hierarchy. This downward sequence continues as long as the student fails to answer correctly.

Figure 7.2 is a flow chart showing a branching strategy for the instructional goal "Capitalize proper nouns" that appeared in Figure 3.3. The flow chart indicates that the first items presented require the student to capitalize proper nouns. If the student correctly answers these items, no more items are presented and the test is over. On the other hand, if the student does not correctly answer these items, then items are presented for enabling skill 10. If these items are answered correctly, then items for enabling skill 2 are presented. If these items are answered correctly as well, then the test is over. However, if the student misses items related to enabling skill 10, then items for enabling skill 9 are presented. The test continues down through the enabling skills until the student reaches a skill that he or she has mastered.

This computerized format is a very useful testing tool. It is excellent for diagnostic pretests. Programs that enable you to put messages on the screen following a student's response are very helpful for practice tests. For example, a student answering an item correctly may receive feedback, such as "Good

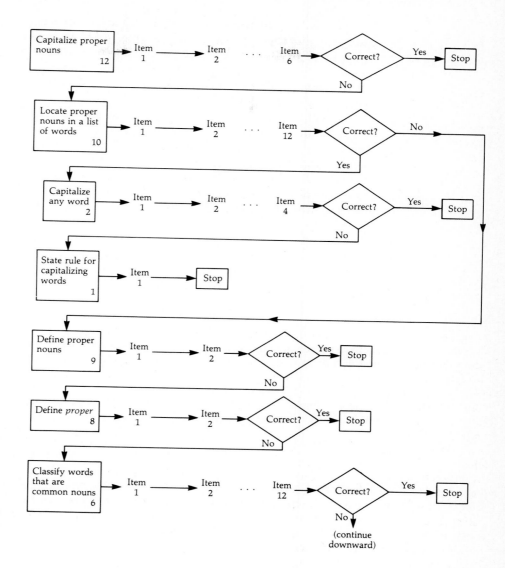

FIGURE 7.2
Flowchart for
Selecting Item
Bank Test Items
Based on a
Student's
Previous
Responses

job'' or ''Keep up the good work.'' If a student answers incorrectly, information explaining why the response chosen was wrong may appear on the screen. Following this instructional message, the screen can display a similar item measuring the same skill to test whether the student benefited from the corrective message. In addition, the computer can summarize students' performances on the practice test that will help you plan additional instruction and evaluate the quality of the items on the test.

Many computer programs permit you to include such resources as tables and figures for the items, and some enable you to address the student taking the test by name. For example, a second correct response might produce the message, "You're right again, Vicky!" Many students like such personal touches. If your school has computer resources, you should learn more about using them in your testing program.

Whether you decide to use a card file, a computerized word-processing or spread-sheet program, or a computerized testing program for your item bank, most of the work involves developing your goal framework and behavioral objectives and writing your test items. Once these tasks are accomplished, you will want to increase your flexibility and save yourself time and work. The best way to make test development easier is to use all the resources available in your school and school district.

SUMMARY

Multiple-choice items have two components: (1) a stem that poses a question or problem and (2) a set of responses that includes the correct answer and two or more distractors. Although these items can be written in a variety of formats, they all require students to select a response from among specified alternatives.

Because of their versatility, multiple-choice items are the most popular form of selected-response test items. They can measure verbal information and a wide variety of intellectual skills, including those subordinate to attitudes and motor skills. They permit a teacher to measure a broad range of skills in a relatively short time period, and they can be conveniently and reliably scored. They can be adapted easily for computer administration and scoring. Finally, they can be stored in item banks and used to create multiple test forms to measure the same objectives.

The suggestions for writing good multiple-choice items are summarized in Table 7.4. Included are the general criteria for writing test items, as well as specific suggestions for writing the stem, the correct answer, and the distractors. Table 7.4 also includes suggestions for organizing responses and for avoiding unintended clues.

Item banks can increase your flexibility in creating multiple test forms to measure the skills in an instructional goal framework and can save you hours of repetitive work. These pools of items enable you to create alternative test forms for pretests, practice tests, unit tests, comprehensive exams, and makeup tests used with the same class. They are also an excellent resource for teachers who must test several classes over the same goals within a short time span.

Card files, word-processing or spread-sheet programs, and computer-based testing programs can be used in creating item banks. To develop an item bank, you should write several items for each behavioral objective in the goal framework. A numbering code will help you store and retrieve items more efficiently. This numbering code should key each item to its objective, enabling skill, and goal. In addition, codes can be used to identify other item information, such as the item format and learning level. After you have developed a table of specifications for a test, you can select items from the bank to match the prescribed objectives, format, and number of items.

TABLE 7.4 Summary of Suggestions for Writing Multiple-Choice Items

A. General Criteria
1. The item should be congruent with the conditions, behavior, and content in the objective.
2. The vocabulary, context, and complexity of the item should be appropriate for students in the class.
3. The wording of the item should be clear and precise, and grammar and punctuation should be correct.
4. Each item should pose only one problem.
5. Different items should be used on subsequent tests that measure the same objective.

B. Stem
1. The complete problem or question should be posed in the stem.
2. Negative words should be underlined for emphasis.
3. Stems that are complete questions or statements are easier for students to understand.
4. When stems are embedded in directions, they should precede instructions for marking answers.

C. Correct Answer
1. The correct response should grammatically fit the stem.
2. Textbook language should be paraphrased.
3. When multiple responses are correct, another response that names all the correct ones should be used.
4. The options "All of the above are correct" and "None of the above are correct" should be used with caution because it is difficult to use them without providing clues to the correct answer.

D. Distractors
1. Each distractor should reflect a common misconception or problem that students have.
2. All distractors should logically answer the problem posed in the stem.

3. Distractors should grammatically fit the stem.
4. Adding key words from the stem will increase the attractiveness of a distractor to a student who is guessing.

E. Set of Responses
1. A set of responses should be homogeneous.
2. When all responses in a set repeat a common word(s), it should be removed and placed in the stem.
3. Responses should be in alphabetical, chronological, or numerical order when possible.
4. Numeric responses should be keyed to alphabetical response codes when separate answer sheets are used.
5. When machine-scored answer sheets are used, the response code beside the item numbers should be used instead of the one heading the column. (Suggestion 4 is an exception to this rule.)
6. When responses are embedded within sentences or paragraphs, instructions for indicating the correct response should be clear.

F. Unintended Clues
1. The correct response should not be the only one that contains key words from the stem.
2. Distractors should not be consistently longer or shorter than the correct answer.
3. Distractors and the correct response should be equally detailed and technical.
4. Such answers as "Both A and C are correct" should *not* be used only when they are correct.
5. The position of correct answers within sets of responses should vary.

PRACTICE EXERCISES

I. Writing Multiple-Choice Items
1. Which of the following characteristics is *unique* to multiple-choice items?
   A. A complete statement that asks a question or poses a problem
   B. A complete statement that is correct in grammar and punctuation
   C. A set of three or more responses from which a student must select the answer
   D. An item that matches the conditions, behavior, and content specified in the objective
   E. Both C and D are correct
2. What part of a multiple-choice item contains the problem statement?
   A. Distractor
   B. Foil
   C. Responses
   D. Stem
3. Which of the following terms is used for incorrect responses?
   A. Distractor
   B. Foil
   C. Response Set
   D. Stem
   E. Both A and B are correct
4. Which of the following statements reflects a *positive* feature of multiple-choice items? They can be used to measure
   A. Various types of learning including attitudes.
   B. Students' ability to make fine discriminations.
   C. A student's unique or novel solutions to a problem.
   D. Both A and B are correct.
5. Which of the following statements reflects *limitations* of multiple-choice items? They *cannot* be written to
   A. Measure complex intellectual skills.
   B. Measure several levels of learning.
   C. Diagnose misconceptions and problems students have.
   D. Avoid the probability of students guessing the correct answer.
   E. Measure the intellectual skills that are subordinate to a motor skill.

   Directions: The following items may have more than one correct answer. Indicate the responses that apply.
6. Which of the following characteristics does a good stem have?
   A. It is congruent with the behavioral objective.
   B. The vocabulary, the context, and the complexity are appropriate for the students being tested.
   C. It clearly poses the question or problem.
   D. The grammar and punctuation are correct.
7. Which of the following suggestions would help you develop correct responses for multiple-choice questions?
   A. Repeat key words from the stem in the answer.
   B. Use statements as they appear in the textbook.
   C. Do *not* use such options as "Both A and B are correct" as the answer.
   D. Ensure that the answer is grammatically consistent with the stem.

8. Which of the following suggestions would help you write good distractors?
   A. Construct responses that are plausible to students.
   B. Ensure that distractors are grammatically consistent with the stem.
   C. Include common misconceptions and problems students may have with the skill measured.
   D. Construct them to be either longer or shorter than the correct answer.
9. Which of the following characteristics does a good set of responses have?
   A. They are homogeneous.
   B. They all contain the same key words from the stem.
   C. When the responses are numerals, the answer code should also be a numeral for consistency.
   D. They are placed in a logical order.
10. Which of the following statements describes clues commonly found in multiple-choice items?
   A. Distractors are consistently longer or shorter than the correct answer.
   B. Using such responses as "Both A and C are correct" only when this is the correct response.
   C. Key words in the stem appear in one or more of the distractors.
   D. The correct answer frequently appears in the same position in the set.
11. Which of the following suggestions would help you arrange multiple-choice items on a test?
   A. List responses horizontally on a line.
   B. Place resource materials between the directions and the questions when they are on the same page.
   C. Place resources that require a lot of space, or that are needed for questions on several pages, on a separate, unattached page.
   D. For economy, place some or all of the responses on the page following the one containing the stem.

Directions: Evaluate each of the following multiple-choice items using the suggestions for writing items included in this chapter. List problems you believe the items contain in the center column of a chart like the one in Figure 7.3, and write a revised item in the right-hand column to correct the problems. There are many ways the items could be corrected. An example revision is included for each in Figure 7.3(F) in the Feedback section. Assume that students will respond, using a separate answer sheet, with the codes A, B, C, D, and E heading the columns and 1, 2, 3, 4, and 5 beside the item numbers.

FIGURE 7.3 Evaluate Multiple-Choice Items

Items	Problems	Revised Items

12. A nickel equals:
   1. Two cents
   2. Ten cents
   3. Five cents
   4. Fifteen cents
   5. Twenty-five cents		

(continued on next page)

FIGURE 7.3   *(continued)*

Items	Problems	Revised Items

13. How many <u>cents</u>
   does a quarter
   equal?
   1. Twenty pennies
   2. Twenty-five
      cents
   3. One nickel
   4. Two dimes

14. Three quarters
   equal:
   1. Two quarters,
      two dimes, and
      a nickel
   2. Seven dimes
      and a nickel
   3. One fifty-cent
      piece and two
      dimes
   4. More than one
      is correct

15. *Directions:* Choose
   the correct
   punctuation mark
   to close the
   following
   sentences.
   1. They have
      planned a hike
      for Saturday___
      1..,2.!,3.?,4.,
   2. Where are the
      broom and dust
      pan___
      1..,2.!,3.?,4.,

16. *Directions:* Choose
   the underlined
   word in the
   following
   sentences that is a
   verb:
   1. She returned
      1   2
      the roller
      3   4
      skates.
      5

(continued on next page)

FIGURE 7.3 *(continued)*

Items	Problems	Revised Items

2. He jogs early
   1 2   3
   every morning.
   4   5

17. *Directions:* Select the word that best completes the sentence.
    Tom _____ to go to church last Sunday.
    1. is choosing
    2. chooses
    3. chose
    4. will choose

18. Order the following sentences.
    1. He toasted the marshmallows over the flame.
    2. He built a roaring fire in the fireplace.
    3. He got the marshmallows from the pantry.
    4. He ate twelve marshmallows.
       1. 1–3–2–4
       2. 2–3–4–1
       3. 3–2–1–4
       4. 2–3–1–4

19. The following objectives are based on some of the capitalization instructional goals included in Table 4.5. For each objective, write the prescribed number of multiple-choice items. Before beginning to write the items, imagine a particular group of students. Then write the items so they are appropriate in vocabulary, context, and complexity for the group. In addition, write directions for your set of items to explain to students how they should respond. Compare your test with the one included in Table 7.5, which was created for students in the upper elementary grades.

Goals	Objectives
1	Given sentences without the first word capitalized, select the word that should be capitalized. (2 items)
2	Given sentences without the pronoun *I* capitalized, select the word that should be capitalized. (2 items)
3	Given sentences without proper nouns capitalized, select the word that should be capitalized. (4 items)
4	Given sentences without proper adjectives capitalized, select the word that should be capitalized. (2 items)

Directions: Multiple-choice items frequently require resources, such as paragraphs, illustrations, or other types of materials. For each of the following three objectives:

A. Develop the resource specified in the objective.
B. Write three multiple-choice questions based on the objective that require the resource.
C. Write directions that explain how to respond to the items.

Before beginning, imagine a group of students and design your materials so they are appropriate in vocabulary, context, and complexity for the group. Use your own paper for these items.

Objectives:

20. Given a five-sentence paragraph, identify the topic, supporting, and concluding sentences. (Compare your materials with those in Table 7.6.)
21. Given a mileage table, locate the number of miles between two given towns. (Compare your materials with those in Table 7.7.)
22. Given a mileage scale with 1 inch equal to 100 miles, estimate the distance between two specified towns that is:
    a. one-half the length of the scale.
    b. the same length as the scale.
    c. two and one-half times the length of the scale.
    (Compare your materials with those in Table 7.8.)

II. Item Banks
23. What are two other names for item banks?
24. List two ways in which item banks can shorten test development time.
25. Why should you develop a coding system for test items in your item bank?
26. What types of information might you want to include in an item code?

III. Enrichment
27. Review the goal framework, objectives, and table of specifications you developed for your own content area. Based on your materials, do the following:
    1. Write two multiple-choice items for objectives that can be measured using this format.
    2. Use the suggestions in Table 7.4 to evaluate and revise your items.
28. Develop a coding system for your goal framework, objectives, and items.
29. Inquire about the computer resources available in your school, or school district, that you can use for developing item banks, producing tests, scoring

tests, or administering tests. Keep these resources in mind as you design and develop your tests.

FEEDBACK

I. Writing Multiple-Choice Items

Questions	1	2	3	4	5	6	7	8	9	10	11
Responses	C	D	E	B	D	A	D	A	A	A	B
						B		B	D	B	C
						C		C		D	
						D					

FIGURE 7.3(F)

Items	Problems	Revised Items

12. A nickel equals:
  1. Two cents
  2. Ten cents
  3. Five cents
  4. Fifteen cents
  5. Twenty-five cents
	1. The stem is not a complete question or statement.
	2. The responses do not list money values in order.
	3. The item requires an answer that is a number between one and five, yet numbers are used for response codes.
	4. Repeating the word *cents* in each response is redundant.
	5. Numerals could be used to replace the words that refer to numbers.
		12. How many <u>cents</u> does a nickel equal?
		  A. 2
		  B. 5
		  C. 10
		  D. 15
		  E. 25

13. How many <u>cents</u> does a quarter equal?
  1. Twenty pennies
  2. Twenty-five cents
  3. One nickel
  4. Two dimes
	1. Distractors 1, 3, and 4 are not consistent with the problem posed in the stem.
	2. The correct response is the only one that repeats a key word from the stem.
	3. Numerals could be used to streamline the responses, and letters should be used as response codes.
		13. How many <u>cents</u> does a quarter equal?
		  A. 5
		  B. 10
		  C. 25
		  D. 50

(continued on next page)

FIGURE 7.3(F)   (*continued*)

Items	Problems	Revised Items
14. Three quarters equal: 1. Two quarters, two dimes, and a nickel 2. Seven dimes and a nickel 3. One fifty-cent piece and two dimes 4. More than one is correct	1. The stem does not provide adequate direction for responding. 2. The fourth distractor should be more specific. 3. Using letters as answer codes would reduce the amount of numbers involved.	14. Which of the following sets of coins equal the same value as three quarters? A. Two quarters, two dimes, and a nickel. B. Seven dimes and a nickel. C. One fifty-cent piece and two dimes. D. Both A and B are correct.
15. *Directions:* Choose the correct punctuation mark to close the following sentences. 1. They have planned a hike for Saturday _____ 1..,2.!,3.?,4., 2. Where are the broom and dust pan _____ 1..,2.!,3.?,4.,	1. The responses are listed horizontally rather than vertically. 2. Each response does not begin on a separate line. 3. The punctuation required to separate items becomes confused with the response punctuation. 4. Since all items in the set require the same responses, the set may be written as keyed items rather than repeating the responses for each item.	15. *Directions:* Choose the correct punctuation mark to close the following sentences. Responses: (1) . (2) ! (3) ? (4) , 1. They have planned a hike for Saturday _____ 2. Where are the broom and dust pan _____

16. *Directions:*   Choose the underlined word in the following sentences that is a verb:
1. She returned
    1   2
the roller
 3   4
skates.
 5
	1. The directions on how to respond precedes the problem statement in the directions.	16. *Directions:* Locate the verb in the following sentences. Circle the number beneath the word that is a verb.
		1. She returned the
		   1 2 3
		roller skates.
		 4 5

(*continued on next page*)

FIGURE 7.3(F)   *(continued)*

Items	Problems	Revised Items

2. He jogs early
   1   2   3
every morning.
   4   5
		2. He jogs early
		   1 2 3
		every morning.
		   4 5

Items	Problems	Revised Items
Directions: Select the word that best completes the sentence. 17. Tom _____ to go to church last Sunday. 1. is choosing 2. chooses 3. chose 4. will choose	1. The directions specify choosing a word whereas two answer choices contain two words. 2. The context related to church on Sunday may be inappropriate for some students in the group.	*Directions:* Select the verb, or verbs, that best complete(s) the sentence. 17. Tom _____ to go to the picnic last Sunday. 1. is choosing 2. will choose 3. chooses 4. chose

18. Order the following sentences.
1. He toasted the marshmallows over the flame.
2. He built a roaring fire in the fireplace.
3. He got the marshmallows from the pantry.
4. He ate twelve marshmallows.
   1. 1–3–2–4
   2. 2–3–4–1
   3. 3–2–1–4
   4. 2–3–1–4
	1. The directions should explain better how to answer the question.
	2. The sentences in the sequence do not have one correct order. For example, he could get the marshmallows before he makes the fire, and he could eat some marshmallows before he toasts any.
	3. Both the sentences and the response codes are numerals, which creates too many numbers.
		18. Choose the order in which these events would happen.
		A. He toasted twelve marshmallows over the embers.
		B. He built a roaring fire in the fireplace.
		C. While the fire burned down, he got marshmallows from the pantry.
		D. He ate all twelve marshmallows.
		Responses:
		   1. A–D–C–B
		   2. A–B–C–D
		   3. B–C–A–D
		   4. B–A–D–C

19. See Table 7.5 for sample items and directions. The material in the example is intended for children in the third or fourth grade.
20. See Table 7.6 for a sample paragraph and items. The paragraph and items are intended for high school students.
21. See Table 7.7 for sample questions. The material in this example is intended for children in the upper elementary grades.

TABLE 7.5   Multiple-Choice Items for Capitalization Objectives

Directions: Locate the <u>mistakes</u> in capitalization in the following sentences. If you think an <u>underlined</u> word is a mistake, circle the letter below the word. If you believe all the underlined words in a sentence are capitalized correctly, circle the letter <u>E</u> below the word <u>none</u> at the end of the sentence.

1. <u>none</u> of the <u>planets</u> are as interesting to <u>me</u> as <u>Saturn</u>. <u>None</u>
    A   B   C   D   E

2. <u>perhaps</u> <u>they</u> will <u>come</u> by <u>Thanksgiving</u>. <u>None</u>
    A   B   C   D   E

3. <u>It</u> was <u>Tuesday</u> <u>evening</u> before <u>i</u> finished. <u>None</u>
    A   B   C   D   E

4. <u>Elma</u> and <u>i</u> plan to play <u>tennis</u> on <u>Monday</u>. <u>None</u>
    A   B   C   D   E

5. The <u>puppy</u> belongs to <u>tom's</u> <u>sister</u>. <u>None</u>
    A B   C   D   E

6. <u>They</u> decided to <u>visit</u> <u>Lincoln</u> <u>zoo</u>. <u>None</u>
    A   B   C   D   E

7. <u>Lucy</u> met her <u>aunt</u> at <u>Memorial</u> <u>library</u>. <u>None</u>
    A   B   C   D   E

8. The favorite <u>cereal</u> of <u>Tommy</u> and his <u>father</u> is <u>wheaties</u>. <u>None</u>
           A   B   C   D   E

9. <u>Annie</u> enrolled in <u>spanish</u> <u>class</u> <u>today</u>. <u>None</u>
    A   B   C   D   E

10. We <u>saluted</u> the <u>american</u> <u>flag</u> at the <u>assembly</u>. <u>None</u>
      A   B   C   D   E

TABLE 7.6   Multiple-Choice Items for the Objective "Given a Five-Sentence Paragraph, Identify the Topic, Supporting, and Concluding Sentences

Directions: Locate the topic, supporting, and concluding sentences in the following paragraph. After you have analyzed the sentences, choose the one, or ones, that best answers the questions following the paragraph. Mark your answers on the answer sheet.

Paragraph

Thanksgiving is a happy time at my house. The whole family gathers to share a meal and stories even though several members travel many miles for the occasion. During dinner last Thanksgiving, we each told a story about something during the past year that made us grateful. Listening to the conversations, I realized that I was most grateful for my family and the opportunity to be together again. Perhaps sharing is what makes Thanksgiving such a happy time.

1. Which of the following words begin(s) a concluding sentence in the paragraph?
   A. Thanksgiving
   B. The and Listening
   C. During and Perhaps
   D. Listening
   E. Perhaps

(continued on next page)

TABLE 7.6   (*continued*)

2. Which of the following words begin(s) a topic sentence?
   A. Thanksgiving
   B. Thanksgiving and The
   C. Thanksgiving and Perhaps
   D. Perhaps
3. Which of the following words begin(s) a supporting sentence?
   A. Thanksgiving, The, and During
   B. The, During, and Listening
   C. During, Listening, and Perhaps
   D. Thanksgiving, Listening, and Perhaps

TABLE 7.7   Multiple-Choice Items for the Objective "Given a Mileage Table, Locate the Number of Miles between Two Given Towns"

Directions: Locate the distance between towns using the following mileage table. Questions 1, 2, and 3 are based on the table. Record your answers on the answer sheet provided.

Mileage Table

	Adams	Brown	Carter	Doyle	Emory
Adams		25	50	75	100
Brown			35	55	105
Carter				45	60
Doyle					110
Emory					

1. How many miles is it from Doyle to Emory?
   A. 45
   B. 55
   C. 75
   D. 100
   E. 110
2. How many miles is it from Adams to Carter?
   A. 25
   B. 35
   C. 50
   D. 75
   E. 100
3. How many miles is it from Carter to Brown?
   A. 35
   B. 45
   C. 50
   D. 60
   E. The mileage is not included in the table.

22. See Table 7.8 for sample questions. This exercise is intended for children in the upper elementary grades.

TABLE 7.8   Multiple-Choice Items for the Objective "Given a Mileage Scale with 1 Inch Equal to 100 Miles, Estimate the Distance between Two Specified Towns"

Directions: Estimate the distance between towns using a mileage scale. Use Figure 1 and your ruler to estimate the distances requested in items 1, 2, and 3. Mark your answers on the answer sheet.

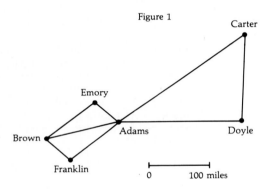

Figure 1

1. How many <u>miles</u> is it from Carter to Adams?
   A. 50
   B. 100
   C. 200
   D. 250
   E. 300
2. How many <u>miles</u> is it from Adams to Emory?
   A. 25
   B. 50
   C. 75
   D. 100
3. How many <u>miles</u> is it from Adams to Franklin?
   A. 50
   B. 100
   C. 150
   D. 200

II. Item banks
   23. Two other names for item banks are item files and item pools.
   24. Item banks can shorten test development because:

    a. it is usually quicker to write several items for one objective at the same time rather than at different times during the unit.

    b. you can create several different forms of the test using relatively few items for each objective.

    c. you can use word-processing or spread sheet programs to reduce the amount of typing and proofreading required.

25. Coded items can be keyed to instructional goals in the curriculum guide, systematically stored, and easily retrieved.

26. You might want to code:
    1. The goal area
    2. The goal number from the curriculum guide
    3. The enabling skill number from the goal framework
    4. The objective number
    5. The item number
    6. The item format
    7. The level of learning
    8. The type of test the item would best suit (e.g., pretest, practice test, posttest)

SUGGESTED READING

Ebel, R. L., and Frisbie, D. A. (1986). *Essentials of educational measurement.* Englewood Cliffs, N.J.: Prentice-Hall, pp. 160–89, 327–8.

Gronlund, N. E. (1985). *Measurement and evaluation in teaching.* New York: Macmillan Publishing Company, pp. 169–212, 257–8.

Mehrens, W. A., and Lehmann, I. J. (1984). *Measurement and evaluation in education and psychology.* New York: CBS College Publishing, pp. 151–75.

Nitko, A. J. (1983). *Educational tests and measurement.* New York: Harcourt, Brace, Jovanovich, pp. 190–211, 286.

Popham, W. J. (1981). *Modern educational measurement.* Englewood Cliffs, N.J.: Prentice-Hall, pp. 251–60.

CHAPTER 8

Constructing and Using Essay and Product Development Tests

OBJECTIVES

1. Define essay and product development tests.
2. Describe the types of skills typically measured using essay and product development tests.
3. Discuss the positive and negative features of essay and product development tests.
4. Write essay questions and product development instructions.
5. Select and include relevant information in directions.
6. Define global scoring and describe its uses.
7. Define analytical scoring and describe its uses.

8. Develop a checklist for analytical scoring.
9. Develop a rating scale for analytical scoring.
10. Use a rating scale to score given products.
11. Describe typical errors associated with constructing and scoring essay and product development tests.
12. Summarize and analyze group performance on essay and product development tests.
13. Describe benefits of students using checklists and rating scales to evaluate their own work.

Curriculum guides often contain complex instructional goals that require students to demonstrate their ability to create a unique response. In constructing unique responses, students need to determine how they will approach a given problem, plan and organize their responses, and present their ideas. Objective tests do not require students to produce original pieces of work that demonstrate these capabilities.

Often these complex goals can be measured with essay questions, which typically require students to discuss, analyze, compare for similarities and differences, synthesize, or evaluate. For example, students may be asked to discuss a product, a procedure, an event, a political action, a natural phenomenon, historical characters, a scientific experiment, a piece of literature, or a philosophical viewpoint. They may be expected to analyze and describe the components of a concrete or defined concept, rule, or principle, or to analyze and describe the steps in a procedure or the components in a system. Essay questions also can be used to measure their ability to compare or contrast concepts, theories, systems, procedures, events, people, and numerous other subjects. They can measure students' abilities to synthesize pieces of literature, articles, events, or other phenomena. In addition, students may be asked to evaluate the quality of a product or event, the execution of some procedure or motor skill, or an instance of behavior.

Some instructional goals cannot be adequately measured by either objective or essay questions. To demonstrate their skill, students need to develop some type of product either with pencil and paper or by some other method. Such products include letters, themes, poems, abstracts, term papers, flow charts, computer programs, original songs, photographs, videotapes, maps, bookcases, blueprints, and drawings. Each student's product will be unique and will vary in complexity, originality, and accuracy. Even when students are following detailed instructions, their responses will vary.

Both essay and product development tests require students to synthesize many enabling skills in their responses. For example, students writing a summary of a book must form sentences and paragraphs, write legibly, select ideas and information, and organize their presentation. One advantage of these tests is the teacher's ability to separate and comment on particular elements of students' responses, such as their approach, organization, logic, and accuracy.

Unfortunately, this type of testing has several major drawbacks. First, a teacher must spend considerable time selecting the task, writing the instructions, scoring the products, analyzing students' work, and evaluating both individual and group performance. Second, more class time is usually required for essay and product exams than for objective-style exams, which often limits the breadth of the material tested. Third, because responses vary, only experts can make the fine distinctions that determine whether an answer is acceptable. Responses cannot be machine scored or given to an aide or student assistant for scoring. Finally, scoring is less reliable on these exams than on objective exams for several reasons. Teachers' standards may shift during scoring, and fatigue can cause lapses in concentration. Scoring bias is another serious problem. Some teachers tend to be lenient whereas others consistently give all the students average or below average marks. A teacher's perceptions of individual students also can bias the scores they assign. In addition, students with excellent verbal and organizational skills can bluff an answer and often receive better scores than less verbally skilled students whose answers contain superior content. Because of these limitations, you should use essay and other product development tests only when the pre-scribed skills cannot be measured with objective tests.

WRITING QUESTIONS AND INSTRUCTIONS

Many of the suggestions for writing objective test items also apply to essay questions and instructions for product development. Questions and instructions should match the behavior, content, and conditions specified in the behavioral objective; the vocabulary, complexity, and context should be appropriate for target students; and questions and instructions should be clearly written using correct grammar and punctuation.

An essay question or set of instructions should describe the type of response that you expect. For example, if students are to compare two things, the instructions should begin with the word *compare*. If they are to critique something, the instructions should begin with the word *critique*. Students should know the meaning of these words and the ways they can demonstrate these skills. If all or some students do not understand what these terms are, their responses may reflect their misunderstanding of what they are told to do.

Providing Guidance

The amount of guidance in the question or instructions depends on the skill being measured and the sophistication of the students. Related to the skill, instructions may require students to discuss or compare things using components they select themselves, or the instructions may specify which components they are to use. Students may have to select and use evaluation criteria, or they may be given the criteria to apply. Related to students' characteristics, older students and high achievers tend to work well with minimum guidance. However, younger students and average or below-average achievers need more structure in the directions.

Students' responses will depend on the amount of guidance in the instructions. Consider the amount of guidance provided in the three essay questions included in Table 8.1. The questions in the left-hand column have the content removed to illustrate the item format. Any content could be substituted for the letters X and Y and the numbers 1, 2, and 3. The questions in the right-hand column use the same format, but content is included in each.

Notice that the three sets of instructions vary considerably in the amount of guidance provided. The first question requires students to decide which aspects of the pretest and posttest they will compare and how they will com-

TABLE 8.1   Degrees of Guidance in Essay Questions

1. Compare X and Y.

2. Compare X and Y for the following:
   1.
   2.
   3.

3. Compare the similarities of and differences between X and Y for the following:
   1.
   2.
   3.

1. Compare *pretests* and *posttests*.

2. Compare *pretests* and *posttests* for the following:
   1. the test's relationship to the goal framework
   2. the time the test is administered
   3. uses for test scores

3. Compare the similarities of and the differences between *pretests* and *posttests* for the following:
   1. the tests' relationship to the goal framework
   2. the time the test is administered
   3. uses for test scores

pare them. This is the most complex question because students must determine all the elements in their response. The lack of guidance will produce greater variety in students' answers.

The second question is more restrictive. Students are told which aspects of pretests and posttests they are to compare. The third set directs students' responses even more by specifying that students compare similarities and differences. Each question is of value. The amount of guidance to include in an essay question depends on whether you want students to recall the facets to be compared or whether you want to provide them. In determining the appropriate amount of guidance, you should always consider what skills you want to measure and the skill level of students being tested.

The amount of guidance to include is also a consideration when writing instructions that require development of a product. For example, the instructions for producing a paragraph can vary considerably in the amount of guidance provided. Consider the following three sets of instructions:

1. Write a paragraph about a fire drill.
2. Write a paragraph about a fire drill. Your paragraph should include:
   a. A topic sentence
   b. At least four supporting sentences
   c. A concluding sentence
3. Write a paragraph that describes fire drill procedures. Your paragraph should include:
   a. A topic sentence
   b. At least four supporting sentences
   c. A concluding sentence

Each set of directions will undoubtedly produce very different paragraphs. The second set is more specific than the first and the third more specific than the second. The third set limits the topic to fire drill procedures and specifies the number and types of sentences to be included. To determine which set of instructions would be best, you would first need to decide how much guidance should be provided for a particular group of students and what skills you want to measure. Specific instructions like those in the third set would not be appropriate if you wanted to measure whether students remembered to include topic and concluding sentences in their paragraphs. However, they would be appropriate for measuring students' skill in ordering events in a prescribed procedure (such as a fire drill). Regardless of the test's purpose, the directions must include enough information to provide clear and unambiguous guidance for the task.

Providing Organizational Information

Besides specifying the nature of the task to be performed, instructions can include additional information to help students determine the relative importance of different questions or sections of the test. Information that can help students organize their work includes (1) the length and scope of the response sought, (2) the number of points each question is worth, and (3) the time available for completing the test or the recommended time students should spend on each question. This type of information is incorporated in the paragraph test in the following example:

1. Write a paragraph that describes fire drill procedures. Your paragraph should include six to ten sentences. Be sure to include:
   a. A topic sentence (5 points)
   b. At least four supporting sentences (8 points)
   c. A concluding sentence (4 points)
   You will have 20 minutes to write and revise your paragraph.

Essay tests can include several questions that require relatively brief answers, or they may contain only one or two questions that require lengthy responses. Whatever the number of questions, the entire class should be directed to answer all the questions included on the test. One relatively common practice in developing essay tests, which is *not* recommended by test specialists, is to provide several questions on an essay test and allow students to select a subset of questions to answer. This practice would be similar to letting students answer twenty of thirty objective items. Both essay and objective test items represent only a few of those a teacher could construct, and the same sample should be used to evaluate all students. When students' responses are not comparable, your ability to evaluate your instruction and students' performance is compromised.

DEVELOPING SCORING PROCEDURES

Teachers typically use two types of scoring procedures to evaluate the quality of students' responses to essay questions and products. With *global* scoring (also called *holistic* scoring) the teacher uses general impressions to judge the quality of an answer or product. A teacher using *analytical* scoring divides a response into its relevant components and evaluates each part separately.

Global Scoring of Essay and Product Tests

Global scoring is appropriate whenever a test is *not* used to provide corrective feedback to students or to evaluate instruction. Its purpose is to sort students' responses into categories that indicate quality. For example, global scoring would be sufficient for a writing test used to place students in an English class. When a teacher has many papers to score, and it is not important to communicate the nature of the errors, global scoring is adequate.

The procedure for global scoring consists of the following seven steps.

1. *Establish the scoring categories you will use.* For example, you may have responses that fall into such categories as pass or fail; good, adequate, and poor; or excellent, good, adequate, poor, and unacceptable. The number of categories selected depends on the purpose for the evaluation and on your ability to place similar responses consistently into the same category. If you create too many categories or do not carefully define each category, you will find scoring difficult.

2. *Characterize a response that fits each category.* If, for example, you were to use the three categories, excellent, adequate, and poor, you should describe the particular characteristics that a response should have to be classified into one of the categories. What characteristics should be present for a response to be considered excellent? What would be absent or present in an adequate response? What would be absent in a poor response? Listing these characteristics helps you classify responses more consistently.

3. *Read each response rapidly and form an overall impression.* During the reading, look for the characteristics you used to describe each rating category.

4. *Sort the responses into the designated categories.*

5. *Reread the papers that have been placed within a category.* After all papers have been classified, you should consider only those within a set for their comparability.

6. *Move any clearly superior or inferior responses to other categories.*

7. *Assign the same numerical score to all responses within a category.* For example, papers in the excellent category can be assigned a score of

five, those in the adequate category can be assigned a score of three, and so forth.

Although global scoring is relatively fast and reliable, two limitations make it less appropriate for classroom tests. First, it does not provide students with adequate feedback about their work. Most students will want to know why they received the assigned score and will not be satisfied with a global rating. Second, global evaluations do not permit the teacher to analyze the responses and identify specific instructional problems. Thus, students do not have the information they need to correct their mistakes, and teachers cannot classify errors and relate them to problems in their lessons.

Analytical Scoring of Product Tests

Analytical scoring is more time consuming than global scoring, but it is a superior method for instructional purposes. This procedure helps a teacher focus on relevant aspects of students' responses and provides a systematic way to assign partial credit. Just as important, it allows students to see where they lost points. Using this method, teachers can summarize the group's performance on main components, analyze errors, and use the error analysis to evaluate and revise instruction.

At the same time, analytical scoring also has some disadvantages. First, constructing a scoring instrument and marking responses take considerable time. If the teacher has not identified and sequenced all the components desired in an answer in the order they are likely to appear in students' responses, searching for these components in students' work will take even longer. Second, developing a flexible scoring procedure that accommodates unanticipated responses can also be difficult. Teachers using analytical scoring may struggle with the problem of scoring correct, unusual answers that do not fit the structure and that cannot be compared to other students' responses.

Analytical scoring can be simplified by using a form that indicates the desired elements of a response and the number of points to be awarded for each. To construct such a form, first identify and order the desired components and subcomponents of each response. The major components you select should always be based on an instructional goal and its framework of subordinate skills. In addition to these skills, you may want to use other elements, such as the students' approach, organization, and originality, to judge their work. Some teachers believe that grammar, neatness, punctuation, and spelling should always count whereas others choose not to emphasize these elements in every task. If you choose to include elements not contained in the goal framework and not included in instruction for the unit, you should inform students of this intention in the test directions.

The process of selecting and ordering components can be demonstrated with an example. Figure 8.1 shows the framework of enabling skills for the goal, "Write a paragraph on a given topic that contains a topic sentence, supporting sentences, and a concluding sentence." Although most of the twenty-eight enabling skills can be measured with objective test items that require students either to write a short answer or select a response, the instructional goal requires that students write a paragraph. The goal framework indicates that students' paragraphs should contain (1) indentation, (2) a topic sentence, (3) supporting sentences, and (4) a concluding sentence. These four elements make up the main components included on the evaluation form. Both sequence and transition are considered within the supporting sentences component.

Next, you need to identify relevant subcomponents for each main component. Indentation is a simple skill that has no subcomponents. Writing a topic sentence is a more complex skill that includes at least two subcomponents. First, the topic sentence should be a general statement that introduces a topic, and second, it should be appropriately placed in the paragraph. Writing supporting sentences is even more complex so it has more subcomponents. The supporting sentences should all relate to the topic, should be logically sequenced, and should contain transition words. These three criteria are subcomponents for supporting sentences. Finally, you need to identify relevant subcomponents for a concluding sentence. Subcomponents could include whether the sentence adequately summarizes the topic and whether it is logically placed in the paragraph. Main components and their subcomponents should be sequenced in the order they are most likely to appear in the paragraphs.

Once you have selected and ordered the evaluation criteria from the goal framework, you must decide whether skills not included in the framework will also be judged. If you want to score prerequisite skills, such as complete sentences, correct verb tenses, spelling, and punctuation, you must add these to your list of criteria. Your completed outline of criteria taken from the goal framework would appear as follows:

    I. Indentation
   II. Topic Sentence
       A. Introduces topic
       B. Logically placed   Criteria from the goal framework

  III. Supporting Sentences
       A. Directly related to topic
       B. Logically sequenced
       C. Includes transition words
  IV. Concluding Sentence
       A. Summarizes topic
       B. Logically placed

FIGURE 8.1 Instructional Goal Framework for Writing a Paragraph

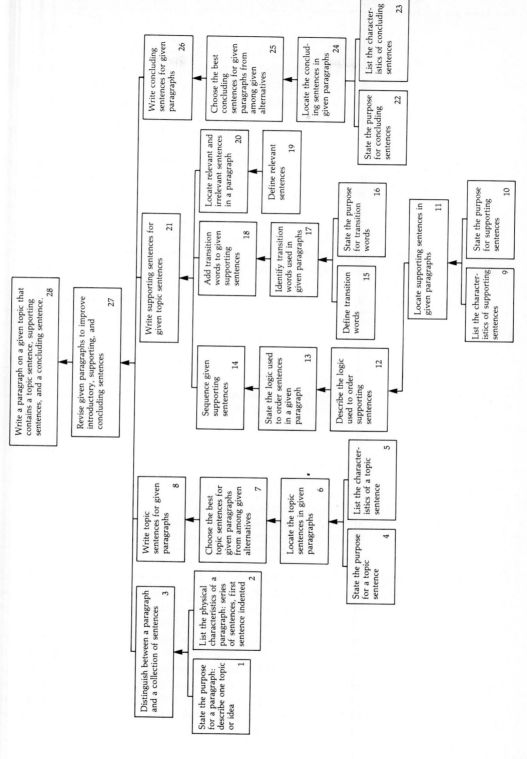

V. Grammar and Spelling
    A. Complete sentences   Criteria based on
    B. Correct spelling   prerequisite skills for the
    C. Correct punctuation   goal framework

This outline of criteria is the basis for either a *checklist* or a *rating scale*.

Checklists   A checklist permits you to judge only the presence or absence of each component. To score a written product that students developed, simply check each component that appears in a response and add up the checkmarks to obtain a total score. In the paragraph examples, the components in the outline become evaluation criteria on the checklist. A student receiving eight check marks receives a perfect score. Table 8.2 illustrates how a paragraph checklist might appear. Only criteria taken from the goal framework are included in the example.

TABLE 8.2   Checklist for Evaluating Students' Paragraphs

Name _____ Date _____ Score _____
                                                Total   (8)

Criteria	*Yes*
I. Indentation (1 point)	
A. Paragraph is indented	_____
II. Topic Sentence (2 points)	
A. Topic sentence is included	_____
B. Topic sentence is appropriately placed	_____
III. Supporting Sentences (3 points)	
A. They directly relate to the topic	_____
B. They are logically sequenced	_____
C. They contain transition words	_____
IV. Concluding Sentence (2 points)	
A. Concluding sentence is included	_____
B. Sentence is appropriately placed	_____

Rating Scales   The rating scale, an extension of the checklist, lets you judge not only the presence of a component but also its quality. A rating scale contains all the criteria on the checklist as well as a sequence of numbers that represent degrees of quality. Table 8.3 shows a rating scale for evaluating paragraphs. Each rating category on the scale includes both a number and a description of quality. A zero indicates the absence of a component or a subcomponent. Zeros should be used for rating only when the rated component can be absent. For example, they should not be used to rate such elements as spelling or organization because some degree of this type of element will be present. Such components as a topic sentence may be missing altogether, so using a zero to represent this absence would be appropriate.

TABLE 8.3 Rating Scale for Evaluating Paragraphs

Name _____ Date _____ Score _____

Total   (17)

I. Indentation (1 point)

	Not Indented	Clearly Indented	
	0	1	

II. Topic Sentence (4 points)

	Not Present	Vague	Clearly Introduces Topic
A. Content	0	1	2
B. Location	Not Present 0	Misplaced 1	Logically Placed 2

III. Supporting Sentences (8 points)

	Some Irrelevant Information	All Relevant Information	Thoroughly Develops Topic
A. Relevance	1	2	3
B. Sequence	Illogical Order 1	Some Order 2	Logical Order 3
C. Transition words	No Transition 0	Some Transition 1	Smooth Transition 2

IV. Concluding Sentence (4 points)

	Not Present	Not Comprehensive	Clearly Summarizes Topic
A. Content	0	1	2
B. Location	Not Present 0	Misplaced 1	Logically Placed 2

The number of rating categories included for each element will depend on your ability to distinguish clearly between adjacent categories. A scale that includes too many categories will affect your rating consistency and thus the reliability of the scores. The words you use to describe each number will also aid the consistency of your rating. Descriptors, such as *inadequate, adequate,* and *good,* may be sufficient, but other terms related to the characteristics of the component measured may help you be more precise. Vague descriptors often reflect vague understanding of each number, and both affect the consistency of your ratings.

Look at the descriptors accompanying each number in the rating scale in Table 8.3. Rather than including vague terms, such as *inadequate, adequate,* and *good,* the descriptors relate to characteristics of the component to be rated. For example, the descriptors for the relevance of supporting sentences (III.A) indicate that students who include irrelevant information in their supporting sentences will be assigned a score of one. Those who include only relevant sentences will receive a score of two. Students whose supporting sentences are relevant and also develop the topic thoroughly will receive a maximum rating of three. Such descriptors for each score help you judge the quality of paragraphs consistently and clearly communicate each rating to students.

Checklists and rating scales may also be used to evaluate other types of student products, such as a bookcase or a picture frame constructed in an industrial arts class, a dress or meal produced in a home economics class, or a mobile constructed in either a math or art class. For example, students being tested on the goal "Construct a mobile" would need to construct mobiles to demonstrate their skill even though the principles involved could be measured at the knowledge and comprehension levels using an objective test. The instructional goal framework should be used as the basis for both objective tests and the product evaluation form. A goal framework that a math teacher might develop is illustrated in Figure 8.2. Table 8.4 is a corresponding

TABLE 8.4   Checklist for Evaluating Mobiles

Name _____ Date _____ Score _____
                                                 Total   (15)

I. Mobile with 1:1 weight ratio between two objects
   _____ 1. Objects correctly selected by weight
   _____ 2. Objects correctly positioned on crosswire
   _____ 3. Fulcrum found on crosswire

II. Mobile with 1:2 weight ratio between two objects
   _____ 1. Objects correctly selected by weight
   _____ 2. Objects correctly positioned on crosswire
   _____ 3. Fulcrum found on crosswire

III. Mobile with 1:3 weight ratio between two objects
   _____ 1. Objects correctly selected by weight
   _____ 2. Objects correctly positioned by crosswire
   _____ 3. Fulcrum found on crosswire

IV. Mobile having three objects of unequal weight and two crosswires
   _____ 1. Objects correctly selected by weight
   _____ 2. Wires correctly selected by length
   _____ 3. Objects attached to correct crosswires
   _____ 4. Objects positioned correctly on crosswires
   _____ 5. Fulcrum found on lower crosswire
   _____ 6. Fulcrum found on upper crosswire

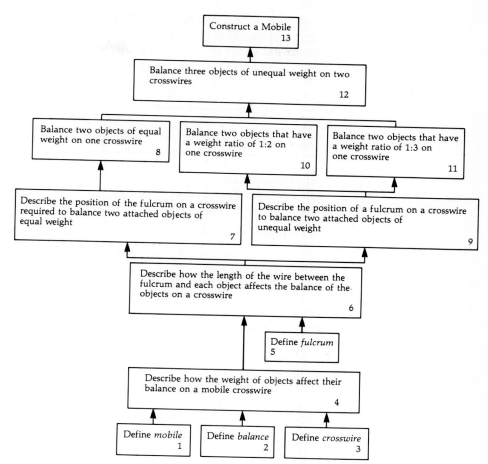

FIGURE 8.2
Instructional
Goal Framework
for Constructing
a Mobile

checklist for evaluating students' mobiles. Notice that the criteria included on the checklist are observable and reflect the teacher's judgment of major components that should be included. An instructional goal framework and checklist created by an art teacher would undoubtedly be different than these examples because art teachers would need to include additional enabling skills related to the artistic quality of the mobile.

Plans for Weighting Components

After you have developed a checklist or rating scale for some type of product, you may need to weight the scores assigned for each criterion. You may want to add points to more important criteria or give more credit for complex or time-consuming skills. You might also want to weight skills that were emphasized during instruction more than skills such as spelling or neatness.

To weight different components, first look at the points each component receives on your checklist or rating scale. For example, Figure 8.3 shows the points already assigned in the checklist in Table 8.2 and the rating scale in Table 8.3.

FIGURE 8.3   Component Points

	Possible Points	
Component	Checklist	Rating Scale
I. Indentation	1	1
II. Topic Sentence	2	4
III. Supporting Sentences	3	8
IV. Concluding Sentence	2	4
	8	17

In both scoring plans, indentation receives the least amount of credit; topic and concluding sentences receive more credit than indentation; and supporting sentences receive the most credit. This balance may not reflect the values you would like each component to have. If you want to adjust the weighting, you need to determine the relative value of each component. For example, you might want the topic sentence, the supporting sentences, and the concluding sentences to be the same value and indentation to count much less than these three. In this case, you could multiply each of the sentence components by a factor that would give them equal weight in the total score.

Table 8.5 shows two different weighting plans. The first illustrates the weighting just described. Components II, III, and IV on the checklist are multiplied by a factor that makes each equal to six points; component I, indentation, is multiplied by 1, which keeps its total the same. The original 8 points have now become 19, with indentation assuming a much smaller portion of the total. On the rating scale, components II and IV are multiplied by a factor of 2, which makes each sentence component worth 8 points. The total score is now 25, with indentation counting only a very small percentage of the score.

The lower section of Table 8.5 shows a plan for the checklist and rating scale that weights the topic sentence and concluding sentence twice as much as the supporting sentences. On the checklist, components II and IV are weighted by a factor of 6, which gives each component a value of 12 points. Components I and III are weighted by a factor of 2, which gives them one-sixth and one-half the value of the other two components. On the rating scale, weightings of 4, 2, and 1 are used to weight indentation one-eighth and supporting sentences one-half the value of the topic and concluding sentences.

Table 8.6 shows a completed rating scale that weights topic, supporting, and concluding sentences equally. The scores for one student are inserted to

TABLE 8.5 Two Plans for Weighting Scores

Component	Checklist					Rating Scale				
	Original		Weight		Total	Original		Weight		Total
I. Indentation	1	×	1	=	1	1	×	1	=	1
II. Topic Sentence	2	×	3	=	6	4	×	2	=	8
III. Supporting Sentences	3	×	2	=	6	8	×	1	=	8
IV. Concluding Sentence	2	×	3	=	6	4	×	2	=	8
Total Points	8				19	17				25

Results: On the checklist, components II, III, and IV are of equal value and each counts six times as much as component I. On the rating scale, components II, III, and IV are equal and each counts eight times as much as component I.

Component	Checklist					Rating Scale				
	Original		Weight		Total	Original		Weight		Total
I. Indentation	1	×	2	=	2	1	×	2	=	2
II. Topic Sentence	2	×	6	=	12	4	×	4	=	16
III. Supporting Sentences	3	×	2	=	6	8	×	1	=	8
IV. Concluding Sentence	2	×	6	=	12	4	×	4	=	16
Total Points	8				32	17				42

Results: In both cases, components II and IV have equal value and count twice as much as component III and significantly more than component I.

illustrate how the form would be completed. To score the student's paragraph, you would circle the score assigned for each subcomponent and then sum these scores to obtain the original component score. This component score is placed in the Original Score column and then multiplied by the assigned weight. Finally, you would add the numbers in the Total column to determine the student's weighted score. As the scale indicates, this student received 21 of 26 possible points.

Analytical Scoring of Essay Tests

The preceding examples illustrate the development of checklists and rating scales for scoring students' products. An extension of these same procedures is used to develop analytical scoring forms for essay tests. Scoring forms for essay tests differ somewhat because these tests usually contain several questions that represent broader content areas. The basic procedure for developing the scoring form for each question is the same as that previously described, that is (1) identify and sequence the main components and subcomponents for each question, (2) determine whether a checklist or rating scale would be most useful, and (3) develop the form weighting each component according

TABLE 8.6   Weighted Rating Scale for Evaluating Paragraphs

Name _Katy Augustine_   Date _10/14_   Score _21_
                                             Total _(26)_

Components	Quality			Original Score × Weight	Total
I. Indentation	Not Indented 0	Clearly Indented ①		_1_ × 2 =	_2_
II. Topic Sentence A. Quality	Not Present 0	Vague 1	Clearly Introduces Topic ②	_4_ × 2 =	_8_
B. Location	Not Present 0	Misplaced 1	Logically Placed ②		
III. Supporting Sentences A. Content	Some Irrelevant Information 1	All Relevant Information ②	Thoroughly Develops Topic 3	_5_ × 1 =	_5_
B. Sequence	Illogical Order 1	Some Order ②	Logical Order 3		
C. Transition	No Transition 0	Some Transition ①	Smooth Transition 2		
IV. Concluding Sentence A. Content	Not Present 0	Not Comprehensive 1	Clearly Summarizes Topic ②	_3_ × 2 =	_6_
B. Location	Not Present 0	Misplaced ①	Logically Placed 2		

                                                        Total _21_

to a plan. In addition, you may need to assign relative weights to each question to ensure that it contributes the desired weight to the overall test score.

The rating form for an essay test might contain a rating scale for each question, a checklist for each question, or a combination of the two formats. In fact, the rating plan for one question might contain some components to be checked as present and others to be rated on a quality scale. Consider the hypothetical rating form in Table 8.7 for a four-question essay test. A checklist containing five components is used to score the first question; the second and third questions are scored using rating scales that contain 16 points each; and a checklist worth 6 points is used to score the fourth question. Using such a form, the topic of each question can be inserted beside the question number, and the components can be inserted beside the capital letters. The number of points a student earns can be inserted in the space beside each question and then multiplied by the desired weight, if additional weighting is needed to balance the questions. In the example, weights were chosen to increase the value of questions 1 and 4 to approximate the value of questions 2 and 3. Using such a rating form to score the questions on an essay test will help you be more objective during scoring, show students where they earned and lost points, and aid your analysis of the group's responses, which is necessary for evaluating instruction and planning review sessions.

TABLE 8.7   Hypothetical Rating Form for an Essay Test Containing Four Questions

Name _____   Date _____   Score ___53.5___

(62)

Question 1 (Checklist)

Present	Component		Score	Weight	=	Total
✓ A.	_____					
✓ B.	_____					
✓ C.	_____		$\frac{4}{(5)}$	×	$\frac{3}{\text{Wt.}}$ =	12
___ D.	_____					
✓ E.	_____					

Question 2 (Rating Scale)

Components   Ratings

		(1)	(2)	(3)	(4)				
A.	_____	___	✓	___					
B.	_____	___	___	✓			$\frac{15}{(16)}$	×	$\frac{1}{\text{Wt.}}$ = 15
C.	_____	___	___	___	✓				
D.	_____	___	___	✓					
E.	_____	___	___	✓					

Question 3 (Rating Scale)

Components   Ratings

		(1)	(2)	(3)	(4)				
A.	_____	___	___	✓					
B.	_____	___	✓	___			$\frac{14}{(16)}$	×	$\frac{1}{\text{Wt.}}$ = 14
C.	_____	___	___	___	✓				
D.	_____	___	✓	___					
E.	_____	___	___	✓					

Question 4 (Checklist)

Present	Component		Score	Weight	=	Total
✓ A.	_____					
___ B.	_____					
✓ C.	_____		$\frac{5}{(6)}$	×	$\frac{2.5}{\text{Wt.}}$ =	12.5
✓ D.	_____					
✓ E.	_____					
✓ F.	_____					

Evaluating Checklists and Rating Scales

Before you use a checklist or rating scale to score students' work, you should evaluate the form and revise it if necessary. First, select two or three students' responses or products and rate their work using the form. Determine whether the components on the form are observable and whether they are listed on the form in the sequence they most frequently occur in the products. Delete components that are not observable, change the sequence of components if necessary, and add components observable in the products that you may have inadvertently overlooked. When adding components, be sure they are appropriate for the instructional goal measured and not an artifact of the particular subset of responses you have chosen. Adjust students' scores on the few products rated to reflect any changes made in the rating form. Second, score each paper again. It is good to allow some time to lapse between the two ratings so you forget the scores assigned the first time. Compare the two ratings you assigned each paper and locate any inconsistencies. Where inconsistent scores occur, either revise the form to include fewer categories of quality that need to be differentiated or write more descriptive titles for each of the categories.

You might also ask a colleague to rate the same papers using the form. Compare your ratings with those of your colleague; discuss any inconsistencies; locate ways in which the form can be changed to improve consistency; and revise the form as needed. Once you begin to score students' work, do not alter the form. Any changes at this point may produce inconsistent ratings.

AVOIDING COMMON ERRORS IN TEST DEVELOPMENT, SCORING, AND GRADING

Development Errors

In producing essay and product development tests, teachers tend to commit two kinds of errors. First, some teachers teach skills at the lower levels of learning and test them at the higher levels. You should not teach lessons at the knowledge and comprehension levels and then expect students to perform at an application level on the test. Likewise, you should not teach at the comprehension and application levels and then write tests to measure skills at the analysis, synthesis, or evaluation levels. If students are required to develop a product or analyze a piece of literature, they should have been instructed at these levels, and been given ample opportunity to practice these skills before the posttest. To avoid this problem, make sure that novel items used on the posttest mirror those used on practice tests.

Teachers also err in constructing essay and product development tests when the items or directions do not provide adequate guidance. One way to ensure that items and directions are clear and the task posed is feasible is to construct the evaluation form before you administer the test. Constructing the evaluation form will help ensure that you have a clear notion of what you are asking students to do. After the evaluation form is complete, recheck your questions and directions to see whether they provide adequate guidance for the responses you anticipate.

Scoring Errors

Two common scoring errors are inconsistency and bias. Even when teachers use checklists and rating scales they can score students' responses inconsistently. They may become stricter or more lenient as they work through a set of papers, and their attitudes can change when they become tired, hurried, or bored. You can avoid such inconsistencies in several ways. First, instead of marking all the essay questions on one student's paper, score all the students' responses to one question before going on to the next question. Complete the scoring of one question during one marking period rather than in several. After you have completed all the papers on each question, check your consistency by again scoring the first few papers. If a student's first and second scores are the same, your scoring was probably consistent for all students. Noticeable inconsistencies in marking might indicate that your attitude, rather than the quality of students' work, determined test scores. If the scores are different, you should rescore the tests.

Besides attitude, the inclusion of too many quality categories for each component can lead to inconsistent scoring. For example, on the paragraph rating scale in Table 8.6, the topic, supporting, and concluding sentence components were each assigned a weighted score of eight. However, this value was created by breaking down each component into subcomponents, limiting the number of quality categories for each, and using a weighting factor to arrive at a score of eight. A teacher who decided that this was too much work might have developed the scale shown in Figure 8.4. Although it would take much less time to develop such a scale, the probability of the teacher's marking paragraphs inconsistently is considerably greater. It would be more dif-

FIGURE 8.4 Rating Scale

Component	Rating		
	Inadequate		Excellent
I. Topic Sentence	1 2 3 4 5 6 7 8		
II. Supporting Sentences	1 2 3 4 5 6 7 8		
III. Concluding Sentence	1 2 3 4 5 6 7 8		

ficult to identify distinct quality descriptors for all eight category numbers. It would also be more difficult to differentiate consistently between adjacent categories (e.g., determining when a student should receive a 3 instead of a 4 or a 6 instead of a 7). When inconsistencies are present, you might want to revise your rating scale besides using strategies to minimize potential attitude shifts before rescoring tests.

Scoring bias is another common problem. Some teachers give all the students high test scores regardless of quality. Others give all average or all very low marks. In your own marking, you should compare the range of scores you assign with the heterogeneity or homogeneity of the group. If you have a homogeneous group of students, a small range of high, average, or low scores may accurately reflect the quality of students' work. If you are assigning similar scores to a heterogeneous group, however, your marking may be biased.

Teachers' opinions of individual students can also bias their scoring. Teachers are often inclined to score particular students' papers more leniently than they score others, and disruptive or uncooperative students sometimes receive scores lower than they deserve. Students who are struggling can evoke a great deal of sympathy, and teachers who want to encourage their efforts may score these students' papers quite leniently. However you choose to justify unearned scores, keep in mind that they are, indeed, unearned.

Because teachers are often unaware of their bias, they may find it difficult to avoid. Test specialists recommend that teachers maintain objectivity by dissociating students' names from their responses. For example, you could instruct your students to put their names on the backs of their papers or you could cover their names with removable labels until you finished scoring the papers. Students could also write their names and an identifying number on a separate sheet of paper and indicate only the identifying number on their work. If you have difficulty scoring papers that do not identify the student, your impressions of students are probably influencing the way you score. If this is the case, you should keep in mind that you are scoring responses and not individuals.

A Grading Error

One common grading error is to count practice tests as posttests and include them in the term grade. This tends to happen more on essay and product development practice tests than on objective-style practice tests because of the time and effort required for essay and product tests by both the teacher and students. But the required effort is not what differentiates between practice exercises and posttests. The purposes of practice tests, regardless of the format, are to provide students with the opportunity to rehearse skills and to provide them with corrective feedback. Despite the degree of effort required, students' scores on essay and product development practice tests should not be considered when calculating term achievement grades.

SUMMARIZING TEST SCORES AND EVALUATING PROGRESS

The scores students receive on checklists and rating scales can help a teacher determine the quality of instruction. To pinpoint problems and instructional needs, however, you will require more detailed information than can be obtained by reviewing each student's scores separately. A summary of students' performance by component will help you analyze the data efficiently.

Summarizing Test Data

Table 8.8 shows a class performance form with all the students' scores listed by component. Students' names are listed in the left-hand column and the evaluation criteria appear across the top. The students' scores on each component have been entered in the appropriate cells. The far right-hand column records students' total scores on the test. With the data thus arranged, you can summarize the group's performance for each quality category within a component. One summary method is illustrated in Table 8.9. The components are listed in the left-hand column and the categories for each component appear across the top. Empty cells indicate categories not used on the rating

TABLE 8.8   Class Performance on the Paragraph Test

Students	I Indented	II Topic Sentence		III Supporting Sentences			IV Concluding Sentence		Total Points
		Content	*Loc.*	*Rel.*	*Seq.*	*Trans.*	*Content*	*Loc.*	*(17)*
Baker	1	2	2	3	2	1	2	1	14
Brown	1	2	2	3	3	1	0	0	12
Egan	1	1	2	2	1	1	1	1	10
Ford	1	0	0	2	1	1	2	1	8
Graham	1	2	2	3	2	1	2	2	15
Little	1	1	1	1	1	2	0	0	7
Martinez	1	2	2	3	1	0	1	2	12
Smith	1	0	0	1	1	0	0	0	3
Taylor	1	2	2	3	3	2	2	2	17
Williams	1	2	1	1	1	1	2	2	11

form. To complete this table, the teacher would refer to the class performance form, count the students who received each rating, and record that number in the appropriate cell. With this summary, the teacher can then assess the effectiveness of instruction for each component.

A teacher looking at the summary in Table 8.9 sees that all students indented their paragraphs properly. Most students remembered to include both a topic and a concluding sentence. The numbers for the third component, supporting sentences, indicate a problem. Although most students included relevant material in their paragraphs, eight of ten students did not properly sequence their sentences. Likewise, only two of the ten students effectively used transition words. Obviously, the instruction on sequencing sentences and using transition words was not as effective as it could have been.

TABLE 8.9   Summary of Students Receiving Each Rating

Class Second Period   Date of Test 10–15   Number of Students 10

Component		Rating Categories				Total Students
		0	1	2	3	
I. Indentation			10			10
II. Topic	A. Content	2	2	6		10
Sentence	B. Location	2	2	6		10
III. Supporting	A. Relevance		3	2	5	10
Sentences	B. Sequence		6	2	2	10
	C. Transition	2	6	2		10
IV. Concluding	A. Content	3	2	5		10
Sentence	B. Location	3	3	4		10

A class summary form like the one in Table 8.9 can also help a teacher detect problems with the rating scale. Blank cells on a completed form may indicate that one or two components had too many rating categories. Blanks might also mean that, on that particular occasion, no one submitted work that deserved those ratings. In using your own summary forms, note blank cells and check students' performances on subsequent tests. If you never use a particular rating, you should either redefine or remove it.

Evaluating Progress

Teachers can also summarize performance data across tests to evaluate students' progress over a period of time and to judge the effectiveness of instruction and review activities. Students' skills in the same area are often measured using pretests, practice tests, and posttests, and data can be summarized across all measures to observe progress over time. Language arts is one subject in which teachers administer a series of posttests to measure progress on the same skills, such as writing sentences, paragraphs, and themes.

Table 8.10 presents a class progress form for the paragraph skills already described. The components are again listed in the left-hand column, the rating

TABLE 8.10 Class Progress Form

Class _____ Number of Students _____

Components	Dates Tested	Rating 0	1	2	3
I. Indentation	10–15		10	____	____
	10–22		10	____	____
	10–29		10	____	____
	11–5		10	____	____
II. Topic Sentence					
A. Content	10–15	2	2	6	____
	10–22	1	2	7	____
	10–29		3	7	____
	11–5		2	8	____
B. Location	10–15	2	2	6	____
	10–22		1	9	____
	10–29			10	____
	11–5			10	____
III. Supporting Sentences					
A. Relevance	10–15	____	3	2	5
	10–22	____	1	4	5
	10–29	____		4	6
	11–5	____		2	8
B. Sequence	10–15	____	6	2	2
	10–22	____	7	2	1
	10–29	____	2	6	2
	11–5	____	1	4	5
C. Transition	10–15	2	6	2	____
	10–22	5	1	4	____
	10–29	1	3	6	____
	11–5	1	2	7	____
IV. Concluding Sentences					
A. Content	10–15	3	2	5	____
	10–22	3	3	4	____
	10–29	3	3	4	____
	11–5		3	7	____
B. Location	10–15	3	3	4	____
	10–22	3	4	3	____
	10–29	3	3	4	____
	11–5		2	8	____

categories appear across the top, and unused values boxes contain a short horizontal line. Four different testing dates appear beside each component to indicate that students wrote paragraphs on October 15, 22, 29, and November 5. The data for component I show that all ten students received the total possible points on all four tests. After the first test, the lessons emphasized quality in topic sentences, with a resulting improvement of performance on the second test. This time, all ten students included a topic sentence, and only one student's sentence was too specific. Their skill in placing topic sentences also improved.

In writing supporting and concluding sentences, the students' skills changed very little. After the second test, the teacher emphasized supporting sentences and transition words. On the third test, the students kept their level of performance on topic sentences and wrote better supporting sentences. Their concluding sentences received ratings similar to those on the first two tests. After the third test, the teacher focused on summarizing ideas and on writing concluding sentences. The data for test four show that students improved their skills for this component. Even though many students still did not write perfect paragraphs after the fourth week, the teacher's data indicate that the lessons on paragraph writing were effective.

USING PRODUCT RATING FORMS AS AN INSTRUCTIONAL TOOL

Used as self-assessment tools, rating scales and checklists can help students identify and use appropriate criteria for developing their responses. During practice exercises, they can use an evaluation form to rate the quality of their work and to compare their ratings with yours. You can then discuss differences in ratings with students who have difficulty finding problems in their work. Students can also use the rating forms to evaluate example answers and products that you provide. They can discuss similarities and differences among their evaluations and between theirs and yours. Using the criteria when developing their responses for practice exercises and when reviewing work samples will help students focus on the important aspects of a skill. Such involvement should help them not only produce better work, but also feel a greater sense of responsibility for the quality of their work and the scores they receive.

SUMMARY

Essay tests and product development tests measure students' skills in producing original responses. Essay questions can ask students to discuss, explain, analyze, summarize, or evaluate something. Product development tests can be used to measure students' skill in producing a variety of verbal products, such as paragraphs, book reports, and themes. Product tests can also be used to measure students' skill in creating such objects as mobiles, photographs, and maps.

Essay and product tests allow students to select their approach to a given problem, the information they will include, and the methods of organization and presentation they will use. (Such skills cannot be measured using objective tests.) These tests enable a teacher to determine both what and how students think. Test drawbacks include the time required to develop, analyze, and score them; difficulties in scoring responses consistently and without bias; and the advantage essay tests give to students with well-developed verbal skills.

The procedure for developing and using essay and product development tests consists of four phases: (1) writing questions and directions; (2) developing scoring procedures; (3) scoring students' responses; and (4) summarizing group performance.

The criteria for developing valid and reliable test items also apply to essay questions and directions for products. The behavior, content, and conditions included should match those in the objectives; the complexity, context, and vocabulary should be appropriate for students; and grammar, punctuation, and sentence structure should be correct. Good questions and directions also provide adequate guidance for responding. Questions and directions that provide little guidance require students to exercise considerable judgment in responding. A lot of guidance guarantees that students will address specific issues, but it also limits the approaches they can take. Considering the main purpose for your test and the skill level of students will help you select an appropriate amount of guidance.

Besides describing the task to be performed, you should provide information that can help students determine the scope of the anticipated responses. You might want to include such information as how long their response should be, the amount of time they should spend, and the number of points each question or section is worth. Developing an evaluation form before administer-

ing the test will help you evaluate the clarity and feasibility of your questions or directions.

Essay and product development tests can be scored using either global or analytical scoring methods. Global scoring provides information on the overall quality of students' responses. Analytical scoring provides information on the quality of specific components and subcomponents of a response. Although analytical scoring is more time consuming than is global scoring, it provides students with better feedback and teachers with specific information they can use to analyze and evaluate the quality of instruction.

Analytical scoring requires the use of either a checklist or rating scale. Both should list the components and, if needed, the subcomponents of a skill to direct your attention to particular aspects of a response. The components and subcomponents should be taken directly from the enabling and prerequisite skills in the instructional goal framework. A checklist allows you to mark the presence or absence of a component, whereas a rating scale enables you to differentiate various quality categories for each component using a scale. The number of quality categories included on the scale should not exceed the number you can consistently judge. Verbal descriptors should be written for each quality category. Once the checklist or rating scale is designed, review the number of points allocated to each component. If the value assigned does not contribute an appropriate amount to the total score, use weighting schemes to adjust the relative value of components.

When the evaluation form is complete, review the questions and directions to ensure that they provide students with the guidance necessary to produce the responses you anticipate. At this point, revisions can be made in the questions, directions, or evaluation form as needed. After the test is administered, the rating form should again be evaluated using a few tests. Determine whether the components listed are observable in students' responses; whether they are sequenced in the most efficient order on the form; and whether you can score responses consistently. Make necessary revisions before beginning to score students' work.

Teachers experience two problems when rating students' responses: inconsistent scoring and bias. Inconsistent scoring can be caused by shifts in attitude that may lead to stricter or more lenient scoring. It can also result when you include more categories of quality for each component than you can consistently judge or use vague descriptors for each category. Bias results from marking all students as good, average, or poor regardless of the quality of their work. Bias also results when you consider not only the nature of the response, but also the characteristics of the student who made the response. After scoring all papers, rescore the first two or three to see whether you were consistent. Also check to see whether the range of scores assigned is reasonable given the heterogeneity or homogeneity of the group. If inconsistency or bias is detectable, you should rescore the papers.

Information about a group's test performance can help you evaluate the instruction students received. After scoring is completed, make a table to summarize students' scores by component and subcomponent. Areas of poor performance will become obvious, and instruction for related components can be reviewed and revised. When multiple tests are administered to measure the same skills, make a table to summarize students' scores across measures. Such summaries enable you to monitor the group's progress.

PRACTICE EXERCISES

1. Which of the following skills could be measured only with essay or product development tests?
   a. Recall verbal information
   b. Design a solution to a problem
   c. Discriminate among examples and nonexamples of a concept
   d. Use a rule to solve a problem
   e. Decide how two or more things should be compared and make the comparisons
   f. Evaluate a rule, a principle, an object, or a product
   g. Synthesize facts and information
   h. Organize facts and information
   i. Follow rules to produce an original piece of work
   j. Recall, select, organize, and present information
2. Table 8.11 summarizes information and rules for outlining a passage. Use the table to:
   a. Write instructions for a test that measures students' skills in outlining given passages. Assume that the given passages each have three main topics, three secondary ideas, and no level-three or level-four ideas.
   b. Develop an evaluation form for scoring students' outlines. (See Table 8.15 in the Feedback section.)
   c. Develop a class performance form that includes each student's rating on each component listed on your rating scale. (See the top part of Table 8.12 for feedback.)
   d. Develop a class summary form that can be used to summarize the number of students who received each rating. (See the bottom part of Table 8.12 for feedback.)
3. Summarize the class performance data in Table 8.12.
   a. Count the students who received each rating and record the number on the summary form at the bottom of the table. (See Table 8.16 in the Feedback section.)
   b. Review your completed summary form and identify the components that require more instruction.

TABLE 8.11 **Information and Rules for the Instructional Goal "Outline a Passage"**

Components	Define Levels	Paraphrase Entries	Sequence Entries within Level	Label Entries	Align Entries in Outline
Main topics	Define main topics as key main ideas in total passage.	Use sentence or topic outline. Do not mix sentences and phrases in one outline.	Place entries in order defined by passage.	Use Roman numerals to label main ideas.	Place all main topics flush with left margin.
Secondary topics	Define secondary topics as key ideas within each main topic. There should be at least two entries.	Make all entries within a main topic parallel in structure. Structure may differ from that of main topics and from that of secondary topics for other main ideas.	Place secondary topics in order defined by passage.	Use capital letters to label secondary topics.	Indent secondary entries five spaces from left margin and align.
Level-three topics	Define level-three topics as key ideas within each secondary level topic. There should be at least two entries.	Make all entries within a secondary level topic parallel.	Place level-three topics in order defined by passage.	Label level-three topics with Arabic numerals.	Indent all level-three topics ten spaces from left margin and align.
Level-four topics	Define level-four topics as key ideas within each level-three topic. There should be at least two entries.	Make all entries within a level-three topic parallel.	Place level-four topics in order defined by passage.	Label level-four topics with lower case letters.	Indent all level-four topics fifteen spaces from left margin and align.

4. Score the three paragraphs entitled "Washing a Dog" in Table 8.13 using the paragraph rating form in Table 8.14. Assume the paragraphs were written by sixth-grade students. Record your scores for each paragraph on a separate sheet. When you have finished:
   a. Compare the scores you assigned with those of classmates.
   b. Discuss inconsistencies and try to determine why the scores were different.
   c. If you attribute differences to inadequacies in the rating scale, suggest ways to improve the form.
   d. Compare your scores to those in Table 8.17 (in Feedback section) that reflect the judgment of another rater.

Enrichment

5. Select a skill from your own field that can only be measured with an essay or product development test and do the following:

TABLE 8.12   Class Performance and Performance Summary Forms for the Outline Test

I. Class Performance Form

Students	Main Ideas						Secondary Ideas							Total Score
	A	B	C	D	E	F	A	B	C	D	E	F	G	
Allen	3	2	1	2	2	2	3	3	2	1	2	2	2	27
Baker	1	2	1	2	2	2	1	2	2	1	2	2	2	22
Carter	1	2	1	2	2	2	1	2	2	1	2	2	2	22
Doyle	2	2	1	2	2	2	1	2	2	1	2	2	2	23
Egan	3	2	1	2	2	2	3	3	2	1	2	2	2	27
Frank	1	1	1	1	2	2	1	1	1	1	1	2	2	17
Garcia	3	1	1	2	2	2	3	3	1	1	2	2	2	25
Howe	1	1	1	2	2	2	2	2	1	1	2	2	2	21
Jackson	3	2	1	2	2	2	3	2	2	1	2	2	2	26
Little	3	2	1	2	2	2	3	1	2	1	2	2	2	25

II. Class Summary Form

Class _____   Date _____   Number of Students _____

	Rating Categories				Total Students
	0	1	2	3	
I. Main Ideas					
A. Main ideas identified	—				
B. Clearly paraphrased	—				
C. Parallel structure	—				
D. Consistent order	—				
E. Consistent labels	—			—	
F. Alignment	—			—	
II. Secondary Ideas					
A. Secondary ideas identified	—				
B. Related to main ideas	—				
C. Clearly paraphrased	—				
D. Parallel structure	—				
E. Consistent order	—				
F. Consistent labels	—		—		
G. Alignment				—	

a. Analyze the skill to identify its subordinate skills and create a goal framework that illustrates the relationship among the skills.
b. Write a behavioral objective for the skill; be sure to include relevant conditions.
c. Write an essay question or questions or the instructions for product development. Include adequate guidance for the skill being measured and for the sophistication of target students.
d. Develop a scoring checklist or rating scale.
e. If you have students' work available, score their work using your form.
f. Revise the rating form if necessary.
g. Develop a class performance form and summary form that will illustrate students' performance on each component of the test.

FEEDBACK

1. b, e, i, j
2. a. Instructions for a test of outlining skills.
   Example 1
   Read the article titled _____ . Make a <u>topic</u> outline of the information in the article. You have 20 minutes to complete the task.
   Example 2
   Make a <u>sentence</u> outline of the information in the article entitled _____ . You have 30 minutes to complete the following:
   1. Read the article.
   2. Review the rating form attached to the article that will be used to score your outline.
   3. Select and organize the information you think should be included.
   4. Write your outline.
   5. Use the rating form to:
      a. review your outline and <u>correct</u> any problems you find.
      b. <u>score</u> your outline.
   6. Turn in both your outline and your completed rating form when you have finished.
   b. See Table 8.15.
   c. See the top part of Table 8.12 (in Practice Exercises).
   d. See the bottom part of Table 8.12 (in Practice Exercises).
3. a. See Table 8.16.
   b. You may have concluded that:
      1. Approximately half the class had difficulty differentiating between main and secondary ideas. Thus, you need to provide more instruction on the levels of ideas.
      2. All students had problems with parallel structure. They need more instruction on constructing parallel entries.
      3. Eight students had problems relating secondary ideas to the main idea. They need additional instruction in sorting secondary ideas by topic.
      4. Three students need more instruction on paraphrasing ideas for a topic outline.
4. Compare your scores with those of classmates and students included in Table 8.17.

TABLE 8.13　Three Paragraphs Entitled "Washing a Dog"

Paragraph 1

One of my chors on Saturday is to wash my dog Rover. I use warm water to get him wet all over. Then I rub him with a special soap that doesn't hurt his eyes and keeps his coat glossie. When he is clean, I rinse him twice to make sure all the soap is gone. After he shakes off most of the water, I rub him with a clean old towel. He thinks I do a good job.

Paragraph 2

Put a wash tub in the yard. Fill it with water and sope. Put the dog in the tub. Scrub the dog. Rinse the dog with a hose. Stand back when the dog gets out of the tub.

Paragraph 3

My dog hates to get a bath. When anyone gets out the tub she runs and hides. It is easy to find her because she always hides in the same place. You have to hold her the whole time or she will run away again. She shivers and barks the whole time. My cousin's dog likes to get a bath.

TABLE 8.14   Rating Scale for Evaluating Paragraphs

Components			
I. Indentation	Not Indented 0	Clearly Indented 1	
II. Topic Sentence			
A. Quality	Not Present 0	Vague 1	Clearly Introduces Topic 2
B. Location	Not Present 0	Misplaced 1	Logically Placed 2
III. Supporting Sentences			
A. Content	Some Irrelevant Information 1	All Relevant Information 2	Thoroughly Develops Topic 3
B. Sequence	Illogical Order 1	Some Order 2	Logical Order 3
C. Transition	No Transition 0	Some Transition 1	Smooth Transition 2
IV. Concluding Sentence			
A. Content	Not Present 0	Not Comprehensive 1	Clearly Summarizes Topic 2
B. Location	Not Present 0	Misplaced 1	Logically Placed 2

TABLE 8.15   **Rating Scale for Evaluating Outlines**

Name _____ Date _____ Score _____

                                                  Total   (35)

I. Main ideas

A. Main ideas identified	Secondary ideas included 1	Some ideas missing 2	All main ideas included 3
B. Clearly paraphrased	Some meaning changed 1	Too brief/ wordy 2	Clearly paraphrased 3
C. Parallel structure	Mixed sentence/ phrase 1	All sentences or phrases 2	Consistent word format 3
D. Consistent order	Out of order 1	Most in order 2	All in order 3
E. Consistent labels	Inconsistent 1	Consistent 2	
F. Alignment	Flush with left margin 1	Aligned 2	

II. Secondary ideas

A. Secondary ideas identified	Main ideas included 1	Some ideas missing 2	All secondary ideas included 3
B. Related to main idea	Scrambled placement 1	Most within right topic 2	All within right topic 3
C. Clearly paraphrased	Some meaning changed 1	Too brief/ wordy 2	Clearly paraphrased 3
D. Parallel structure	Mixed sentence/ phrase/word 1	All sentences, phrases, or words 2	Consistent word format 3
E. Consistent order	Out of order 1	Most in order 2	All in order 3
F. Consistent labels	Inconsistent 1	Consistent 2	
G. Alignment	Not indented 0	Indented five spaces 1	Aligned 2

TABLE 8.16 Class Summary Form for Outline Test

Class _____ Date _____ Number of Students _____

Component	0	1	2	3
I. Main ideas				
A. Main ideas identified	——	4	1	5
B. Clearly paraphrased	——	3	7	
C. Parallel structure	——	10		
D. Consistent order	——	1	9	
E. Consistent labels	——		10	——
F. Alignment	——		10	——
II. Secondary ideas				
A. Secondary ideas identified	——	4	1	5
B. Related to main idea	——	2	5	3
C. Clearly paraphrased	——	3	7	
D. Parallel structure	——	10		
E. Consistent order	——	1	9	
F. Consistent labels	——		10	——
G. Alignment	——		10	——

TABLE 8.17 Completed Ratings for Paragraphs Entitled "Washing a Dog"

Components				Parag. 1	Parag. 2	Parag. 3
I. Indentation	Not Indented 0	Clearly Indented 1		1	0	0
II. Topic Sentence						
A. Quality	Not Present 0	Vague 1	Clearly Introduces Topic 2	2	0	2
B. Location	Not Present 0	Misplaced 1	Logically Placed 2	2	0	2
III. Supporting Sentences						
A. Content	Some Irrelevant Information 1	All Relevant Information 2	Thoroughly Develops Topic 3	3	3	1
B. Sequence	Illogical Order 1	Some Order 2	Logical Order 3	3	3	2
C. Transition	No Transition 0	Some Transition 1	Smooth Transition 2	2	0	1

TABLE 8.17 (*continued*)

				Parag. 1	Parag. 2	Parag. 3
Components					Scores	
IV. Concluding Sentence						
A. Content	Not Present 0	Not Comprehensive 1	Clearly Summarizes Topic 2	2	0	0
B. Location	Not Present 0	Misplaced 1	Logically Placed 2	2	0	0
			Total Score (Out of 18)	17	6	8

SUGGESTED READING

Ebel, R. L., and Frisbie, D. A. (1986). *Essentials of educational measurement.* Englewood Cliffs, N.J.: Prentice-Hall, pp. 126–36.

Gronlund, N. E. (1985). *Measurement and evaluation in teaching.* New York: Macmillan Publishing Company, pp. 213–28, 383–405.

Mehrens, W. A., and Lehmann, I. J. (1984). *Measurement and evaluation in education and psychology.* New York: CBS College Publishing, pp. 94–124, 203–10.

Nitko, A. J. (1983). *Educational tests and measurement.* New York: Harcourt, Brace, Jovanovich, pp. 141–55, 243–79.

Popham, W. J. (1981). *Modern educational measurement.* Englewood Cliffs, N.J.: Prentice-Hall, pp. 274–84, 309–27.

CHAPTER 9

Rating Student Performance, Attitudes, and Behavior

OBJECTIVES

1. Write instructions for a performance test.
2. Select, paraphrase, and sequence the components to be observed.
3. Develop a rating form and evaluation procedures.
4. Describe procedures for formatively evaluating instructions and rating forms.
5. Rate students' performance.
6. Summarize group performance.
7. Define the attitudes to be evaluated.
8. Select behaviors that reflect these attitudes.
9. Develop a rating form and evaluation procedures.
10. Describe procedures for rating students' behavior.
11. Convert scores into report card categories.
12. Summarize group attitudes and behaviors.

Many skills students learn in school involve some type of performance, such as delivering an oral report, driving a car, changing a tire, operating audio-visual equipment, and performing athletic skills. Teachers can measure and assign grades to these performances just as they do for the skills measured by objective, essay, and product development tests. At the same time, a school district may also want teachers to evaluate particular attitudes students have. For example, many districts have report cards with sections for rating classroom conduct, citizenship, and attitudes toward learning. The procedure teachers use to evaluate students' performance, attitudes, and behavior is similar to that for developing and scoring essay exams and products. Teachers should (1) define and analyze the expected performance, attitude, or behavior; (2) select evaluation criteria; (3) develop an evaluation form and procedures; (4) formatively evaluate the form and procedures; (5) observe and rate students' performances or behaviors; and (6) summarize group performance and behaviors to identify areas requiring additional instruction.

There are important differences in the procedures for evaluating products and performances. One is the timing of the observations and ratings. To evaluate performance, a teacher must observe and score students while they perform. Because students are usually tested individually, considerable class time must be reserved for performance and observation. Another difference is that the teacher always knows the identity of each student evaluated; thus, avoiding rater bias is more difficult. Another critical difference is that no tangible product remains for reconsideration and feedback unless the performance is videotaped. This means that judgments must be quick and that there is usually nothing except the rating form to show students. Finally, the speed with which some skills are performed restricts the time for observation and detailed analysis of components and subcomponents. This means that evaluation forms must be concise, components must be carefully ordered and easy to find, and score marking must be easy.

Rating attitudes and behaviors can be much more difficult than judging essay tests and products. Attitudes and behaviors, such as the attitudes toward learning and classroom conduct, are abstract and difficult to define. In judging a skill, a teacher has to make very few syntheses and inferences. When judging attitudes and behavior, however, a teacher must classify individual instances of behavior over time and synthesize them into a general impression of the underlying attitude. These actions often require inferences about intentions and motives, which is very difficult. The same action or statement can be interpreted many different ways, depending on the context, tone of voice, facial expression, or physical mannerism accompanying the behavior. Because human social behavior is interactive, a teacher must be aware of the effects that the actions and reactions of other group members can have on individual students. Teachers should also have some sense of how their own attitudes and behaviors influence those of students.

The following sections describe general procedures for measuring students' performance, attitudes, and behaviors. The particular steps you take as a teacher will depend on the content of your instruction, your classroom environment, and the characteristics of your students.

MEASURING PERFORMANCE

Performance tests measure skills that require some type of action. They enable teachers to analyze students' performances and to comment on such aspects as timing, speed, precision, sequence, and appearance. Like other types of tests, they provide a basis for evaluating the quality of instruction for separate aspects of the skill. For outgoing students, they are also motivational. Some students enjoy the opportunity to demonstrate their skill for the teacher and their classmates.

At the same time, performance tests have their disadvantages. First, because individuals must be evaluated separately, they are time consuming. Second, teachers have to observe closely because important aspects of the performance may be rapid and difficult to see. Asking students to repeat a performance because something was missed may affect their performance negatively. Third, some students become extremely self-conscious and uncomfortable when they are asked to perform in front of the teacher or the group. If a teacher is not sensitive to the needs and feelings of these students, performance tests might actually inhibit learning and reduce the quality of performance. Finally, a teacher must have excellent classroom management skills in order to (1) maintain a positive atmosphere for the performing student; (2) keep other students engaged in some activity; and (3) focus attention on the performing student. In spite of these limitations, performance tests are the most appropriate method for measuring skills that require action.

Writing Instructions for Performance Tests

Before students are tested, they should understand exactly what they are to do and how they are to do it. Written directions ensure that each student receives the same information, which should include any special conditions of the performance. The suggestions for writing objective, essay, and product development tests are also appropriate for performance tests. The task described should match the behavior, content, and conditions in the objective. Language should be clear and precise, and the vocabulary should be appropriate for target students. It is especially important on performance tests to ensure that (1) the skill is not too complex for target students and (2) the conditions of performance are the same for all students.

After students have read the instructions, they should be allowed to discuss them and ask questions. During discussion, the teacher can clarify the task and correct misunderstandings for the entire group. The teacher can also explain what the students are to do and how they are to behave while individuals are being tested.

The requirement that a skill be tested in a novel or unfamiliar context does not apply to all performance tests. Many performance tests require students to demonstrate the skills in the same sequence and with the same equipment they used during instruction and rehearsal. Obviously, a student who has learned to drive a car with an automatic transmission should not be evaluated on the ability to drive a car with a standard transmission. For students' performance to be a valid indication of their skill, the testing situation should require the same equipment, content, sequence, and conditions as in the instruction.

Selecting and Organizing the Components to Observe

Many of the same procedures for developing essay- or product-rating forms can also be used to develop performance-rating forms. With performance tests, however, you must be especially careful in selecting the components.

The following seven steps are recommended for selecting, sequencing, and paraphrasing the components.

1. Develop an instructional goal framework of the enabling skills and their sequence.
2. Select from the framework the skills you believe will be observable.
3. List these observable skills in the order you believe they will occur.
4. Watch several students who are proficient in the skills and compare the skills on your list with those you are able to observe.
5. Eliminate skills you do not see and add any others you identify during the performance that are not contained on your list.
6. While the students are performing, check your sequence of components and reorder them if necessary.
7. After you have identified and sequenced the components, para-

TABLE 9.1   Behaviors to Evaluate during
Oral Presentation

I. Physical Expression
   A. Posture
   B. Movements and gestures
   C. Facial expression
   D. Eye contact
II. Vocal Expression
   A. Calmness
   B. Intonation
   C. Volume
   D. Speed
   E. Enunciation
III. Verbal Expression
   A. Word flow
   B. Word choice
   C. Repetition
   D. Complete thoughts and ideas
   E. Organization

phrase your verbal descriptions of each component into one or two key words.

The list of behaviors in Table 9.1 and the instructional goal framework in Figure 9.1 show how one teacher identified, sequenced, and paraphrased the components to be judged for the instructional goal "Makes an oral presentation." Notice that the teacher selected only observable skills from the framework. Because the skills had no inherent order, the teacher decided on a sequence that would permit efficient observation.

Paraphrasing is an important aspect of writing component descriptors. Notice that in Table 9.1 each component is paraphrased using only one or

FIGURE 9.1   Framework of Enabling Skills for the Goal "Make an Oral Presentation"

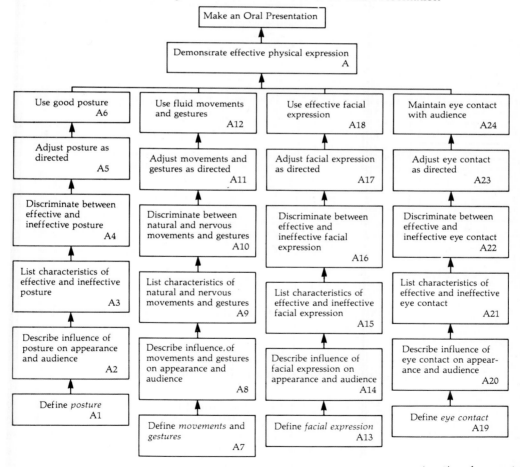

(continued on next page)

FIGURE 9.1 *(continued)*

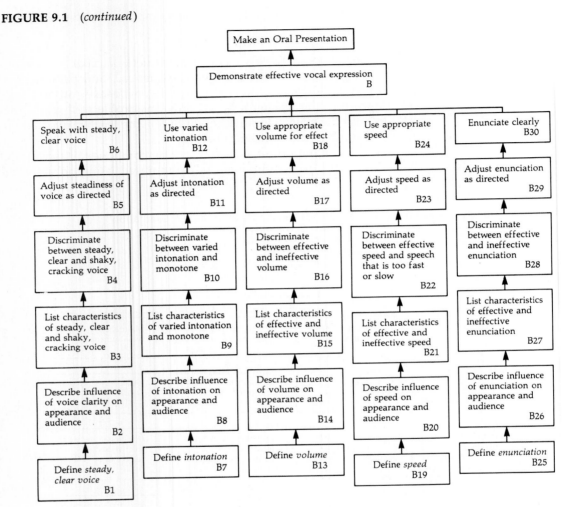

two words. This minimizes the amount of reading required during the students' performance.

Developing a Rating Form and Evaluation Procedures

Although you may choose to use either global or analytical scoring methods, analytical scoring is preferable. It is especially helpful for performance tests because they usually do not have a tangible product to mark and return to students. Analytical scoring enables you to focus on separate aspects of the performances and gather information needed to evaluate the instruction and

FIGURE 9.1   (*continued*)

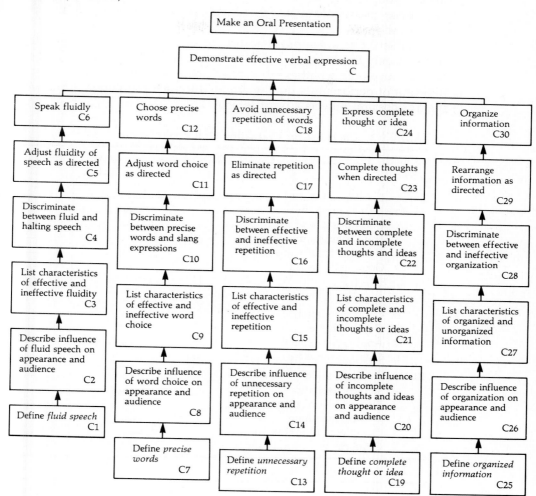

help students understand their scores. You can use a checklist, a rating scale, or a form that combines the two. The form you develop depends on the type of performance you are observing.

To begin, identify a feasible number of quality categories for each component. If an action cannot be broken down into levels of quality, use a checklist that indicates only its presence or absence. On the other hand, if it is possible to distinguish levels of quality for some or all of the components in the time available, the use of a rating scale will provide better information. The quality categories should represent low-to-high levels of proficiency. For each category, write a descriptor of the characteristics used to classify an action. The more carefully you select and describe the categories, the more reliable your ratings will be. Assign a score to each category, with low numbers representing low quality and high numbers representing high performance levels.

Table 9.2 is a sample checklist for evaluating an oral presentation. It contains only two rating categories, No and Yes. A teacher using this format would judge only whether the defined action was acceptable. Notice that an indicator of performance quality is added to each component; thus, checking the Yes column reflects a positive score.

TABLE 9.2   Checklist for Evaluating Oral Presentations

Name _____ Date _____	Score _____	
	Total	(14)
Criteria	No	Yes
I. Physical Expression		
A. Good posture	____	____
B. Fluid, natural movements	____	____
C. Effective facial expression	____	____
D. Good eye contact	____	____
II. Vocal Expression	No	Yes
A. Calm voice	____	____
B. Good intonation	____	____
C. Good volume	____	____
D. Appropriate speed	____	____
E. Clearly enunciates	____	____
III. Verbal Expression	No	Yes
A. Avoids hesitation	____	____
B. Effective word choice	____	____
C. Avoids repetition	____	____
D. Completes thoughts and ideas	____	____
E. Good organization of ideas	____	____
	Total Score	____

One caution is in order. Only positive descriptors should be used with a checklist because mixing positive and negative descriptors will result in an uninterpretable score. Consider the meaning of a score of 2 in the following example:

	(0) No	(1) Yes
A. Good posture	____	✓
B. Awkward movements	____	✓
Total		2

Checking Yes for the presence of each action results in a score that reflects good posture as well as awkward movements. Because a high score is meant to reflect only positive performance, each action should be stated positively. If the second criterion were restated as Fluid movements, a Yes rating would reflect a positive performance for that criterion as well. If you need to rate distracting behaviors, such as lengthy pauses and hesitations or the overuse of certain words, the word *avoids* can be added to these components to make a Yes rating a positive score. A student demonstrating all fourteen behaviors on the checklist would receive a total score of 14 on the test.

Table 9.3 illustrates a rating scale for an oral presentation. The components are listed in the left column and all quality categories are included in the right columns. Four general quality levels are used to rate all fourteen components. The lowest rating is Distracting, which would indicate negative actions for the component. The second category, Sometimes Effective, would be used to score an action that was sometimes distracting and sometimes acceptable. The third category, Generally Effective, indicates that no distracting actions were observed and that the student was consistent in demonstrating the behavior. The fourth category, Very Effective, would be used for students who consistently demonstrated the skill in an effective, polished manner. As students are observed, the assigned rating can be circled. The student's total score could then be obtained by summing the circled numbers.

TABLE 9.3 Rating Scale for Oral Presentations

Name _____ Date _____ Score _____

Total (56)

Component	Distracting 1	Sometimes Effective 2	Generally Effective 3	Very Effective 4
I. Physical Expression				
A. Posture	1	2	3	4
B. Movements/gestures	1	2	3	4
C. Facial expression	1	2	3	4
D. Eye contact	1	2	3	4
II. Vocal Expression				
A. Calmness	1	2	3	4
B. Intonation	1	2	3	4
C. Volume	1	2	3	4
D. Speed	1	2	3	4
E. Enunciation	1	2	3	4
III. Verbal Expression				
A. Word flow	1	2	3	4
B. Word choice	1	2	3	4
C. Repetition	1	2	3	4
D. Thoughts/ideas complete	1	2	3	4
E. Ideas organized	1	2	3	4

A student who received a perfect rating in all fourteen components would earn a total score of 56 points.

If the general categories of quality included in the rating scale in Table 9.3 were not adequate to express the reasons for rating a particular component as distracting or effective, the rating scale could be expanded to allow for additional quality descriptors. For example, the facial expression component could be expanded to differentiate among different types of facial expressions. Such expressions as boredom, lack of expression, frowning, and nervousness could be distracting. In actuality, a student may exhibit one of these negative expressions but not others.

The expanded rating scale in Table 9.4 enables you to differentiate among different types of facial expressions and better explain why students received a low rating in this area. The components are listed in the far left column. Negative and positive descriptions of expression border each end of

TABLE 9.4 Expanded Rating Scale for Oral Presentations

Name _____ Date _____ Score _____
                                                            Total   (60)

		Rating			
	Negative Quality	Distracting	Sometimes Effective	Very Effective	Positive Quality
I. Physical Expression					
A. Posture	1. Slouched	1	2	3	Straight
	2. Awkward	1	2	3	Relaxed
B. Movements/ Gestures	1. Hands trembling	1	2	3	Hands steady
	2. Awkward gestures	1	2	3	Fluid gestures
C. Facial Expression	1. Bored	1	2	3	Interested
	2. Unexpressive	1	2	3	Animated
	3. Frowning	1	2	3	Pleasant
	4. Nervous	1	2	3	Relaxed
D. Eye Contact	1. With few people	1	2	3	With many people
	2. Reading notes	1	2	3	Looks at audience
II. Vocal Expression	A. Wavering/cracking	1	2	3	Steady/calm
	B. Monotonous	1	2	3	Varied
	C. Too loud/quiet	1	2	3	Natural
	D. Too rapid/slow	1	2	3	Natural
	E. Poorly enunciated	1	2	3	Enunciated well
III. Verbal Expression	A. Long pauses	1	2	3	Fluid
	B. Slang expressions	1	2	3	Precise vocabulary
	C. Needless repetition	1	2	3	Effective/varied
	D. Incomplete thoughts	1	2	3	Complete thoughts
	E. Poorly organized	1	2	3	Well organized

the rating scale. Negative descriptors are listed down the left side beside low ratings, and positive ones are listed in the far right column beside high ratings. The ratings of Distracting, Sometimes Effective, and Very Effective are positioned in the middle columns. Such a scale would help you be more precise in marking your ratings and in communicating the meaning of each rating to students. Be careful, however, not to create a scale with so much detail that it is cumbersome to use while observing a student's performance. To use the rating scale, simply circle the rating desired and sum the circled numbers to obtain the total score for each student. A student who received the highest possible rating in each category would earn a total test score of 60 points.

As with rating scales for essay exams and product development tests, you should review the number of points each main component contributes to the total score. In Table 9.4, physical expression contributes 30 points (half of the total 60 points). Vocal expression and verbal expression each contribute 15 points (one-quarter of the total score). Should you wish to equalize the points each main component contributes, you would need to multiply the total for vocal expression and for verbal expression by a factor of two. Weighting the components equally would require the following steps:

Component	Score		Weight		Total
I. Physical expression	30	×	1	=	30
II. Vocal expression	15	×	2	=	30
III. Verbal expression	15	×	2	=	30
			Total Score		90

Formatively Evaluating Instructions and the Evaluation Form

You should not modify the instructions or the evaluation form for a performance test after the test begins. Certainly, you would not want to ask students to repeat a performance because the instructions were unclear or the evaluation form was cumbersome. To avoid an awkward situation, always evaluate and, if necessary, revise both the instructions and evaluation form you plan to use. One evaluation method is to observe students informally as they practice their skills. The information you gather during their rehearsals will help you modify both the assignment and the rating form.

A good place to begin the formative evaluation is with the task itself. Do the students' actions during rehearsal reflect an understanding of what they are to do? Are they able to demonstrate the desired actions in the time set aside for their evaluation? Can you observe and rate all the actions you have delineated? Are you able to differentiate all the quality categories you have included? Are the components in the best order? Answers to these questions will help you revise the form and estimate the amount of time needed to administer the test to all students.

Rating Students' Performance

Students who know they are being scored on a performance are bound to be influenced by the teacher's behaviors. Nonverbal expressions of anger, disappointment, displeasure, surprise, boredom, or fatigue will produce some type of reaction in students. Often, they will adjust their performance according to the behavioral clues they receive from you. Thus, as you evaluate students' performances, you should always appear positive, noncommittal, and interested in the task. Although you want students to perform well, you should also avoid verbal and nonverbal coaching during a performance. Such assistance, although appropriate during rehearsal, is not appropriate during a posttest.

Rating bias is especially problematic on performance tests. The limited time available for scoring each student's performance can contribute to rating patterns that are consistently generous, neutral, or critical on all components, even though the student was better in some areas than others. If you find that each student was rated consistently in all areas, it could reflect the presence of response bias. Being aware of this potential danger will help you differentiate the quality of different aspects of the performance.

Eliminating personal bias from scoring is also difficult because students' identities are not separated from their performance. Thus, a teacher's perception of individual students can influence ratings. Obviously, the more a teacher's biases affect students' scores, the more the validity of the test is threatened. You can help avoid this tricky problem by not forming expectations for each student's performance. Although easier said than done, you can try to find positive indicators in a typically weak student's performance and problems in a typically strong student's performance. If you only look for the type of performance you expect, your ratings may not accurately reflect the performance.

A final problem in performance tests is the tendency of students to demonstrate their skills inconsistently. In athletic skills, they may be inconsistent in their ability to serve a tennis ball, shoot baskets, pitch a softball, or execute a particular dive. When such skills are being measured, students can be given several opportunities during the test to perform the skill, and the final score can be determined not only by judging their form and execution each time, but also by judging the number of times they succeed in placing a serve or scoring a basket. Some teachers prefer to sum the total scores students receive on each trial and then determine an average score by dividing the sum by the number of trials. Inconsistencies also occur in other types of performances. For example, students delivering oral reports may initially demonstrate nervousness through trembling hands, looking only at their notes, and halting speech. However, as they continue their presentations, some may gain their composure, which will reduce or eliminate these types of behaviors. Others may begin in a composed manner and grow more nervous as they proceed. Inconsistent performance can be communicated to students using a rating category, such as Sometimes Effective or Inconsistent.

Summarizing Group Performance

The procedure for summarizing group performance is the same as that used for essay and product development tests. The purposes are also the same: to help the teacher evaluate the effectiveness of instruction and to determine whether additional instruction is needed for any component. Table 9.5 is a group performance summary form based on the rating scale in Table 9.3. You can use a blank copy of your rating scale to tally scores if there is enough space. If not, a separate form is easy enough to construct.

The summary form in Table 9.5 lists the behaviors in the far left column and the rating categories across the top. The class totals fifteen students, and the number of students who earned each rating is tallied in the cells. The teacher could infer from the data that the class needs more coaching and rehearsal in making oral presentations. Regarding physical expression, they especially need to work on eye contact. Speed seems to need the most work in their vocal expression, and in verbal expression, they need to work most

TABLE 9.5   Group Performance Summary Form for Oral Presentation Rating Scale in Table 9.3

	Distracting	Sometimes Effective	Generally Effective	Very Effective
I. Physical Expression				
A. Posture	111	11	卌	卌
B. Movements/gestures	11	1	1111	卌 111
C. Facial expression	111	11	1111	卌 1
D. Eye contact	卌 1	111	11	1111
II. Vocal Expression				
A. Calmness	1111	111	卌	111
B. Intonation	11	卌	1111	111
C. Volume	1		卌 111	卌 1
D. Speed	卌 1	111	11	1111
E. Enunciation	1111	11	11	卌 11
III. Verbal Expression				
A. Word flow	卌 1	卌	111	1
B. Word choice	1111	111	卌 1	11
C. Repetition	卌 111	11	1111	1
D. Thoughts/ideas complete	1111	1111	卌	11
E. Ideas organized	111	11	卌	卌

Note: This summary is based on fifteen students.

on unnecessary repetition. Data summaries like these permit you to identify problem areas and plan additional coaching and rehearsal.

MEASURING ATTITUDES AND CLASSROOM BEHAVIOR

In addition to measuring students' achievement of verbal information, intellectual skills, and motor skills, teachers are often expected to measure students' attitudes and classroom behavior. The report cards of many school districts have sections to record students' progress in such areas as citizenship, classroom conduct, and attitudes toward learning. Even though teachers often have difficulty defining attitudes and behavior that fit such categories, they should still attempt to do so. Chapter 3 presents Gagné's definition of an attitude and suggests procedures for analyzing an attitude's three components. Reviewing this and other information about the nature of attitudes should help you identify, evaluate, and report the attitudes and behaviors requested by your school district.

Defining the Attitudes to Be Evaluated

Because most curriculum guides focus on the achievement of verbal information, intellectual skills, and motor skills, they do not identify the student attitudes and behaviors that teachers may be asked to report. This information usually appears only on the school district's report card. Occasionally, related information will be included in a student or teacher handbook. Report cards typically indicate categories of attitudes to be rated, and the handbooks explain school policy and rules of student conduct. Some teachers add rules to those specified by the district to suit their subject area, classroom environment, and particular students.

Students to be rated on certain attitudes and behaviors need to understand the meaning of each category of behavior on a report card. Teachers required to judge attitudes and behaviors should define them for students and explain how the ratings will be done.

To define a district's affective goals to students and parents, a teacher must first understand the categories and have evaluation procedures already developed. The most appropriate place to begin is with the information on the report cards. Although report cards often vary from school to school, and typically from district to district, most list attitudes or behaviors on which students are to be rated. Consider the secondary-level report card shown in Table 9.6. In addition to grading achievement, teachers in this district are required to evaluate a student's citizenship, attitude toward learning, and study habits for each grading period. Teachers using such report cards must decide what attitudes and behaviors a mark in each category would reflect.

TABLE 9.6 **Secondary School Report Card for One Semester**

STUDENT PROGRESS REPORT

_____ _____ _____
(Name) (School District) (Year)

_____ _____
(School) (Home Room)

Course	Per	Teacher	Grading Period I					Grading Period II					Semester I	
			GRD	CIT	ATL	SH	ABS	GRD	CIT	ATL	SH	ABS	EX	SAG
	1													
	2													
	3													
	4													
	5													
	6													
	7													

Abbreviations _Grade Codes_

PER = Class period during day
GRD = Achievement grade
CIT = Citizenship
ATL = Attitude toward learning
SH = Study habits
ABS = Absences (frequency)
EX = Semester exam score
SAG = Semester average grade

A = Excellent (93–100%)
B = Good (85–92%)
C = Fair (77–84%)
D = Poor (69–76%)
F = Failure (68% and below)

I = Incomplete work
P = Pass
S = Satisfactory
N = Needs improvement
U = Unsatisfactory

Table 9.7 illustrates the behaviors that elementary-level teachers in two different school districts are expected to rate. Besides achievement grades in the subjects studied, teachers using report card A must comment on students' conduct, citizenship, and work habits. Rather than including just these general categories, Citizenship is divided into five specific behaviors that must be rated and Work Habits includes four separate categories. Teachers report students' progress in each area using the ratings of satisfactory, needs improvement, and unsatisfactory. Elementary report card B includes nine categories of behavior that are not organized according to areas. Similar to report card A, teachers use satisfactory, needs improvement, and unsatisfactory to rate each of the nine areas. A comparison of the nonachievement categories included on the secondary and two elementary examples shows that these

TABLE 9.7   Attitudes and Behaviors Rated on Two Elementary-Level Report Cards

Report Card A		Report Card B	
Attitude/Behavior	Rating	Attitude/Behavior	Rating
I. Conduct		1. Practices self-discipline	
II. Citizenship		2. Works independently	
A. Respects authority		3. Works well in group activities	
B. Uses self-control		4. Makes good use of time	
C. Respects property		5. Respects persons and property	
D. Respects others' rights		6. Is thoughtful and considerate	
E. Obeys school rules		7. Completes classroom assignments	
III. Work Habits		8. Completes homework assignments	
A. Listens attentively		9. Respects authority	
B. Works quietly			
C. Follows directions			
D. Completes assignments			

Scale:
S = Satisfactory
N = Needs improvement
U = Unsatisfactory

Scale:
S = Satisfactory
N = Needs improvement
U = Unsatisfactory

three school districts are interested in reporting similar types of behaviors to students and parents.

After you have reviewed the report card you will be using, you need to define the attitudes you have to rate and list the observable behaviors that reflect each attitude. For example, the secondary report card in Table 9.6 has one attitude category called Attitude Toward Learning and another called Study Habits. In what ways do students' attitudes toward learning differ from their study habits? Elementary report card A in Table 9.7 includes both Conduct and Citizenship. If you were using this report card, how would you distinguish between the two? As a teacher in this district, you would need to determine what these terms mean and how they relate to each other, to the subject taught, to the classroom environment, and to your students. Your interpretations will undoubtedly differ from those of other teachers due not only to the abstractness of the terms, but also to differences in students' ages, classroom environments, and subjects.

Consider, for example, one teacher's definitions of the following categories:

1. *Citizenship* is the social interactions students have with their peers and with their teacher. It includes their individual contributions to the classroom society.
2. *Conduct* relates to observing established school and classroom rules of behavior (e.g., safety, property, and permissable actions).

3. *Attitude toward learning* relates to the student's approach to learning new ideas and skills.
4. *Study habits* relates to the procedures a student uses to accomplish assigned work.

Selecting Behaviors That Reflect the Attitudes

The previous definitions partially explain the four categories. A list of related behaviors, both positive and negative, would further clarify each category. Table 9.8 lists behaviors the same teacher developed for the category, Attitude toward learning.

TABLE 9.8   Teacher-Constructed List of Behaviors That Reflect a Student's Attitude toward Learning

Positive Behaviors	*Negative Behaviors*
1. Appears interested in the topics being studied	1. Appears disinterested in or bored by topics being studied
2. Shows curiosity by asking questions or seeking more information	2. Rejects ideas presented and does not seek additional information
3. Demonstrates confidence in ability to learn new information and skills; is eager to try	3. Lacks confidence in ability to perform new tasks; resists trying
4. Works independently	4. Quits working on tasks when not monitored
5. Demonstrates perseverance in accomplishing tasks	5. Becomes frustrated and quits before completing tasks
6. Seeks and accepts corrective feedback; adjusts performance accordingly	6. Rejects corrective feedback and resists adjusting performance

In considering behaviors that might be related to a student's approach to learning, the teacher selected the concepts of interest, curiosity, confidence, independence, perseverance, and acceptance. A list of behaviors based on these concepts would exclude such behaviors as lesson preparation and following directions, which relate more to study habits.

After you develop a list of behaviors for each rating category, you need to determine if the behaviors are representative of only one of the main categories to be judged, observable in the classroom, and significant. Any redundant, unobservable, or irrelevant behaviors should be eliminated.

Developing an Evaluation Form and Rating Procedures

The type of rating form you develop depends on the behaviors you are observing and the number of times you plan to evaluate students. The behaviors on your list probably range from very abstract to very concrete, and each type of behavior requires a different evaluation method. For example, you may wish to record the number of times a student fails to turn in a homework assignment or fails to bring required materials to class. If you assign homework fifteen times during a grading period, your form should permit you to record the number of times a student either submits incomplete assignments or fails to turn in an assignment. The totals for each student can then be converted to descriptors, such as always, usually, and rarely.

Abstract behaviors, such as displays interest in topic, are much more difficult to evaluate. A rating form might include two or three rating categories for such a behavior. For example, the categories Disinterested/Bored, Easily distracted, and Interested/Engaged might be used to rate students on their interest. If you include too many categories for an abstract behavior, you undoubtedly will have difficulty scoring students consistently.

The rating scale in Table 9.9 shows three rating categories for six be-

TABLE 9.9 Rating Scale for Attitude toward Learning

Name _____ Date _____ Score _____
                                                Total   (18)

Behavior	Rating		
	Disinterested/ Bored	Easily distracted	Interested/ Engaged
1. Interest	1	2	3
	Does not seek additional information	Occasionally questions topic	Seeks resources, enrichment
2. Curiosity	1	2	3
	Resists trying	Apologizes for questions/work	Eager to try
3. Confidence	1	2	3
	Needs encouragement to begin	Quits working when unmonitored	Begins promptly, works independently
4. Independence	1	2	3
	Easily frustrated, usually quits	Occasionally frustrated and quits	Works steadily, completing tasks
5. Perseverance	1	2	3
	Ignores comments, does not correct work	Occasionally argues, sometimes corrects work	Seeks correction, adjusts work
6. Accepts corrective feedback	1	2	3

haviors under the general heading, Attitude toward Learning. Notice that each rating category has both a number and a verbal descriptor. The verbal descriptors help a teacher discriminate among the levels of behavior, and the numbers add up to produce a score for the attitude category. Because the scale permits positive and negative observations, the behaviors are stated neutrally. Mixing positive and negative statements of behavior in the left column would cause scoring problems and thus should be avoided.

Rating Students' Attitudes and Behavior

The number of times during a term that students' behavior is formally rated must be determined. Although students are informally observed on a daily basis, formal observations need not be as frequent. The number of evaluations will depend on the nature of the behavior observed. Concrete behaviors, such as submitting or completing assignments and bringing required materials to class, should be recorded at the appropriate time. Behaviors that are used to infer attitudes, such as attitude toward learning and citizenship, are not usually measured as frequently. Certainly, you want to rate the behaviors you have chosen to reflect these attitudes more than once during a grading term. Multiple ratings help ensure that students' term marks reflect their attitude throughout the term, not just the week preceding report card distribution. Some teachers choose to rate students weekly, some biweekly, and others less frequently. The number of times you choose to rate students' behavior formally depends in part on the subject and on the students you teach. A good rule of thumb is to have at least three measures of behaviors that reflect attitudes. This helps ensure that the ratings students receive on report cards are not peculiar to a special set of circumstances.

Select times when you are fresh, unhurried, and in a positive mood to do your ratings. Because of the degree of inference required, teachers' ratings can reflect their own attitudes more than those of students. As with performance tests, rating bias can affect the validity of students' attitude scores. While rating students' behavior, you should be aware of the potential bias from rating patterns and from general impressions of students and try to be as objective as possible.

Summarizing Group Behavior

A summary of a group's behavior during a term will help you identify positive and negative behavior patterns in the group and plan needed instruction or discussions. The procedures for summarizing behavior are the same as those for summarizing performance, product, and essay test results. Table 9.10

illustrates a group summary form for behaviors related to attitude toward learning.

TABLE 9.10   Group Summary Forms for Behaviors Representing Students' Attitude toward Learning

I. Group Summary Form

	Rating								
	1			2			3		
Component	9–15	9–30	10–15	9–15	9–30	10–15	9–15	9–30	10–15
1. Interest	111ᵃ	11	111	1111	卌	11	111	111	卌
2. Curiosity	–	–	–	卌 1	卌	1111	1111	卌	卌 1
3. Confidence	11	11	11	111	111	111	卌	卌	卌
4. Independence	卌 1	卌	1111	111	111	11	1	11	1111
5. Perseverance	11	11	1	卌	卌	卌 1	111	111	111
6. Acceptance	–	1	1	111	11	111	卌 11	卌 11	卌 1

ᵃ The total number of students who received a rating of 1 on September 15.

This particular form is designed to summarize students' ratings over three evaluations. The behaviors are listed in the left column and the rating categories are listed across the top. The dates of the evaluations are listed within each category. The tallies within the cells were taken from individual students' evaluation forms. Table 9.10 includes data for ten students. Of particular interest in analyzing the data is the shift in the number of students within each category across the rating periods. Within the lowest category, the teacher would hope for a decrease in the number of students across the rating periods. Likewise, the number of students in the highest category would hopefully increase during the term. The data show that the number of students in the lowest category decreased for independence and perseverance, which reflects a positive result. The teacher would probably be disappointed that strides were not made in the interest, confidence, and acceptance behaviors. In the highest category, the teacher would be pleased that more students received this rating in interest, curiosity, and independence. However, no gains were observed in confidence, perseverance, and acceptance. These data underscore areas in which students are not progressing and for which interventions should be planned.

SUMMARY

The procedure for evaluating student performances and behaviors consists of four major steps: (1) select the behaviors to be observed; (2) design the rating form and procedures; (3) rate the students' performances or behaviors; and (4) summarize the data for the group. Each major step can be broken down into two or more substeps. For example, to select the skills to be observed during a performance test:

1. Analyze the goal framework and select only those skills you believe can be observed during a performance.
2. Observe someone performing the task and verify that the chosen skills are observable and that none has been omitted.
3. Sequence the skills in the order they can be observed most efficiently.
4. Paraphrase each skill using only one or two key words. Either make all statements neutral or all statements positive.

To select the behaviors to observe for an attitude or behavior rating form:

1. Locate the attitudes and behaviors to be rated on the report card.
2. Define each attitude and behavior to differentiate among them.
3. Generate a list of observable behaviors that would reflect a positive attitude and one that would reflect a negative attitude for each attitude or behavior to be rated.
4. Compare behavior lists for the different attitudes to ensure that you have not included the same behavior on more than one list.
5. Evaluate each list of behaviors and remove those that are unobservable, redundant, and irrelevant.
6. Paraphrase the list of behaviors using only key words. Ensure that each behavior is either stated neutrally or positively.

To design a rating form for either a performance test or a set of behaviors:

1. List the paraphrased actions or behaviors in the left column.
2. Select the number of quality categories that you can consistently distinguish for each.
3. Write a descriptor for each category and assign each a number, with low numbers representing inadequate performance or negative behaviors.
4. Determine the relative value of each component rated and devise a weighting plan, if needed.

Rating students' performances and behaviors requires both professional judgment and self-awareness. Unlike evaluating essay and product development tests, you usually cannot check previous ratings of the same performance to determine whether you are consistently judging behaviors. Therefore, it is very important not to have more categories of quality for each action or behavior than you can clearly differentiate. Additionally:

1. Review the range and location of scores you have assigned a class and determine whether they are realistic given the group's characteristics. When the range of scores appears restricted and inappropriately high, average, or low for a given group, your judgments may have been biased.
2. Be aware of how your perceptions of individual students can influence the scores you assign. Take care to look for good qualities in the performance of students who usually score lower than others and look for problems in the performance of students who usually score high. This will help you avoid seeing what you expect to see when it is not there.
3. When judging a performance test, be especially careful not to exhibit nonverbal gestures that will influence a student's performance.
4. Be careful not to coach students during a performance posttest because coaching will tend to alter their performance.
5. When judging students' behaviors that reflect an attitude, select a time when you are *not* fatigued, disappointed, or unhappy. Your own attitude will influence your interpretation of students' behaviors and attitudes.

The final step in the evaluation process is to summarize the group's performance or behaviors. This entails (1) summarizing the data by tallying the number of students receiving marks in each rating category, and (2) analyzing the summaries to identify areas where additional instruction or discussions are warranted.

By following these steps, you can evaluate students as objectively as possible; provide students with specific, corrective feedback; and have the information you need to evaluate the quality of your instruction.

PRACTICE EXERCISES

I. Rating Students' Performances
   A. Use Figure 3.4, "A Partial Analysis of a Motor Skill Goal: Execute a Golf Swing," to develop either a checklist or a rating scale for evaluating students' overlap grip. Compare your evaluation form with the example checklist provided in Table 9.11 in the Feedback section.
   B. Design a performance summary form for your "grip" evaluation form that would permit you to tally the data. If your rating form can be used to summarize group performance, there is no need to design a different form.

II. Rating Attitudes and Behaviors
   A. Many school districts require teachers to report students' progress in citizenship. Develop a rating scale you could use to judge behaviors you believe reflect citizenship. In developing your rating scale, follow these steps:
      1. Write a definition for the term *citizenship* that can be used to guide your work.
      2. List the positive behaviors you believe reflect good citizenship and the negative behaviors that demonstrate a student's lack of citizenship. Your list should be appropriate for the students and subject you teach or plan to teach.
      3. Evaluate the list and remove behaviors that are redundant, unobservable in the classroom, and irrelevant.
      4. Paraphrase and list selected behaviors on the left side of a sheet of paper. Check to ensure that all are either neutrally or positively worded.
      5. Select rating categories for each behavior and write a verbal description for each.
      6. Assign a number for each category with low numbers reflecting negative or inappropriate categories.
      7. Design the form so you can rate students' behavior three times during a term.
      Compare your definition and rating scale with those included in Table 9.12 (see Feedback). Because definitions, subjects, grade levels, classroom environments, and target students vary, your form will undoubtedly differ from the example provided.

B. Design and develop a behavior summary form for your citizenship rating scale. Be sure to include space for summarizing three evaluations during the term. Compare your summary form with the one included in Table 9.13 (see Feedback).

C. Using the steps outlined in II.A, develop a behavior rating scale for study habits. Compare the definition and rating scale you develop with the one in Table 9.14 (see Feedback).

III. Enrichment

A. Rating Student Performance

1. Select an active performance skill that is relevant for the subject and grade level you teach or plan to teach.
2. Analyze the skill to identify the main components and subcomponents within each main step.
3. Develop either a rating scale or checklist for the skill.
4. Use your evaluation form to rate students or other individuals as they perform the skill.
5. Evaluate the form's feasibility and convenience and revise it if necessary.
6. Use the rating form to develop an appropriate performance summary form.

B. Rating Attitudes and Behaviors

1. Locate the attitudes and behaviors to be communicated on a report card for your subject and grade level.
2. Locate the rating categories for the attitudes and behaviors on the report card.
3. Define each attitude and behavior category.
4. Develop rating forms for evaluating the attitudes and behaviors.
5. If you are teaching a class, use the forms to evaluate the behavior of students in the class. Revise the form as needed for feasibility and convenience.
6. Use the evaluation forms to develop behavior summary forms.
7. Develop standards for converting students' scores to the rating categories defined on the report card.
8. If you have evaluated a class, summarize their behavior using your summary form and analyze the results to identify areas where instruction or discussion is needed.

FEEDBACK

I. Rating Students' Performances
   A. See Table 9.11.
   B. A blank copy of the checklist in Table 9.11 can be used as a summary form.

TABLE 9.11   Checklist for Rating an Overlap Grip[a]

Name _Joseph Augustine_   Period **2**   Date _10/15_ Score __12__
                                                    Total   (15)

Observed No	Yes	
		A. PLACEMENT OF LEFT HAND
	X	1. Hand toward top of club
	X	2. Back of hand toward target
	X	3. Back of hand perpendicular to target line
	X	4. Grip diagonally across palm
	X	5. Thumb down topside of shaft
	X	6. Fingers curled comfortably
X		7. Club grasped lightly
		B. PLACEMENT OF RIGHT HAND
	X	1. Hand just below left hand
	X	2. Palm facing target
	X	3. Palm perpendicular to target line
	X	4. Middle and ring finger curled around shaft
X		5. Little finger overlapping left hand
	X	6. Right palm and thumb over left thumb
	X	7. Right thumb pointed down topside of shaft
X		8. Club grasped lightly
Total	12	

[a]This checklist is for a right-handed person. For a left-handed person,
the right and left hands would be reversed.

II. Rating Attitudes and Behaviors
   A. See Table 9.12.
   B. See Table 9.13.
   C. See Table 9.14.

TABLE 9.12 Definition and Behavior Rating Scale for Citizenship

Definition: Citizenship is the social interactions that students have with their peers and with their teacher. It includes their contributions to the classroom society.

Name _____ Term _____ Score _____
                                                            Total   (153)

	Dates	Totals
I. Citizenship		
A. Self-discipline		
1. Minds own affairs	____ ____ ____ ____	
2. Controls emotions	____ ____ ____ ____	
3. Is honest	____ ____ ____ ____	
4. Is truthful	____ ____ ____ ____	
B. Interactions with peers		
1. Shows interest in classmates	____ ____ ____ ____	
2. Listens to classmates	____ ____ ____ ____	
3. Helps and encourages classmates	____ ____ ____ ____	
4. Shares resources and materials	____ ____ ____ ____	
5. Contributes to group activities	____ ____ ____ ____	
C. Interactions with teacher		
1. Listens when teacher is talking	____ ____ ____ ____	
2. Follows directions	____ ____ ____ ____	
3. Seeks guidance and help	____ ____ ____ ____	
4. Accepts suggestions and comments about classroom interactions	____ ____ ____ ____	
D. Support of a positive classroom environment		
1. Helps define and analyze class problems	____ ____ ____ ____	
2. Suggests solutions for class problems	____ ____ ____ ____	
3. Accepts responsibility for personal contributions to class problems	____ ____ ____ ____	
4. Helps maintain class property	____ ____ ____ ____	
Totals		

Scale: 1 = Rarely; 2 = Inconsistently;
       3 = Almost always

TABLE 9.13   Behavior Summary Form for Citizenship Rating Scale

Class _____ Term _____

Behavior	Rarely			Inconsistently			Almost Always		
	9–15	9–30	10–15	9–15	9–30	10–15	9–15	9–30	10–15
A. Self-discipline									
1. Affairs	——	——	——	——	——	——	——	——	——
2. Emotions	——	——	——	——	——	——	——	——	——
3. Honesty	——	——	——	——	——	——	——	——	——
4. Truthfulness	——	——	——	——	——	——	——	——	——
B. Interactions with Peers									
1. Interest	——	——	——	——	——	——	——	——	——
2. Listens	——	——	——	——	——	——	——	——	——
3. Encourages	——	——	——	——	——	——	——	——	——
4. Shares	——	——	——	——	——	——	——	——	——
5. Contributes	——	——	——	——	——	——	——	——	——
C. Interactions with Teacher									
1. Listens	——	——	——	——	——	——	——	——	——
2. Directions	——	——	——	——	——	——	——	——	——
3. Guidance	——	——	——	——	——	——	——	——	——
4. Suggestions	——	——	——	——	——	——	——	——	——
D. Support Positive Environment									
1. Analyze	——	——	——	——	——	——	——	——	——
2. Solutions	——	——	——	——	——	——	——	——	——
3. Responsibility	——	——	——	——	——	——	——	——	——
4. Maintenance	——	——	——	——	——	——	——	——	——

TABLE 9.14   Definition and Rating Scale for Study Habits

Definition: Study habits are the procedures students use to accomplish assigned work.

Name _____ Term _____ Score _____

Behavior	Dates			*Totals*
I. Class Preparation				
A. Reads assignments before class	__	__	__	__
B. Brings required materials to class	__	__	__	__
II. During presentations/demonstrations				
A. Listens	__	__	__	__
B. Takes notes	__	__	__	__
C. Follows instructions	__	__	__	__
III. During class work				
A. Organizes material	__	__	__	__
B. Works carefully and accurately	__	__	__	__
C. Uses time productively	__	__	__	__
Totals	__	__	__	__

Number of homework assignments during term: _____

IV. Homework
  A. Number submitted on time   _____
  B. Number submitted complete   _____
  C. Number accurate   _____

Scale: 1 = Rarely; 2 = Inconsistently;
3 = Almost always

SUGGESTED READING

Gronlund, N. E. (1985). *Measurement and evaluation in teaching.* New York: Macmillan Publishing Company, pp. 383–405.

Mehrens, W. A., and Lehmann, I. J. (1984). *Measurement and evaluation in education and psychology.* New York: CBS College Publishing, pp. 205–45.

Nitko, A. J. (1983). *Educational tests and measurement.* New York: Harcourt, Brace, Jovanovich, pp. 243–79, 564–80.

Popham, W. J. (1981). *Modern educational measurement.* Englewood Cliffs, N.J.: Prentice-Hall, pp. 309–27.

CHAPTER 10

Performing a Test Item Analysis

OBJECTIVES

1. Define, calculate, and interpret indices of item difficulty.
2. Define, calculate, and interpret indices of item discrimination.

3. Define, calculate, and interpret data for a distractor analysis.
4. Use item analysis data to evaluate test items.

In developing classroom tests, teachers must synthesize many factors related to the skills to be measured, the instruction delivered, and the characteristics of target students. The tests they develop reflect their perceptions of the best way to measure prescribed skills. Teachers often check their perceptions of the clarity and technical accuracy of items by asking a colleague and a few students to review new items. These reviews help them detect problems and revise the items before administering new tests.

Like classroom teachers, test specialists have content experts and sample students review new items they write. However, they also administer new tests to a large, representative group of students before the tests are finalized. Using data from these field trials, test specialists usually find problems in the items that were not detected during item reviews. Defective items are then revised or eliminated before a new test is actually used.

Since defective items are commonly found during field trials, it is unfortunate that most teachers do not have the time or resources to conduct such trials before administering new tests in the classroom. Even though defective items cannot always be identified before a test is administered, teachers can use the item analysis procedures used by test specialists to locate defective items after the test is administered. Teachers who simply score, record, and return test papers without performing item analyses are missing opportunities to identify and discount defective items, improve their item-writing skills, and evaluate the quality of their test and instruction.

Item analysis procedures are commonly used in the development of standardized norm-referenced tests; however, they are also useful for evaluating and refining the criterion-referenced tests developed and administered by teachers. Most school districts today have computer-scoring services for selected-response tests that quickly calculate and summarize the data teachers need to perform item analysis. If computer-scoring services are available in your district, and your class is mature enough to manage a separate answer sheet, use them. When machine scoring is not feasible, item analysis can be performed manually, although it is time consuming.

Whether or not you use machine-scoring services, the arrangement of items on your test is an important consideration. Items that measure the same enabling skill should be clustered together on the test, and enabling skills related to the same instructional goal should be side by side whenever possible. If items that measure the same skill are scattered throughout the test, organizing item data for the analysis becomes more difficult. Item data need to be arranged by enabling skill and goal, both for the analysis procedures presented in this chapter and for the individual student performance analysis described in Chapter 12.

Item analysis procedures fall into three categories: item difficulty analysis, item discrimination analysis, and distractor analysis. The following sections describe how to organize data and perform these analyses by hand for two reasons. First, if you can organize, calculate, and interpret item data that you generate, you can certainly interpret the same data provided by a test-scoring service. Second, developing the skill required to perform these analyses by hand eliminates any mystery and thoroughly prepares you to request the information from data-processing personnel when these services are not currently available. The chapter concludes with a discussion of typical item analysis forms provided by test-scoring services.

ORGANIZING TEST DATA FOR ITEM ANALYSIS

Before beginning an item analysis, the test results need to be organized and summarized using a worksheet. The first steps in creating the worksheet are to reserve space for students' names in the left-hand column and to list information that identifies each item across the top. Column titles for the worksheet are illustrated in Table 10.1. Items are usually grouped according to objective, enabling skill, or instructional goal. If the items are not so grouped

TABLE 10.1 Worksheet for Summarizing Item Data and Calculating Difficulty and Discrimination Indices

Goals	Goal 1		Goal 2		Goal 3			
Enabling skills	*1.A*	*1.B*	*2.A*	*2.B*	*3.A*	*3.B*	*3.C*	*Total Score*
Item Number	1 2	3 4	5 6 7	8 9	1 1 1 0 1 2	1 1 3 4	1 1 5 6	16
Correct Answer	3 2	3 1	2 2 3	1 4	2 4 3	1 2	1 4	
Jones			2					15
Baldwin			1	3				14

on your test, rearrange them as you prepare your table. The example worksheet is for a test that includes three instructional goals, each with two or three enabling skills. The top row is used to identify the goals and the second row to identify the enabling skills. The third row identifies the item numbers, and the fourth row identifies the correct response.

The second step in creating the worksheet is to select the students whose test results will be recorded and analyzed. Although most teachers have classes that contain more than twenty students, measurement specialists recommend using only twenty for item analysis. The particular students you should include are the ten with the highest overall test scores and the ten with the lowest overall scores. Limiting the analysis to twenty students does not affect the quality of the information you obtain, but it does reduce the amount of work and make the required calculations much easier. After students' tests are scored and each student's total score is calculated, you should rank order all the test papers, from the highest to the lowest earned score. Counting from the highest score, select the top ten papers. Then, counting from the lowest score, select the bottom ten papers. Occasionally you will find that several students have the same raw score, yet you need only one or two of them to complete your groups. Should this happen, include only the number of papers you need. It does not matter which of the students' papers you choose when their total scores are equal.

The third step is to record the item data in the table for the selected students. Within the upper and lower groups, arrange the papers in order based on their total score. Beginning with the upper group, enter the data for the student with the highest score first. Usually, to save time, only the number or letter of an incorrect response is recorded. Blank cells will then indicate correct responses. The data for two students in Table 10.1 illustrate this method. The first student, Jones, missed only one item on the test. Instead of selecting the correct answer, 3, for item 7, Jones picked distractor 2. The only data recorded for Jones is a 2 beneath item 7. The second student, Baldwin, missed two items. The incorrect response, 1, is inserted beneath item 5, and the incorrect response, 3, is inserted beneath item 9. After you have recorded the data for the ten students in the upper group, skip several rows and record the item data for students in the lower group, beginning with the highest score in this set. The visual separation of scores in the upper and lower groups makes your calculations easier.

If a test contains some or all completion items rather than selected-response items, you identify and categorize the types of errors students made on each item as you score the papers. Each error category can be assigned an identifying number or letter that can be recorded in the summary table. For such tests, create an error legend for reference during scoring and analysis.

The next step in creating the worksheet is to count and record the number of students in the upper group who answered each item correctly. Repeat this procedure for the students in the lower group. Record these item totals in a row just beneath each group's data.

With the item data organized and summarized in this manner, you have all the information you need to calculate and record the difficulty and discrimination indices on your worksheet. Usually two additional rows are included at the bottom of the worksheet to record these indices.

Table 10.2 contains a completed item summary worksheet for a posttest on capitalization. Notice in this example that the items measuring each goal were not grouped together on the test but were rearranged for the analysis. Items 7, 11, and 14 measure capitalizing the first word of a sentence. The top half of the table lists the item data for students in the upper group; the bottom half of the table shows the item data for the lower group. The numbers in the rows labeled R_U and R_L represent the number of students in the upper and lower groups who answered each item correctly. Notice that each column total represents the number of blank cells or correct answers. For example, eight students in the upper group and two students in the lower group answered item 13 correctly.

Notice that two rows, labeled p and d are included at the bottom of the worksheet. These rows contain the difficulty index, p, and the discrimination index, d, for each item. Before discussing these indices, the text describes the procedures for calculating and interpreting them.

ITEM DIFFICULTY ANALYSIS

The item difficulty index, p, is the proportion or percentage of students in the analysis group who answer the item correctly. Difficulty indices expressed as proportions can range from .00 to 1.00, and those expressed as percentages can range from 0 to 100 percent as follows:

TABLE 10.2 Item Summary Table for Posttest on Capitalization

Goals / Items #	First Word 7	11	14	Pronoun I 3	9	17	Proper Nouns 1	5	13	16	8	19	Proper Adjectives 2	6	10	18	Days and Months 4	12	15	20	Total Score
Correct Answers	1	1	1	3	3	2	4	4	4	3	3	2	2	3	2	3	3	4	3	4	
Rogers																					20
Jackson																					20
Ayres																					20
Augustine																					20
Deddens																					20
Talbot												3									19
McCoy												3									19
Jensen												3									19
Prince								3				3									18
Rust								2				3									18
R_U	10	10	10	10	10	10	10	8	10	10	10	5	10	10	10	10	10	10	10	10	
Wilson											3	3		1							17
Boyd											3	3			3						17
Merrill									2	2	1				3						16
Jones									1	2	1				3						16
Hart										1	2				3				2	2	15
Little								2			1				3				1	2	15
Moyle								2		3					3				2	3	15
Brown									3	3	3				3				4	1	14
Bentley								2		2				1	3		2		2	2	13
Rogers									3	2	2				3		1	3	2	3	12
R_L	10	10	10	10	10	10	10	7	8	4	4	8	10	8	1	10	8	9	4	4	
p	1.00	1.00	1.00	1.00	1.00	1.00	1.00	.85	.50	.80	.70	.65	1.00	.90	.55	1.00	.90	.95	.70	.70	
d	.00	.00	.00	.00	.00	.00	.00	.30	.60	.40	.60	-.30	.00	.20	.90	.00	.20	.10	.60	.60	
Item Number	7	11	14	3	9	17	1	5	13	16	8	19	2	6	10	18	4	12	15	20	

	Very Difficult	Difficult	Very Easy
Proportion	.00	.50	1.00
Percentage	0%	50%	100%

As the illustration shows, the higher the p value, or difficulty index, the easier the item for a group.

Calculating Item Difficulty Indices

To calculate an item difficulty index, you need to know (1) the number of students in the upper group who answered the item correctly (R_U), (2) the number of students in the lower group who answered the item correctly (R_L), and (3) the number of students in the analysis group (N). You then substitute these numbers in the following formula to find p, or the proportion of students in the analysis group who answered the item correctly. This proportion can be converted to a percentage by multiplying it by 100.

Item Difficulty Formula:

$$p = \frac{R_U + R_L}{N}$$

The examples in Figure 10.1 show how to calculate a difficulty index for items 7, 13, and 19 in Table 10.2

The calculation for item 7 indicates that all students in both groups (10 + 10) answered the item correctly. The total (20) is divided by the number of students (20) in the group. The result is a difficulty index of 1.00. This is the highest difficulty value possible and indicates that the item was very easy for the class. To find the percentage of the group passing the item, multiply the difficulty index by 100. For item 7, $1.00 \times 100 = 100$ percent.

For item 13, eight students in the upper group and two students in the lower group answered the question correctly. This calculation produces a difficulty index of .50, or 50 percent. Because only half the class answered the item correctly, it was a difficult item for the group.

FIGURE 10.1 Difficulty Index Calculations

$$\text{Item 7: } p = \frac{10 + 10}{20} = \frac{20}{20} = 1.00$$

$$\text{Item 13: } p = \frac{8 + 2}{20} = \frac{10}{20} = .50$$

$$\text{Item 19: } p = \frac{5 + 8}{20} = \frac{13}{20} = .65$$

Sixty-five percent of the class ($p = .65$) answered item 19 correctly. This value indicates a question that was easier than item 13, but much more difficult than item 7. The difficulty index for each item is calculated in the same manner.

Evaluating Items Using the Item Difficulty Index

The difficulty index is a *measure* of each item's difficulty for the students tested. This measure can be used to describe the difficulty of the item (e.g., this item is very easy, moderately easy, fairly difficult, or very difficult for this group). It can also be used to evaluate or judge the quality of the item using criteria and standards. Evaluation requires that you identify variables that influence the difficulty index and standards for judging the quality of the item. In essence, you are judging the reasonableness of the measure considering the variables that influence it. When an observed difficulty index does not seem reasonable given the circumstances, then you have evidence to question the quality of the item. The following four variables can be used to evaluate the item using the difficulty index:

1. The complexity of the skill measured
2. The achievement characteristics of the group
3. The comparability of difficulty indices for multiple items that measure the same objective
4. The comparability of difficulty indices for items that measure hierarchically related skills

Skill Complexity   To determine whether an observed difficulty index is reasonable, you should first estimate the complexity of the skill measured by the item and set expectations for the percentage of students likely to answer correctly. For example, if a test item requires students to recall simple verbal information, make a relatively obvious discrimination, or perform a simple calculation, you would expect most of the students to answer the item correctly. If, on the other hand, the item measures a complex skill, some students undoubtedly will miss the item. If many students miss an item you believe measures a simple skill, then you have reason to believe that something is wrong either with the item or with the instruction. Likewise, a very high proportion of correct responses for a relatively complex task may signal the presence of a clue in the item. Therefore, the reasonableness of an observed difficulty index depends in part on the complexity of the skill measured.

The Group's Achievement Characteristics   In addition to the complexity of the skill measured, interpreting difficulty indices requires considering the group's achievement characteristics. Given the same skill complexity and item to measure the skill, you would adjust the anticipated difficulty index depending on whether the group was heterogeneous or homogeneous. The expected proportion of students who answer the item correctly in a very heterogeneous group should be lower than that expected for a homogeneous group of high achievers. The expected difficulty index for a homogeneous, high-achieving group should be higher than one for a homogeneous group of average achievers. Likewise, a homogeneous group of average achievers should have a higher expected difficulty index than a homogeneous group of low-achieving students.

Using information about the complexity of the task measured and about the group's achievement characteristics, you can make decisions about the reasonableness of an observed difficulty index. In a group of high achievers, a large proportion of students would probably answer an item correctly, regardless of task complexity, if instruction was adequate and the item was clearly written. In a group of average achievers, items measuring easy skills would probably produce a high proportion of correct responses; items measuring more complex skills would produce a smaller proportion of right answers. You might expect most students in a group of low achievers to answer complex items incorrectly and to produce high difficulty indices only on very easy questions. Similarly, you would not expect all of the students in a heterogeneous group to answer an item correctly, unless the task was very simple or the item contained a clue. Item difficulty indices that seem unrealistically high, given the task's complexity and the group's characteristics, usually signal clues in the items; those that seem unreasonably low signal either defective items or inadequate instruction.

Multiple Items for the Same Objective   Comparing the difficulty indices for different items that measure the same objective can usually help you determine whether problems detected are caused by the item or by instruction. Test items that measure the same objective should result in approximately the same difficulty indices. For example, if you include three items on a test to measure the same objective, and all students answer one item correctly whereas only 60 percent answer the other two items correctly, you should look for a clue in the easy item. On the other hand, if only 55 percent of the students answer one of a set of three items correctly, and more than 90 percent answer the other two items correctly, it might signal a complexity in the difficult item not experienced by students in the easier ones. The following example illustrates this situation. The set of five items requires students to select words that are nouns. Notice that the difficulty index is at about the same level on all but one item.

	Difficulty Index
Word	p
1. barn	.70
2. busy	.65
3. brown	.75
4. barrel	.70
5. barrister	.40

The first four items have difficulty indices between .65 and .75. Item 5, however, is obviously more difficult than the other four. The atypically low proportion of correct responses to this item suggests some sort of problem. From this example, you would probably conclude that most students did not know the meaning of the word *barrister*, which influenced their responses.

Locating an atypical difficulty index in a set of items does not always pinpoint the defective item. You should also use your estimation of a reasonable difficulty index in deciding whether the atypical item is the one posing the problem. Consider, for example, a set of three items that measures a rather complex skill administered to a very heterogeneous group of students. If you estimated that approximately two-thirds of the class had mastered the skill yet observed difficulty indices of .60, .90, and 1.00 for the three items, you probably would not conclude that the more difficult item contained inadvertent complexity. Instead, you might review the two easier items to see whether they contained clues to the correct answer. Although this type of situation is possible, the atypical difficulty index usually reflects the problem item.

Hierarchically Related Items   In interpreting difficulty indices, it is also important to compare them for items that measure hierarchically related skills. For instance, students may be required to:

1. State the identifying characteristics of nouns
2. Select nouns from a list of words containing nouns and other parts of speech
3. Select proper nouns from a list of nouns
4. Capitalize proper nouns

Obviously, students who do not know the characteristics of nouns cannot consistently separate nouns from other parts of speech. If they cannot recognize nouns, they will not be able to recognize proper nouns without clues. Also, if they cannot recognize proper nouns, they can only guess which nouns should be capitalized. Consider the following reasonable difficulty indices for three test items based on each of the skills in Figure 10.2.

FIGURE 10.2   Difficulty Indices for Hierarchical Tasks

Difficulty Indices			Skills
Item 1	*Item 2*	*Item 3*	
.60	.60	.65	Capitalize proper nouns
.65	.60	.65	Select proper nouns from a list of nouns
.70	.75	.70	Select nouns from a list of nouns and other parts of speech
.80			State the identifying characteristics of nouns

In Figure 10.2, 80 percent of the group correctly answered the item that required them to state the characteristics of nouns. Therefore, no more than 80 percent should correctly answer higher-level skills. Seventy percent correctly selected nouns, and fewer, or 60 percent, correctly selected proper nouns. All the students who were able to identify proper nouns could also capitalize them. Considering the hierarchical relationship among these skills, the difficulty indices for the items seem reasonable.

Now, compare these data with a second set of unreasonable difficulty indices in Figure 10.3. Here, 90 percent or more of the students could locate proper nouns, yet only 80 percent knew the characteristics of nouns and only 70 percent could correctly select nouns from a list of words containing nouns and other parts of speech. These illogical percentages can be explained in two ways. First, proper noun items may have contained clues, for example, being capitalized when other words in the list were not. The other possibility could be faulty reasoning in establishing the relationship among skills in the hierarchy. If you encounter difficulty indices that imply that higher-level skills have been mastered by more students than have subordinate skills, you should look for (1) clues in items that measure higher-order skills; (2) errors in logic in identifying skills included in the hierarchy; and (3) errors in sequencing skills in the hierarchy.

In summary, interpreting the reasonableness of item difficulty indices requires comparing observed indices with those anticipated given the complexity of the skills measured and the achievement characteristics of the group; comparing difficulty indices for multiple items that measure the same behavioral objective; and comparing difficulty indices for items that measure hierarchically related skills. These comparisons should enable you to pinpoint items that either contain clues or introduce unintended complexity.

You can also use difficulty indices to evaluate the quality of your instruction. If many students incorrectly answer some or all of the items related to an important skill, you need to reconsider the instruction for these behavioral objectives. Although an analysis of item difficulty will not identify the instructional weaknesses, it will indicate where to look for problems.

FIGURE 10.3 Unreasonable Difficulty Indices for Hierarchical Tasks

Difficulty Indices			Skills
Item 1	Item 2	Item 3	
.60	.60	.60	Capitalize proper nouns
.90	.95	.90	Select proper nouns from a list of nouns
.70	.70	.70	Select nouns from a list of nouns and other parts of speech
.80	.80	.80	State the identifying characteristics of nouns

Caution is required when interpreting item difficulty indices. In a small group, one wrong answer or a careless mistake will produce a different difficulty index. Therefore, in making your comparisons, you should look for a reasonable range of scores. A difference of as much as 10 to 15 percentage points in a small group will be due to chance errors on the part of students rather than to actual differences in item difficulty. Thus, you should be concerned only with large, obvious differences in your analysis.

Some measurement specialists recommend comparing the difficulty indices of items on pretests and posttests in order to evaluate the quality of items on criterion-referenced tests. To perform such an item analysis, you need to administer a pretest and posttest that contain the same items. Then calculate the difficulty indices for the items on each test and subtract each item's p value on the pretest from its p value on the posttest. The difference between these values is considered one indicator of item quality. This procedure is illustrated in Figure 10.4.

Items that exhibit high, positive differences, such as 1, 3, and 4, supposedly reflect good technical characteristics. Items that have small or no differences, or negative differences, such as items 2 and 5, supposedly reflect technical problems with the item, the instruction, or both.

Using a pretest–posttest comparison to evaluate the quality of items on your criterion-referenced tests has several limitations. First, pretest data are not always available for comparison. Pretests are usually administered only when teachers have reason to believe that some students in the class already possess some of the enabling skills in the goal framework. When this is the case, pretests are administered to aid in grouping students for instruction or for differentiating between skills that need to be taught and those that simply need to be reviewed. Second, when pretests are used to aid planning, different or novel items should be used on posttests to measure students' accomplishment of the same enabling skills and objectives. When exactly the same items are included on pretests and posttests, it is impossible to determine whether students have learned the enabling skill or simply remember the example used in the previous measure. Third, when different items are used to measure the same skill on the pretest and posttest, comparing them would not make sense because it is impossible to ensure that different items are precisely equal in difficulty. Although comparing students' pretest and

FIGURE 10.4   Comparing Item Difficulty on Pretests and Posttests

Items	Enabling Skill 1				
	1	2	3	4	5
Posttest $_p$	.60	.40	1.00	.85	.20
Pretest $_p$	.20	.40	.50	.50	.80
Difference (post–pre)	.40	.00	.50	.35	. −60

posttest performances is valuable for evaluating the quality of instruction, these comparisons are best made at the objective or enabling skill level rather than at the item level. Procedures for judging students' progress at the objective level are described in Chapter 12. Item analysis for criterion-referenced tests is best accomplished by comparing the reasonableness of observed difficulty indices against your perceptions of the complexity of the skill measured and the achievement characteristics of your class.

ITEM DISCRIMINATION ANALYSIS

Item discrimination analysis is based on the assumption that students who receive high scores on the overall test should score better on an item-by-item basis than students who receive low scores on the overall test. An index of item discrimination permits a teacher to determine whether students' performances on individual items are consistent with their overall performances.

Discrimination indices can range from 1.00 to −1.00 as follows:

Maximum Negative Discrimination between Groups	No Discrimination between Groups	Maximum Positive Discrimination between Groups
−1.00	.00	1.00

A discrimination index of 1.00 for an item indicates maximum positive discrimination between the upper and lower groups. To observe such an index, all ten students in the upper group would have to answer the item correctly whereas all ten students in the lower group would have to miss the item. An index of .00 indicates that the item does not discriminate at all between the upper and lower groups. When the same number of students in each group answer an item correctly, a discrimination index of .00 results. Maximum negative discrimination is −1.00, which results when all ten students in the lower group answer an item correctly and all ten students in the upper group miss it. Generally, high negative discrimination indices reflect problems.

Calculating Item Discrimination

An item's discrimination index, which indicates the difference in the performances of the upper and lower groups, is easy to calculate. The formula for calculating the discrimination index, or d, uses the same information as the difficulty index, but combines it in the following manner:

Discrimination Index Formula:

$$d = \frac{R_U - R_L}{1/2N}$$

In calculating the discrimination index, the number of students in the lower group who answer an item correctly is subtracted from the number in the upper group who answer correctly. The result is divided by one-half of the total number of students in the analysis group. Discrimination indices for items 7, 13, and 19 in Table 10.2 would be calculated as in Figure 10.5.

The discrimination index for item 7 is .00. This value indicates that item 7 does not discriminate between the upper and lower groups. Obviously, if all students in the analysis group answered the item correctly, no discrimination would be present.

On the other hand, item 13 has a discrimination index of .60. This item discriminates between the two groups in a high, positive manner, which indicates students' performance on the item is consistent with their overall test scores.

A negative discrimination index of $-.30$ for item 19 indicates some problem with the item. Any such negative result indicates that students' scores on the item are not consistent with their overall test scores.

Evaluating Items Using the Discrimination Index

There are two main factors to consider in interpreting discrimination indices: the relationship between the difficulty and discrimination indices and the achievement characteristics of the group.

Difficulty and Discrimination Relationship The difficulty and discrimination indices are directly related. Figure 10.6 illustrates the relationship of the two indices for an analysis group of twenty students. In the figure, the difficulty indices are listed in the left-hand column from high to low values. The dis-

FIGURE 10.5 Calculating Discrimination Indices

Item 7:	$\dfrac{10 - 10}{10} = \dfrac{0}{10} = .00$
Item 13:	$\dfrac{8 - 2}{10} = \dfrac{6}{10} = .60$
Item 19:	$\dfrac{5 - 8}{10} = \dfrac{-3}{10} = -.30$

FIGURE 10.6 Difficulty Indices and Corresponding Ranges of Discrimination Indices

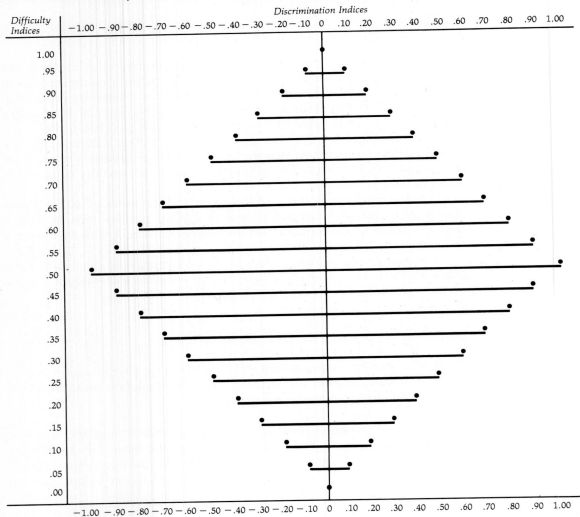

crimination indices are listed across the top and bottom of the figure. The bars inserted in the figure show the possible range of discrimination indices for each difficulty level. The graph illustrates that only a discrimination index of 0 is possible for difficulty indices of 1.00 and 0 because all students performed the same. As difficulty indices drop from 1.00 to .50, the range of possible discrimination indices increases to a maximum of 1.00. As the difficulty indices drop from .50 toward 0, the range of possible discrimination indices gradually decreases.

Table 10.3 illustrates how the range of discrimination indices occurs for difficulty indices of .70 and .30. The difficulty indices appear in the far left column. Columns are included for the number of students in the upper and the lower groups who answer an item correctly, the total number of students who answer correctly, the difference between the upper and lower groups, and the resulting discrimination index. To obtain a difficulty index of .70, fourteen students would need to answer an item correctly ($.70 \times 20 = 14$). The value of the discrimination index depends on how these fourteen students are distributed between the upper and lower groups. If the item is answered correctly by all ten students in the upper group and only four students in the lower group, then the maximum discrimination index, .60, for a difficulty index of .70 will be obtained. As the number of students in the upper group decreases and the number in the lower group increases, the discrimination index drops. When seven students in each group answer correctly, the discrimination index is 0. If more students in the lower group answer an item correctly, then the discrimination index is negative. The maximum possible negative discrimination index for a difficulty index of .70 is $-.60$. This is only observed when all ten students in the lower group and only four students in the upper group answer correctly.

Notice that the range of possible discrimination indices for a difficulty index of .30 is the same as that for a difficulty index of .70. Although only six of the twenty students answer correctly ($.30 \times 20 = 6$), the differences between the upper and lower groups for each possible combination remain

TABLE 10.3 **Possible Values of the Discrimination Index for Two Difficulty Levels**

	Number of Students in Upper Group Who Answer Correctly R_U	Number of Students in Lower Group Who Answer Correctly R_L	Total Correct $R_U + R_L$	Difference between Upper and Lower Groups $R_U - R_L$	Discrimination Index $d = \dfrac{R_U - R_L}{1/2N}$
$p = .70$	10	4	14	6	.60
	9	5	14	4	.40
	8	6	14	2	.20
	7	7	14	0	.00
	6	8	14	-2	$-.20$
	5	9	14	-4	$-.40$
	4	10	14	-6	$-.60$
$p = .30$	6	0	6	6	.60
	5	1	6	4	.40
	4	2	6	2	.20
	3	3	6	0	.00
	2	4	6	-2	$-.20$
	1	5	6	-4	$-.40$
	0	6	6	-6	$-.60$

the same as those for a difficulty index of .70. For a difficulty index of .30, the discrimination index cannot be higher than .60 or lower than − .60. However, it can range between these two limits depending on how the six students are distributed between the upper and lower groups. The range of possible discrimination indices for each difficulty index can be determined in the same manner.

The method of calculating the possible range of discrimination indices just described is too cumbersome to be practical. However, it is included to help you understand the different combinations of R_U and R_L that are possible for each difficulty index and how they influence the discrimination index. Once you understand these relationships, you can use a more practical method to locate the possible range of discrimination indices for each difficulty index. To obtain the ± range of discrimination indices for any difficulty index of .50 and above, subtract the difficulty index from 1.00 and multiply the remainder by 2. For difficulty indices of .49 and below, simply multiply the observed difficulty index by 2. These two methods are illustrated in Figure 10.7. Figure 10.7 shows that the range of possible discrimination indices for a difficulty index of .80 extends from .40 to − .40; for a difficulty index of .45, it extends from .90 to − .90.

The following rules apply in interpreting discrimination indices:

1. The range of possible discrimination indices depends on the value of the difficulty index.
2. Very high and very low difficulty indices have limited discrimination ranges.
3. Maximum discrimination indices of 1.00 and − 1.00 are possible only when the difficulty index is .50.
4. Positive discrimination indices indicate that more students in the upper group answered correctly.
5. Negative discrimination indices indicate that more students in the lower group answered correctly.
6. A discrimination index of 0 indicates no difference in the performance of students in the upper and lower groups.

In addition to using the relationship between p and d and these interpretation rules to interpret discrimination indices, you can use the index to

FIGURE 10.7   Calculating Maximum Possible Discrimination for Given Difficulty Indices

	Procedure	p	Example
Difficulty indices or p values of .50 or above	$2(1.00 - p) = \pm d$	.80	$2(1.00 - .80) = \pm .40$
		.60	$2(1.00 - .60) = \pm .80$
p values of .49 or below	$2p = \pm d$	.45	$2 \times .45 = \pm .90$
		.30	$2 \times .30 = \pm .60$

describe an item's discrimination power as strong, moderate, or weak. Items that have discrimination indices close to the maximum possible (d_{max}) for any given difficulty index can be classified as strong discriminators. Items that have discrimination indices close to one-half the maximum possible ($\frac{1}{2}d_{max}$) can be classified as moderate discriminators; and items that have discrimination indices close to one-quarter the maximum possible ($\frac{1}{4}d_{max}$) can be classified as weak discriminators. For example, the maximum discrimination possible for an item that has a difficulty index of .60 is .80, or $2(1.00 - .60)$. For such an item, a discrimination index close to .80 would reflect strong discrimination; one close to .40 (or $\frac{1}{2}d_{max}$) would reflect moderate discrimination; and one close to .20 (or $\frac{1}{4}d_{max}$) would reflect weak discrimination.

Group Achievement Characteristics   Besides describing the degree of discrimination, the discrimination index can be used to evaluate the quality of an item. However, evaluation requires setting a standard in order to judge items as being either good, adequate, or poor in quality. The group's achievement characteristics and overall test performance should be used in setting this standard. For example, if a group's overall test performance is very heterogeneous, then your standard for good items would undoubtedly be set at close to maximum possible discrimination, given the difficulty index, for each item on the test. In this situation, if you observe moderate discrimination for an item, you would probably judge the item adequate. Similarly, an item that resulted in weak discrimination, given heterogeneous group performance, would be judged as poor. Consider the following examples for a heterogeneous group:

Observed Difficulty	d_{max}	Observed Discrimination	Item Quality Good	Adequate	Poor
.60	.80	.80	X		
.60	.80	.40		X	
.60	.80	.20			X

Your standard for judging the quality of an item would be different if your group's performance were only somewhat heterogeneous. In this case, moderate discrimination ($\frac{1}{2}d_{max}$) would reflect good items; weak discrimination ($\frac{1}{4}d_{max}$) would reflect adequate items; and no discrimination would reflect poor items. Consider the following examples for a somewhat heterogeneous group:

Observed Difficulty	d_{max}	Observed Discrimination	Item Quality Good	Adequate	Poor
.60	.80	.40	X		
.60	.80	.20		X	
.60	.80	.00			X

Your standard for judging items would also be different if your group's overall performance were very homogeneous. In this situation, weak discrimination ($\frac{1}{4}d_{max}$) would reflect a good item, and no discrimination would reflect an adequate item. If you observe a moderate discrimination index for such a group, you can usually consider the item to be good. On the other hand, a maximum discrimination index would cause you to question such an atypical result. Consider the following examples for a very homogeneous group:

Observed Difficulty	d_{max}	Observed Discrimination	Item Quality		
			Good	Adequate	Poor
.90	.20	.10	X		
.80	.40	.10	X		
.70	.60	.00		X	
.60	.80	.20	X		
.60	.80	.80			?

Thus, strong discrimination does not always reflect a good item, and weak discrimination does not always reflect a defective one. The standards you set for judging item quality based on the discrimination index should fluctuate to reflect the achievement characteristics of the group tested and their overall performance on the test.

Because the number of students included in the item analysis is small, guessing behaviors and careless mistakes can produce small differences between your expected discrimination indices and those you calculate. Ignore minor discrepancies as suggested where interpreting difficulty indices.

SUMMARIZING AND INTERPRETING DIFFICULTY AND DISCRIMINATION INDICES FOR A TEST

Difficulty and discrimination indices can be organized in many ways to help you interpret the data. One way is to create a summary table that organizes items by difficulty indices. You could create different categories for item difficulty to help you visually separate the data. For example, you might classify items that have difficulty indices between .90 and 1.00 as easy for the group; items that have difficulty indices between .70 and .89 as moderately easy; items that have difficulty indices between .50 and .69 as fairly difficult; and those that have difficulty indices of .49 or below as very difficult because the majority of the class missed them. A table that visually separates items into these four difficulty categories will aid your data interpretation. Additionally, a summary table that lists the possible range of discrimination indices for each difficulty level will help you interpret the data. The structure for such a summary table is shown in Table 10.4.

TABLE 10.4 Structure for Organizing Item Data

Difficulty Classification	Easy			Moderately Easy				Fairly Difficult				Very Difficult
Maximum + d	.00	.10	.20	.30	.40	.50	.60	.70	.80	.90	1.00	.90–.00
Observed p	1.00	.95	.90	.85	.80	.75	.70	.65	.60	.55	.50	.45–.00
Goals Items												

Table 10.4 contains columns to identify goals and items and a column for each difficulty index. Above each difficulty index is listed the highest possible discrimination index for each. To complete the table, locate the cell corresponding to each item's calculated difficulty and record the calculated discrimination index. There is no need to record the difficulty index because the location of the discrimination index provides this information. Since only one column is included for very difficult items, both the difficulty and discrimination indices should be recorded in these cells.

In Table 10.5, all the item data from the bottom rows of Table 10.2 are recorded in the appropriate cells. Notice how organizing the data in this manner aids interpretation. For example, if you have a heterogeneous group, and if a skill measured by an item is easy, you expect to find the item data in the far left columns. Likewise, if a skill is moderately complex, you expect to locate data for it within the moderately easy columns. As the skills increase in complexity, you expect to see the item data located farther to the right. If the data do not appear within the expected region of the table, it denotes potential item problems.

The expected and observed discrimination indices can also be compared quickly using the summary table. For heterogeneous groups, you would generally expect discrimination indices recorded on the left side of the table to be small (or near 0) and those on the right side of the table to be larger. For homogeneous groups, however, you would expect them to be relatively small throughout the table.

The following discussion illustrates how the item data summarized in Table 10.5 would be interpreted for the class that took the capitalization test. First, determine whether the class was heterogeneous or homogeneous. This determination can be made by reviewing the range of overall test scores earned by students in the group. The students' overall test scores ranged from a high of 20 to a low of 12. Additionally, students' scores did not fall into high or low clusters but reflected the entire range. This information would lead you to conclude that the class is relatively heterogeneous. Therefore, you should expect to see at least moderate discrimination between the upper and lower groups for items in which the discrimination index can vary.

Second, estimate the complexity of skills measured by the test, set expectations for difficulty indices based on skill complexity, and compare the

TABLE 10.5 Summary Table for Organizing and Interpreting Difficulty and Discrimination Indices

Difficulty Classification		Easy			Moderately Easy				Fairly Difficult				Very Difficult
Maximum + d		.00	.10	.20	.30	.40	.50	.60	.70	.80	.90	1.00	.90–.00
Values of p		1.00	.95	.90	.85	.80	.75	.70	.65	.60	.55	.50	.45 ↓
Goals	**Items**												
Capitalize: First word of sentence	7	.00											
	11	.00											
	14	.00											
Pronoun *I*	3	.00											
	9	.00											
	17	.00											
Proper nouns PR	1	.00											
PL	5				.30								
PL	13											.60	
PL	16					.40							
TH	8							.60					
TH	19								− .30				
Proper adjectives	2	.00											
	6			.20									
	10										.90		
	18	.00											
Days and months	4			.20									
	12		.10										
	15							.60					
	20							.60					

observed indices with those anticipated. Goals related to capitalizing the first word of a sentence, the pronoun *I*, proper adjectives, and days and months were judged to be quite easy. Therefore, the difficulty indices for these skills should be very high. Reviewing the data in Table 10.5, you can see that the anticipated difficulty levels were obtained. One goal, Capitalizing Proper Nouns, was considered more complex. Within this goal, items related to people's names were judged to be very easy; those related to naming places were judged to be more complex; and those related to naming things were judged to be most difficult, but not too difficult for the majority of the group. With these expectations in mind, review the data for capitalizing proper nouns in Table 10.5. The difficulty indices for this goal ranged across the difficulty categories, which is not surprising. Item 1(PR) included a person's name, and as expected, it was very easy for the group. Items 5, 13, and 16 related to places (PL) and were considered more complex. As anticipated, the *p* values for these items were observed within the moderately easy and fairly difficult ranges. Two items, 8 and 19, related to things (TH). Again, as anticipated, the difficulty indices for these items fell within the moderately easy and fairly difficult ranges.

Once you have compared the anticipated and observed difficulty indices for each skill area, compare those within an area for consistency. Difficulty indices were consistent for First Word of a Sentence, Pronoun *I*, and Proper Nouns (TH) items. However, item difficulties were not consistent for Proper Nouns (PL), Proper Adjectives, or Days and Months items. Within the Proper Nouns (PL) area, item 13 is much more difficult than the other two items. You might want to review this item to ensure that it contains words that all class members understand. Within the Proper Adjectives category, there appears to be a potential problem with item 10, which is atypically more difficult than the other items in the set. Finally, you might want to check items 15 and 20 in the Days and Months area to see whether the increased complexity there is warranted or unintentional.

Next, review the discrimination indices for all items under the easy category to see whether the observed discrimination is reasonable, given the relatively heterogeneous nature of the group. Comparing the observed discrimination with the maximum possible discrimination for each difficulty level, you can see that all items but one, 19, show good discrimination between the upper and lower groups. Item 19 has a difficulty index of .65, which means that maximum positive discrimination for this item is .70. For this somewhat heterogeneous group you should obtain a discrimination index somewhere around $\frac{1}{2}d_{max}$, or .30 to .40, at this difficulty level. Thus, a discrimination index of $-.30$ for item 19 is unacceptable. This item should be reviewed carefully and revised before reuse. If you are unable to locate the problem by reviewing the item and its directions, ask several students in the upper group why they answered as they did. Their explanations should provide clues to the problem. In summary, items 13, 10, 15, and 20 should be reviewed for potential problems; item 19 should be reviewed to locate the existing problem.

ITEM DISTRACTOR ANALYSIS

An item distractor analysis is performed for selected-response items to review items judged to be problematic during difficulty and discrimination analyses, to evaluate the plausibility of distractors, and to identify areas in which instruction needs to be revised.

Selecting Items for Distractor Analysis

Although a distractor analysis of all items would be beneficial for improving test quality, many teachers find their time too limited. Therefore, they often select a subset of items for analysis. Obviously, you should review items identified as potentially problematic during the difficulty and discrimination analyses. You might also have time to review the items that measure relatively complex skills. Analyzing these items will help you determine whether all the distractors were plausible or reflected misconceptions and problems students had.

For the capitalization test, four items (10, 13, 15, and 20) were considered potentially problematic because they proved to be more difficult for students than anticipated. Additionally, they were more difficult than other test items measuring the same skills. These items would be selected for review to determine whether the observed complexity was warranted or unintentional. A review of item 19 is warranted because of its negative discrimination. A distractor analysis should help you locate the problem.

Given time, you might also review the items for capitalizing the names of places and things. Analyzing these items will help you judge the quality of your distractors and perhaps improve the test's diagnostic potential.

Organizing the Data for Distractor Analysis

To perform a distractor analysis for the selected items, determine how many students in the upper and lower groups selected each distractor. Creating a distractor analysis table will help you summarize this information. Table 10.6 summarizes distractor data for the selected items from the item worksheet in Table 10.2. The left-hand column lists the reason for the review; the center columns identify the goals, items, and groups; and the columns on the right contain the response options for each item. The cells contain the number of students in the upper and lower groups who selected each option. An asterisk is used to identify correct answers.

Reviewing the distractor data in Table 10.6 for items that were more difficult than anticipated, you can see that all ten students in the upper group answered the three items correctly. All nine students who missed item 10 chose only distractor number 3. There are two possible explanations for this finding. First, distractors 1 and 4 may have appeared illogical to them. To check this possibility, review the contents of these distractors and judge whether they represent plausible choices. If you find them unrealistic, revise the item before you use it again. However, if you believe distractors 1 and 4 represent logical alternatives to the correct answer, then the second explanation for the data is more probable: distractor 3 reflects a common misconception held by a large portion of the class. This explanation requires revising your initial instruction to include information on how to avoid the problem.

TABLE 10.6 Summary of Distractor Data for Selected Items on the Capitalization Posttest

Reason for Review	Goal	Item	Group	Responses 1	2	3	4	5
Items more difficult than anticipated	Capitalize proper adjectives	10	U		10*			
			L	X	1*	9	X	
	Capitalize days and months	15	U			10*		
			L	1	4	4*	1	
		20	U				10*	
			L	1	3	2	4*	
Items initially judged to be complex	Proper nouns	5	U				10*	
			L	X	3	X	7	
		13	U		1	1	8*	
			L	1	1	6	2*	
		16	U			10*		
			L	1	3	6*	X	
		8	U			10*		
			L	3	2	4*	1	
Item discriminates negatively		19	U	X	5*	5	X	
			L	X	8*	2	X	

* Correct answers

Distractor analysis also enables you to tailor subsequent instruction and reviews to the specific needs of the class.

For items 15 and 20, note that (1) all the distractors included in these items appeared logical for the group, and (2) no common misconception or problem appears to be present. Because both items measured the same skill, and students' response patterns were similar, you would probably conclude that either both items were faulty or the instruction resulted in confusion. Therefore, both should be reviewed.

For the items initially judged to be complex, the distractors not chosen by anyone are indicated by a large "X"; they should be reviewed for plausibility. Item 19 discriminates negatively between the upper and lower groups, and all students who missed the item selected distractor 3. Evidently the problem is located in distractor 3. Either responses 2 and 3 are both correct or something in response 3 confused the students.

Following the distractor analysis, both items and instruction can be revised as needed. Items that are confusing or contain serious construction errors can be eliminated from the test. Students' overall test scores should be adjusted to reflect the corrections before analyzing the group's overall achievement or assigning grades.

USING MACHINE-SCORING SERVICES

Many schools have machine-scoring services that can produce data summaries for selected-response tests. These services are a valuable resource for teachers who believe that item analysis is worthwhile. Most machine printouts show each student's response to each item and, in addition, the difficulty index. Some provide discrimination indices as well.

Although the formats of machine-scored summaries vary, most are similar to the following one:

Item:	1	2	3	4	5	6	7	8	9	10	11	12	13	14	15	Raw Score	%
Answer:	3	2	1	2	4	1	3	3	5	5	1	3	2	4	2	15	100
Anderson	•	•	•	1	•	•	•	•	3	•	•	•	•	•	1	12	80
Baldwin	—	•	•	—	•	•	•	•	3	•	•	•	*	—	•	10	67

Where:

    • = a correct answer
1,3 = selected distractors
  — = no answer selected
   * = multiple answers selected for one question

In addition to illustrating how each student responded to each item, the summary reports each student's raw score and percentage of items answered correctly. If the scoring service in your school does not provide discrimination indices, you can obtain them by having the tests scored twice. After the first scoring, rank order the answer sheets by raw score, then select the papers with the ten highest and ten lowest scores. Have the tests for the upper group and lower group scored separately the second time, as though they were different tests. The second set of printouts will present the data for the two groups separately, which will aid in calculating the discrimination index and organizing data for the distractor analysis.

To aid distractor analysis, most scoring services provide another printout that illustrates the percentage of students who select each response. The following illustration shows the type of information generally included:

		Responses					No
Objective	Item	1	2	3	4	5	Response
1	1	5	5	80*	5	5	
	2	60*	35				5

The two left columns identify the objective, enabling skill, or goal and the item numbers. When the items on your test are sequenced by objective or goal, the data will be automatically organized for the analysis. The numbers within each item row indicate the percentage of students who select each response, and the asterisk identifies the correct answer. As the illustration shows, 80 percent of the students selected the correct answer for item 1, and all four distractors were chosen by 5 percent of the group. Sixty percent of the students answered item 2 correctly, 35 percent selected distractor 2, and no one chose distractors 3, 4, or 5. Five percent of the class failed to answer the item. The responses with the asterisks are the difficulty indices (p) since they reflect the percentage of students who answered the item correctly.

This printout can be used to obtain discrimination indices quickly when they are not provided. After having the tests scored separately for the upper and lower groups, simply subtract the percentage of students in the lower group who answered an item correctly from the percentage of students in the upper group who also got the answer right. For example, if the printout indicates that 80 percent of the students in the upper group and 60 percent in the lower group answered an item correctly, you calculate the discrimination index as follows:

$$d = \overset{U}{.80} - \overset{L}{.60} = .20$$

Notice that this index is the same as the one you would obtain if you used frequencies.

$$d = \frac{8 - 6}{10} = \frac{2}{10} = .20$$

Because most machine-scored printouts provide percentages, this calculation method is easier than the one presented earlier in the chapter.

Selected-response tests scored by machine provide you with a treasure chest of data that would require many hours to produce by hand. Scoring services score your tests and provide you with each student's raw score and percentage of items correct; the response matrix that illustrates the particular incorrect responses chosen by each student; the difficulty index for each item; the percentage of the group that selected each distractor; and, frequently, the discrimination index as well. When it is not provided, the discrimination index can be calculated easily using the difficulty index. Scoring services also provide a group's score distribution and calculate the measures of central tendency and variability, which are described in the next chapter on group performance evaluation. Additionally, they provide the response matrix required for the analysis of an individual's performance (described in Chapter 12).

Learning how these data are obtained by hand should convince you that a test-scoring service is important for teachers. If your school district does not currently provide such a service, request it immediately! Otherwise you may be overwhelmed with scoring tests, summarizing data, and calculating indices. Eventually you will be tempted to skip these analyses altogether, which is unfortunate but not uncommon. Without these analyses, it is difficult for teachers to evaluate the quality of their tests and instruction and to refine their teaching skills.

SUMMARY

Due to limited time and resources, teachers usually cannot field test and revise items before a test is administered to a class. However, analyzing test items after students have taken the test can help teachers locate faulty or ineffective items and identify areas where instruction might be improved.

The three types of item analysis are item difficulty analysis, item discrimination analysis, and distractor analysis. The difficulty index is a measure of the difficulty of an item for a given group of students; it is the proportion of students who answer the item correctly; and it can range from 0 to 1.00. To describe the difficulty of an item using this measure, the indices can be classified into four categories: easy ($p = .90–1.00$), moderately easy ($p = .70–.89$), fairly difficult ($p = .50–.69$), and very difficult ($p = .00–.49$). The overall difficulty of a test depends on the number of items falling into each category. The difficulty index can be used to evaluate an item by comparing (1) an item's difficulty with the difficulty anticipated, given the skill's complexity and the group's achievement characteristics; (2) the difficulty indices for items measuring the same objective; and (3) the difficulty indices for hierarchically related items. Difficulty measures that are very different from those anticipated signal a problem with the item, the instruction, or your perception of the circumstances.

Item discrimination analysis compares the performances of students who earn higher overall test scores with those of students earning lower total scores. Discrimination indices can range from 1.00 to −1.00. Positive numbers indicate that students with higher overall scores performed better on an item than did students with lower test scores. A discrimination index of 0 indicates that the upper and lower groups performed the same on an item; a negative index indicates that the lower scoring group performed better.

Evaluating an item using the discrimination index depends on two factors: the difficulty level of the item and the group's achievement characteristics. For homogeneous groups, relatively little discrimination is anticipated for an item, regardless of its difficulty level. For heterogeneous groups, little or no discrimination is anticipated for items that are extremely easy or extremely difficult. However, moderate-to-high, positive values should be anticipated for midrange difficulty indices.

Distractor analysis is performed for selected-response items. It provides information about the plausibility of distractors, helps teachers identify common misconceptions, and pinpoints parts of an item that are causing problems. In performing a distractor analysis, the number or percentage of students in the upper and lower groups who select each response are identified and analyzed. If teachers have ample time, they analyze the distractors for all items. However, when time is limited, they analyze only items that were (1) less difficult or more difficult than anticipated, (2) negative discriminators, and (3) designed to measure relatively complex skills.

Item analysis data do not indicate what is wrong with an item. Instead, they suggest that an item and perhaps the related instruction need to be reconsidered. Before calculating group performance data or students' grades, you should eliminate items found to be defective as they tend to distort the results and affect the validity of your interpretations.

PRACTICE EXERCISES

I. In the following exercise, column 1 contains descriptions of item analysis activities and column 2 names the three types of item analyses. Match each activity with its corresponding type of analysis.

1. Analysis Activities

1. Calculate the proportion of students who answer each item correctly.
2. Summarize the number or proportion of students in the upper and lower groups who select each response option.
3. Compare the proportion of the upper and lower groups who answer each item correctly.
4. Compare the perceived item complexity with the proportion of students who answer correctly.
5. Locate responses that were not plausible as well as common misconceptions.
6. Compare the proportion of students who correctly answer items related to the same objective.

2. Types of Item Analysis

A. Difficulty analysis
B. Discrimination analysis
C. Distractor analysis

II. Calculate the difficulty (p) and discrimination (d) indices using the formulas and item data in Figure 10.8:

FIGURE 10.8

Item	R_U	R_L	p $\dfrac{R_U + R_L}{N}$	d $\dfrac{R_U - R_L}{1/2N}$
1	10	6		
2	8	7		
3	6	6		
4	4	7		

III. Given that an item analysis group contains twenty students, what are all the possible discrimination indices for an item that has a difficulty index of .80? Answer the following questions to obtain this information:

1. How many of the 20 students would need to answer the item correctly for the difficulty index to be .80? .80 × 20 = _____
2. To obtain maximum, positive discrimination, how many students in the upper and lower group would need to answer the item correctly? R_U = _____ , R_L = _____
3. Given these values for R_U and R_L, what are all the possible combinations of R_U and R_L for an item with a difficulty index of .80? Record these combinations and the related discrimination indices for each in a chart with the following column headings:

| | | | Discrimination |
| R_U | R_L | Difference | Index |

4. If a group were very homogeneous, which of the preceding discrimination indices would you anticipate for an item with a difficulty index of .80?
5. If a group were heterogeneous, which of the preceding discrimination indices would you anticipate?

IV. Table 10.7 contains an item analysis worksheet for a twenty-item test on capitalization. The goals include capitalizing (1) the names of regions of the country,

TABLE 10.7 Item Worksheet for a Second Test on Capitalization

Goals Capitalize: Items	Regions of the Country				Family Relationship				People's Titles				Artistic Works				Quotations				Raw Score
	1	2	3	4	5	6	7	8	9	10	11	12	13	14	15	16	17	18	19	20	20
Correct Answers	3	1	2	4	3	3	1	4	2	3	1	3	2	4	1	2	4	3	1	2	
Rogers																					20
Jackson																					20
Ayres								1													19
Augustine								1													19
Deddens								1					1								18
Talbot			3										1								18
McCoy											2		1								18
Jensen		2	3					1													17
Prince		2	3								2										17
Rust			3					1			2										17
R_U																					
Wilson			1	2							3										17
Boyd			4	1					2	3											16
Merrill			1	1										2	3						16
Jones			1	3					2	3											16
Hart			3							3							3	2	1		15
Little			4						2								1	2	1		15
Moyle				1						3							2	1	1		15
Brown			3	3					2								2	4	1		14
Bentley			3	2				2		3							3	2	1		13
Rogers			4	3				3		2			1	3			3	1	1		11
R_L																					
Diff. p																					
Disc. d																					

(2) words for family relationships, (3) people's titles, (4) the names of artistic works; and (5) quotations. Complete the worksheet by:

1. Counting and recording the number of students in the upper group who answered each item correctly (R_U).
2. Counting and recording the number of students in the lower group who answered each item correctly (R_L).
3. Calculating and recording the difficulty index (p) for each item.
4. Calculating and recording the discrimination index (d) for each item.

V. Use Table 10.8 to organize the difficulty and discrimination indices calculated in Table 10.7. For each item, locate the appropriate column for the observed

TABLE 10.8 Summary Table for Difficulty and Discrimination Indices (from Item Worksheet in Table 10.7)

Difficulty Classification	Easy			Moderately Easy				Fairly Difficult				Very Difficult
Maximum $+d$ *Values of p*	.00 1.00	.10 .95	.20 .90	.30 .85	.40 .80	.50 .75	.60 .70	.70 .65	.80 .60	.90 .55	1.00 .50	.90–.00 .45–.00

Goals:

Capitalize:	Items												p/d
Regions of the country	1												
	2												
	3												
	4												
Family relation-ships	5												
	6												
	7												
	8												
People's titles	9												
	10												
	11												
	12												
Artistic works	13												
	14												
	15												
	16												
Quotations	17												
	18												
	19												
	20												

difficulty index. Then record the obtained discrimination index in the intersecting cell.

VI. Use your data summary in Table 10.8 to locate test items that you believe should be reviewed. Since you have no way to establish anticipated difficulty levels in this situation, look for items that you consider to be (1) much more difficult than other items in the set, and (2) much less difficult than other items in the set. You should also identify any items that have a negative discrimination index. Record in Table 10.9 the items you believe should be reviewed. Place the item numbers beside the reason you believe they should be reviewed.

TABLE 10.9   Items Selected for Distractor Analysis

Reason for Review	Goal	Item	Group	Responses			
				1	2	3	4
More difficult than others in the set	Regions of the country		U				
			L				
			U				
			L				
	Family relationships[a]		U				
			L				
	People's titles		U				
			L				
Less difficult than others in the set	Quotations		U				
			L				
Negative discriminators	Artistic works		U				
			L				
	Regions of the country		U				
			L				

[a] Item 8 is both more difficult than others in the set and a negatively discriminating item.

VII. When you have the items selected for the distractor analysis, return to the item worksheet in Table 10.7 to identify the number of students in the upper and lower groups who chose each response for these items. Record these data in Table 10.9 in the far right columns. When you have finished recording the response data, shade the response cells for distractors chosen by no one in the group. Using your completed table, answer the following questions:

1. For items 3 and 4, related to regions of the country, indicate all of the following explanations that could apply.
   a. Students' difficulties seem to be related to one common problem or misconception.
   b. All distractors included in these items were plausible.
   c. These items should be compared with others in the set to identify how they differ.

        d. If the differences between the items represent unintended complexity, items 3 and 4 should be revised to eliminate the problem.

  2. For item 8, indicate all of the following explanations that could apply.

      a. Students' difficulties seem to be related to one common problem.

      b. All distractors included were obviously plausible.

      c. Distractor 1 should be checked to see whether it is also correct.

      d. Distractor 1 possibly contains information that is misleading or confusing.

  3. For item 11, indicate all of the following explanations that could apply.

      a. Students' difficulties seem to be related to one common problem or misconception.

      b. All distractors included were obviously plausible.

      c. The item could possibly be improved by replacing distractor 4.

      d. The item should be compared with others in the set to determine how it differs.

      e. If the difference represents unintended complexity, the item should be revised.

  4. For item 19, indicate all of the following explanations that could apply.

      a. The item should be compared with others in the set to determine how it differs.

      b. There is possibly a clue to the correct answer.

      c. The distractors are illogical.

  5. For item 13, indicate all of the following explanations that could apply.

      a. Distractors 3 and 4 are not plausible and should be revised.

      b. Distractor 1 should be checked for misleading or confusing information.

      c. The item does not contain any construction problems.

VIII. Enrichment. Perform an item analysis for a test that either you or someone else has administered to at least twenty students. Proceed in the following manner:

  1. Create a student-by-item worksheet.

      a. Group items that measure the same objectives and goals, and list items across the top of the worksheet.

      b. Rank order students' papers by raw scores and divide the papers into two groups, one containing the ten highest scores and the other containing the ten lowest scores.

      c. Record these students' incorrect responses in the table. You will need to classify errors for any completion or short-answer items on the test before recording incorrect responses for them.

  2. Calculate R_U, R_L, the difficulty index (p), and the discrimination index (d) for each item.

  3. Create a summary table to organize the difficulty and discrimination indices.

      a. List possible difficulty indices in descending order from left to right across the top of the table.

      b. Record the highest possible discrimination index for each difficulty index just above the difficulty index.

      c. Separate the difficulty indices into categories by difficulty levels: easy, .90–1.00; moderately easy, .70–.89; fairly difficult, .50–.69; and very difficult, .49 and below.

      d. List goals, objectives, and items in the far left columns.

      e. Locate the appropriate column for each item's calculated difficulty index and insert its calculated discrimination index in the intersecting cell.

4. Using your summary table, identify items that:
   a. Are either easier or more difficult than anticipated.
   b. Have difficulty indices much different from other items measuring the same objective.
   c. Do not discriminate between the upper and lower groups when they should.
   d. Have negative discrimination indices.
5. Analyze the distractors for items identified in step 4 using a distractor analysis table.
   a. Create the table by:
      1. Listing the reasons for reviewing items, the objectives measured, the particular items to analyze, and the groups in columns on the left side and the possible responses to each selected item in columns on the right side of the table.
      2. Recording the number of students in the upper and lower groups who selected each response to chosen items.
   b. Locate potential problems by:
      1. Locating and reviewing distractors not chosen by any class members.
      2. Locating and reviewing distractors selected by many of the students in the group.
      3. Locating and reviewing distractors selected by more students in the upper group.
6. Revise items you consider faulty.

FEEDBACK

I. Questions   1   2   3   4   5   6
   Answers   A   C   B   A   C   A

II. **FIGURE 10.8(F)**

Item	R_U	R_L	p	d
1	10	6	.80	.40
2	8	7	.75	.10
3	6	6	.60	.00
4	4	7	.55	−.30

III. 1. 16
     2. $R_U = 10; R_L = 6$

3.

R_U	R_L	Difference	Discrimination Index
10	6	4	.40
9	7	2	.20
8	8	0	.00
7	9	−2	−.20
6	10	−4	−.40

4. You could anticipate discrimination indices between .20 and −.20.
5. You would anticipate a discrimination index from .20 to .40.
IV. See Table 10.7(F)
V. See Table 10.8(F)

TABLE 10.7(F)

Items	1	2	3	4	5	6	7	8	9	10	11	12	13	14	15	16	17	18	19	20
R_U	10	8	6	10	10	10	10	5	10	10	7	10	7	10	10	10	10	10	10	10
R_L	10	10	1	2	10	10	10	8	10	6	3	10	9	9	9	9	4	4	10	4
p	1.00	.90	.35	.60	1.00	1.00	1.00	.65	1.00	.80	.50	1.00	.80	.95	.95	.95	.70	.70	1.00	.70
d	.00	−.20	.50	.80	.00	.00	.00	−.30	.00	.40	.40	.00	−.20	.10	.10	.10	.60	.60	.00	.60

TABLE 10.8(F)   Difficulty and Discrimination Indices for Table 10.8

Difficulty Classification	Easy			Moderately Easy				Fairly Difficult				Very Difficult
Maximum $+d$ Values of p	.00 1.00	.10 .95	.20 .90	.30 .85	.40 .80	.50 .75	.60 .70	.70 .65	.80 .60	.90 .55	1.00 .50	.90–.00 .45–.00

Goals: Capitalize:	Items	Easy			Mod. Easy				Fairly Diff.				Very Diff. (p/d)
Regions of the country	1	.00											
	2		−.20										
	3												.35/.50
	4									.80			
Family relation-ships	5	.00											
	6	.00											
	7	.00											
	8								−.30				
People's titles	9	.00											
	10					.40							
	11											.40	
	12	.00											
Artistic works	13					−.20							
	14		.10										
	15		.10										
	16		.10										
Quotations	17							.60					
	18							.60					
	19	.00											
	20							.60					

VI. See Table 10.9(F)
VII. See Table 10.9(F)

TABLE 10.9(F)   Distractor Analysis for Selected Items on the Second Capitalization Test

Reason for Review	Goal	Item	Group	Responses 1	2	3	4
More difficult than others in the set	Regions of the country	3	U		6*	4	
			L	3	1*	3	3
		4	U				10*
			L	3	2	3	2*
	Family relationships[a]	8[a]	U	5			5*
			L		1	1	8*
	People's titles	11	U	7*	3		X
			L	3*	1	6	X
Less difficult than others in the set	Quotations	19	U	10*	X	X	X
			L	10*	X	X	X
Negative discriminators	Artistic works	13	U	3	7*	X	X
			L	1	9*	X	X
	Regions of the country	2	U	8*	2	X	X
			L	10*		X	X

* Correct response
[a] This item also discriminates negatively between the upper and lower groups.

Questions	1	2	3	4	5
Answers	b	b	c	a	a
	c	c	d	b	b
	d	d	e	c	c

SUGGESTED READING

Crocker, L., and Algina, J. (1986). *Introduction to classical and modern test theory.* New York: CBS College Publishing, pp. 311–36.

Ebel, R. L., and Frisbie, D. A. (1986). *Essentials of educational measurement.* Englewood Cliffs, N.J.: Prentice-Hall, pp. 223–41.

Gronlund, N. E. (1985). *Measurement and evaluation in teaching.* New York: Macmillan Publishing Company, pp. 243–60.

Hills, J. R. (1981). *Measurement and evaluation in the classroom.* Columbus, Ohio: Charles E. Merrill Publishing Company, pp. 75–94.

Mehrens, W. A., and Lehmann, I. J. (1984). *Measurement and evaluation in education and psychology.* New York: CBS College Publishing, pp. 189–201.

Nitko, A. J. (1983). *Educational tests and measurement.* New York: Harcourt, Brace, Jovanovich, pp. 283–302.

Popham, W. J. (1981). *Modern educational measurement.* Englewood Cliffs, N.J.: Prentice-Hall, pp. 293–308.

CHAPTER 11

Evaluating Group Performance

OBJECTIVES

1. Set expectations for the distribution of scores, measures of central tendency, and measures of variability based on:
   a. The complexity of the tasks measured,
   b. The achievement characteristics of the group, and
   c. The perceived quality of the instruction and the test.
2. Describe the group's performance by:
   a. Creating a frequency distribution,
   b. Calculating measures of central tendency, and
   c. Calculating measures of variability.
3. Evaluate the group's performance by comparing the anticipated to the calculated measures.

After you have analyzed your items and corrected students' raw scores by eliminating defective items, you are ready to evaluate a group's performance. In order to evaluate a group's performance, you need to calculate several measures of their performances and then compare these measures with criteria and standards you establish. You need to answer one basic question, Are these measures reasonable given the circumstances? There are four main factors to consider when establishing your criteria for judging the reasonableness of the measures, including:

1. The complexity of the tasks measured,
2. The achievement characteristics of the group,
3. The quality of the instruction, and
4. The quality of the test.

The first two factors are relatively fixed, that is, your instruction is not likely to change the nature of the task or the characteristics of the group. However, the quality of your instruction and test can make a difference in how students perform.

When estimating levels of performance, teachers generally assume that their instruction was effective and their test was good. Therefore, expectations for group performance are set using only the complexity of the tasks and the group's characteristics. Should the group's performance not meet the expected levels, then the instruction and test are usually reviewed to locate the cause for the discrepancy.

Three main areas of indicators are used to describe a group's test performance. They are (1) the location and shape of the raw score distribution; (2) measures of central tendency, including the mean, median, and mode; and (3) measures of variability, including the range and standard deviation. The following sections present procedures for calculating and interpreting these measures to describe a group's performance. In addition, there are procedures for identifying criteria and setting standards for evaluating a group's performance. Practically speaking, calculating these group performance indicators by hand is tedious and unnecessary. However, basic paper-and-pencil methods are illustrated to ensure that you understand the logic behind the indices. Without this understanding, your ability to interpret the data would be affected. Whenever possible, obtain these indices from machine-scoring services and spend your time interpreting rather than calculating. When machine scoring is not feasible, use an inexpensive hand calculator with the capacity to compute measures of central tendency and variability from raw scores.

DESCRIBING THE DISTRIBUTION OF TEST SCORES

To describe the distribution of test scores, you can use either a frequency table or a frequency polygon.

Creating a Frequency Table

Table 11.1 shows a frequency table for the capitalization test data presented in Table 10.2. The first column lists all the possible scores starting with the highest and ending with the lowest. A second column ("Tally") indicates the number of times each score occurs. The third column indicates frequencies, or the total number of times each score appears. Notice that the term *raw score* and the symbol X are used to represent the number of items each student answered correctly. These widely accepted terms are used to represent students' individual scores throughout the chapter. Summarizing the scores on such a table will permit you to determine the highest and lowest scores quickly and to identify the score distribution pattern.

TABLE 11.1   Frequency Distribution of Scores on the First Capitalization Test

	Raw Scores X	Tally	Frequency
Highest Possible Score	20	11111 111	8
	19	11	2
	18	11	2
	17		0
	16	11	2
	15	111	3
	14	1	1
	13	1	1
	12	1	1
	.		
	.		
Lowest Possible Score	0		

Creating a Frequency Polygon

A frequency polygon is a graph that provides the same information as a frequency table. Plotting a graph of the frequency of scores will help you determine the shape of the distribution, which you can then use to interpret the results. A frequency polygon has a horizontal axis and a vertical axis placed at right angles to each other. Each point on the horizontal axis represents a possible raw score, and each point on the vertical axis represents the frequency or the number of times each score occurs. To complete the graph, place a dot at the intersection of each raw score and its frequency. Figure 11.1 shows how the frequency of one score is plotted. The dot at the intersection of a raw score of 5 on the horizontal axis and the frequency 4 on the vertical axis indicates that four students in the group answered five of twenty items correctly.

After you have plotted the frequency of each raw score, you would connect the dots to complete the polygon as shown in Figure 11.2. This graph indicates that (1) everyone in the group answered more than eight and fewer than twenty items correctly, (2) one person correctly answered nine items

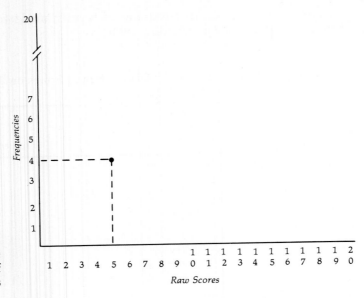

FIGURE 11.1
Plotting the
Frequency of
Raw Scores

and two correctly answered ten items, and (3) thirteen correct items was the most frequently earned score.

Figure 11.3 contains a frequency polygon for the raw scores on the capitalization test summarized in Table 11.1. The slashes at the beginning of the horizontal axis indicate that no students earned raw scores from 0 to 11. The graph begins with a raw score of 12 and ends with 20, the maximum score possible.

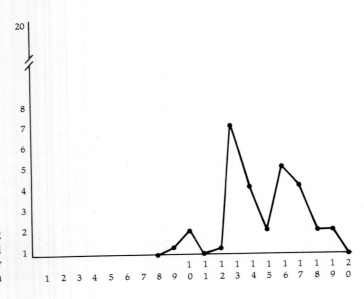

FIGURE 11.2
Completed
Frequency
Polygon

FIGURE 11.3   Frequency Polygon for Students'
Scores on the First Capitalization Test

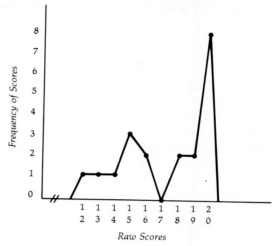

Raw Scores

Table 11.1 and Figure 11.3 both illustrate the distribution of raw scores for the class. To interpret this distribution, you need to understand the different shapes that distributions can take and what these shapes indicate.

General Shapes of Test Score Distributions

A test score distribution reflects one of several commonly observed shapes. It can be *symmetrical, skewed, unimodal, bimodal,* or *multimodal.* The normal distribution (sometimes called the *bell-shaped curve*), the rectangular distribution, and the U-shaped distribution illustrated in Figure 11.4 are all symmetrical. In a normal distribution, most scores are near the center of the distribution. The low and high ends of the score scale contain very small

FIGURE 11.4   Symmetrically Shaped Test Score Distributions

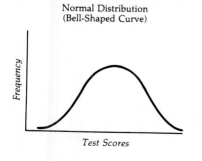

Normal Distribution
(Bell-Shaped Curve)

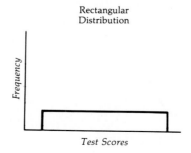

Rectangular
Distribution

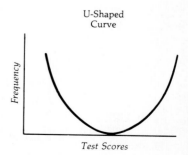

U-Shaped
Curve

frequencies of scores. The rectangular distribution, while also symmetrical, indicates that an equal number of students received each score. There is no common area of performance. In the U-shaped distribution, a large number of scores occur at the low and the high ends, but none or few occur in the middle of the distribution.

In a skewed distribution, more scores occur at either the high or low end of the score scale. When most scores occur at the high end of the scale, the distribution is *negatively skewed*. Notice that in the negatively skewed distribution in Figure 11.5, the highest frequencies appear to the right of the midpoint on the raw score scale. If the curve were folded in half at the midpoint, the two sides of the distribution would not be equal. A negatively skewed distribution indicates that more students received high scores than low scores. For this reason, it is sometimes called a *mastery curve*.

A distribution in which most scores appear toward the lower end of the score scale is positively skewed. A positively skewed distribution is illustrated to the right in Figure 11.5. Such a distribution indicates that a test was difficult for most of the class.

Distributions can also be unimodal, bimodal, or multimodal. The raw score that occurs most frequently in a distribution is called the *mode*. If only one score appears most frequently, the distribution is unimodal. The bell-shaped curve in Figure 11.4 and the skewed distributions in Figure 11.5 are examples of unimodal distributions. If two scores, some distance from each other on the scale, have higher frequencies than the scores surrounding them, the distribution is bimodal. The center distribution in Figure 11.6 represents a bimodal curve. The right-hand illustration represents a multimodal distribution in which more than two scores have atypically high frequencies compared to the scores around them.

Interpreting a Score Distribution Using Its Location and Shape

To interpret test results, consider both the location and the shape of the distribution on the raw score scale. The distribution can spread out across the range of possible test scores, or it can cover only a small portion of the

FIGURE 11.5
Skewed
Distributions of
Test Scores

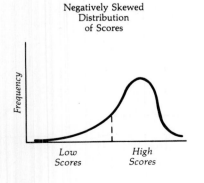

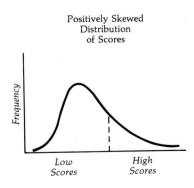

FIGURE 11.6 Unimodal, Bimodal, and Multimodal Distributions of Test Scores

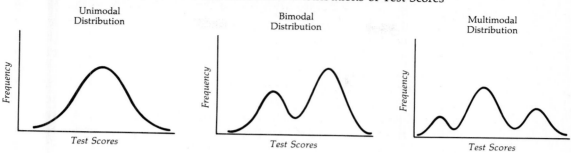

scale. Tall, narrow shapes indicate homogeneous group performance; a wide distribution of scores reflects heterogeneous performance. High, narrow distributions located at the upper end of the score scale represent high achievement; those toward the lower end of the scale suggest inadequate achievement. Consider the shapes and locations of the score distributions in Figure 11.7. Although all three distributions are unimodal, bell-shaped curves, each reflects a different level of performance. The distribution in illustration A is short and wide, reflecting heterogeneous group performance. The one in illustration B is high and narrow and located toward the high end of the scale, indicating homogeneous, high test performance. Such a distribution suggests that the group was made up of high-achieving students; or that the skills tested were very easy for the group; or that the instruction was very effective. The distribution in illustration C is also tall and narrow but located toward the lower end of the scale. This distribution indicates that the group contained low-achieving students; or that the skills tested were too complex for the group; or that the test, the instruction, or both were inadequate.

Evaluating a Group's Performance Using the Score Distribution

In order to use the observed score distribution to evaluate a group's performance, you need to judge whether the observed distribution is reasonable

FIGURE 11.7 Width and Location of Score Distributions

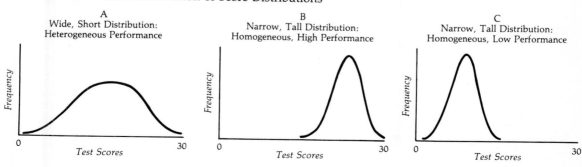

given the circumstances. Two factors can be used to establish reasonable levels of performance: the complexity of the tasks measured by the test and the achievement characteristics of the group. Using your perceptions related to these two factors, estimate a reasonable score distribution for the situation. When the distribution you observe does not resemble one you anticipate, investigate the cause.

Reconsider the class that took the capitalization test. The class was previously described as heterogeneous, and the skills measured by the test were described as relatively easy. Therefore, you would expect to see a relatively wide distribution of scores to reflect the group's heterogeneity. However, since the tasks were considered relatively easy, the shape should be negatively skewed. Now, review the distribution obtained for the test in Figure 11.3. As expected, the distribution is relatively wide. It is also located in the top half of the raw score scale, making it negatively skewed. This means that the instruction was effective and the test good, as anticipated.

A score distribution considered reasonable for one group may not be acceptable for another. For example, if the class taking the capitalization test contained only high achievers, the teacher would undoubtedly be disappointed with the score distribution in Figure 11.3. Instead of this shape, the teacher would have expected a narrow, tall distribution located toward the high end of the scale. This mismatch between the anticipated and obtained distributions would cause the teacher to question the instruction and test.

USING MEASURES OF CENTRAL TENDENCY

Measures of central tendency that identify the center of a score distribution include the *mean* and the *median*. The mean is a group's average raw score, and the median is the central point in the distribution of scores.

Calculating the Mean and Median

To calculate the mean for a set of raw scores, add all the scores together and divide the sum by the number of students in the group. For example, if raw scores for a group of five students were 5, 6, 7, 8, and 9, you would calculate the mean as follows:

1. Add
   5
   6
   7
   8
   +9
   ——
   35

2. Divide
   $\dfrac{35}{5} = 7$

Seven is the mean score for the set of scores.

The following formula is used to represent this calculation:

$$\overline{X} = \frac{\sum X}{N}$$

In the formula, the symbol $\overline{X}$ represents the mean; the symbol $\sum$ means to sum the raw scores, represented by X; and N is the number of scores, or students, in the group.

The median is a point that divides the distribution of scores in half. You can approximate a median by locating the middle score in an ordered set of scores. For example, the median for the scores 5, 6, 7, 8, and 9 is the middle score, or 7. For an uneven number of scores, the median is simply the middle score. The median for an even number of scores is a point halfway between the two middle scores. For example, the median for the scores 5, 6, 7, 8, 9, and 10 is halfway between 7 and 8, which are the two middle scores. Thus, the median for this set of scores is 7.5.

When there are several tied scores in a distribution, calculating the median is a bit more complex. In this situation, each score is considered to extend .5 points below and .5 points above the actual scores. For example, a score of 18 would extend from 17.5 to 18.5. The score 17.5 is called the *lower real limit* for the observed score 18. The median is calculated using the following formula:

$$\text{Median} = L + \frac{\dfrac{N}{2} - \text{Sum of students below the score containing the median}}{\text{Frequency of students at the score containing the median}}$$

where:

L = The lower real limit of the raw score containing the median
N = The number of students in the group

Figure 11.8 illustrates the use of this formula to calculate the median for a set of scores.

Now, review the data for the capitalization test in Table 11.1 and calculate the mean and median. To find the mean, add all the raw scores together ($\sum X$). You should have eight scores of 20, two scores of 19, two scores of 18, and so on. Next, divide the sum of the scores by 20, the number of students in the group. Your calculation should look like this:

1. Sum scores.

   20 + 20 + 20 + 20 + 20 + 20 + 20 + 20 + 19 + 19 + 18 + 18 + 16 + 16 + 15 + 15 + 15 + 14 + 13 + 12 = 350

FIGURE 11.8   Calculating the Median

X	f
20	1
19	1
18	111
17	1111
16	11111
15	1111
14	111
13	11
12	1
11	1
10	1
N = 26	

1. The number in the group is 26 and half this number is 13. Therefore the median will divide the scores such that 13 scores are below and above it.
2. Count from the bottom of the distribution to locate the raw score that contains the thirteenth and fourteenth scores. In this example, the raw score 16 contains these scores.
3. The median is then calculated using the formula:

$$\text{Median} = 15.5 + \frac{\frac{26}{2} - 12}{5} = 15.5 + \frac{1}{5} = 15.5 + .20 = 15.70$$

2. Divide the sum by the number of students.

$$\overline{X} = \frac{350}{20} = 17.5$$

The group's average score on the capitalization test is 17.5.

You may have already concluded that multiplying each raw score by its frequency and then adding the products is a faster way to obtain $\sum X$. Whenever you use a frequency table to calculate a mean, you can save time by doing some simple multiplication as illustrated in Table 11.2.

Because there is an even number of scores (20), the median will be halfway between the two middle scores. The tenth score from the top of the distribution is 19, and the tenth score from the bottom is 18. Thus the median is halfway between 18 and 19, or 18.5.

Relating the Mean and Median to the Distribution of Scores

To interpret measures of central tendency, you can compare (1) the relative positions of the mean and median in the distribution, (2) their distance from the highest earned score, and (3) their distance from the highest possible raw score.

The illustrations in Figure 11.9 show the relative positions of the mean and median in three distributions. In distribution A, which is normal and

TABLE 11.2 Calculating the Mean Using a Frequency Table

1. Multiply each score by its frequency and sum the products.

	Raw Scores X		Frequency f		Product fX
	20	×	8	=	160
Median →	19	×	2	=	38
	18	×	2	=	36
	17	×	0	=	0
	16	×	2	=	32
	15	×	3	=	45
	14	×	1	=	14
	13	×	1	=	13
	12	×	1	=	12
			$\Sigma X =$		350

2. Divide ΣX by the number of students (20).

$$\overline{X} = \frac{350}{20} = 17.5$$

symmetrical, the mean and median occupy the same central point. In a negatively skewed distribution, like the one in example B, the atypically low scores in the group produce a mean lower than the median. A positively skewed distribution, as the one in example C, has a few extremely high scores that raise the mean above the median. These illustrations show that the mean is influenced by the size of each raw score in the distribution whereas the median is not. Extreme scores raise or lower the mean, but they have no effect on the median. In the latter case, very high or very low scores are simply scores, regardless of their values. The relative position of the mean and me-

FIGURE 11.9 Relative Positions of the Mean and Median in Score Distributions

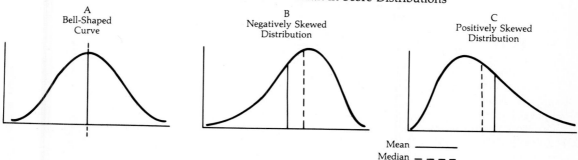

| A Bell-Shaped Curve | B Negatively Skewed Distribution | C Positively Skewed Distribution |

Mean _____
Median _ _ _ _

dian in a distribution helps you determine whether its shape is symmetrical or skewed, and if skewed, in what direction.

To assess the difficulty of a test for a group, you can compare the mean, the highest earned score, and the highest possible raw score for the test. When the mean is relatively close to the highest earned score, you have evidence that the overall group's performance was rather similar. Additionally, when the highest earned score is the same as, or close to, the highest possible score, you have evidence that the group performed similarly and well on the test. This situation is illustrated in example A of Figure 11.10.

When the mean score is close to the highest earned score (X_H), yet the highest earned score is quite a bit below the highest possible score, then a different interpretation would result. This finding would indicate that the group's performance was rather homogeneous and that the test was rather difficult. This situation is illustrated in example B of Figure 11.10.

Another pattern could emerge in which the highest earned and the highest possible scores were the same, or similar, yet the mean score was quite a bit below them on the scale. This result, illustrated in example C, would tend to reflect heterogeneous group performance on relatively complex tasks.

Evaluating a Group's Performance

To evaluate the group's performance using measures of central tendency, you need to estimate reasonable values for the mean and median and compare the estimated scores with those observed. In deciding what to expect, you

A   Total possible points = 50
    Highest earned score (X_H) = 50
    Mean score ($\bar{X}$) = 43 (86%)

B   Total possible points = 50
    Highest earned score (X_H) = 43 (86%)
    Mean score ($\bar{X}$) = 38 (76%)

C   Total possible points = 50
    Highest earned score (X_H) = 50 (100%)
    Mean score ($\bar{X}$) = 38 (76%)

FIGURE 11.10 Describing a Group's Performance Using the Mean, Highest Earned Score, and Highest Possible Score on a Test

should again consider the difficulty of the tasks measured and the achievement characteristics of the group. For example, if you have a homogeneous group of high achievers and relatively complex tasks, then you would expect to find the mean and median relatively close to the highest possible score. When the tasks measured are judged to be relatively easy for such a group, you might expect to see these scores located even closer to the highest possible score. Your expected mean and median would be lower for a homogeneous, average group and even lower for a homogeneous, below-average group. When setting expectations for the mean and median, you should select an area in which these scores will fall rather than particular scores because estimating precise scores would be very difficult. When the mean and median fall outside a reasonable area, you have reason to question the instruction and test.

Now, use the measures of central tendency to evaluate the group's performance on the capitalization test (Table 11.2). As previously described, the group is heterogeneous, and most of the tasks are relatively easy. These two factors would lead you to anticipate that:

1. The mean and median will be relatively close to the highest earned and the highest possible scores.
2. The mean will be lower than the median to reflect the anticipated negatively skewed curve.

Comparing the mean (17.5) and the median (18.5) with the highest earned score (20) and the highest possible score (20), you find that the obtained scores fall within the area anticipated. Comparing the relative positions of the mean and median, you find that the mean is lower than the median, which reflects the anticipated negatively skewed distribution. Therefore, the measures of central tendency reflect that the group's performance on the capitalization test is reasonable given the circumstances.

USING MEASURES OF VARIABILITY

The variability of performance among students in the group is indicated by the range and standard deviation. The range is set by the two extreme scores, and the standard deviation is a calculation of the average difference between the mean and each score in the set. Both measures reflect the amount that individual performances differ and thus describe the homogeneity or heterogeneity of a group's performance.

Calculating the Range

Some measurement specialists define the range (R) as the difference between the highest score and the lowest score earned on a test. The formula for this calculation is:

$$\text{Range } (R) = X_H - X_L$$

Other specialists define the range as including all observed scores in the set. Using this definition, the formula for calculating the range is:

$$R = (X_H - X_L) + 1$$

The latter procedure ensures that the range extends to include all scores. For example, if the highest observed raw score on a test is 28 and the lowest is 12, then the range would be:

$$R = 28 - 12 = 16$$
$$R = (28 - 12) + 1 = 17$$

Whether you use the first or second calculation method is a matter of personal choice although most teachers use the first one. For all practical purposes the interpretation of the index would be the same.

Interpreting the Range

One caution should be made about using the range to interpret a group's performance. Because the range is based only on the two extreme scores in a set, an atypical high or low score for the group will distort your interpretation. Atypical scores are called *outliers*; they reflect the performance of an atypical student rather than overall group performance. Thus, before calculating and interpreting the range, determine that the high and low scores are not extreme compared to the other scores in the distribution. If you find an outlier score on either end of your distribution, eliminate it and calculate the range using the next closest score to it in the set.

There are some rules of thumb you can use to interpret a range. A range that covers about one-quarter or less of the total raw score scale generally reflects homogeneous performance. Thus, if a test contains forty items and the range is about ten, then the group's performance can be considered homogeneous. As the width of the range increases, so does the heterogeneity of the performance. A range spanning about one-third of the raw score scale indicates a somewhat heterogeneous group performance; one that spans about one-half of the raw score scale signals a very heterogeneous group performance. Therefore, for a forty-item test, a range of about thirteen (or one-third of forty) would reflect somewhat heterogeneous group performance; a range of about twenty would reflect very heterogeneous performance.

As previously noted, the group's achievement characteristics and the complexity of the tasks measured should be considered when using the range to evaluate a group's performance on a given test. Again considering the data from the capitalization test (Table 11.2), you would expect to see a range that spans between one-third to one-half the raw score scale because the group is heterogeneous. One-third of the raw score scale is 6.6, or 20 (items) divided by 3. The observed range is 8, or 20 minus 12. Therefore, the observed range comes close to the expected range, indicating that the group's performance is rather heterogeneous. Like the performance indicators previously described, the range reflects the group's overall test performance was as anticipated.

Calculating the Standard Deviation

Because all scores in the distribution and the mean are used in calculating the standard deviation, the procedure is more complex. It involves the following series of steps:

1. Calculate the mean score ($\overline{X}$).
2. Subtract the mean score from each raw score (X) to find the deviation score (x).
3. Square each deviation score (x^2).
4. Add together all the squared deviation scores ($\sum x^2$).
5. Divide the sum by the number of scores (N) to obtain the average.
6. Find the square root of the average squared deviation scores.

The formula for calculating the standard deviation is:

$$SD = \sqrt{\frac{\sum(X - \overline{X})^2}{N}}$$

Although this procedure appears complicated, you can easily master it with practice. Moreover, most hand calculators can automatically square numbers and calculate square roots.

Working through an example will help you understand this procedure. Given a set of five raw scores (5, 6, 7, 8, and 9), rank and list the scores from highest to lowest. Next, add all the scores and divide by the number of scores to obtain the mean. The sum of the five scores is 35, and the mean is 7, or 35 divided by 5. The next step is to calculate the deviation score (x), and the easiest way to do this is to set up a table of columns as follows:

Raw Scores (X)		Mean ($\overline{X}$)		Deviation Score x
9	−	7	=	2
8	−	7	=	1
7	−	7	=	0
6	−	7	=	−1
5	−	7	=	−2

Notice that the mean score, 7, is subtracted from each raw score. The resulting figures are the deviation scores.

The reason for the next step, squaring each deviation score, now becomes obvious. The sum of 2, 1, 0, −1, and −2 is 0. Zero divided by the number of scores is also 0. To eliminate this problem, change all the negative deviation scores to positive numbers by squaring each score. Next, the squared deviations should be summed to obtain $\sum x^2$. Your calculations should appear as follows:

$(X - \overline{X})$	x	x^2
9 − 7	2	4
8 − 7	1	1
7 − 7	0	0
6 − 7	−1	1
5 − 7	−2	4
	$\sum x^2 =$	10

Now you can calculate the standard deviation using the formula:

$$SD = \sqrt{\frac{\sum(X - \overline{X})^2}{N}}$$

You already have the numerator, 10, which is the sum of your x^2 column. Divide 10 by 5, which is the number of scores in the set. Your formula now is:

$$SD = \sqrt{\frac{10}{5}} \text{ or } SD = \sqrt{2}$$

Use your calculator to find the square root of 2, which is 1.41. This standard deviation of 1.41 for this set of scores is the average distance between the mean and all raw scores in the set.

Table 11.3 presents the calculations needed to figure the standard deviation for the first capitalization test. The first and second columns list the raw scores and the mean score, 17.5. The third column contains each deviation score, and the fourth column the squared deviation scores. Below the fourth column is the sum of the squared deviation scores, 141. The standard deviation, 2.66, is the square root of 141 divided by 20, the number of scores in the set.

TABLE 11.3   Calculating the Standard Deviation for the First Capitalization Test

$(X - \overline{X})$	x	x^2	
20 − 17.5 =	2.5	6.25	*Formula*
20 − 17.5 =	2.5	6.25	
20 − 17.5 =	2.5	6.25	
20 − 17.5 =	2.5	6.25	$SD = \sqrt{\dfrac{\Sigma(X - \overline{X})^2}{N}}$
20 − 17.5 =	2.5	6.25	
20 − 17.5 =	2.5	6.25	
20 − 17.5 =	2.5	6.25	$= \sqrt{\dfrac{141}{20}}$
20 − 17.5 =	2.5	6.25	
19 − 17.5 =	1.5	2.25	$= \sqrt{7.05}$
19 − 17.5 =	1.5	2.25	
18 − 17.5 =	.5	.25	$= 2.66$
18 − 17.5 =	.5	.25	
16 − 17.5 =	−1.5	2.25	
16 − 17.5 =	−1.5	2.25	
15 − 17.5 =	−2.5	6.25	
15 − 17.5 =	−2.5	6.25	
15 − 17.5 =	−2.5	6.25	
14 − 17.5 =	−3.5	12.25	
13 − 17.5 =	−4.5	20.25	
12 − 17.5 =	−5.5	30.25	
	$\Sigma x^2 = 141$		

Interpreting the Standard Deviation

Two factors influence the size of the standard deviation: the range and the distribution of scores within the range. Because both the range and the standard deviation are measures of a group's variability, larger ranges will produce larger standard deviations. A wide range and standard deviation both reflect heterogeneous performance, and narrow ones reflect performances that are more similar.

For a given range size, the size of the corresponding standard deviation will vary based on the distribution of scores within the range. For example, the ranges and mean scores are the same in the score distributions illustrated in Figure 11.11, yet the score patterns within these distributions are very

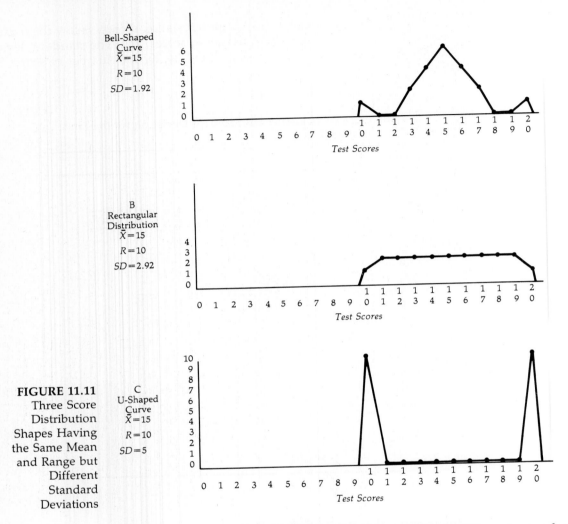

different. These different score patterns produce different standard deviations.

Most scores are close to the mean score in the bell-shaped curve in example A. In distributions in which there is a short distance between the mean and most other scores in the set, the standard deviation will be small for the range. A relatively small standard deviation for a given range reflects rather similar performance for most students in the group. The scores in the rectangular distribution, illustration B, are farther from the mean. The standard deviation for such a distribution will be larger than one for a distribution in which most of the scores are clustered in one area. A rectangular distribution reflects heterogeneous performance within the range with no area of similar performance. The bimodal, U-shaped distribution in example C produces the largest standard deviation because the average distance between the mean and other scores in the set is greater. This distribution reflects two divergent groups within the class.

You can estimate the distribution of scores within the range using a few quick calculations and comparisons. The largest possible standard deviation for any given range is the range divided by two. Such a large standard deviation would reflect a U-shaped distribution (see example C in Figure 11.11). Although so large a standard deviation is unlikely, you can use this figure as a basis of comparison for the obtained standard deviation value. The following rules will help you determine the variability of a group's performance within the range.

1. A standard deviation close to one-half of the range indicates that the group's performance is very diverse within the range.
2. A standard deviation close to one-third of the range reflects scores that are dispersed throughout the range.
3. A standard deviation spanning one-quarter or less of the range indicates that most scores are clustered within an area.

For example, if the range were 20, an observed standard deviation approaching one-half this value, or 10, reflects two diverse groups in the class. An observed standard deviation of around 6.6, or one-third of the range, reflects a more even distribution of scores throughout the range. However, a standard deviation of about 5 or less, one-quarter of the range, reflects a majority of scores clustered within an area.

Evaluating a Group's Performance

To evaluate a group's performance using the standard deviation, you should first decide what value you expect. Using the previously obtained information for the capitalization test, you would undoubtedly expect a standard deviation somewhere around one-third to one-quarter of the range because, although the group is heterogeneous, the tasks were relatively easy. Given the range of 8 for the test, you would expect the standard deviation to be between 2.66 and 2, rather than between 2.66 and 4. Once you have selected an area for the standard deviation, you should compare it with the one obtained. The standard deviation calculated for the capitalization test is 2.66 (see Table 11.3), and the expected standard deviation is about 2.66. Therefore, the scores are distributed within the anticipated range and reflect the heterogeneous nature of the group.

The machine-scoring services available for selected-response tests eliminate the tedium of calculating the mean and standard deviation. These scores are usually provided on the printout and need only be compared with those you anticipate.

Estimating the Standard Deviation

When machine-scoring services are not available, you may want to estimate, rather than calculate, the standard deviation. This estimation procedure is recommended by Hills (1981). It is most accurate when the students in your group typically produce a rather normal distribution of test scores, or bell-shaped curve. The formula for estimating the standard deviation is:

$$SD_E = \frac{R}{k}$$

SD_E stands for the estimated standard deviation, R represents the range of scores, and k is a predetermined constant based on the size of the class. In estimating standard deviations for your own tests, you should use a constant from the following list. In selecting the appropriate constant for your group, consider your class size. For example, if your class contains fifteen students, then the constant 3 should be used because the group size of 9 listed is closest to your class size. If your class contains between eighteen and sixty-two students, you should use the constant 4. If your group contains more than sixty-two students, the constant 5 should be used.

Number of Students in the Group	Recommended k Value
4	2
9	3
27	4
98	5

Referring to Table 11.3, estimate the standard deviation for the capitalization test. The range of scores is 8, and the constant to use is 4 because the group contains twenty students. Using these numbers in the formula, you should obtain the following estimate:

$$SD_E = \frac{8}{4} = 2$$

In this case, the estimated standard deviation underestimates the calculated standard deviation, 2.66, because the observed distribution was skewed rather than bell-shaped.

One caution is that this estimation procedure does not allow for the unique achievement characteristics of all group members because only the range and group size are used. However, if your group is rather typical, meaning that it usually produces short, bell-shaped or slightly skewed distributions rather than extremely skewed, rectangular, or U-shaped ones, then the estimation is a reasonable substitute. In addition, an estimated standard deviation cannot be used to detect discrepancies between what you anticipate and what actually occurred because the estimated standard deviation does not reflect the actual score pattern within the range.

SUMMARY

The following outline summarizes the procedure used to describe and evaluate a group's test performance.

A. Describe and compare test results.
   1. Create a frequency table or frequency polygon of the test scores.
   2. Compare the location of the highest and lowest earned scores with the highest possible score and decide whether they are reasonable, given the complexity of the tasks measured by the test and achievement characteristics of the group.
   3. Calculate and compare measures of central tendency.
      a. Calculate the mean and note its position in the score distribution.
      b. Locate the median and note its position in the score distribution.
      c. Locate any mode (or modes) and note its position in the score distribution.
      d. Compare the mean, median, and mode and describe the distribution as being symmetrical or skewed based on these measures.
   4. Compare the observed measures of central tendency and their location in the score distribution to those you would expect, given the complexity of the tasks and the achievement characteristics of the group.
   5. Calculate and compare the measures of variability.
      a. Calculate the range.
      b. Calculate the standard deviation.
   6. Compare the variability measures with those you would expect, given the complexity of the tasks and the group's characteristics.
B. Note any discrepancies between measures you expected and those you observed.
C. Try to explain any discrepancies you find. Discrepancies are usually caused by misjudging the quality of instruction or the test. They are also potentially related to misinterpreting the complexity of the tasks or the group's achievement characteristics.
D. Judge the group's performance as being better than expected, as expected, or lower than expected.

Table 11.4 summarizes the group's performance on the capitalization test. The performance indicators are listed in the far left column, and the teacher's estimations for the class are listed in the second column. The observed results are listed in the third column, and any discrepancies between the estimated and observed measures are listed in the last column. Comparing the information summarized in the table, you can see that the teacher was very good in synthesizing factors that relate to group performance since there are no discrepancies between the estimated and observed measures. This teacher would undoubtedly conclude that the group's test performance was as expected and very good for a heterogeneous class.

TABLE 11.4 Summary of the Estimated and Observed Measures of Group Performance on the First Capitalization Test

Performance Indicator	Estimation Based on Relatively Easy Tasks and a Heterogeneous Group	Observation	Discrepancy
Location of highest earned score	Highest possible score	Highest possible score	None
Location of lowest earned score	Slightly more than half the number of items correct	12 (or 60%) of the items correct	None
Location of mean score	Close to the high end of the distribution	17 (or 85%) correct	None
Location of median score	Higher than the mean score	18.5	None
Location of mode	Around the mean and median	Around the mean and median	None
Range	Between one-third and one-half of the total number of items $\frac{20}{3} = 6.66$ $\frac{20}{2} = 10$	8	None
Standard deviation	Somewhere around one-third of the range $\frac{8}{3} = 2.66$	2.66	None
Distribution shape	Negatively skewed	Negatively skewed	None

PRACTICE EXERCISES

A. Test Score Distributions
  1. Use the following raw scores, taken from the second capitalization test in Table 10.6, to complete the frequency table and frequency polygon in Figure 11.12.
     20, 20, 19, 19, 18, 18, 18, 17, 17, 17, 17, 16, 16, 16, 15, 15, 15, 14, 13, 11
  2. Which of the following descriptions fits the distribution of raw scores in Figure 11.12?
     a. Symmetrical; unimodal
     b. Rectangular; no mode
     c. Negatively skewed
     d. Positively skewed

FIGURE 11.12

Frequency Table		*Frequency Polygon*

X   Tally   Total

20
19
18
17
16
15
14
13
12
11

Frequency

6
5
4
3
2
1

10 11 12 13 14 15 16 17 18 19 20
Test Scores

B. Measures of Central Tendency
   3. What is the name of the average score in a set of test scores?
       a. Mode
       b. Standard deviation
       c. Mean
       d. Median
   4. Fifty percent of the scores fall below which point in a distribution:
       a. Mean
       b. Median
       c. Mode
       d. A score half way between the highest and lowest raw score

Column *A* contains the location of the mean and median in a distribution of test scores. Column *B* contains the shapes of score distributions. Match the location of the mean and the median with the corresponding distribution shape.

A	*B*
5. The mean and median are the same value.	a. Positively skewed
	b. Negatively skewed
6. The mean is greater than the median.	c. Symmetrical, bell-shaped
7. The median is greater than the mean.	d. Symmetrical, rectangular
	e. Both c and d

8. Calculate the mean for the set of scores in item 1 using the following formula:

$$\overline{X} = \frac{\Sigma X}{N}$$

9. Calculate the median for the set of scores using the frequency table in item 1 and the following formula:

$$\text{Median} = L + \frac{\frac{N}{2} - \text{Sum of students below}}{\text{Frequency of students within}}$$

10. Compare the mean and median calculated in items 8 and 9. What distribution shape does this location of the mean and median reflect?
    a. An extremely negatively skewed distribution
    b. A slightly negatively skewed distribution
    c. A symmetrical distribution
    d. An extremely positively skewed distribution
    e. A slightly positively skewed distribution

C. Measures of Variability
11. Use the following formula to calculate the range for the raw scores in Figure 11.12.

$$R = X_H - X_L$$

12. The range for this set of scores covers approximately half of the raw score scale. Therefore, how would you describe the group's performance on the test?
    a. Very homogeneous
    b. Slightly heterogeneous
    c. Heterogeneous

Column A describes distributions of scores within a range. Column B lists possible values of the standard deviation for a range of 9. Match each distribution with the standard deviation value that would reflect it.

	A		B
13.	The majority of the scores in the set are located close to the mean.	a.	$\frac{9}{2} = 4.5$
14.	The scores are spread throughout the range.	b.	$\frac{9}{3} = 3$
15.	The scores are divided between the upper and lower end of the range reflecting a bimodal, U-shaped distribution.	c.	$\frac{9}{4} = 2.5$

16. Use Table 11.5 to calculate the standard deviation for the second capitalization test.

TABLE 11.5 Raw Scores for the Second Capitalization Test Arranged for Calculating the Standard Deviation

$N = 20$

$(X - \overline{X})$	$= x$	x^2
20 − 16.55		
20 − 16.55		
19 − 16.55		
19 − 16.55		
18 − 16.55		
18 − 16.55		
18 − 16.55		
17 − 16.55		
17 − 16.55		
17 − 16.55		
17 − 16.55		
16 − 16.55		
16 − 16.55		
16 − 16.55		
15 − 16.55		
15 − 16.55		
15 − 16.55		
14 − 16.55		
13 − 16.55		
11 − 16.55		

$$SD = \sqrt{\frac{\Sigma(X - \overline{X})^2}{N}}$$

$\Sigma x^2 =$ _____

17. Since the calculated standard deviation for the second capitalization test is 2.24 and the range is 9, how would you describe the group's distribution of scores within the range?
    a. Most scores are located close to the mean score (one-fourth of the range equals 2.25, or 9 divided by 4).
    b. The scores are widely distributed throughout the range (one-third of the range equals 3, or 9 divided by 3).
    c. The scores are divided between the upper and lower end of the range (one-half of the range equals 4.5, or 9 divided by 2).
18. Estimate the standard deviation using the following formula:

$$SD_E = \frac{R}{k}$$

The recommended constant (k) for a group size of 20 students is 4.

D. Enrichment
    19. Use a test you have developed and administered to complete the following exercises.
        a. Use information about the complexity of the tasks measured and the

achievement characteristics of the group to estimate the group's performance. You should estimate:
1. The areas in which the highest and lowest raw scores will occur.
2. The area between the highest and the lowest scores in which the mean
   will be located.
3. The area in which the median will occur.
4. The shape of the distribution.
5. The range.
6. The standard deviation based on the estimated range.
b. Determine the shape of the distribution, measures of central tendency, and
   measures of variability.
c. Use the observed measures to describe the group's performance.
d. Compare the anticipated and observed performances and try to explain
   any discrepancies.

FEEDBACK

A. Test Score Distributions. See Figure 11.12(F).

1. FIGURE 11.12(F)   Frequency Table

X	Tally	Total
20	11	
19	11	
18	111	
17	1111	
16	111	
15	111	
14	1	
13	1	
12		
11	1	

N = 20

Frequency Polygon

2. c, negatively skewed

B. Measures of Central Tendency

Item:	3	4	5	6	7
Answer:	c	b	e	a	b

8. $\overline{X} = \dfrac{331}{20} = 16.55$

9.

$$\text{Median} = 16.5 + \frac{\frac{20}{2} - 9}{4} = 16.5 + \frac{1}{4} = 16.5 + .25 = 16.75$$

10. b

C. Measures of Variability

Items:	11	12	13	14	15
Answers:	R = 9	c	c	b	a

16.

$$SD = \sqrt{\frac{100.90}{20}}$$
$$= \sqrt{5.04}$$
$$= 2.24$$

17. a

18.

$$SD_E = \frac{R}{k} = \frac{9}{4} = 2.25$$

In this situation the estimated standard deviation closely approximates the actual standard deviation of 2.24.

REFERENCES

Hills, J. R. (1981). *Measurement and evaluation in the classroom*. Columbus, Ohio: Charles E. Merrill Publishing Company.

SUGGESTED READING

Crocker, L., and Algina, J. (1986). *Introduction to classical and modern test theory*. New York: CBS College Publishing, pp. 16–42.

Ebel, R. L., and Frisbie, D. A. (1986). *Essentials of educational measurement*. Englewood Cliffs, N.J.: Prentice-Hall, pp. 47–68.

Gronlund, N. E. (1985). *Measurement and evaluation in teaching*. New York: Macmillan Publishing Company, pp. 491–503.

Hills, J. R. (1981). *Measurement and evaluation in the classroom*. Columbus, Ohio: Charles E. Merrill Publishing Company, pp. 425–32.

Mehrens, W. A., and Lehmann, I. J. (1984). *Measurement and evaluation in education and psychology*. New York: CBS College Publishing, pp. 247–64.

Nitko, A. J. (1983). *Educational tests and measurement*. New York: Harcourt, Brace, Jovanovich, pp. 51–88.

Popham, W. J. (1981). *Modern educational measurement*. Englewood Cliffs, N.J.: Prentice-Hall, pp. 66–97.

CHAPTER 12

Evaluating Individual Performance and Instruction

OBJECTIVES

1. Perform a norm-referenced analysis and also an evaluation of an individual's test performances.
2. Perform a criterion-referenced analysis and an evaluation of an individual's test performances.
3. Evaluate the quality of instruction for each goal.

Once you have analyzed a group's performance, you need to interpret each individual's performance. A test score by itself has little meaning. To interpret a student's score, you can compare it with scores of other students or relate it to the number of skills measured by the test. Comparing a student's performance with that of other students is called *norm-referenced analysis*. Teachers use this type of analysis to determine whether a student's test performance is above average, average, or below average compared to classmates. Norm-referenced analysis can be used to interpret students' scores from any test, regardless of the logic used in the test design. *Criterion-referenced analysis* refers only to the interpretation of test scores obtained from criterion-referenced tests. Remember that the design of a criterion-referenced test is based on the carefully specified set of enabling skills that make up an instructional goal framework. Thus, a high score on a criterion-referenced test reflects that the student has mastered the criterion or set of skills embedded in the goal.

Likewise, a low score reflects that a student has made little, if any, progress on the criterion. Since the classroom tests described in this chapter are criterion-referenced, both criterion-referenced and norm-referenced analyses can be performed.

Each of these analyses provides a different type of information. For example, if a criterion-referenced analysis indicated that a student had mastered only half of the skills measured, you might consider the student's performance inadequate. If you then performed a norm-referenced analysis and discovered that the same student's performance was well above average in the class, your interpretation of the score would probably change. In addition to evaluating individual performances, you should evaluate the group's performance on each goal, enabling skill, or objective. Information from this analysis will help you evaluate the quality of the instruction and identify lessons or portions of lessons that were not effective.

CONDUCTING A NORM-REFERENCED ANALYSIS

To compare an individual's performance to the group's, you need to determine whether (1) the student's performance is above average, average, or below average and (2) the student's performance is consistent with her or his past performance.

Comparing Individual Performance to the Group

An easy way to compare a student's performance to that of the group is to divide the raw scores into categories of above average, average, and below average, and then compare the student's score with these categories. You can use the mean and the standard deviation to categorize the scores. First, establish the upper end of the average category by adding one standard deviation to the mean score. Then subtract one standard deviation from the mean score to locate the bottom of the average category. These two scores represent the boundaries of the average scores on the test. Scores above this range can be considered above average, and those below it can be considered below average. All that remains is to place each student's score in the appropriate category.

Consider, for example, the following categories for a forty-item test. Remember the following symbols: X_H = the highest earned score, X_L = the lowest earned score, $\overline{X}$ = the mean, and SD = the standard deviation. The standard deviation in the example is 4.27. This value, 4.27, is added to and subtracted from the mean score, 30, to locate the upper and lower boundaries of the average range.

Score Category:	Below-Average Performance		Average Performance		Above-Average Performance
Scores:	20	25.73	30	34.27	40
	X_L	-1 SD	$\overline{X}$	$+1$ SD	X_H

According to this chart, scores of 35 and above would be above average; scores between 26 and 34 would be average; and scores of 25 and below would be below average.

If your class is very heterogeneous, and you wish to make even finer distinctions in the above- and the below-average categories, you can add two more categories to the scale. To do this, two standard deviations should be added to or subtracted from the mean. The categories in the example would then appear as follows:

Score Category:	Very Low		Below Average		Average Performance		Above Average		Very High
Scores:	20	21.46		25.73	30	34.27		38.54	40
	X_L	-2 SD		-1 SD	$\overline{X}$	$+1$ SD		$+2$ SD	X_H

In this example, scores of 39 and 40 are classified as very high and scores of 20 and 21 are classified as very low.

On the first capitalization test described in previous chapters, the highest score was 20, the lowest score was 12, the mean was 17.5, and the standard deviation was 2.66 (see Table 11.3). The performance categories for this test would be:

Score Category:	Below-Average Performance		Average Performance	
Scores:	12	14.84	17.50	20.16
	X_L	-1 SD	$\overline{X}$	X_H
				$+1$ SD

Students who earned scores of 12, 13, or 14 on the test would be below average, and those who earned scores between 15 and 20 would be average. Because the highest score was within one standard deviation of the mean, no students had an above-average performance. For this test, an average performance of 17, 18, or 19 would be very good.

Comparing Current with Past Performances

Comparing a student's performance with the group's performance provides a general indication of how the student is performing. To interpret properly a student's performance that is classified as above average, average, or below average, you need to compare it with his or her usual or typical performance level. For example, an average test performance can be considered as not good, typical, or excellent depending on the student's previous record. An average-level performance would undoubtedly be considered good for a student who typically earns below-average scores. Likewise, an average performance would be viewed negatively for a student who typically earns one of the highest scores in the group.

The achievement characteristics of the group will also influence your interpretation of high, average, and low performance. An average performance in a high-achieving, homogeneous group is different than an average performance in a heterogeneous group. Because norm-referenced interpretations are relative, you should also evaluate students on the number of skills they have mastered.

CONDUCTING A CRITERION-REFERENCED ANALYSIS

All the performance analysis procedures presented thus far use students' raw scores. Raw scores alone do not provide the type of information you need to evaluate a student's progress on prescribed skills. Consider, for example, the test performances of J. Allen and T. Baker shown in Figure 12.1. Both answered eighteen of twenty-four test items correctly. If the mean score on the test is also 18, you might conclude that their performances are the same and that they are average for the group. After looking at the students' prior performance records you might also conclude that their test performances are typical for them. Now, compare the two students' responses by objective and item.

Although both students answered eighteen items correctly, their performances on the objectives were quite different. Allen correctly answered three of four items for each objective. Baker, however, correctly answered all of the items for four of the objectives, failed objective four completely, and answered half the items correctly for objective six. This information sheds new light on the divergence of the students' performances and suggests very different instructional needs.

FIGURE 12.1   Student Performance by Objective and Item

Objective	1	2	3	4	5	6	Total	
							Raw	
Item	1 2 3 4	5 6 7 8	9 0 1 2	3 4 5 6	7 8 9 0	1 2 3 4	Score	%
Answer	3 2 1 4	4 3 1 4	2 3 5 1	2 2 1 3	5 1 4 3	2 1 1 5		
Allen, J.	2	1	4	1	2	3	18	75
Baker, T.			1 3 2 2			3 3	18	75

Reviewing your students' response patterns can help you determine their mastery of the objective, enabling skills, or goals you are measuring. By using such a mastery analysis, you can better judge the quality of each student's performance and prescribe appropriate follow-up activities.

To perform a mastery analysis you need to:

1. Sort items by objective, enabling skills, or goal. This procedure is described in detail in Chapter 10. The only difference here is that you need to have the response data for all students in the class, not just for the twenty students in the high and low groups. Such a response matrix can be obtained automatically when you use machine scoring. In this case, all you need to do is to draw vertical lines in the matrix to separate the items by objective.
2. Determine the number of correct answers that will indicate minimal mastery of each skill.
3. Determine whether each student mastered each objective.
4. Prescribe follow-up activities.
5. Develop a student progress chart.
6. Evaluate students' performances.

Establishing Mastery Criteria

After you have sorted the test items, decide the level of performance on each skill that you consider mastery. If a skill is represented by multiple test items, minimal mastery is generally defined as correctly answering a majority of the items. If a skill is measured by only one or two items, the student would need to answer one or both items correctly. For example, the test just described measured six different objectives with four items each. Students would have had to answer three of the four items correctly to master each objective. If a skill is extremely important or includes a variety of subskills, you might want to set the criterion at a level higher than a simple majority of correct items.

Determining Individual Mastery of Skills

To determine an individual student's mastery of the skills, you need to (1) count the items that the student answered correctly for each skill and (2) count the number of skills that the student mastered. Referring to the example test in Figure 12.1, if a student missed two or more items per objective, you should circle these items on your chart. Next, count the number of objectives mastered and record them in the right-hand column of your chart. Your mastery chart should appear as in Figure 12.2 for the two students.

FIGURE 12.2 Describing Students' Mastery

Objective	1		2		3		4		5		6		Total	Total Obj.
					1 1 1 1	1 1 1 1	1 1 2 2	2 2 2					Raw	
Item	1 2 3 4	5 6 7 8	9 0 1 2	3 4 5 6	7 8 9 0	1 2 3 4							Score %	
Answer	3 2 1 4	4 3 1 4	2 3 5 1	2 2 1 3	5 1 4 3	2 1 1 5							24	6
Allen, J.	2 1			4 1		2		3					18 75	6
Baker, T.				(1 3 2 2)		(3 3)							18 75	4

According to the chart, Allen correctly answered a majority of the items for each objective, achieving at least minimal mastery on all six objectives. For Baker, objectives four and six are circled. The number in the right-hand column indicates that this student mastered only four of the six objectives.

The mastery analysis shown in Table 12.1 uses information from the item worksheet for the first capitalization posttest (see Table 10.2). The criterion for mastering goals related to capitalizing the first word of a sentence, the pronoun *I*, proper adjectives, and days and months was established as answering the majority of the items in each set correctly. However, the criterion for mastering the capitalize proper nouns goal was set at answering five of the six items correctly. This higher criterion was used because students could miss two items related to the same category of nouns and fail a major portion of the goal. Responses that do not meet these criteria are circled in the table, and the total number of goals each student mastered appears in the far right-hand column.

Prescribing Follow-Up Activities

To prescribe appropriate follow-up activities, you need to consider the importance of the skills that students failed and the students' previous achievement. For example, if subsequent lessons build on a particular skill, a student who failed to master the skill will undoubtedly have difficulty. The simplest way to avoid such problems is to divide the group into two categories: students who have mastered the goals and students who need more instruction and practice. You can then prescribe enrichment activities for the first group and developmental activities for the second. Regarding the capitalization test, you might individualize subsequent activities as shown in Figure 12.3.

Eight students in the class mastered, at least minimally, all five capitalization goals, and you would probably want to prescribe enrichment activities for these students. The eleven students who failed to master the capitalize proper nouns goal need additional instruction and practice in this area.

TABLE 12.1 Mastery Analysis of Students' Performances on the First Capitalization Posttest

Goals / Items #	First Word			Pronoun I			Proper Nouns						Proper Adjectives				Days and Months				Total Score	Goals Mastered
	7	11	14	3	9	17	1	5	13	16	8	19	2	6	10	18	4	12	15	20		
Correct Answers	1	1	1	3	3	2	4	4	4	3	3	2	2	3	2	3	3	4	3	4	20	5
Rogers, T.																					20	5
Jackson																					20	5
Ayres																					20	5
Augustine																					20	5
Deddens																					20	5
Talbot											3										19	5
McCoy											3										19	5
Jensen											3										19	5
Prince									3		3										18	4
Rust									2		3										18	4
Wilson									3		3			1							17	4
Boyd									3		3			3							17	4
Merrill									2	2	1			3							16	4
Jones									1					3					2	2	16	4
Hart										1	2			3					1	2	15	3
Little	2									1				3					2	3	15	3
Moyle	2	3												3					4	1	15	3
Brown	2	3								1				3					2	2	14	3
Bentley	2	3	2							4			1	3		2					13	3
Rogers, B.		3	2	2										3			1	3	2	3	12	3
Number who mastered goal		20			20					9				19				14				
Percentage who mastered goal		100			100					45				95				70				

FIGURE 12.3 Prescribed Instructional Activities for Capitalization Based on Mastery Analysis

	Additional Instruction and Practice		
Enrichment	*Proper Nouns*	*Proper Adjectives*	*Days and Months*
Augustine	Bentley	Bentley	
Ayres	Boyd		
	Brown		Brown
Deddens	Hart		Hart
Jackson	Little		Little
Jensen	Merrill		Jones
McCoy	Moyle		Moyle
	Prince		
Rogers, T.	Rogers, B.		Rogers, B.
	Rust		
Talbot	Wilson		

Only one student, Bentley, needs additional instruction and practice on capitalizing proper adjectives. Six members of the group need additional help on capitalizing days and months. Review and practice can be much more efficient when tailored to the specific needs of students.

In establishing follow-up activities, also consider each student's previous achievement. If a student's test performance is inconsistent in terms of the number of goals or objectives typically mastered, determine what factors contributed to the sudden decline or improvement in achievement.

Developing a Student Progress Chart

Some teachers like to keep a student progress chart indicating the skills that remain to be mastered by each student. This type of chart usually lists all student names in the left-hand column and indicates the objectives, enabling skills, or goals to be mastered across the top. The teacher can either post the chart on a bulletin board for student use or refer to the chart during private consultations with students or their parents. A student progress chart for the first capitalization posttest appears in Table 12.2. An X represents a goal the student has mastered. The blank cells indicate that the student failed the skill on the first posttest. As the students master the goals on subsequent posttests, the teacher can place an X in the blank cell.

Evaluating Students' Performances

Students' performances can be evaluated by comparing the raw scores and the number of skills mastered. Reviewing either of these scores independently

TABLE 12.2   **Student Progress Chart for the First Capitalization Posttest**

Students	\ Capitalization Goals				
	First Word	Pronoun I	Proper Nouns	Proper Adjectives	Days and Months
Augustine	X	X	X	X	X
Ayres	X	X	X	X	X
Bentley	X	X			X
Boyd	X	X		X	X
Brown	X	X		X	
Deddens	X	X	X	X	X
Hart	X	X		X	
Jackson	X	X	X	X	X
Jensen	X	X	X	X	X
Jones	X	X	X	X	
Little	X	X		X	
McCoy	X	X	X	X	X
Merrill	X	X		X	X
Moyle	X	X		X	
Prince	X	X		X	X
Rogers, B.	X	X		X	
Rogers, T.	X	X	X	X	X
Rust	X	X		X	X
Talbot	X	X	X	X	X
Wilson	X	X		X	X

does not provide the same insight. Earning a high test score and mastering all skills would obviously be considered a good test performance. Likewise, earning a low score and failing several skills would be judged an inadequate performance. However, it is not uncommon to find rather average test scores for students who have mastered all the skills, at least at a minimum level. When such a pattern is found, the student's overall performance can be judged as good because mastering all the skills reflects good work. However, the student may have a reading problem, may not be motivated to be very careful in answering questions, or may work too quickly. Such a pattern warrants a student conference to investigate and hopefully resolve the problem.

EVALUATING THE QUALITY OF INSTRUCTION

Analyzing individual performances provides useful information about each student's progress. To evaluate the quality of instruction, however, you need to analyze the entire group's mastery of each goal. To conduct a group mastery analysis, you need to:

1. Establish a minimum standard for group mastery of each skill
2. Describe the proportion of the group that mastered each one
3. Compare the group's performance to the minimum standards
4. Evaluate the quality of the instruction for each skill.

Setting Minimum Standards for Group Performance

To set minimum standards for the group, again consider the achievement characteristics of the students and the complexity of the skills measured. In addition, consider each skill's importance as a prerequisite for subsequent goals. For example, if a class contains average and above-average students, and if the skills measured are relatively easy, you might reasonably expect 80 percent or more of the students to master each skill. However, if the skills are important prerequisites for subsequent lessons, you might raise your criterion to 100 percent. If you have a very low-achieving group of students who are learning rather complex skills, you might lower your criterion to 75, 70, or 60 percent of the group passing. The mastery criteria you set are relative and should reflect all the factors just described. You can set one mastery criterion for all skills measured or establish a different minimum standard for each.

Describing Group Performance on Each Skill

You can easily calculate a group's performance on each skill using a mastery analysis like the one in Table 12.1. Simply count the number of students who mastered each skill and write the total at the bottom of the table. To find the percentage who mastered the skill, divide the number who passed the skill by the total number of students and then multiply the proportion by 100. Using the information in Table 12.1, group totals on the capitalization goals are as shown in Figure 12.4.

FIGURE 12.4   Evaluation of Instruction Based on Percentage of Students Mastering Each Capitalization Goal

Goal	Total Number of Students Mastering Goal	Percentage of Students Mastering Goal
Capitalize		
1. First word	20	100
2. Pronoun I	20	100
3. Proper nouns	11	45
4. Proper adjectives	19	95
5. Days and months	14	70

Comparing a Group's Performance to Minimum Standards

If 80 percent of the group passing each goal was set as the minimum acceptable standard for each skill, then you can see that group performance on two goals, capitalizing proper nouns and capitalizing days and months, did not meet the standard. The percentage of students passing the other three goals was well above the minimum standard.

Evaluating the Quality of the Instruction

As the previous example shows, a group's performance reflects the quality of instruction much more than does individual achievement. When group performance on a skill exceeds your minimum criterion, you can conclude that instruction was very effective. If group performance barely meets the minimum standard, the instruction can be judged as acceptable. If a group fails to meet the established minimum, however, you should review and revise instruction that produced such a poor posttest performance. In the example, instruction related to capitalizing proper nouns and capitalizing the names of days and months should be revised. By revising ineffective lessons throughout the year, you improve the quality of your instruction and, hopefully, raise the level of subsequent group performances.

SUMMARY

Test data can be used to analyze and evaluate an individual's performance, a group's performance, and the quality of instruction.

Individual's scores can be evaluated using both norm-referenced and criterion-referenced analysis. To make norm-referenced comparisons, you need to create performance categories of above average, average, and below average. You can then compare each student's score with these categories and with the levels earned by the student on previous tests.

Using criterion-referenced analysis, you can evaluate individual student's progress on prescribed instructional goals, enabling skills, or objectives. To conduct such an analysis you need to organize items within objectives, enabling skills, or goals; establish minimum criteria for mastering each; and determine whether each student mastered each skill. This information can be used to prepare follow-up activities and to judge the quality and consistency of each student's performance. Progress charts will help you keep track of skills that individual students still need to learn.

Evaluating the quality of instruction requires a third type of analysis. First, prescribe the minimum percentage of students who must master each skill for instruction to be considered adequate. Next, calculate the percentage of students who pass each skill and compare these figures with the established minimums. If the percentage of students who pass a skill exceeds the minimum standard, then instruction is considered good; if the minimum is met, instruction is considered adequate. However, if the proportion passing does not meet the minimum standard, the instruction is considered inadequate, and you should analyze and revise related lessons.

Although these analyses procedures may seem complex and time consuming, they are easily mastered with practice. Today, machine-scoring services can provide most of the required data summaries that you need. Once you recognize the value of these analyses for aiding your evaluation and planning, you will want to use them whenever possible.

PRACTICE EXERCISES

A. Norm-Referenced Analysis of a Student's Performance. In Chapter 11, you calculated the following measures for the second capitalization test:

$$X_H = 20 \qquad \overline{X} = 16.55$$
$$X_L = 11 \qquad SD = 2.24$$

1. Use these measures to divide the range of scores into categories of above
average, average, and below average performance.

Score Category:	Below Average	Average Performance			Above Average
Scores:	X_L	-1 SD	$\overline{X}$	$+1$ SD	X_H

2. Using these categories, judge the performance of those students with the raw
scores indicated in Figure 12.5.

B. Criterion-Referenced Analysis of a Student's Performance. Table 12.3 repeats the
item worksheet for the second capitalization test.

3. Use the item information in Table 12.3 to set a minimal mastery criterion for
each goal.
4. Count the number of items answered correctly for each goal by each student.
Circle the items for each goal *not* mastered by each student.
5. Count and record in the right-hand column the number of goals mastered by
each student.
6. On a chart like Figure 12.6, indicate the students from Table 12.3 who should
receive the prescribed follow-up activities.
7. Table 12.4 contains a skill progress chart for all of the capitalization goals with
results from the first posttest already recorded. Add the mastery data for the
second capitalization test that appear in Table 12.3. If a student mastered the
goal, place an X in the appropriate cell. If the student did *not* master the goal,
shade the block. Finally, place the total number of goals that each student
mastered in the right-hand column.

C. Mastery Analysis of the Group's Performance on Each Goal

8. In Table 12.3, calculate the frequency and percentage of students who mas-

FIGURE 12.5 Performance Compared to Class

Student	Score	Below Average	Average	Above Average
Merrill	16			
Talbot	19			
Bentley	13			
Wilson	17			
Jackson	20			

tered each goal. Record the frequency and percentage data in the bottom two rows of the table.

9. Assume that you have set 80 percent of the students passing as the minimum acceptable criterion for each goal. Compare this criterion with the percentage of the group who passed each goal (see Table 12.3). On Figure 12.7, indicate whether instruction for each goal was good, adequate, or inadequate.

10. Which lessons related to the five capitalization goals need to be reviewed and revised?

D. Enrichment

11. For a test you have developed and administered, complete the following:
    a. Establish above-average, average, and below-average categories of scores using the mean and the standard deviation.
    b. Compare each student's score to the established categories and determine whether the performance is above average, average, or below average within the group.
    c. Establish criteria for minimal mastery of each skill measured and:
       1) Determine the number of skills each student mastered.
       2) Prescribe follow-up activities for each student. Identify students who should receive enrichment activities and those who need additional instruction and practice on each skill.
    d. Evaluate instruction
       1) Establish a criterion for the minimal percentage of students who should master each skill.
       2) Calculate the percentage of students who master each skill.
       3) Compare the percentage who passed each skill to the criterion established and judge instruction as good, adequate, or inadequate.
       4) Revise lesson plans for ineffective instruction.

FEEDBACK

A. Norm-Referenced Analysis of a Student's Performance
   1. The categories are:

Score Category:	Below Average	Average Performance			Above Average
Scores:	11	14.31	16.55	18.79	20
	X_L	-1 SD	$\overline{X}$	$+1$ SD	X_H

The upper and lower boundaries of average performance were obtained by adding the standard deviation, 2.24, to the mean score, 16.55, and subtracting it from the mean score.

   2. Each student's performance compared to the group's performance is:

B. Criterion-Referenced Analysis of a Student's Performance
   3. Four items are used to measure each of the five goals. If the mastery criterion

TABLE 12.3   Mastery Analysis of Students' Performances on the Second Capitalization Posttest

Goals: Capitalize:	Regions of the Country				Family Relationship				People's Titles				Artistic Works				Quotations				Raw Score	Goals Mastered
Items	1	2	3	4	5	6	7	8	9	10	11	12	13	14	15	16	17	18	19	20	20	5
Correct Answers	3	1	2	4	3	3	1	4	2	3	1	3	2	4	1	2	4	3	1	2		
Rogers, T.																					20	
Jackson																					20	
Ayres							1														19	
Augustine							1														19	
Deddens							1						1								18	
Talbot			3																		18	
McCoy										2			1								18	
Jensen		2	3				1														17	
Prince		2	3							2											17	
Rust			3				1			2											17	
Wilson			1	2						3											17	
Boyd			4	1					2	3											16	
Merrill			1	1											2	3					16	
Jones			1	3					2	3											16	
Hart			3							3							3	2	1		15	
Little			4						2								1	2	1		15	
Moyle				1						3							2	1	1		15	
Brown			3	3					2								2	4	1		14	
Bentley			3	2				2		3							3	2	1		13	
Rogers, B.			4	3				3		2			1	3			3	1	1		11	
Number who mastered goal																						
Percentage who mastered goal																						

FIGURE 12.6   Follow-up Activities

Enrichment	Additional Instruction and Practice in Capitalization			
	Regions of the Country	Person's Title	Artistic Works	Quotations

TABLE 12.4 Student Progress Chart for All the Capitalization Skills

	First Word	Pronoun I	Proper Nouns	Proper Adjectives	Days and Months	Regions of Country	Family Relationship	Person's Title	Artistic Works	Quotations	Number of Capitalization Goals Mastered (10)
Students											
Augustine	X	X	X	X	X						
Ayres	X	X	X	X	X						
Bentley	X	X	—	—	X						
Boyd	X	X	—	X	X						
Brown	X	X	—	X	—						
Deddens	X	X	X	X	X						
Hart	X	X	—	X	—						
Jackson	X	X	X	X	X						
Jensen	X	X	X	X	X						
Jones	X	X	X	X	—						
Little	X	X	—	X	—						
McCoy	X	X	X	X	X						
Merrill	X	X	—	X	X						
Moyle	X	X	—	X	—						
Prince	X	X	—	X	X						
Rogers, B.	X	X	—	X	—						
Rogers, T.	X	X	X	X	X						
Rust	X	X	—	X	X						
Talbot	X	X	X	X	X						
Wilson	X	X	—	X	X						
Frequency	20	20	9	19	14						
Percentage	100	100	45	95	70						

FIGURE 12.7

Goal Capitalize:	Percentage Passing Goal	Instructional Quality		
		Good (above 80%)	Adequate (about 80%)	Inadequate (below 80%)
Regions of the country	55%			
Family relationships	100%			
People's titles	90%			
Artistic works	90%			
Quotations	70%			

TABLE 12.3(F) Mastery Analysis of Students' Performances on the Second Capitalization Posttest

Goals: Capitalize:	Regions of the Country	Family Relationship	People's Titles	Artistic Works	Quotations	Raw Score	Goals Mastered
Items	1 2 3 4	5 6 7 8	9 10 11 12	13 14 15 16	17 18 19 20	20	5
Correct Answers	3 1 2 4	3 3 1 4	2 3 1 3	2 4 1 2	4 3 1 2		
Rogers, T.						20	
Jackson						20	
Ayres		1				19	
Augustine		1				19	
Deddens		1		1		18	
Talbot	3			1		18	
McCoy			2	1		18	
Jensen	(2 3)	1				17	
Prince	(2 3)		2			17	
Rust	3	1	2			17	
Wilson	(1 2)		3			17	
Boyd	(4 1)	(2 3)				16	
Merrill	(1 1)			(2 3)		16	
Jones	(1 3)	(2 3)				16	
Hart	3		3		(3 2 1)	15	
Little	4		2		(1 2 1)	15	
Moyle	1		3		(2 1 1)	15	
Brown	(3 3)		2		(2 4 1)	14	
Bentley	(3 2)	2	3		(3 2 1)	13	
Rogers, B.	(4 3)	3	2	(1 3)	(3 1 1)	11	
Number who mastered goal	11	20	18	18	14		
Percentage who mastered goal	55	100	90	90	70		

is answering a majority of the items correctly for each goal, the students need to answer correctly three items for each.
4. See Table 12.3(F).
5. See Table 12.3(F).
6. Your chart should be similar to the one in Figure 12.6(F).
7. See Table 12.4(F).
C. Mastery Analysis of a Group's Performance on Each Goal
8. See Table 12.3(F).
9. Your chart should appear as in Figure 12.7(F).
10. The capitalization lessons related to names of regions of the country and quotations need to be revised.

FIGURE 12.5(F) Performance Compared to Class

Student	Score	Below Average	Average	Above Average
Merrill	16		X	
Talbot	19			X
Bentley	13	X		
Wilson	17		X	
Jackson	20			X

FIGURE 12.6(F) Follow-Up Activities

	Additional Instruction and Practice in Capitalizing			
Enrichment	Regions of the Country	Person's Title	Artistic Works	Quotations
Augustine	Bentley			Bentley
Ayres	Boyd	Boyd		
Deddens	Brown			Brown
Jackson	Jensen			Hart
McCoy	Jones	Jones		Little
Rogers, T.	Merrill		Merrill	Moyle
Rust	Prince			
Talbot	Rogers, B.		Rogers, B.	Rogers, B.
	Wilson			

FIGURE 12.7(F)

Goal: Capitalize:	Percentage Passing Goal	Instructional Quality		
		Good (above 80%)	Adequate (about 80%)	Inadequate (below 80%)
Regions of the country	55%			X
Family relationships	100%	X		
People's titles	90%	X		
Artistic works	90%	X		
Quotations	70%			X

TABLE 12.4(F)   Completed Student Progress Chart for All the Capitalization Skills

Students	First Word	Pronoun I	Proper Nouns	Proper Adjectives	Days and Months	Regions of Country	Family Relationship	Person's Title	Artistic Works	Quotations	Number of Capitalization Goals Mastered (10)
Augustine	X	X	X	X	X	X	X	X	X	X	10
Ayres	X	X	X	X	X	X	X	X	X	X	10
Bentley	X	X	—	—	X	—	X	X	X	—	6
Boyd	X	X	—	X	X	—	X	—	X	X	7
Brown	X	X	—	X	—	—	X	X	X	—	6
Deddens	X	X	X	X	X	X	X	X	X	X	10
Hart	X	X	—	X	—	X	X	X	X	—	7
Jackson	X	X	X	X	X	X	X	X	X	X	10
Jensen	X	X	X	X	X	—	X	X	X	X	9
Jones	X	X	X	X	—	—	X	—	X	X	7
Little	X	X	—	X	—	X	X	X	X	—	7
McCoy	X	X	X	X	X	X	X	X	X	X	10
Merrill	X	X	—	X	X	—	X	X	—	X	7
Moyle	X	X	—	X	—	X	X	X	X	—	7
Prince	X	X	—	X	X	—	X	X	X	X	8
Rogers, B.	X	X	—	X	—	—	X	X	—	—	5
Rogers, T.	X	X	X	X	X	X	X	X	X	X	10
Rust	X	X	—	X	X	X	X	X	X	X	9
Talbot	X	X	X	X	X	X	X	X	X	X	10
Wilson	X	X	—	X	X	—	X	X	X	X	8
Frequency	20	20	9	19	14	11	20	18	18	14	
Percentage	100	100	45	95	70	55	100	90	90	70	

SUGGESTED READING

Crocker, L., and Algina, J. (1986). *Introduction to classical and modern test theory.* New York: CBS College Publishing, pp. 410–30.

Dick, W., and Carey, L. M. (1985). *The systematic design of instruction.* Glendale, Ill.: Scott Foresman, pp. 222–55.

Ebel, R. L., and Frisbie, D. A. (1986). *Essentials of educational measurement.* Englewood Cliffs, N.J.: Prentice-Hall, pp. 27–9.

Gronlund, N. E. (1985). *Measurement and evaluation in teaching.* New York: Macmillan Publishing Company, pp. 463–7.

Nitko, A. J. (1983). *Educational tests and measurement.* New York: Harcourt, Brace, Jovanovich, pp. 444–63.

Popham, W. J. (1981). *Modern educational measurement.* Englewood Cliffs, N.J.: Prentice-Hall, pp. 371–99.

PART III

Communicating Student Progress

CHAPTER 13

Grading and Reporting Student Progress

OBJECTIVES

1. Design a gradebook based on your teaching assignment.
2. Create a daily record to record and summarize instances of behavior and manage classroom business.
3. Create a posttest record to document and summarize students' progress on instructional goals during the term.
   a. Combine individual posttest scores into a composite score.
   b. Convert composite scores to term grades.
4. Create a conduct record to document and summarize students' scores on conduct rating scales.
5. Identify factors that confound achievement grades and result in invalid interpretations.
6. Create a performance summary form to use as a reference during parent-teacher conferences.

Teachers are usually expected to monitor and report three types of student behavior: achievement, attendance, and conduct. School districts use report cards to communicate this information to students, parents, school personnel, and other interested parties. Students use their achievement grades and other marks to verify the quality of their work and the acceptability of their conduct. Parents use report cards to help determine the amount of study time their children need and to make educational plans. School personnel also use grades, along with other information, for a number of purposes.

1. To review the scope and sequence of the curriculum
2. To plan supplementary programs
3. To help students plan their education
4. To determine students' eligibility for special programs
5. To compare with standardized achievement test scores
6. To manage students' promotion

Employers and admission officers for colleges and universities use grades to determine whether an individual will be hired or admitted. Because grades can significantly influence decisions about a student's future, teachers should ensure that students' achievement grades and marks for conduct accurately reflect their behavior.

DESIGNING A GRADEBOOK

Teachers use a gradebook to document students' progress throughout a year. Although teaching assignments and information requirements vary, most teachers need a daily record of students' attendance and other information related to daily classroom management, a record of posttest scores, and a record of conduct scores obtained from behavior rating scales. Like most efficient accounting systems, the gradebook should separate the different types of information to reduce the probability of recording and analysis errors.

Your gradebook's design should reflect the nature of your teaching assignment. For example, an elementary teacher who teaches five different subjects to the same group needs to create one daily record, one conduct record, and a different posttest record for each subject. On the other hand, a teacher who is assigned five different groups needs a gradebook that contains a daily record, a posttest record, and a conduct record for each class.

Although commercially produced gradebooks are available, many are scanty and contain inadequate space for good documentation. You may be more satisfied with a gradebook you construct yourself using a loose-leaf notebook; large block, two-sided graph paper; and divider pages with tabs. After students' names are recorded on the first page, subsequent pages can be trimmed so the names remain visible as new pages are added. Such a gradebook has several advantages. You can add new pages as needed, remove and store information from previous terms, and insert records you might generate using the various computer programs available for gradebooks. If you are skilled in using a personal computer and spreadsheet programs that enable you to design a record for summarizing and manipulating data, you will want to use these resources to create and manage your gradebook. Commercial gradebook computer programs are now available; however, they are often not as flexible as a tailor-made spreadsheet program. Keep in mind the availability of these resources as you study the procedures recommended in this chapter.

CREATING THE DAILY RECORD

The daily record is used to document information related to daily classroom management. It contains information about attendance, homework and classroom assignments, particular instances of conduct you want to record, and other school matters. This record helps you complete behavior rating scales throughout the term, complete the attendance section of the report card, and conduct conferences with parents, students, and others. Your notations can help you explain the term marks for study habits and conduct and can also help identify factors, such as attendance or lack of participation, that contributed to students' posttest scores.

Selecting Symbols

In creating this section, you need to select symbols you can use to record information. For example, you can use symbols like those in Figure 13.1 to record instances of behavior related to attendance, study habits, participation, and conduct.

Symbols should be selected for their efficiency and convenience. Consider the symbols in the attendance column of Figure 13.1. When you first record attendance, you can use the symbol / to note a student is absent. Should the student appear during the class session with an acceptable excuse for the lateness, the symbol can be converted to an X to indicate an excused tardiness. If the student does not have an adequate excuse, a circle can be placed around the X to signal an unexcused tardiness. However, if the student does not appear, the symbol / will indicate that the student was absent that day. If the student brings an acceptable excuse for the absence, no other mark is necessary. However, if the student does not present a legitimate excuse for the absence, a circle can be placed around the / to signify an unexcused absence.

FIGURE 13.1   Symbols for Recording Behaviors

Attendance	Study Habits	Participation	Conduct
/ = Absent	H = Homework	M = Materials	A = Aggressive
Ⓛ = Unexcused absence	Ⓗ = Homework accurate	not present	D = Disruptive
X = Tardy	XH = No homework	C = Clothing inadequate	CT = Cheating on test
Ⓧ = Unexcused tardy	IH = Inaccurate homework	P = Did not participate	
	CH = Homework not complete	T = Time wasted	
	LH = Late homework		

FIGURE 13.2 Sample Daily Record

Dates	9–1	2	3	4	5		8		9	10	11		12
Students								H				Trip	
Allen, B.					⊘		X	IH	X	P		ok	
Baker, J.								H	/			ok	

You need to create a legend in the daily record that explains each symbol. Otherwise, you might use different symbols for the same behavior or forget what a particular symbol means. You can create new symbols as needed and add them to the legend.

Labeling Columns and Recording Information

In creating the daily record, you should reserve at least two rows at the top of the page to label columns. The date of each class session can be recorded in the top row. The second row can be used to label specific types of information: for example, homework due, parent permission slips due, laboratory fees paid, or materials borrowed from a class resource center. Since more than one column may be needed for some dates, it is best to complete this record on a day-to-day basis. An example of a daily record is shown in Figure 13.2.

Summarizing Information

At the end of the grading period, you need to summarize the information. The two rows at the top of this record can be used to organize the data. The first row can identify the behavior category, and the second row can label the particular type of behavior within each category. The total number of times a student exhibits each behavior can be recorded in the remaining rows. Figure 13.3 is a sample summary section of a daily record.

FIGURE 13.3 Sample Summary Section of Daily Record

Students	Attendance					Study Habits				Participation				Conduct		
	/	⊘	X	Ⓧ	Ⓗ	XH	IH	CH	LH	M	C	P	T	A	D	CT
Allen, B.	0	1	1	0	12	2	1	0	0	1	0	0	0	0	0	1
Baker, J.	3	0	1	0	2	4	6	1	2	7	0	2	0	0	1	0

CREATING THE POSTTEST RECORD

The posttest section is used to record information about students' progress on instructional goals and objectives studied during the term. Keeping adequate posttest records saves you time at the end of a grading term by providing the information needed to analyze tests, combine scores, and assign term grades. Adequate records also help you conduct conferences with students, parents, and other school personnel. To ensure that you have all the information needed, you should include the following items for each posttest:

1. The title and format of the test and the date it was administered
2. The total number of items or points
3. The group's mean score and standard deviation
4. The specific goals and the number of goals measured
5. Each student's raw score, percentage of items correct or points earned, number of goals or objectives mastered, and assigned grade

At first, this amount of information may seem unreasonable. At the end of the term, however, you will need this information in order to analyze the relationship among tests, devise a plan for combining scores, and calculate term grades. You may also need to explain the nature and meaning of particular test scores to other people. Referring to the information in your gradebook will be much easier than reconstructing it by sorting through your files.

Formatting the Information

You can reduce recording time by designing a systematic way to record test information. Reserve at least three rows at the top of the page to label columns and record general information about the test. The remaining rows can be used to record individual's performances. Consider the sample record for one student shown in Figure 13.4.

The top row is used to identify the test; it includes the test format, title, and date. In this example in Figure 13.4, the O indicates that the test was

FIGURE 13.4 Sample Posttest Record

	O Unit 1 9–10					O Unit 2 9–17				
	$\overline{X}$ / SD	%	Wt.	1–3		$\overline{X}$ / SD	%	Wt.	4–6	
Students	16 / 3	20		3	G	21 / 3	25		3	G
Allen, B.	14	70		2	C	19	76		2	C
	(1)	(2)	(3)	(4)	(5)	(1)	(2)	(3)	(4)	(5)

objective, covered the goals in unit 1, and was administered on September 10. Each test has five columns. The first column contains the symbols for the mean and standard deviation in the top row, these measures for the group in the second row, and students' raw scores in the remaining rows. From this information you can see that Allen's raw score of 14 was below the mean score, but not one standard deviation below. The second column contains the percentage symbol in the top row, the total number of items or points on the test in the second row, and students' percentage scores in the remaining rows. The third column, labeled *Wt.*, is reserved for calculating weighted scores at the end of the term (described later in this chapter). The fourth column identifies the particular goals measured by the test in the top row, the number of goals measured by the test in the second row, and the number of goals mastered by each student in the remaining rows. The fifth column is used to record students' assigned grades. To include additional information about each test, you can add other columns.

Combining Posttest Scores into a Composite Score

At the end of each term, you need to combine posttest scores into a *composite score* that reflects each student's achievement throughout the term. A composite score is created by combining two or more test scores. The steps in creating a composite score include (1) analyzing the relationship among posttests administered during the term to determine the weight each posttest should contribute to the composite score; (2) identifying weighting factors and calculating weighted scores so each test contributes the desired amount; and (3) combining weighted scores into the composite score.

Analyzing the Relationship among Posttests   When combining scores from multiple tests in a composite score, you need to decide how much weight each test will contribute. Analyzing the relationship among the tests will help you determine an appropriate weight for each one. There are at least two factors to consider in analyzing tests: their interdependence and their complexity.

The first comparison is whether tests measure different or overlapping sets of instructional goals. For example, if only unit tests are administered, each will most likely measure a different set of goals and objectives. However, posttests are frequently interdependent because they overlap in the goals measured. Suppose you administer quizzes, unit tests, midterm exams, and a final exam. Unit tests will measure many of the goals previously measured by quizzes; midterm exams will overlap unit tests; and comprehensive finals will overlap all previous tests. When posttests are interdependent, you should compare them across these categories as well as within each category.

A second comparison is the relative complexity of the tests. Factors that influence a test's complexity are its scope and the difficulty level of goals it measures. The scope of tests can be compared using the number of goals measured and the length of time between instruction and testing. Difficulty can be compared using the relative complexity of the goals measured by each test.

Comparing tests on the basis of scope, quizzes administered immediately following instruction that measure the objectives for only one goal are undoubtedly the least complex. A unit test that measures more goals and spans more time is more complex. Similarly, a comprehensive final exam that measures all the goals studied during the term and spans many weeks of study is more complex than any other test during the term. Based on these differences in complexity, you might decide that (1) a comprehensive final should contribute more to the composite score than any midterm exam; (2) a midterm exam should contribute more than any unit test; and (3) a unit test should contribute more than any quiz.

In addition to scope, the relative difficulty of goals measured is used to compare tests. Most likely, the goals measured by different tests are unequal in difficulty. For example, one test may measure students' skills in capitalizing the pronoun *I* and the first word of a sentence whereas another measures their skill in capitalizing proper nouns and the titles of artistic works. Obviously, the goals measured by the second test are more difficult. The format of a test can sometimes provide a clue to the difficulty of the skills measured. For instance, essay tests, product development tests, and performance tests that require recall, analysis, organization, synthesis, and presentation skills might be judged more difficult than some objective tests. Based on differences in skill difficulty, you might decide to assign more weight to tests that measure more difficult goals.

Although tests may differ in the number and difficulty of goals measured, their overall complexity might be considered equal. For example, one test that measures several less difficult goals might be considered comparable in overall complexity to another that measures fewer more difficult ones. Thus, based on overall complexity, you might decide to assign them equal weight in the composite score.

You need to summarize information about posttests in order to compare them. Table 13.1 contains two summary charts for nine tests administered during a term. The information required to create such a summary should be available in the gradebook. In the top chart, the left-hand column identifies the test, and the second column identifies its format. The next set of columns identifies the instructional goals studied during the term, and the particular goals measured by each test are identified using an X. The right-hand column lists the total number of goals measured by each test.

Using the information in the top chart, tests can be compared for interdependence. From the table, the following relationships are evident:

1. Tests 1, 2, 3, 5, 6, and 7 are independent in the goals they measure. They appear to be unit tests because each measures either two or three goals. Collectively, they measure all sixteen goals.
2. Test 4 measures goals previously measured by unit tests 1, 2, and 3.

TABLE 13.1 Summary of Posttests Administered during One Term

Test	Format	1	2	3	4	5	6	7	8	9	10	11	12	13	14	15	16	Total Goals
							Goals Measured											
1	Objective	X	X	X														3
2	Objective				X	X	X											3
3	Objective							X	X	X								3
4	Objective	X	X	X	X	X	X	X	X	X								9
5	Objective										X	X	X					3
6	Objective													X	X			2
7	Objective															X	X	2
8	Objective										X	X	X	X	X	X	X	7
9	Objective	X	X	X	X	X	X	X	X	X	X	X	X	X	X	X	X	16

Test Categories

	Unit Tests						Midterm Exams		Comprehensive Final
Test Number	1	2	3	5	6	7	4	8	9
of Goals	3	3	3	3	2	2	9	7	16
Format Difficulty	0	0	0	0	0	0	0	0	0
of Goals					X^a	X		X	X

[a] An X reflects more complex goals.

3. Test 8 measures the same goals as unit tests 5, 6, and 7.
4. Together, tests 4 and 8 measure all sixteen goals.
5. Test 9 measures all sixteen goals studied during the term.

This example includes three categories of interdependent tests: (1) six unit tests, numbers 1, 2, 3, 5, 6, and 7; (2) two midterm exams, tests 4 and 8; and (3) one comprehensive final exam, test 9. Based on the fact that the tests are interdependent, you could first compare categories to determine how much weight each category should contribute to the term composite score. Once the weight for each category is selected, you can compare tests within each category to determine how much weight to assign each one.

To compare categories, consider the number and complexity of goals measured by tests across categories. In this example, all three categories measure the same sixteen goals. Therefore, one category probably would not be considered more complex than another, and they would be weighted equally in the composite score. To weight the categories equally, the unit tests collectively would contribute one-third, or 33.3 percent, to the composite score; the two midterm exams together would contribute one-third; and the final exam would contribute one-third, as illustrated in Figure 13.5.

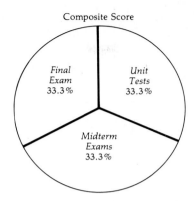

Composite Score

Final
Exam
33.3%

Unit
Tests
33.3%

Midterm
Exams
33.3%

FIGURE 13.5
Percentage
Contributed to
the Composite
Score by Each
Test Category

When you have determined the percentage each category is to contribute to the composite score, the next step in the analysis is to compare the tests within a category. The purpose for this comparison is to determine how much weight each test should contribute to the total percentage allotted for the category. The lower portion of Table 13.1 contains information about the nine tests' scope and difficulty arranged by category.

Comparing unit tests by scope, tests 1, 2, 3, and 5 all measure three goals whereas tests 6 and 7 measure only two. Comparing them by the relative difficulty of goals measured, tests 6 and 7 are considered more difficult than the other four tests. If you decide that scope is balanced by skill difficulty and that the overall complexity of the six tests is approximately equal, then each test should contribute an equal percentage to the composite score.

The percentage that each unit test will contribute to the composite score can now be determined. The total percentage allocated for unit tests (33.3 percent) is divided by the number of tests (6) to identify the percentage for each. Therefore, each unit test will contribute 5.55 percent to the term composite score.

The midterm exam category contains two tests to be compared. Test 4 measures nine skills whereas test 8 measures only seven; however, the goals measured by test 8 are considered more complex. Thus, balancing scope and skill difficulty, you might decide to weight the two midterm exams equally.

To determine the percentage each midterm exam will contribute to the composite score, divide the percentage allocated for midterm exams (33.3 percent) by the number of exams (2). In this case, each midterm exam will contribute 16.65 percent to the composite score.

The percentage of weight assigned to categories and to individual tests is illustrated in Figure 13.6. Note that each of the three categories contributes an equal amount to the composite score (the six unit tests combined and the two midterm exams combined contribute equal amounts). Notice also that the final exam contributes more weight than either midterm exam and that each midterm exam contributes more weight than any unit test.

FIGURE 13.6 Percentage Contributed to the Term Composite Score by Each Test Category and Individual Test

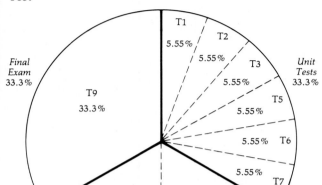

Usually, the manner in which you weight your tests is a matter of professional judgment. Some school districts, however, have grading policies that prescribe the weight final exams are to contribute to the composite score. Should your district prescribe the percentage allotted to final exams, you would assign weights to individual tests using a procedure similar to the one described in the previous example.

Suppose your district's grading policies state that final exams must contribute 25 percent to the composite score. With this given, you need to determine how the remaining 75 percent will be divided among the other tests. Using the nine tests in the preceding example and the same decisions about their relative weights, you could assign percentages to categories and to individual tests as follows:

1. Assign 25 percent to the final exam.
2. Divide the remaining 75 percent by the number of categories (2) and assign 37.5 percent to the unit test and the midterm exam categories.
3. Divide the percentage allocated for unit tests (37.5 percent) by the number of tests (6), and assign 6.25 percent to each unit test.
4. Divide the 37.5 percent allocated for midterm exams by 2, and assign 18.75 percent to each midterm.

Figure 13.7 illustrates the percentages assigned to each category and test. The unit test category and the midterm exam category each contribute more weight to the composite score than the final exam. However, the final exam contributes more than either midterm exam, and each midterm exam contributes more than any unit test. Thus, the assigned weights should reflect the relative complexity of the tests.

Identifying Weighting Factors and Calculating Weighted Scores After selecting the weight each test will contribute to the term composite score, the next tasks are to select weighting factors and calculate weighted scores. Each test score needs to be multiplied by a weighting factor so it contributes the desired percentage to the composite score. Weighting factors are easily identified by dividing the smallest percentage allocated for any test into each of the assigned percentages.

The weighting factors for each of the nine tests are calculated in Table 13.2. The first column identifies the tests; the second column, the assigned percentages; and the third column, the weighting factors. The assigned percentages used in this example are those that weight the three test categories equally. Because 5.6 percent is the smallest percentage, it is divided into each of the assigned percentages to obtain the weighting factors. Unit tests 1, 2, 3, 5, 6, and 7 will be weighted by a factor of 1. Midterm exams 4 and 8 will be weighted by a factor of 3, and the final exam will be weighted by a factor of 6.

FIGURE 13.7 Weight Assigned to Nine Tests Using School District Policy

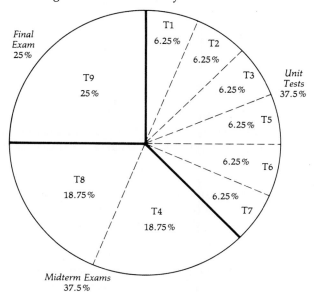

TABLE 13.2   Weighting Factors for Each Test

Test	Percentage Allocated	Weighting Factor
1	5.6	$\frac{5.6}{5.6} = 1$
2	5.6	$\frac{5.6}{5.6} = 1$
3	5.6	$\frac{5.6}{5.6} = 1$
4	16.7	$\frac{16.7}{5.6} = 2.98; 3$
5	5.6	$\frac{5.6}{5.6} = 1$
6	5.6	$\frac{5.6}{5.6} = 1$
7	5.6	$\frac{5.6}{5.6} = 1$
8	16.7	$\frac{16.7}{5.6} = 2.98; 3$
9	33.3	$\frac{33.3}{5.6} = 5.94; 6$
		Total Units of Weight 18

The next step in the procedure is to calculate weighted scores. Before calculating weighted scores, however, you need to convert the raw scores on each test to a common scale. Teachers traditionally use a 100-point scale and convert raw scores to this scale by calculating the percentage of items correct, or points earned, on each test. Since your gradebook already contains the percentage scores for each test, this conversion has already been made.

To calculate weighted scores, record the weighting factor for each test in the second row of the column reserved for weighted scores in the gradebook. This column is headed by the label *Wt.* The students' percentage scores for each test are then multiplied by the assigned weighting factor to obtain the weighted scores, which are then recorded in the *Wt.* column.

Table 13.3 contains the weighted scores for two students for all nine tests in the example. The students' weighted scores on the unit tests are the same as the percentage scores because the weighting factor was one. However, the weighted scores for the remaining tests are greater than the percentage scores because the weighting factors were greater than one. For example, the weighted scores of 258 and 282 on test 4 were obtained by multiplying the students' percentage scores by the weighting factor of three.

TABLE 13.3   Weighted Scores for the Nine Posttests

	O Test 1 9–10					O Test 2 9–17					O Test 3 9–24				
	$\overline{X}$/SD	%	Wt.	1–3	G	$\overline{X}$/SD	%	Wt.	4–6	G	$\overline{X}$/SD	%	Wt.	7–9	G
Students	16/4	20	(1)	3	X	21/3	25	(1)	3	X	24/3	30	(1)	3	X
Allen, B.	14	70	70	2	C	19	76	76	2	C	22	73	73	2	C
Baker, J.	18	90	90	3	A	25	100	100	3	A	28	93	93	3	A

	O Test 4 10–1					O Test 5 10–8					O Test 6 10–15				
	$\overline{X}$/SD	%	Wt.	1–9	G	$\overline{X}$/SD	%	Wt.	10–12	G	$\overline{X}$/SD	%	Wt.	13–14	G
Students	43/4	50	(3)	9		16/2	20	(1)	3		16/3	20	(1)	2	X
Allen, B.	43	86	258	7	B	15	75	75	2	C	15	75	75	2	C
Baker, J.	47	94	282	9	A	20	100	100	3	A	19	95	95	2	A

	O Test 7 10–22					O Test 8 11–3					O Test 9 11–5				
	$\overline{X}$/SD	%	Wt.	15–16	G	$\overline{X}$/SD	%	Wt.	10–16	G	$\overline{X}$/SD	%	Wt.	1–16	G
Students	26/3	30	(1)	2	X	38/4	45	(3)	7		42/5	50	(6)	16	X
Allen, B.	25	83	83	2	B	39	87	261	6	B	45	90	540	14	A
Baker, J.	27	90	90	2	A	42	93	279	7	A	50	100	600	16	A

Combining Weighted Scores into the Composite Score   With the weighted scores calculated for each test, you can calculate the composite score using the following procedure:

1. Sum the weighting factors to obtain the total units of weight.
2. Sum the weighted scores to obtain the total weighted score.
3. Divide the total weighted score by the total units of weight to obtain the composite score on a 100 point scale.

You should reserve columns in the gradebook to record the summary data. You will need one column to record the total units of weight and weighted scores, one column for the composite score, one column for the total number of goals mastered, and one for the assigned grade. The summary section for the nine tests in the example is shown in Figure 13.8.

Notice that the total units of weight, 18, is recorded at the top of the Total column. The total weighted score for Allen is 1511. This sum divided by the total units of weight gives this student a composite score of 84. The total weighted score for Baker is 1729, which divided by 18 is 96. The total number of goals mastered during the term is 14 for Allen and 16 for Baker. When tests are interrelated, you should calculate mastery using the latest, most comprehensive test. If the comprehensive final had not measured all 16 goals, you could have based mastery on the midterm exams instead.

Table 13.4 illustrates that the selected weighting factors for the nine tests result in the desired percentage or weight for each test. The first column identifies the test; the second, the percentage each test contributes to the composite score; the third, the assigned weighting factor; the fourth, the total number of points for each test on a 100-point scale; the fifth, the weighted scores; and the sixth, the percentage each weighted score contributes to the total weighted score. Multiplying each score, 100, by the assigned weighting factor, you obtain the weighted scores for each test. Summing these, you obtain the total weighted score, 1800, for the nine tests. Then, dividing each weighted score by the total weighted score, you obtain the proportion each test contributes to the composite. Multiplying this proportion by 100 results in the percentage. Notice that the assigned percentage in column 2 is the same as the actual percentage in column 6.

Converting Composite Scores into Term Grades

After calculating the composite scores, you need to convert them to grades. This conversion requires selecting a range of composite scores for each grade. These score ranges are called *grading standards*. Some school districts have policies that set common grading standards throughout the district. When this is the case, each grade and the range of composite scores required to earn it are described on the report card or in the teacher's manual. The three sets of grading standards shown in Table 13.5 are common.

FIGURE 13.8   Term 1 Summary

	Total	Composite	Goals	Grade
Students	(18)		16	
Allen, B.	1511	84	14	
Baker, J.	1729	96	16	

TABLE 13.4 Percentage of the Total Weighted Score Contributed by Each Test

1 Test	2 Assigned Percentage	3 Assigned Weighting Factor	4 Total Score on 100-Point Scale	5 Weighted Scores	6 Percentage of Total Weighted Score
1	5.6	1	100	100	$\dfrac{100}{1{,}800} = .055;\ 5.6$
2	5.6	1	100	100	
3	5.6	1	100	100	
4	16.7	3	100	300	$\dfrac{300}{1{,}800} = .166;\ 16.7$
5	5.6	1	100	100	
6	5.6	1	100	100	
7	5.6	1	100	100	
8	16.7	3	100	300	
9	33.3	6	100	600	$\dfrac{600}{1{,}800} = .333;\ 33.3$
			Total Weighted 1,800 Score		

These standards differ in the range of composite scores assigned for each grade. The first set assigns the highest eleven scores a grade of *A*, and the *B*, *C*, and *D* grade categories each contain ten scores. It is the most lenient of the three standards. The grades in the second set have equal score ranges, but they include only eight points instead of ten. The third set differs from the first two in that it has unequal score ranges for the grades. The range of scores for an *A* is only six points, the range for a *B* is seven points, and the range for both *C* and *D* grades is nine points. Therefore, this set is more rigorous at the high than at the low end of the scale.

TABLE 13.5 Three Sets of Grading Standards

Grade	Standards or Range of Corresponding Composite Scores		
	Standard 1	Standard 2	Standard 3
A	90–100	93–100	95–100
B	80–89	85–92	88–94
C	70–79	77–84	79–87
D	60–69	69–76	70–78
F	59 and below	68 and below	69 and below

Converting your students' composite scores to grades is easy when your district prescribes grade standards. You simply locate and assign the grade that corresponds to the earned composite scores. For example, if your district prescribed the first set of grade standards, B. Allen, who earned a composite score of 84, would receive a *B*. However, this student would be assigned a *C* if the second or third set of standards were applied. J. Baker, who earned a composite score of 96, would be assigned an *A* using any of the three grade standards.

When the district does not prescribe composite score ranges for grades, you need to set your own. There are two options to use in setting grade standards. One is to set standards based solely on students' achievement of the goals, called *criterion-referenced grading*. The other is to set standards based on students' relative performances, called *norm-referenced grading*. Criterion-referenced grading is preferable because it more clearly communicates the amount of information and skills each student has achieved.

Using Criterion-Referenced Standards   Setting standards for criterion-referenced grading is a matter of professional judgment. You need to select the composite score ranges that reflect outstanding, good, questionable, and inadequate achievement. You also need to select a score below which students will be assigned a failing grade. An outstanding, or *A* grade, should communicate to other people that a student has mastered all the skills covered and has done so at a high level. A grade of *B* should communicate that a student has mastered all or most skills, at least at a minimum level. A grade of *C* should reflect that the student has mastered the majority of the skills, but is struggling. A grade of *D* should reflect that the student is having difficulty with many of the skills, and an *F* should reflect that the student has made little, if any, progress on the goals studied during the term.

To set your own grading standards, you need to select the lowest composite score that reflects each of the five grade levels. The minimum score for each grade can be set by (1) predicting a score range within which you believe the minimum score should fall; (2) reviewing the number of goals mastered by students who earn composite scores within the chosen range; and (3) selecting a cut-off score that best reflects that grade. For example, you might predict that the cut-off score for an *A* should be somewhere between 90 and 95. The total goals mastered column in the gradebook should be reviewed for students who earn composite scores in this range to determine whether they have mastered all the goals. If students who earn scores of 90 have mastered all the goals, then 90 could be set as the minimum score. However, if students who earn this score fail to master some of the goals, then you might want to set a higher cut-off score for an *A*. The same procedure can be followed to select the minimum score for each grade.

An alternative method for setting cut-off scores that is quicker, but not as thorough, is to (1) establish the lower limit for *A* and *D* grades, using the previously described method; (2) find the score range between the minimum

A and *D* grades; and (3) divide this range by 3 to set the score ranges for the *D*, *C*, and *B* grades. For example, if you set 90 as the cut-off score for an *A* and 65 as the cut-off score for a *D*, the difference between these two scores is 25 points (90 minus 65). Dividing 25 by 3, you obtain 8.3 points. Therefore, the *D*, *C*, and *B* ranges will each contain about 8 points.

Next, you need to locate the minimum score for each grade. You can do so using the following steps:

1. Select the exact number of points for each grade. Assume you decide to make the *D* and *B* ranges equal 8 points and the *C* range equal 9 points.
2. Subtract the assigned number of points for a *B* (8) from the lowest *A* score (90) to identify the minimum score for a *B* (90 − 8 = 82).
3. Subtract the assigned number of points for a *C* (9) from the lowest *B* score to identify the minimum score for a *C* (82 − 9 = 73).
4. Subtract the assigned number of points for a *D* (8) from the lowest *C* score to identify the minimum score for a *D* (73 − 8 = 65). This score should match the one initially selected as the minimum *D* score, 65, which it does.

Thus, your grading standards would be the following:

Grade	Composite Score Range
A	90–100 (11 points)
B	82–89 (8 points)
C	73–81 (9 points)
D	65–72 (8 points)
F	64 and below

After establishing a range of scores for each grade, you can convert each student's term composite score to the matching letter grade. Using these standards, B. Allen, who earned a term composite score of 84 in the preceding example, would be assigned a grade of *B*; J. Baker, who earned a composite score of 96, would be assigned an *A*.

Using Norm-Referenced Standards   Although it is not recommended, some teachers prefer to assign term grades based on the relative performance of students in the group. If you wanted to use a purely norm-referenced grading system, you would need to convert students' raw scores on each test to standard scores before combining them in the composite score. This procedure is described later in this section. However, if you have calculated composite scores using the percentage score as a basis, there are two norm-referenced procedures you can use to convert composite scores to grades. One is to decide what proportion of the class will receive each grade and then make grade assignments based on the students' ranked scores. The other is to use the mean and standard deviation to set cut-off scores for above-average, average, and below-average performance. Table 13.6 includes term composite scores for one class used to illustrate both these procedures.

TABLE 13.6   Frequency Distribution of a Group's Composite Scores

Composite Score	Frequency	Composite Score	Frequency	Composite Score	Frequency
100		86	111	72	
99		85		71	1
98		84	1111	70	1
97		83	1	69	
96	1	82		68	1
95		81	1	67	
94	111	80	11	66	
93		79		65	1
92	1	78	1	64	
91		77	1	63	
90	111	76		62	1
89		75	11	61	
88	1111	74		60	1
87	1	73	1	44	1

N = 36

To assign grades based on a set percentage of the group, you can use the following procedure:

1. Decide what proportion of the class is to receive each grade.
2. Multiply the total number of students in the class by the assigned proportion to identify the number of students that will receive each grade.
3. Create a frequency distribution of composite scores.
4. Beginning at the top of the distribution, count down the number of scores that are to receive an A. Then, using the remaining scores, count down the number of scores that are to receive a B, and so on.

Suppose you wanted 15 percent of the class to receive As, 20 percent to receive Bs, 30 percent Cs, 20 percent Ds, and 15 percent Fs. The number of students that receive each grade would be obtained as follows:

Grade	Percentage of Students	Number of Students
A	15	$.15 \times 36 = 5.4$
B	20	$.20 \times 36 = 7.2$
C	30	$.30 \times 36 = 10.8$
D	20	$.20 \times 36 = 7.2$
F	15	$.15 \times 36 = 5.4$

The next steps are to create a frequency distribution of composite scores and count down the number of scores designated for each grade. Referring to the frequency distribution in Table 13.6, begin with the highest score, 96, and count down five students. The fifth score down is 92; thus, students who earn scores between 96 and 92 will be assigned an *A*. Seven students are to receive a *B*, and beginning with a composite score of 90, seven students' scores fall between 90 and 88. Twelve students' scores fall between 87 and 80; thus, these students will be assigned a grade of *C*. The seven students whose scores fall between 78 and 70 will be assigned a *D*, and the remaining five students will be assigned an *F*.

The second norm-referenced procedure is to use the mean and standard deviation of the composite scores to set cut-off scores for each grade. The mean of the composite scores in Table 13.6 is 81 and the standard deviation is 11. By adding and subtracting increments of the standard deviation to and from the mean score, you might locate score ranges that you consider suitable for the class. The following scores are obtained by adding one and two standard deviations to the mean score and subtracting them from the mean score.

Composite Scores	59	70	81	92	103
Standard Deviations	$\overline{X} - 2SD$	$\overline{X} - 1SD$	$\overline{X}$	$\overline{X} + 1SD$	$\overline{X} + 2SD$

The easiest way to proceed would be to set the cut-off score for an *A* grade at 92, a *B* grade at 81, a *C* grade at 70, and a *D* grade at 59. Using this plan, the following grade standards and number of students in Table 13.6 who receive each grade would result.

Grade	Range of Composite Scores	Frequency of Students Earning Each Grade
A	92–100	5
B	81–91	17
C	70–80	9
D	59–69	4
F	58 and below	1

If you feel that the average score, 81, should equal a *C* instead of a *B*, then you could set your standards using the following procedure:

1. Add and subtract one-fourth of the standard deviation to the mean score to set the *C* range around the mean and make it about one-half a standard deviation wide.

$81 + 2.7 = 83.7$, or 84
$81 - 2.7 = 78.3$, or 78

2. Add one-half a standard deviation to the upper boundary of a *C* grade, 84, to locate the upper boundary of a *B* grade.

$$84 + 5.5 = 89.5, \text{ or } 90$$

3. Subtract one-half a standard deviation from the lower boundary of a *C* grade to locate the lower boundary of a *D* grade.

$$78 - 5.5 = 72.5, \text{ or } 72$$

This plan would result in the following grade standards and number of students in Table 13.6 who receive each grade.

Grade	Range of Composite Scores	Frequency of Students Earning Each Grade
A	91–100	5
B	85–90	11
C	78–84	9
D	72–77	4
F	71 and below	7

Should you want to expand the range of composite scores for the *C* and *D* grades, consider the following plan:

1. Set the lower limit for an *A* grade at the mean plus one standard deviation (81 + 11 = 92).
2. Set the lower limit for a *B* grade at the mean plus one-half a standard deviation (81 + 5.5 = 86.5 or 87).
3. Set the lower limit of a *C* grade by subtracting one-half a standard deviation from the mean (81 − 5.5 = 75.5 or 75).
4. Set the lower limit of the *D* grade by subtracting one and one-half a standard deviation from the mean (81 − 16.5 = 64.5 or 64).

This plan would result in the following grade standards and frequency of students earning each grade.

Grade	Range of Composite Scores	Frequency of Students Earning Each Grade
A	92–100	5
B	87–91	8
C	75–86	15
D	64–74	5
F	63 and below	3

Using Standard Scores Purely norm-referenced grading requires the conversion of raw scores on each test to standard scores before combining them in the composite scores. A standard score is a derived score based on the individual's raw score, the group's average score, and the group's variability as measured by the standard deviation. Thus, students' raw scores on each test are modified to reflect their group standing.

These norm-referenced scores are called standard scores because they convert all posttest scores to a standard scale that has a constant mean and a constant standard deviation. Holding these measures constant facilitates comparing students' relative performance across tests. One standard score, the z score, has a constant mean of 0 and a constant standard deviation of 1. Another commonly used standard score is the T score, which has a constant mean of 50 and a constant standard deviation of 10.

The standard score scale for z and T scores is illustrated in the following diagram:

T Scores	20	30	40	50	60	70	80
z Scores	−3	−2	−1	0	1	2	3
Standard Deviations	−3SD	−2SD	−1SD	$\overline{X}$	+1SD	+2SD	+3SD

A z score of 0 and a T score of 50 both reflect that the student earned the mean score. A z score of 1 and a T score of 60 both are one standard deviation above the mean; therefore, they reflect above-average performance. Likewise, a z score of −1 and a T score of 40 both are one standard deviation below the mean and reflect below-average performance. Scores farther from the mean in either direction reflect performance farther removed from average. Thus, regardless of the original raw scores, original mean scores, or original standard deviations on the tests, the standard scores can be used to locate the students' comparative performance levels.

The formulas for calculating the z and T scores are:

$$z = \frac{X - \overline{X}}{SD} \qquad T = 10z + 50$$

The z score is calculated by subtracting the mean score on the test from the student's raw score. This difference, or the amount the individual's score deviates from the mean, is divided by the group's standard deviation to determine how much larger or smaller the individual's deviation is than the group's average deviation. In other words, a z score of .5 or −.5 indicates that a student's deviation from the mean is half as large as the group's average deviation. Negative numbers reflect deviation below the mean. A z score of 1 or −1 indicates that the student's deviation from the mean is the same as the group's average deviation. Scores of 1.5 and −1.5 indicate that a student's deviation from the mean is one and one-half times larger than the group's average deviation.

The T score is calculated from the z score. The z score is multiplied by 10 to change the size of the standard deviation from 1 to 10. This product is added to 50 to change the size of the mean from 0 to 50. These T scores have the same meaning as z scores. Scores of 45 or 55 indicate that a student's deviation from the mean is only half as large as the group's deviation.

Using the students' raw scores, the group's mean scores, and the group's standard deviations from test 1 and test 2 in Table 13.3, the z and T scores for the two students are calculated in Figure 13.9.

The location of the students' standard scores on the two tests is illustrated in the following diagram. Allen's scores are labeled A1 (test 1) and A2 (test 2). Baker's scores are labeled B1 (test 1) and B2 (test 2). Allen's performance on both tests was lower than the mean; however, his performance was lower on test 2, compared to the group, than on test 1. Baker's performance on both tests was above the mean. Comparing his performance on the two tests, his performance on test 1, compared to the group, was lower than on test 2.

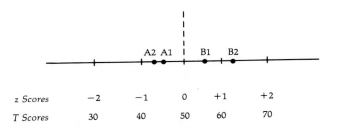

You can use either the z or T score to calculate the term composite scores. An additional column would need to be reserved in the gradebook to record the standard scores for each posttest. At the end of the term, analyzing the tests and selecting weighting factors are accomplished as previously de-

FIGURE 13.9 z and T Score Calculations

Students	z Scores	T Scores
	$z = \dfrac{X - \overline{X}}{SD}$	$T = 10z + 50$
Allen, B. Test 1	$\dfrac{14 - 16}{4} = \dfrac{-2}{4} = -.50$	$(10 \times -.50) + 50 = -5 + 50 = 45$
Test 2	$\dfrac{19 - 21}{3} = \dfrac{-2}{3} = -.66$	$(10 \times -.66) + 50 = -6.6 + 50 = 43$
Baker, J. Test 1	$\dfrac{18 - 16}{4} = \dfrac{2}{4} = .50$	$(10 \times .50) + 50 = 5 + 50 = 55$
Test 2	$\dfrac{25 - 21}{3} = \dfrac{4}{3} = 1.25$	$(10 \times 1.25) + 50 = 12.5 + 50 = 63$

scribed. Because standard scores are already on a common scale, they can be multiplied by the selected weighting factor to obtain the weighted score for each test. As with weighted percentage scores, they are summed to obtain the total weighted score. This score divided by the total units of weight is the composite score on a standard scale. These composite scores can be converted to grades using either of the norm-referenced conversions previously described.

One difficulty with norm-referenced grading is that it can be used to mask inadequate instruction and low levels of student performance. Inadequate lesson preparation and instruction rarely yield the composite scores necessary for an *A* or *B* grade under a criterion-referenced grading system, even for high-ability students. Suppose that instead of the composite scores illustrated in Table 13.6, the group's scores ranged between 44 and 74; the mean score was 65; and the standard deviation was 7. If the group contained several high-ability students, assigning grades using a criterion-referenced system would cause an immediate reaction from students and parents. In spite of the differences in the two sets of scores, however, the same grades could be assigned using a norm-referenced system. Students who earn *A*s and *B*s rarely question their grades even though they realize they did not learn much in the course, and parents do not know they should question the grades. Thus, accountability for students' true progress on the goals can be avoided.

Calculating Semester and Annual Grades

At the conclusion of two or more terms, you need to combine term grades into a semester grade; at the end of the year, you may need to combine semester grades into an annual grade. Suppose you teach in a school district that has two terms in a semester and a comprehensive semester exam that contributes 25 percent to the semester grade. In your gradebook you need to create semester summary columns for the composite score for each term, the semester exam raw score and percentage score, the weighted scores for each measure, the total weighted score, the semester composite score, and the semester grade.

The first step is to identify the percentage each measure is to contribute to the semester composite score. Since the semester exam contributes 25 percent to the semester grade, the term composite scores will contribute the remaining 75 percent. Undoubtedly, you will want to weight the terms equally, so each term composite score will contribute one-half the 75 percent, or 37.5 percent.

The second step is to identify weighting factors that can be used to ensure that each measure contributes the assigned percentage. Since 25 percent is the smallest weight assigned, it is divided into each of the other percentages to obtain the weighting factors. The weighting factor for the semester

FIGURE 13.10   Semester 1 Summary

Students	Term 1 Comp. Score	Term 1 Wt. (1.5)	Term 2 Comp. Score	Term 2 Wt. (1.5)	Semester Exam X	Semester Exam 50 %	Semester Exam Wt. (1)	Total (4)	Composite	Grade
Allen, B.	84	126	86	129	42	84	84	339	85	B
Baker, J.	96	144	93	140	45	90	90	374	94	A

FIGURE 13.11   Annual Summary

Students	Semester 1 Composite (1)	Semester 2 Composite (1)	Total (2)	Composite	Grade
Allen, B.	85	80	165	83	B
Baker, J.	94	95	189	95	A

exam is 1 (25/25 = 1), and the weighting factor for the term composite scores is 1.5 (37.5/25 = 1.5).

Next, you should (1) calculate the weighted scores, (2) sum them to obtain the total weighted score, (3) sum the units of weight, and (4) calculate the composite score. These calculations for two students are illustrated in Figure 13.10.

The weighted scores for each test are added to obtain the total weighted scores, 339 and 374. These scores are then divided by the total units of weight, 4, to obtain the semester composite scores of 85 and 94.

The last task is to convert these semester composite scores to semester grades using the scale established for term grades. The same process is used to calculate annual grades. Usually, the two semesters are weighted equally when combined into a composite score for the year. Figure 13.11 illustrates how semester composite scores are combined to obtain the annual grade.

The students' composite scores for the two semesters are added to obtain the total weighted scores of 165 and 189. These scores are divided by the total units of weight, 2, to obtain the annual composite scores of 83 and 95. These scores are then converted to the annual grade using the established grading scale.

CREATING THE CONDUCT RECORD

In addition to reporting achievement, teachers are often expected to measure and report students' conduct in such areas as study habits, attitude toward learning, and citizenship. The procedures for developing behavior rating scales to judge conduct are described in Chapter 9. During the grading period, you would follow an observation schedule and use the rating scales to score students' behavior. Similar to achievement test scores, these conduct scores should be recorded in the gradebook, combined into composite scores, and converted to the marks prescribed on the report card.

Recording Scores

Since different behaviors are reported separately, you can create an area for each in the conduct section of the gradebook. For example, if you are expected to report attitude toward learning, study habits, and citizenship, you would need three separate areas in the record. The number of columns required for each behavior depends on the number of times it was rated during the term. If you rated each behavior three times, you would need three columns to record students' scores. To accommodate your work at the end of the term, you should reserve three additional columns: one for the total score, one for the composite score, and one for the assigned mark. The gradebook section for attitude toward learning might appear as follows:

Behavior			Attitude toward Learning			
Date	9–21	10–10	10–30	Total	Composite	Grade
Weights						
Allen, B.	12	13	14			
Baker, J.	18	16	18			

The behavior is identified in the top row, and the dates when students were rated and column titles appear in the second row. The third row is reserved for weighting factors, and students' scores are listed in the remaining rows.

Combining Scores into a Composite Score

There are two factors to consider before combining scores into a composite score: converting all scores to a common scale and determining the amount of weight each measure should contribute. Relative to a common scale, the same rating scale is usually used each time a behavior is scored, and no conversion should be necessary. Also, you will probably want each measure to contribute an equal amount of weight to the term composite score. Therefore, each score can be assigned a weight of 1. If you want to weight the measures differently, you should identify weighting factors as you did for posttest scores, reserve space in the gradebook for weighted scores, and convert raw scores to weighted scores before summing them.

Composite scores for conduct are calculated the same way as composite scores for achievement. The steps are as follows:

1. Sum the individual scores to obtain the total weighted score.
2. Sum the units of weight to obtain the total units of weight.
3. Divide the total weighted score by the total units of weight to obtain the composite score.

The following example illustrates the calculation of composite scores for B. Allen and J. Baker.

Behavior			Attitude toward Learning			
Date	9–21	10–10	10–30	Total	Composite	Grade
Weights	(1)	(1)	(1)	(3)		
Allen, B.	12	13	14	39	13	
Baker, J.	18	16	18	52	17	

Converting Composite Scores to Marks

The final step in the procedure is to convert term composite scores into marks. The marks used to communicate conduct are generally described on the report card. Some school districts use a three-category scale whereas others use four- or five-category scales. The three-category scale is often S for satisfactory, N for needs improvement; and U for unsatisfactory. The four-category scale might use E for excellent, G for good, N for needs improvement, and U for unsatisfactory. The five-category scale might use A through F, or 1 through 5, to communicate different levels of behavior.

One way to convert composite scores to report card marks is to (1) identify the possible range of composite scores, (2) divide this range by the number of grade categories prescribed by the district, and (3) assign a relatively equal number of scores to each category. Suppose the highest possible composite score for attitude toward learning is 18 and the lowest possible score is 6. You have a potential range of 13 points including the lowest and highest scores. This range of 13 points might be divided in the following ways for scales that include three, four, and five categories.

Three-Category Scale		Four-Category Scale		Five-Category Scale	
Mark	Score Range	Mark	Score Range	Mark	Score Range
S	15, 16, 17, 18	E	16, 17, 18	A	16, 17, 18
N	11, 12, 13, 14	G	13, 14, 15	B	13, 14, 15
U	6, 7, 8, 9, 10	N	9, 10, 11, 12	C	10, 11, 12
		U	5, 6, 7, 8	D	8, 9
				F	6, 7

Based on a three-category scale, B. Allen's composite score, 13, would be converted to an *N*; J. Baker's composite score, 17, would be *S*. On the four-category scale, Allen would receive a *G* and Baker, an *E*. On the five-category scale, Allen and Baker would receive a *B* and an *A*, respectively. The standards you select should be recorded in the gradebook for reference.

CONFOUNDING THE ACHIEVEMENT GRADE

In their efforts to create a comprehensive index of students' progress, some teachers mix conduct and achievement. Although they may believe that mixing these variables improves the accuracy of students' grades, exactly the opposite occurs. The term used to describe mixing variables is *confounding*. When conduct is confounded with achievement, the meaning of the achievement grade is compromised, and valid interpretation becomes difficult, if not impossible. Four common ways that teachers confound achievement grades are (1) treating practice tests as posttests, (2) administering unannounced posttests, (3) reducing posttest scores for misbehavior, and (4) using extra-credit assignments to alter grades.

It is not uncommon to find teachers who treat practice tests and routine homework assignments as posttests. This is typically done to encourage students to complete their assignments and to do so carefully. When practice tests are used as posttests, students' initial attempts to perform skills are confounded with their progress following instruction, practice, and feedback. Since the purpose for practice tests is rehearsal, they are premature measures of achievement; and students' scores on practice tests tend to be lower than their scores on legitimate posttests. Thus, practice test scores negatively influence the composite score. Teachers who confound practice and achievement usually attempt to minimize this negative influence by reducing the percentage that practice tests contribute to the composite score, eliminating the lowest practice test score, providing opportunities for extra-credit work, or a combination of these three strategies.

A second confounding practice is administering unannounced posttests, sometimes called *pop quizzes*. The usual explanation teachers give for using such tests is to keep students studying on a regular basis rather than cramming just before a scheduled test. This practice, however, confounds study habits and actual achievement. Low scores could be attributed to the fact that either students did not study or they were experiencing difficulty learning the skills. The consequence of administering unannounced posttests is that these scores tend to be lower than scores on scheduled tests. Thus, they also have a negative influence on composite scores and grades. Like teachers who use practice tests as posttests, those who use unannounced tests generally need to develop strategies to counter their negative influence.

A third practice that confounds conduct and achievement is reducing earned posttest scores for unacceptable behavior. These unacceptable behaviors can include habitually submitting product development tests late, talking or being otherwise disruptive during a test, or cheating on a test. The reason usually given for altering the earned scores is to teach students that such misbehaviors will not be tolerated. However, this practice confounds achievement with lack of judgment and immaturity. Students caught cheating on a test should be required to take another form of the test so that a legitimate measure of their progress is obtained. Alternative strategies, besides reducing earned scores, should be sought for encouraging promptness, consideration, and honesty.

A fourth practice that confounds achievement and conduct is using extra-credit assignments to alter grades. Extra-credit assignments are those not required of all students in the regular conduct of the class. The reason typically given for altering grades using extra-credit is to give students who are not satisfied with their earned scores an opportunity to improve their grades. However, this practice confounds students' achievement of the prescribed goals and their effort. For example, some students may want a higher grade than their test performance warrants. When given an extra-credit option, these students will complete the additional work to improve their grades. Suppose that students who demonstrated mastery at good (*B*) and questionable (*C*) levels are permitted to raise these grades one letter by completing an extra report, paper, or project. Does completing the assignment mean that they have now mastered the skills studied during the term at a higher level? Probably not. Instead, it means they have mastered the skills at the measured level but are willing to expend additional effort to obtain a higher grade. Thus, the higher grade masks their mastery level.

Any one of these confounding practices confuses the meaning of the grade. However, when two or more of them are used, the grade's meaning becomes increasingly distorted. The grade no longer reflects students' mastery level, but this level plus rehearsal, study habits, misbehavior, and effort. Parents and school administrators will undoubtedly misinterpret such grades. It is also unlikely that confounded grades will correlate very well with students' scores on district-wide or standardized tests that measure the same skills. The best practice is to assign achievement grades solely for achievement. You can communicate students' inadequate study habits, misbehavior, and outstanding effort using the space for such conduct on the report card.

PREPARING FOR CONFERENCES

Many school districts schedule parent–teacher conferences following the distribution of report cards. These conferences permit teachers to explain students' grades and answer questions parents may have about their child's achievement, conduct, and attendance.

To prepare for these individual conferences, you need to review each student's record, select the information to present, and decide how you will present your observations. Preparing for conferences will be easier if you develop a generic term summary form that can be completed from data in the gradebook as conferences are scheduled. You might include the following information on the form:

1. The goals covered during the term
2. The goals mastered by the student
3. The student's percentage score on each posttest administered during the term
4. The student's composite score
5. The group's average composite score, standard deviation, and range

A sample generic form is illustrated in Table 13.7. The top row contains space for the student's name, the term, and the grade earned. Section A contains space for listing the goals covered during the term. The block preceding each goal can be used to indicate whether the student mastered it. Section B contains a percentage scale for recording the student's posttest

TABLE 13.7 Generic Performance Summary Form for Parent Conferences

Name _____ Term _____ Grade _____

A. *Instructional Goals*

____ 1. _____	____ 11. _____
____ 2. _____	____ 12. _____
____ 3. _____	____ 13. _____
____ 4. _____	____ 14. _____
____ 5. _____	____ 15. _____
____ 6. _____	____ 16. _____
____ 7. _____	____ 17. _____
____ 8. _____	____ 18. _____
____ 9. _____	____ 19. _____
____ 10. _____	____ 20. _____

B. *Posttest Scores*

Percentage
Scores _____

      10   20   30   40   50   60   70   80   90   100

Tests _____

C. *Term Composite Score*

Composite
Scores _____

      10   20   30   40   50   60   70   80   90   100

$\overline{X}$ = _____
SD = _____
Range = _____

scores on each test. The area beneath this scale can be used to list quizzes, unit tests, midterm exams, and the final exam. Section C includes another scale that can be used to illustrate the student's composite score, as well as the class mean, standard deviation, and range.

At the conclusion of each term, a master form for the term can be completed by inserting the particular goals studied in section A; listing the posttests administered in section B; and inserting the class mean, standard deviation, and range for the class composite scores in section C. Multiple copies of the master form can be made and then completed for each student as conferences are scheduled.

Table 13.8 contains a sample form completed for Brian Allen for the first term. To complete the form, his name and term grade are inserted in the top

TABLE 13.8   Performance Summary Form

Name _____*Allen, Brian*_____ Term ___*I*___ Grade ___*B*___

A.   Instructional Goals (X's indicate at least minimal mastery)

X	1. Group common words or objects		X	11. Select adjectives to modify nouns
X	2. Name synonyms			12. Select adverbs to modify verbs, adjectives, & adverbs
X	3. Name antonyms		X	13. Write plural forms of singular words & vice versa
X	4. Add prefixes to root words		X	14. Match singular subjects and verbs
	5. Add suffixes to root words		X	15. Match plural subjects and verbs
X	6. Form contractions		X	16. Select the correct verb tense
X	7. Use coordinating conjunctions			17.
X	8. Use correlative conjunctions			18.
X	9. Use subordinating conjunctions			19.
X	10. Substitute pronouns for nouns			20.

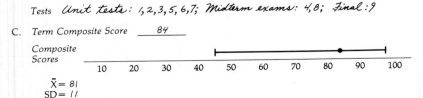

B.   Posttest Scores

Percentage
Scores

```
                                              6
                                              5           8
                                         1  3 2    7 4  9
        10    20    30    40    50    60    70    80    90    100
```

Tests   *Unit tests: 1, 2, 3, 5, 6, 7; Midterm exams: 4, 8; Final: 9*

C.   Term Composite Score ___*84*___

Composite
Scores

```
                              |————————————•————|
        10    20    30    40    50    60    70    80    90    100
```

$\bar{X} = 81$
SD $= 11$
Range $= 44$ *to* 96

row; the goals he mastered are checked in section A; the location of his percentage score on each posttest is inserted in section B; and the location of his composite score is added to section C.

During the conference, the form can be used as a reference for presenting and discussing his progress. For example, section A can be used to describe the skills studied during the term and Brian's mastery or failure of each. Section B can be used to explain the level and consistency of his performance throughout the term. Trends in his progress, such as his improved test performance toward the end of the term, will be obvious from the location and sequence of the scores. Section C can be used not only to describe his achievement level, but also to compare his progress to that of the class. Although completing such a form will take only a couple of minutes, it will help ensure that you are prepared for conferences and can present factual data for discussion.

SUMMARY

Each grading term, teachers are expected to evaluate and report students' progress in achievement and conduct as well as to report their attendance. To document and summarize student data, you need to design a gradebook that matches your teaching assignment.

The gradebook should include a daily record in which you document events that occur during each class session. To prepare this section, select the information you will document; choose symbols that represent each type of information; create a legend for the symbols; list class dates; and record the selected behaviors. You will also need a summary section in which to record the frequencies of selected behaviors. Information in the daily record will help you summarize attendance, complete behavior rating scales, and perhaps explain the grades and other marks students earn.

The gradebook should also contain a posttest record. This section is used to record and summarize students' posttest performance. In documenting achievement you should record general information about each test, such as (1) the format, title, and date; (2) the group's average score and standard deviation; (3) the number of items or points included on the test; and (4) the particular goals and number of goals measured. This information is used to compare tests at the end of the term and to interpret students' scores on each test. To document students' performance, record their raw scores, percentage scores, the number of goals they mastered, and the grade earned. You should also reserve a column for weighted scores.

At the end of the term, you need to synthesize individual test scores into a term composite score. The steps in this procedure include: (1) analyzing the relationship among posttests; (2) selecting the percentage each test should contribute to the composite score; (3) identifying weighting factors; (4) calculating weighted scores; and (5) calculating composite scores.

The next task is to convert composite scores to term grades using standards. Grade standards are often prescribed by district policy; when they are not, you need to set your own. Standards can be set using either criterion-referenced or norm-referenced methods, although criterion-referenced methods are preferred. Criterion-referenced standards are based on the level of students' performance on the goals studied during the term, and norm-referenced standards are based on relative group performance.

Most school districts also require you to assign marks for conduct in such areas as attitude toward learning, study habits, and citizenship. A third section of the gradebook should be reserved for recording students' scores from behavior rating scales. Similar to posttest scores, conduct scores should be combined into a composite score at the end of the term. These scores are converted to district-prescribed marks using standards you set yourself.

Some teachers confound achievement grades by combining conduct and achievement. This happens when posttest achievement is confounded with rehearsal, study habits, misbehavior, or effort. Such practices should be avoided because they make valid interpretation of the achievement grade impossible.

Teacher–parent conferences are usually scheduled after report cards are sent home. In preparing for these conferences, you need to select the information you want to communicate and decide how to present it. To save time, prepare a generic summary form that includes the selected information. The form can be completed for each student and used as a basis for discussion during scheduled conferences.

PRACTICE EXERCISES

I. The Gradebook. Identify the section of the gradebook in which each of the following types of information should be recorded.

Gradebook Sections
   A. The Daily Record
   B. The Posttest Record
   C. The Conduct Record

Information to Record
   1. Scores from behavior rating scales
   2. The particular goals and number of goals measured
   3. Materials checked out from the resource center
   4. Dates of class sessions
   5. The format, title, and dates of tests given
   6. Particular instances of conduct
   7. The number of items or points on a test
   8. Attendance
   9. Parent permission granted for a field trip
   10. Raw scores
   11. Group performance measures including the mean and standard deviation
   12. The percentage of items correct

II. Recording Posttest Information. Information about one posttest is given below. On a piece of graph paper, label columns and insert the test information as you would in the gradebook. Remember to reserve several columns on the left side to record students' names and a column to record weighted scores at the end of the term.

Posttest Information
   1. The test was objective and covered goals 1, 2, 3, and 4 in the punctuation unit.
   2. It was administered on December 5.

3. The test included 30 items, and the average score and standard deviation were 25 and 3, respectively.

4. John Anker's raw score was 28, he mastered all four goals, and he earned an *A*.

5. Alice Brown's raw score was 20, she mastered two of the goals, and she earned a *D*.

III. Identifying the Percentage Each Test Will Contribute to the Composite Score. Suppose that during one term you administered five quizzes, three unit tests, and a comprehensive final exam. Based on an analysis of the tests, you decided that:

1. The five quizzes should contribute 25 percent to the composite score.
2. The three unit tests should contribute 50 percent.
3. The final exam should contribute 25 percent.
4. The five quizzes should be weighted equally.
5. The three unit tests should be weighted equally.
  A. What percentage will each quiz contribute to the composite score?
  B. What percentage will each unit test contribute to the composite score?

IV. Identifying Weighting Factors for Each Test
  A. Using the percentage allocated for each test, identify the weighting factor for each quiz, each unit test, and the final exam.

FIGURE 13.12

Test	Percentage	Weighting Factor
Quizzes		
Unit Tests		
Final Exam		

V. Calculating Weighted Scores. The posttest record for the nine tests is included in Table 13.9.
  A. Insert the selected weighting factors in the appropriate columns for each test.
  B. Calculate weighted scores for each test for the two students illustrated.

VI. Calculating Composite Scores. A section, Term 2 Summary, is located at the bottom of Table 13.9.
  A. Label columns in this section to record term summary information.
  B. Calculate the term composite scores for the two students and record them in this section.
  C. Sum the number of goals mastered by each student.

VII. Setting Standards for Assigning Grades
  A. Grade standards that are based on the number of goals mastered and points earned during a term are called _____ .
  B. Grade standards that are based on the relative position of students' composite scores are called _____ .

C. What does each grade mean when criterion-referenced and norm-referenced standards are used? Answer this on a chart like the one in Figure 13.13.

D. Suppose you set 93 as the cut-off score for an *A* grade and 60 as the cut-off score for a *D*.
  1. Set an equal score range for the *B*, *C*, and *D* grades and identify the size of the range for each grade.
  2. Identify the composite scores that will correspond to each grade.

TABLE 13.9   Posttest Record for One Term

Students	O Quiz 1 11–10					O Quiz 2 11–17					O Unit Test 1 11–24				
	$\overline{X}$/SD	%	Wt.	1	G	$\overline{X}$/SD	%	Wt.	2–3	G	$\overline{X}$/SD	%	Wt.	1–3	G
	17/2	20		1	X	12/2	15		2		30/3	35		3	X
Acus, M.	17	85		1	B	12	80		2	C	31	89		3	B
Ayres, J.	20	100		1	A	13	87		2	B	34	97		3	A

Students	E Quiz 3 11–31					O Quiz 4 12–7					O Unit Test 2 12–14				
	$\overline{X}$/SD	%	Wt.	4,5	G	$\overline{X}$/SD	%	Wt.	6	G	$\overline{X}$/SD	%	Wt.	4–6	G
	16/4	20		2	X	21/2	25		1	X	32/4	40		3	X
Acus, M.	17	85		2	B	20	80		1	C	32	80		2	C
Ayres, J.	19	95		2	A	23	92		1	A	38	95		3	A

Students	PD Quiz 5 12–21					O Unit Test 3 1–6					O Final Exam 1–12				
	$\overline{X}$/SD	%	Wt.	8,9	G	$\overline{X}$/SD	%	Wt.	7–9	G	$\overline{X}$/SD	%	Wt.	1–9	G
	16/3	20		2	X	33/4	40		3	X	40/5	50		9	X
Acus, M.	17	85		2	B	35	88		3	B	42	84		8	B
Ayres, J.	20	100		2	A	39	98		3	A	46	92		9	A

Term 2 Summary

Students			
Acus, M.			
Ayres, J.			

FIGURE 13.13

Grade	Criterion-Referenced Standards	Norm-Referenced Standards
A		
B		
C		
D		
F		

Grade		Score Range
A	=	_93_ to _100_
B	=	___ to ___
C	=	___ to ___
D	=	_60_ to ___
F	=	_59_ and below

    E. Using these grading standards, convert the students' composite scores in Table 13.9 to grades.

VIII. Enrichment

    A. Obtain your school district's policies on grading and look for information that describes:

       1. The type and number of measures that are to be used to measure the students' progress.

       2. The percentage a final exam is to contribute to the composite score.

       3. The standards for converting composite scores to grades.

       4. Whether grade standards are to be criterion-referenced or norm-referenced.

    B. Review your school district's report card for your grade level and identify the categories of behavior that are to be reported.

    C. Design a gradebook that will enable you to document the required information.

    D. Select the behaviors you want to record in a daily record and identify symbols you can use to document each one.

    E. Based on your subject and grade level, select the information you need for each posttest. Design a format that can be used to systematically record the information.

FEEDBACK

I. The Gradebook

Items	1	2	3	4	5	6	7	8	9	10	11	12
Answers	C	B	A	A	B	A	B	A	A	B	B	B

II. Recording Posttest Information: Gradebook Section

Students	O	Punctuation			12-5				
	$\bar{X}$ / 30	%	wt.	1-4	G				
	25 / 3	30		4	////				
Anker, John	28	93		4	A				
Brown, Alice	20	67		2	D				

Did you remember to reserve a column for percentage scores? Percentage scores are obtained by:

A. Dividing each student's raw score by the total number of items, or points, on the test to obtain the proportion correct.

B. Multiplying the proportion correct by 100 to obtain the percentage.

John: $\dfrac{28}{30} = .93; .93 \times 100 = 93\%$

Alice: $\dfrac{20}{30} = .666; .67 \times 100 = 67\%$

III. Identifying the Percentage Each Test Will Contribute to the Composite Score

A. Each quiz will contribute 5 percent.

$$\dfrac{\text{Total percentage allocated for quizzes}}{\text{Number of quizzes}} = \dfrac{25}{5} = 5 \text{ percent}$$

B. Each unit test will contribut 16.7 percent.

$$\dfrac{\text{Total percentage allocated for unit tests}}{\text{Number of unit tests}} = \dfrac{50}{3} = 16.66; 16.7 \text{ percent}$$

IV. Identifying Weighting Factors for Each Test

FIGURE 13.12(F)

Test	Percentage	Weighting Factor
Quizzes	5	$\dfrac{5}{5} = 1$
Unit Tests	16.7	$\dfrac{16.7}{5} = 3.3$
Final Exam	25	$\dfrac{25}{5} = 5$

V. Calculating Weighted Scores. See Table 13.9 (F).
  A. The weighting factors for each test are inserted in the second row of the *Wt.* column.
  B. The percentage scores are multiplied by the weighting factors to obtain the weighted score.
VI. Calculating Composite Scores. See Table 13.9(F).

TABLE 13.9(F) Posttest Record for One Term

Students	O Quiz 1 11–10					O Quiz 2 11–17					O Unit Test 1 11–24				
	$\overline{X}$/SD	%	Wt.	1	G	$\overline{X}$/SD	%	Wt.	2–3	G	$\overline{X}$/SD	%	Wt.	1–3	G
	17/2	20	(1)	1	X	12/2	15	(1)	2		30/3	35	(3.3)	3	X
Acus, M.	17	85	85	1	B	12	80	80	2	C	31	89	294	3	B
Ayres, J.	20	100	100	1	A	13	87	87	2	B	34	97	320	3	A

Students	E Quiz 3 11–31					O Quiz 4 12–7					O Unit Test 2 12–14				
	$\overline{X}$/SD	%	Wt.	4,5	G	$\overline{X}$/SD	%	Wt.	6	G	$\overline{X}$/SD	%	Wt.	4–6	G
	16/4	20	(1)	2	X	21/2	25	(1)	1		32/4	40	(3.3)	3	X
Acus, M.	17	85	85	2	B	20	80	80	1	C	32	80	264	2	C
Ayres, J.	19	95	95	2	A	23	92	92	1	A	38	95	314	3	A

Students	PD Quiz 5 12–21					O Unit Test 3 1–6					O Final Exam 1–12				
	$\overline{X}$/SD	%	Wt.	8,9	G	$\overline{X}$/SD	%	Wt.	7–9	G	$\overline{X}$/SD	%	Wt.	1–9	G
	16/3	20	(1)	2	X	33/4	40	(3.3)	3		40/5	50	(5)	9	X
Acus, M.	17	85	85	2	B	35	88	290	3	B	42	84	420	8	B
Ayres, J.	20	100	100	2	A	39	98	323	3	A	46	92	460	9	A

Students	*Term 2 Summary*			
	Total	Composite	Goals	Grade
Acus, M.	(19.9) 1683	85	9 8	B
Ayres, J.	1891	95	9	A

A. Columns were created in the summary section to record the total units of weight and total weighted scores, the composite scores, the total number of goals mastered during the term, and the term grade.

B. The composite scores were calculated using the following procedure:
   1. Sum the total units of weight.
   2. Sum the weighted scores to obtain the total weighted score.
   3. Divide the total weighted score by the total units of weight to obtain the composite score.

VII. Setting Standards for Assigning Grades
   A. Criterion-referenced standards
   B. Norm-referenced standards
   C. **FIGURE 13.13(F)**

Grade	Criterion-Referenced Standards	Norm-Referenced Standards
A	Outstanding number of goals mastered and points earned	Outstanding progress compared to classmates
B	Very good number of goals mastered and points earned	Above-average progress compared to classmates
C	Questionable number of goals mastered and points earned—student is experiencing some difficulty	Average progress compared to classmates
D	Inadequate number of goals mastered and points earned	Below-average progress compared to classmates
F	Unacceptable number of goals mastered and points earned	Very little progress compared to classmates

D. *Grade   Score Range*
   A   = 93 to 100
   B   = 82 to 92
   C   = 71 to 81
   D   = 60 to 70
   F   = 59 and below

These scores were identified using the following steps:
1. Identify the range of scores between the lowest *A* and the lowest *D* (93 − 60 = 33).
2. Divide this range by 3 (there are three grade levels—*B*, *C*, and *D*) to obtain the range of scores for each grade (33/3 = 11).
3. Subtract 11 from 93 to identify the lower limit for a *B* grade (93 − 11 = 82).
4. Subtract 11 from 82 to identify the lower limit for a *C* grade (82 − 11 = 72).

5. Subtract 11 from 71 to obtain the lower limit for a *D* grade (71 − 11 = 60).

E. M. Acus would be assigned a *B*, and J. Ayers would be assigned an *A*.

SUGGESTED READING

Ebel, R. L., and Frisbie, D. A. (1986). *Essentials of educational measurement.* Englewood Cliffs, N.J.: Prentice-Hall, pp. 243–65.

Gronlund, N.E. (1985). *Measurement and evaluation in teaching.* New York: Macmillan Publishing Company, pp. 435–60.

Hills, J. R. (1981). *Measurement and evaluation in the classroom.* Columbus, Ohio: Charles E. Merrill Publishing Company, pp. 282–358.

Mehrens, W. A., and Lehmann, I. J. (1984). *Measurement and evaluation in education and psychology.* New York: CBS College Publishing, pp. 493–523.

Nitko, A. J. (1983). *Educational tests and measurement.* New York: Harcourt, Brace, Jovanovich, pp. 329–50.

Popham, W. J. (1981). *Modern educational measurement.* Englewood Cliffs, N.J.: Prentice-Hall, pp. 400–12.

CHAPTER 14

Interpreting Standardized Test Results

OBJECTIVES

1. Compare criterion-referenced achievement tests, norm-referenced achievement tests, and scholastic aptitude tests using their purposes, design characteristics, and uses.
2. Describe the procedures for developing norm-referenced tests.
3. Calculate and interpret the following standard scores: percentiles, percentile bands, and stanines.
4. Interpret the following standard scores; normalized z and T scores, normal curve equivalent scores, and deviation IQ scores.
5. Interpret the following developmental scores: grade equivalent scores, scale scores, and anticipated achievement scores.
6. Describe the performance of individual students and class groups using their test records.

In addition to preparing and using classroom tests, teachers are usually expected to administer and interpret one or more standardized tests each year. These tests are called *standardized* because the same directions are used for administering them in all classrooms and standard procedures are used for scoring and interpreting them. This standardization permits comparing students' performance across classrooms, across schools, and across school districts. The three types of standardized tests used in schools include criterion-referenced achievement tests, norm-referenced achievement tests, and norm-referenced scholastic aptitude tests. These tests differ in purpose and in how they are developed and interpreted.

CRITERION-REFERENCED ACHIEVEMENT TESTS

Criterion-referenced achievement tests are developed by school districts, state departments of education, and commercial testing companies. These tests measure students' progress in such subjects as language arts, mathematics, science, and social studies. The match between these tests and the prescribed curriculum for a particular grade level and subject is of primary importance. Because these tests correspond directly to the curriculum guide, they can be administered at the beginning of the school year to evaluate the appropriateness of the curriculum for the grade level and to plan instruction tailored to students' needs. At the conclusion of a semester or year, they can be used to evaluate students' progress during the course.

The procedures used to develop criterion-referenced achievement tests are similar to those teachers use to develop classroom tests. The goals prescribed in the curriculum guide are analyzed to identify their subordinate skills, which are divided into prerequisite and enabling skills for each grade. The conditions for performing each skill are identified, and item specifications are written to ensure that each item is at an appropriate level of complexity, elicits the appropriate behavior, and includes the intended content. Item specifications prescribe the characteristics of the stem (or question), the correct answer, and each distractor to be included. Multiple choice items are often used because of their economy, versatility, and objectivity. Tables of specifications are developed to ensure an appropriate balance among goals and their subordinate skills. Using these specifications, a writing team writes many more items than needed for each skill.

The review process used to evaluate these items is more comprehensive than that used by teachers. In addition to the writing team, content experts review the items for congruence with item specifications. Language specialists evaluate the appropriateness of the vocabulary, reading level, and grammar. Representatives from different cultural groups evaluate the items for potential bias in vocabulary and context. Finally, target students are sometimes used to review the items to verify their readability. During the review process, many items are either eliminated or revised.

Items that survive these reviews are assigned to different test forms for a field test. A large, representative sample of students is selected to take each test, which is administered in regular classrooms by the teachers. Like classroom tests, the items are evaluated using their difficulty and discrimination indexes. Related to difficulty, items that are more difficult than anticipated, given the complexity of the task, are eliminated. Likewise, those that do not discriminate well for the obtained difficulty levels are eliminated. Items that meet the criteria are stored in an item bank or item pool. Using the table of specifications, items are selected from the bank for tests as needed.

To help ensure the curricular validity of commercial criterion-referenced tests, publishers have begun to provide custom-made or tailor-made tests. Publishers follow the previously described procedure to create comprehensive item banks for each subject. Working in collaboration with a school district's representatives, they select the goals and objectives to be measured by a test and create a table of specifications tailored to the school's curriculum. Then, using the table of specifications, they select items from their item pool to create tests tailored to the district's curriculum.

Students' performance on criterion-referenced tests is usually reported as nonmastery, partial knowledge, or mastery of each objective. A criterion, or score needed for partial knowledge and mastery, is set using professional judgment. Scores used to report each student's level are either the percentage of items answered correctly for each objective or derived scores created using the number of items correct and other factors, such as the difficulty and discrimination levels of items in a set and the probability of guessing correct answers.

NORM-REFERENCED ACHIEVEMENT TESTS

Norm-referenced achievement tests are used primarily to compare students' achievement to that of a large, representative group of students at the same grade level. This representative group is called a *norm group*. Norm groups can be made up of students from throughout a school district, the state, the region, or the country. The purpose for these tests is to determine whether a student's or a group's achievement level is above average, average, or below average when compared to that of the selected norm group. These tests typically measure students' achievement in basic skills, such as language and mathematics, although other subjects are sometimes included. Norm-referenced tests are extremely time consuming and expensive to develop; therefore, they are usually produced and distributed by commercial test publishers rather than by school districts or state departments of education.

A summary of the process used to develop norm-referenced achievement tests appears in Figure 14.1. There are five main stages in the process: designing, developing, field testing, creating norms, and writing test manuals. During the design of norm-referenced tests, those goals cited most often in curriculum guides throughout the nation are selected to ensure the test's relevance for most school districts. Tasks selected to measure each goal vary in difficulty, for example, some are prerequisite skills, some are enabling skills, and some are too complex for most students at each grade level. Tasks are chosen in this manner to ensure the wide range of scores necessary to discriminate among below-average, average, and above-average achievers.

The item writing and review processes are the same for both criterion-referenced and norm-referenced tests. However, the procedures used to field test and select items for norm-referenced tests are different. During the field test, the different test forms are administered to a large, representative sample of students. Students are selected according to specific characteristics, such

FIGURE 14.1   Process for Developing Norm-Referenced Achievement Tests

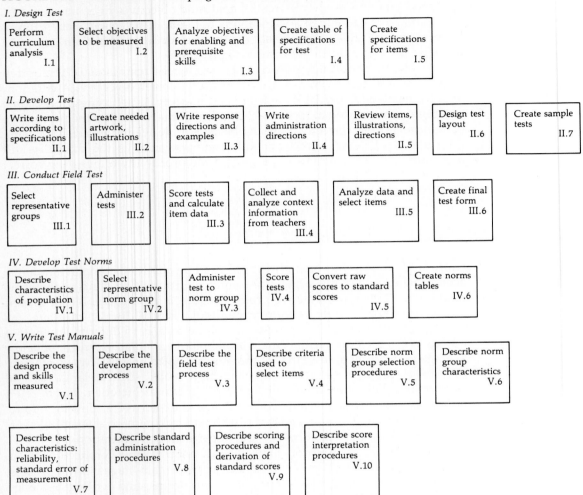

as prior achievement or aptitude, age, gender, cultural group, socioeconomic level, school and community type, and geographic region. A sample of students from the grades immediately preceding and following the target grade may also be included. Teachers administer the tests in selected classrooms and follow the prescribed administration procedures, with one exception. Students are allowed ample time to finish the test. Teachers record the time each student requires, note any items or directions that cause confusion, and describe difficulties observed.

     Data from the field test are analyzed, and items are selected for the final test version using the following four criteria:

1. Objective balance (inclusion of enough items for all skills)
2. Difficulty range (p values ranging from .90 down to .20, with a median value of about .55)
3. Discrimination indices (the highest positive discrimination index for the accompanying difficulty index)
4. Instructional sensitivity (a larger proportion of students answering items correctly at each higher grade level)

The items that best meet these criteria appear on the final test form, which is professionally formatted and produced.

Scores on norm-referenced tests are based on the performance of students in a reference group, or norm group. To select a representative norm group, the team must first define the population (e.g., all third-graders in the United States) and then select variables that accurately describe the group. If the norm group selected does not adequately represent the population, interpretations of individual student's performances are questionable.

To ensure that a cross-section of students is included, the team establishes categories of students and then determines the proportion of the population that falls into each category. For example, the team must know how the population is distributed according to the following characteristics:

1. Achievement or aptitude
2. Age, gender, race, and cultural group
3. Enrollment in public, private, and parochial schools
4. Enrollment in large, medium, and small schools
5. Residence in the different regions of the country
6. Residence in urban, suburban, and rural communities
7. Residence in high-, medium-, and low-income communities

Once the team has determined the characteristics of the population, a sampling plan is used to select the schools that will be included. The norm group usually includes thousands of students who, all together, are representative of the population.

Teachers then use the standardized procedures to administer the test to students in the norm group. At the same time, the team collects data on the group's characteristics. The tests are scored, and derived scores are calculated and reported in norms tables that appear in the test's technical manual and in the administrator's manual. Although raw scores are used to report students' achievement, they are converted to derived scores to facilitate comparing each student's performance to that of the norm group. Commonly used derived scores include percentiles, percentile bands, stanines, normal curve equivalent scores, grade equivalent scores, scale scores, and anticipated achievement scores. Procedures for interpreting these scores are described later in the chapter.

The team's final task is to develop the test manuals. These manuals usually describe the design and development process, the field test procedures, the item selection process, the sampling plan for the norm group, the characteristics of the norm group, and the group's test performance. They also include a list of the goals and objectives measured, directions for administering and scoring the test, and directions for interpreting the scores.

SCHOLASTIC APTITUDE TESTS

Scholastic aptitude tests are developed by commercial test publishers because they too are time-consuming and expensive to develop. Unlike the two types of achievement tests, they do not measure students' achievement in school-related subjects. Instead, their main purpose is to measure students' thinking processes, sometimes called *reasoning skills*. These thinking processes include such skills as recall, concept discrimination, classification, analysis, sequencing, synthesis, inference, and generalization. Students' performances on aptitude tests are used to predict how well they will achieve in given subjects, special training programs, higher education, and careers that require similar reasoning skills.

The procedures used to develop scholastic aptitude tests are similar to those used to develop norm-referenced achievement tests because aptitude tests are norm-referenced. The skills measured vary widely in difficulty to enable discrimination among students who are below average, average, and above average in aptitude. The major difference between these tests is that the foundation or framework of skills measured by the aptitude test involves thinking or reasoning skills rather than curriculum-based skills.

Students' performances on aptitude tests are interpreted by comparing them to the performances of the representative norm group. The scores traditionally used to report performance on aptitude tests are deviation IQ scores. However, percentiles are sometimes reported as well.

Table 14.1 summarizes the characteristics of criterion-referenced and norm-referenced achievement tests and scholastic aptitude tests. Because of the differences in these tests, school personnel carefully select the appropriate test for their purpose. For example, if they want to know how many students in each grade have mastered the skills prescribed in the curriculum guide, they should use a criterion-referenced test. However, if they want to know how their students' general achievement in a subject area compares to the achievement of a norm group, they should use a norm-referenced test. Finally, if they want to know which students are most likely to succeed in a particular subject, they should use an aptitude test that measures the reasoning skills required in the subject.

TABLE 14.1 Characteristics of Criterion-Referenced and Norm-Referenced Achievement Tests and Scholastic Aptitude Tests

	Criterion-Referenced Achievement Tests	Norm-Referenced Achievement Tests	Scholastic Aptitude Tests
Typical developers	School districts State departments of education Commercial publishers	Commercial publishers	Commercial publishers
Primary purpose	To measure students' achievement of curriculum-based skills	To measure students' achievement of curriculum-based skills	To measure students' general thinking or reasoning skills
Foundation or item basis	Grade or course-specific curricular goals and their subordinate skills	Curricular goals from multiple grade levels	Generic thinking or reasoning skills
Criteria for including items	Balanced representation of goals and objectives Measured difficulty levels are within bounds for perceived skill complexity Measured discrimination levels are high, positive for given difficulty levels	Balanced representation of goals and objectives Wide range of difficulty levels, from .90 to .20 with a median about .55 Measured discrimination levels are high, positive for given difficulty levels Sensitivity to instruction	Balanced representation of thinking or reasoning skills Wide range of difficulty levels, from .90 to .20 with a median about .55 Measured discrimination levels are high, positive for given difficulty levels
Scores typically reported	Minimum scores for partial and total mastery of main skill areas Number of items correct Percentage of items correct Derived score based on items correct and other factors	Percentile ranks Percentile bands Stanines Normal curve equivalent scores Grade equivalent scores Scale scores Anticipated achievement scores (in conjunction with aptitude scores)	Deviation IQ scores Percentiles
When administered	Before instruction After instruction	After instruction	With achievement tests Before selecting students for courses of study

(continued on next page)

TABLE 14.1 (*continued*)

	Criterion-Referenced Achievement Tests	Norm-Referenced Achievement Tests	Scholastic Aptitude Tests
Use	Assess the curriculum Plan instruction Evaluate progress Group students for instruction	Classify students' achievement as above average, average, or below average for a given grade Create homogeneous or heterogeneous class groups	Classify students' aptitude as below average, average, or above average for a given age Predict achievement in subjects, and courses of study that require similar reasoning skills

One type of test cannot serve all three purposes equally well; however, it is not uncommon to find a norm-referenced achievement test used for all three. For example, the publishers of norm-referenced tests have begun to report criterion-referenced or mastery scores in addition to the traditional norm-referenced scores. Using these mastery scores, though, potentially can lead to inaccurate judgments about students' mastery. Remember that items are primarily selected for these tests to create a wide range of scores. Thus, many items are purposefully included that are judged to be too complex for most students at a given grade level. This design feature, which is necessary for norm-referenced achievement tests, will result in lower mastery scores for students than will scores produced from legitimate criterion-referenced tests. Norm-referenced achievement tests are also commonly used instead of aptitude tests to predict achievement. This practice is not as problematic since both previous achievement and aptitude have been found to be good predictors of future achievement. One potential problem with this practice is that the subject-based skills in the new curriculum may require different reasoning skills than those measured by previous achievement tests.

NORM-REFERENCED TEST SCORES

Publishers of norm-referenced tests convert students' raw scores into derived scores that permit each student's performance to be compared to that of the norm group. These derived scores are created using only the raw scores of students in the norm group. Later, when students throughout the country take the test, their raw scores are matched with those of students in the norm group, and the corresponding preset derived scores are assigned to individual students.

Using the Normal Curve to Interpret Standard Scores

Most derived scores are based on the standard normal distribution of scores, frequently called the *normal curve*. This distribution is used to give the scores a common meaning that makes interpreting performance much easier. Obviously, if every standardized test used a different score distribution, interpreting the various scores would be a difficult task.

The area under the normal curve is divided into halves with the mean score as the center. Notice that in Figure 14.2, the area between the mean score and one standard deviation above the mean score (+1SD) contains approximately 34 percent of the ranked scores in the distribution (.3413). Because a normal distribution is symmetrical, approximately 68 percent of the ranked scores fall between one standard deviation above (+1SD) and one standard deviation below (−1SD) the mean score (.3413 + .3413). Fourteen percent of the scores fall within the area between one and two standard deviations above the mean, and another 14 percent fall between one and two standard deviations below the mean. The remaining 4 percent of scores are evenly divided between the two remaining plus and minus categories. These percentages total 100 percent of the scores. If you add these percentages cumulatively from left to right, you can locate the proportion of scores that fall below each standard deviation. For example, about 2 percent of the scores fall below two standard deviations below the mean. About 16 percent of the scores fall below one standard deviation below the mean (2 + 14). Likewise, 50 percent fall below the mean (2 + 14 + 34). Eighty-four percent fall below one standard deviation above the mean, and 98 percent fall below two standard deviations above the mean. If you wanted to know the proportion of scores that fall below points between these standard deviation anchors, you

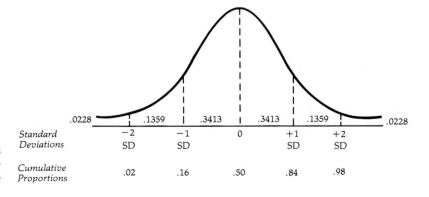

FIGURE 14.2
Areas under the
Normal Curve

could consult a table of areas under the normal curve. These tables are included in most basic statistics books.

Many scores reported on norm-referenced tests are called *normalized scores* because they are converted to fit the standard normal distribution, whatever the actual shape of the raw score distribution. These normalized scores are also called *standard scores*. The most commonly used standard scores are percentiles, stanines, normal curve equivalent scores, and deviation IQ scores.

Interpreting Percentiles

The range for percentiles is 1 to 99. This score indicates the percentage of students in the norm group who earned raw scores below the cumulative frequency at midpoint for each raw score in the distribution. The cumulative frequency at midpoint includes all the students who earned raw scores below a given score plus one-half of the students who earned that raw score. For example, if 38 students earned raw scores lower than 40 and 10 students earned a raw score of 40, the cumulative frequency at midpoint would be 38 plus 5, or 43. A student who earns a percentile score of 62 is said to have performed better than 62 percent of the students in the norm group. (This percentage includes all students who earned lower raw scores and one-half of the students who earned the same raw score.)

Knowing how publishers convert raw scores to percentiles is helpful in interpreting them. Although publishers work with a wide range of raw scores and thousands of students, the simplified frequency distribution in Table 14.2 illustrates the process.

TABLE 14.2   Derivation of Percentiles from Raw Scores

(1) Raw Scores	(2) Frequency of Scores	(3) Cumulative Frequency below		(4) 1/2 Frequency within		(5) Cumulative Frequency at Midpoint	(6) Proportion	(7) Percentage or Percentile
50	1	35	+	.5	=	35.5	35.5/36 = .99	99
49	2	33	+	1	=	34	34/36 = .94	94
48	3	30	+	1.5	=	31.5	31.5/36 = .88	88
47	4	26	+	2	=	28	28/36 = .77	77
46	5	21	+	2.5	=	23.5	23.5/36 = .65	65
45	6	15	+	3	=	18	18/36 = .50	50
44	5	10	+	2.5	=	12.5	12.5/36 = .35	35
43	4	6	+	2	=	8	8/36 = .22	22
42	3	3	+	1.5	=	4.5	4.5/36 = .13	13
41	2	1	+	1	=	2	2/36 = .05	5
40	1	0	+	.5	=	.5	.5/36 = .01	1

N = 36

First, the raw scores are listed from highest to lowest (column 1), and the number of students who earned each score is tallied (column 2). Although there are several ways to proceed from this point, the most commonly used method is:

1. Sum the frequencies of scores falling below each raw score to obtain the cumulative frequency of scores below each raw score (column 3).
2. Divide the frequency of scores at each raw score in half (column 4).
3. Add the frequency of scores below to half the scores at the raw score to obtain the cumulative frequency at midpoint (column 5).
4. Divide this figure by the number of students in the group to obtain the proportion of students at midpoint (column 6).
5. Multiply this proportion by 100 to obtain the percentile for each raw score (column 7).

For example, the percentile for a raw score of 45 in Table 14.2 is 50. This conversion was made by:

1. Summing the frequencies of scores falling below 45 (1 + 2 + 3 + 4 + 5 = 15).
2. Dividing the frequency of scores at 45 in half (6/2 = 3).
3. Adding the frequency of scores below to half the scores at a raw score of 45 (15 + 3 = 18).
4. Dividing the cumulative frequency at midpoint (18) by the total number of students in the group (36) to obtain the proportion at midpoint (18/36 = .50).
5. Multiplying this proportion by 100 to obtain the percentile (.50 × 100 = 50).

There are several factors to consider in interpreting percentiles. One is the distinction between the percentage of correct items and the percentile, since these indices are different. Consider, for example, the percentile and the percentage of correct items for a raw score of 45 in Table 14.2. The percentile for a raw score of 45 is 50 whereas the percentage correct is 90. The percentile score is based on the number of students surpassed, and the percentage correct is based on the number of items correctly answered (see Figure 14.3).

Another factor to consider in interpreting percentile scores is that they are not equal interval scores. An increase of one point on the raw score scale does not correspond to a similar size increase on the percentile scale. For example, in Table 14.2, a 1-point increase on the raw score scale (from 45 to 46) results in a 15-point increase on the percentile scale (from 50 to 65). An increase in raw scores from 46 to 47 results in a 12-point increase on the percentile scale (from 65 to 77). Similarly, an increase in raw scores from 47 to 48 results in an increase on the percentile scale of 11 points. This phe-

FIGURE 14.3   Distinction between Percentile and Percentage Correct

Percentile for a Raw Score of 45	Percentage Correct for a Raw Score of 45
$\dfrac{\text{Cumulative Frequency of Students at Midpoint}}{\text{Total Number of Students in Group}} = \dfrac{18}{36} = .50$ $.50 \times 100 = 50$	$\dfrac{\text{Number of Items Correct}}{\text{Total Number of Items on Test}} = \dfrac{45}{50} = .90$ $.90 \times 100 = 90\%$

nomenon occurs because percentiles are based on the frequency of students who earn each raw score, and this number varies across the raw score scale.

Notice in Table 14.2 that the frequency of students earning each raw score is greater toward the middle of the range than toward the ends of the scale. This uneven distribution of scores across the range influences the correspondence between raw scores and percentiles. Because there are many tied scores in the center of the distribution, small increases in raw scores result in large increases in percentile scores. As the number of tied scores decreases toward the ends of the raw score scale, increases in percentile scores become less dramatic. This uneven correspondence between raw score and percentile increments is not problematic if you know why it occurs and how to explain it to inquiring parents.

Another factor to consider in interpreting percentile scores is that the raw scores of the norm group are the basis for the percentiles. Percentiles based on the performance of a nationwide norm group are called *national percentiles*. If other reference groups, such as all the students in a district, are used, then percentile scores based on this group would be called *district* or *local percentiles*. Percentile scores based on different norm groups are likely to be different even though the underlying raw score is the same for the test. Consider the following data:

Raw Score	National Percentile	District Percentile
40	60	75

When compared to the national norm group, a raw score of 40 reflects lower achievement than it does when compared to the district norm group. This difference reflects that a raw score of 40 ranked higher in the district group than in the national group. As this comparison shows, any interpretation of percentile scores depends on the reference group for the scores.

The final factor to consider in interpreting percentile scores is their relationship to the normal distribution. Because percentile scores reflect the percentage of people in the norm group who earned scores below the midpoint for a raw score, and the areas under the normal curve reflect the percentage of scores falling below a given point on the normal distribution of scores, percentiles can be equated directly to the proportions under the normal curve. The second percentile corresponds to the normal curve cumulative proportion of .02, or two standard deviations below the mean (−2SD). The sixteenth percentile corresponds to the normal curve cumulative proportion of .16, or one standard deviation below the mean (−1SD), and so on. The same correspondence is true for all percentile scores and for all cumulative normal curve proportions. Figure 14.4 illustrates this correspondence. Points between these anchors can be located using a table of areas under the normal curve.

The implication of this correspondence between the percentiles and the normal distribution is that percentiles between plus and minus one standard deviation from the mean are generally interpreted to reflect average test performance. Thus, percentile scores between 16 and 84 are considered within the average range. Those scores above the mean plus one standard deviation, percentiles of 84 or greater, are judged above average. Those scores below the mean minus one standard deviation, percentile scores of 16 or lower, are judged below average.

Interpreting Percentile Bands

Test publishers use an index of their test's reliability, called a *reliability coefficient*, to calculate the test's standard error of measurement. The standard error of measurement (SEM) is an index of the degree of score variability, or inconsistency, that can be expected for each student who takes the test. Lack of perfect reliability, which is a natural characteristic of achievement and aptitude tests, means that a student's score would probably be different if he or she retook the same test. The size of the standard error of measurement reflects the degree of variability that can be expected for a given test. Tests

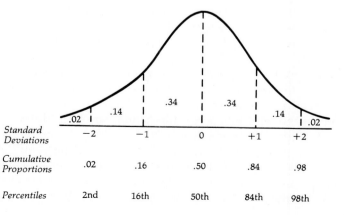

FIGURE 14.4
Relationship of
Percentiles to the
Normal Curve

Standard Deviations	−2	−1	0	+1	+2
Cumulative Proportions	.02	.16	.50	.84	.98
Percentiles	2nd	16th	50th	84th	98th

that have good reliability have a relatively small standard error of measurement.

Publishers usually report the obtained standard error of measurement for a test in the test's technical manual. In addition, many publishers plot percentile bands on students' performance reports to inform teachers of the degree of score variability anticipated. The percentile band encompasses the range of percentile scores within which a student's score could be expected to fall on retesting. The implication of these percentile bands is that teachers should not interpret the percentile score as a precise measure. Instead, it is simply the score obtained by a particular student on a given day.

To aid your interpretation of percentile bands, the method publishers use to create the bands, the characteristics of percentile bands, and the way they are used to compare students' performances are described.

Publishers use the following steps to create percentile bands:

1. Calculate the standard error of measurement for the test.
2. Add one standard error of measurement to the observed raw score to locate the upper limit of the interval.
3. Equate this raw score to its corresponding percentile to identify the upper boundary of the percentile band.
4. Subtract one standard error of measurement from the observed raw score to locate the lower limit of the interval.
5. Equate this raw score to its corresponding percentile to identify the lower boundary of the percentile band.

Table 14.3 illustrates how percentile bands are created and plotted. Section A includes hypothetical raw scores and their corresponding percentile scores. Section B illustrates the scores at the lower and upper ends of the band for three selected scores, 49, 46, and 43, using a hypothetical standard error of measurement of 2. For a raw score of 49, the boundaries of the percentile band are located by adding to and subtracting from this raw score one standard error of measurement (2). The raw scores at the lower and upper boundaries, 47 and 50, are then equated to their corresponding percentiles (93 and 99). Thus, the percentile band for a raw score of 49 and corresponding percentile of 98 extends from a percentile of 93 to one of 99. Section C illustrates the percentile bands for these three scores. The dot above the band is used to locate the position of the observed percentile within the band.

There are two characteristics of percentile bands to consider: (1) the observed percentile score may not fall in the center of the percentile band, and (2) the width of percentile bands varies for different percentiles. These characteristics both result from the fact that there are an unequal number of tied scores at each raw score. The obtained percentile does not fall in the center of the percentile band because there are unequal intervals between percentiles. The area of the band between the observed percentile and the center of the scale, the fiftieth percentile, will be wider than the area between

TABLE 14.3 Using Raw Scores, Standard Error of Measurement, and Percentile Scores to Create Percentile Bands

(A)		(C)	
Raw Scores	Corresponding Percentile Scores		Percentiles
			0 10 20 30 40 50 60 70 80 90 99
50	99		
49	98		
48	96		
47	93		
46	89		
45	84		
44	78		
43	71		
42	63		
41	54		
40	44		

SEM = 2

	Scores at Lower Boundary of Band		(B) Observed Scores		Scores at Upper Boundary of Band	
	Raw	Percentile	Raw	Percentile	Raw	Percentile
1.	47	93	49	98	50	99
2.	44	78	46	89	48	96
3.	41	54	43	71	45	84

the observed percentile and the outer edges of the scale. This occurs because there are more tied raw scores toward the center of the distribution. This characteristic can be observed in the three percentile bands in Table 14.3. Consider the location of the percentile score 98 within its percentile band. There is a difference of only one percentile point between the observed score, 98, and the upper boundary, 99, yet there is a difference of five percentile points between the observed percentile and the lower boundary. The same characteristic can be observed for all three percentile bands.

The second characteristic is that the width of the percentile band varies for different percentile scores. Generally, percentile bands are wider toward the center of the distribution (the fiftieth percentile). This occurs because there are more tied scores at each raw score toward the center of the distribution than there are toward the outer edges of the raw score scale. Remember that many tied raw scores result in dramatic increases on the percentile scale for each increase of one point on the raw score scale. This characteristic can also be observed in the three percentile bands in Table 14.3. The percentile band for a percentile score of 98 is narrower than the one for a percentile score of 89. Likewise, the percentile band for a percentile score of 89 is narrower than the one for a percentile of 71. Farther down the scale toward the mean, the percentile bands would be even wider. Moving from the mean toward the bottom end of the scale, the width of the bands would gradually decrease.

Percentiles are used to compare the performances of several students in a class on one test, as well as the performances of one student across several subtests. When percentile bands overlap on the percentile scale, then observed differences between percentiles are considered negligible, or due to measurement error. In Table 14.3, the bands for percentiles 98 and 89 overlap; thus, this difference would be considered negligible. However, if the bands do not overlap, then the percentiles are considered significantly different. For example, the bands in Table 14.3 for percentiles of 98 and 71 do not overlap. Therefore, the student who earned a percentile of 98 performed significantly better than the student who earned a percentile of 71.

This overlap rule provides an important reminder that rather large differences between percentiles can be based on small differences in raw scores. Using the scores in Table 14.3 as an example, no teacher would be inclined to interpret the performances of students who earned raw scores of 43 and 46 as meaningfully different. However, when percentile scores are used to compare their performances, a percentile of 89 might be interpreted as significantly better than a percentile of 71. The percentile bands and the overlap rule for interpreting them help teachers avoid this inadvertent error.

There is a general rule for comparing percentiles when percentile bands are not provided on students' records. The rule is based on the fact that percentile bands are wider toward the center of the percentile scale than toward the ends. Percentile scores in the center of the distribution (between 30 and 70) should be at least 15 percentile points apart before you consider them different. Percentile scores above 70 and below 30 should be at least 10 percentile points apart. Although this procedure permits only general estimates of differences, it is preferable to assuming that small differences in percentiles are meaningful.

Interpreting Stanines

Stanine scores are another type of standard score used to report students' performance. This discussion of how publishers create them, their characteristics, and their relationship to the normal curve and percentile scores will help you interpret them.

There are nine scores on a stanine scale; a score of 1 reflects low performance, and a score of 9 reflects high performance. Each stanine score represents a set proportion of students in the norm group. The proportion of students that corresponds to each score is as follows:

Stanine scores	1	2	3	4	5	6	7	8	9
Proportion of students assigned each score	.04	.07	.12	.17	.20	.17	.12	.07	.04

Publishers convert raw scores to stanine scores using the following steps:

1. Create a frequency distribution of the norm group's scores by ranking the raw scores from the highest to the lowest and tallying the number of students who earned each score.
2. Convert raw scores to a stanine score of 1.
   a. Multiply the total number of students in the norm group by .04. to identify the number of students that will be assigned a stanine score of 1.
   b. Beginning at the bottom of the score distribution, count up this number of students.
   c. Convert all the raw scores earned by these students to a stanine score of 1.
3. Convert raw scores to a stanine score of 2.
   a. Multiply the total number of students in the norm group by .07 to identify the number of students that will be assigned a stanine score of 2.
   b. Beginning just above the highest raw score converted to a stanine score of 1, count up the number of students to be assigned a stanine score of 2.
   c. Convert all the raw scores earned by these students to a stanine score of 2.
4. Repeat this process, using the prescribed percentages, to convert all raw scores to their corresponding stanine scores.

Besides having only a nine-point scale, there are three characteristics of stanine scores you should consider when interpreting them. First, each stanine score represents a band of raw scores and percentile scores; thus, a different stanine score does not exist for each of the other types of scores. Second, stanine scores toward the center of the distribution include a wider band of percentiles than those toward the outer edges of the scale. Finally, stanines 2 through 8 are each one-half a standard deviation wide and have a fixed position on the normal distribution. Thus, they directly correspond to the normal curve and percentile scores.

Figure 14.5 illustrates the relationship among the stanine scores, the normal distribution, and the percentile scores. Stanine 5 extends one-quarter of a standard deviation on each side of the mean, making it one-half a standard deviation wide. Stanines 2 through 4 and 6 through 8 are also one-half a standard deviation wide. Stanines 1 and 9 are wider and extend to the ends of the distribution. Given this position of each stanine on the normal curve, you can equate stanine scores to the normal curve's standard deviation an-

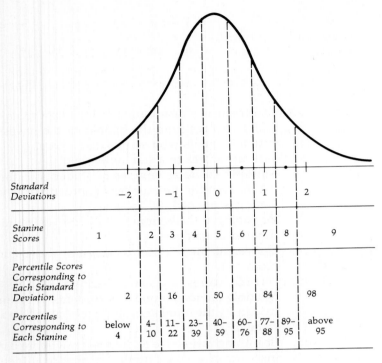

FIGURE 14.5
Correspondence among Stanines, Percentiles, and the Normal Curve

chors and to percentile scores. For example, a stanine score of 1 is equivalent to standard deviations −3 and −2 and to percentiles 1 through 3. A stanine score of 2 is equivalent to a standard deviation of −1 and to percentile scores 4 through 10. Likewise, a stanine score of 5 is equivalent to the mean and to percentile scores 40 through 59. Because of this relationship, if you know the stanine score, you can locate the percentile scores corresponding to it and vice versa.

Interpreting stanines is rather straightforward. Generally, stanines of 1, 2, and 3 reflect below-average performance compared to the norm group. These scores include the bottom 23 percent of the students in the norm group. Stanines 4, 5, and 6 reflect average performance; these scores include the central 54 percent of the norm group. Stanines 7, 8, and 9 reflect above-average performance; these scores include 23 percent of the students at the top end of the scale. School personnel generally use stanines to classify below-average, average, and above-average performance. Although most publishers use both a percentile and a stanine to report students' performance on each subtest, these scores do not provide different information. Instead, they provide the same information in different forms.

Interpreting Normalized *z* and *T* Scores

Two more scores associated with norm-referenced tests are normalized *z* and normalized *T* scores. Chapter 13 described linear *z* and *T* scores that maintain the shape of their raw score distribution, whether it is symmetrical or skewed. Normalized z and T scores are based on a standard normal distribution, regardless of the shape of the corresponding raw score distribution.

Like its linear counterpart, normalized z scores have a mean of 0 and a standard deviation of 1. In creating normalized z scores, raw scores are converted to percentiles to fix their position under the normal curve. Then, based on the location of the percentiles, the conversion is made to z scores. For example, the raw score corresponding to a percentile of 2, or $-2SD$, is equated to a normalized z score of -2; the raw score corresponding to a percentile score of 16, or $-1SD$, is equated to a normalized z score of -1; the raw score corresponding to a percentile of 50 is equated to a normalized z score of 0, and so on.

Normalized T scores are equated to raw scores in the same manner. These scores have a mean of 50 and a standard deviation of 10. The raw score corresponding to a percentile score of 2 is equated to a normalized T score of 30; the raw score corresponding to a percentile of 16 is equated with a normalized T score of 40; and the raw score corresponding to a percentile of 50 is equated to a normalized T score of 50. Scores between these points are matched using a table of areas under the normal curve.

Because of their relationship to the normal distribution and percentile scores, normalized z and T scores are quite easy to interpret. Normalized z and T scores of 1 and 60 and higher reflect above-average performance because these scores are located at one standard deviation or more above the center of the distribution. Those falling between normalized z scores of -1 and $+1$ and normalized T scores of 40 and 60 reflect average performance. Normalized z and T scores of -1 and 40 or lower are below average compared to the norm group. The anchor points for interpreting normalized z and T scores are illustrated in the following chart on performance level:

	Very Low	Below Average	Average Performance	Above Average	Outstanding
Normal Curve Standard Deviations	-2	-1	0	$+1$	$+2$
z Scores	-2	-1	0	1	2
T Scores	30	40	50	60	70

Interpreting Normal Curve Equivalent Scores (NCE)

You might also encounter a standard score called the *normal curve equivalent score* or NCE. As its name implies, this score is also based on the normal curve. It has a fixed mean of 50, a fixed standard deviation of 21.06, and a range from 1 to 99. Thus, an NCE score of 29 is equivalent to one standard deviation below the mean (50 − 21.06), and an NCE score of 71 is equivalent to one standard deviation above the mean (50 + 21.06).

Given these properties, NCE scores are easy to interpret. Those scores between 1 and 29 are considered below average; those between 29 and 71 are considered average; and those of 71 and above reflect above-average performance. The proximity of these scores to their mean and the standard deviation anchors can be used to make inferences about the performance level of each score. The NCE scores corresponding to the normal curve standard deviation anchor points are the following:

	Very Low	Below Average	Average Performance	Above Average	Outstanding
Normal Curve Standard Deviations	−2	−1	0	+1	+2
NCE Scores	7.88	28.94	50	71.06	92.12

When using these scores to compare individual students' performances, be cautious not to attribute undue measurement precision to them. Like percentile scores, these scores should be interpreted as reflecting a probable area of performance rather than a precise point on a scale.

Interpreting Deviation IQ Scores

The deviation IQ score is a standard score used to report students' performance on scholastic aptitude tests. Since it is a standard score, it is interpreted using the properties of the normal distribution. Publishers of aptitude tests use a common mean score of 100; however, some publishers use a standard deviation of 16 points whereas others use one of 15 points. The technical manual for each publisher's test will report which standard deviation value is used in making score conversions.

When the standard deviation is 16, a deviation IQ score of 84 is located one standard deviation below the mean (100 − 16). Thus, scores of 84 and below are considered to reflect below-average performance compared to the norm group. Scores between 84 and 116 are interpreted as reflecting average-level performance. Scores of 116 and above (100 + 16) are considered above average because they reflect scores that are one standard deviation or more above the mean. Scores of 132 are two standard deviations above the mean and reflect performance at the ninety-eighth percentile; these scores reflect outstanding performance compared to the norm group. At the opposite end of the scale, scores of 68 are two standard deviations below the mean and correspond to the second percentile; therefore, they reflect very low performance compared to the norm group. These anchor points for interpreting deviation IQ scores are illustrated in the following diagram on performance level:

	Very Low	Below Average	Average Performance	Above Average	Outstanding
Normal Curve Standard Deviations Deviation	−2	−1	0	+1	+2
IQ Scores	68	84	100	116	132

Interpreting Other Types of Standard Scores

Some publishers use standard scores that are unique to their tests. To interpret any of these scores, you need to consult the test's technical manual to locate the scores that are equivalent to the mean and standard deviation. Interpreting students' performance on these tests is quite easy when these two values are known; otherwise, it can be baffling.

For example, on the Scholastic Aptitude Test (SAT), the College Entrance Examination Board sets the mean at 500 and the standard deviation at 100. Thus, a score of 300 (−2SD) reflects very low performance compared to the norm group; scores between 300 and 400 (−1SD) reflect below-average performance; scores between 400 and 600 reflect average performance; scores between 600 (+1SD) and 700 reflect above-average performance; and those above 700 (+2SD) reflect outstanding performance.

Performance on the Graduate Record Exam (GRE) is reported using a mean score of 1000 and a standard deviation of 200. Thus, scores in the average range extend between 800 to 1200. Scores of 800 and below are considered below average, and those of 1200 and above are considered above average compared to the norm group.

Interpreting Grade Equivalent Scores

Grade equivalent scores enable educators to compare students' variability in each subject within and across grades. Unlike the previously described scores, these scores are not based on the performance of one norm group. Instead, the same test is administered to the norm groups for two or three contiguous grade levels. The mean or median score earned by each group is located and used as the basis for creating all the grade equivalent scores. For example, suppose that the same test is administered to the fourth-, fifth-, and sixth-grade norm groups in September. The grade equivalent scores are matched to raw scores for the test using a chart similar to the one illustrated in Figure 14.6.

Raw scores are ranked vertically from highest to lowest on the left side of the chart. Grade equivalent scores are listed from lowest to highest along the bottom. To begin, three data points are plotted: one at the intersection of the mean or median score earned by fourth graders (20) and the grade equivalent score 4.0; a second at the intersection of the fifth graders' mean or median score (27) and the grade equivalent score 5.0; and the third at the point intersecting the sixth graders' mean or median score (33) and the grade equivalent score 6.0.

All the remaining grade equivalent scores reported for the test are obtained by interpolation and extrapolation. Interpolation is used to match raw scores and grade equivalent scores between the three obtained scores. Extrapolation is used to match raw scores and grade equivalent scores outside the measured area (fourth, fifth, and sixth grades).

To match grade equivalent scores and raw scores within the grades tested, a line is drawn to connect the three observed data points. The area between each set of points is divided into nine equal segments. Each higher segment is assigned a grade equivalent score. For example, between 4.0 and

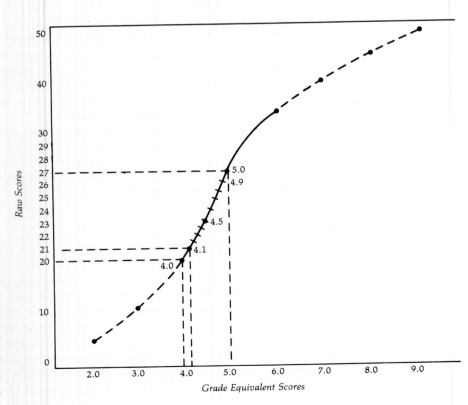

FIGURE 14.6
Matching Grade Equivalent Scores to Raw Scores Using Obtained Mean or Median Scores and the Processes of Interpolation and Extrapolation

5.0, the first segment is assigned the grade equivalent score 4.1, the second is assigned the grade equivalent score 4.2, and so on to 4.9. The segments between 5.0 and 6.0 are assigned grade equivalent scores 5.1 through 5.9. Each grade equivalent score is matched to a raw score by assigning the raw score directly across from the intersecting point for each grade equivalent score. In the example, a raw score of 21 corresponds to a grade equivalent score of 4.1.

The next step is to use extrapolation to match estimated grade equivalent scores and raw scores for grades outside the three grade levels measured. Points to reflect mean or median scores for grades lower than the fourth and higher than the sixth are estimated because students in these grades did not take the test. In order to match scores outside the measured area, the line connecting the three measured points is extended at both ends. In Figure 14.6, these extensions are illustrated using a broken line. Points on the line that reflect the mean or median score for these outside grades are estimated using the observed distances between the three actual scores. The point on the line that is estimated to locate the mean or median point for each grade is used as the intersecting point on the two score scales to equate the grade equivalent scores (2.0, 3.0, 7.0, 8.0, 9.0) to particular raw scores. The interpolation procedures described previously for matching scores between these points is used to complete the matching process.

An important assumption made in creating and interpreting grade equivalent scores is that each grade equivalent score reflects the mean or median score students in the norm group would earn if they took the test in a given month. For example, a grade equivalent score of 4.0 reflects the mean or median score earned by the norm group in September of the fourth grade. A grade equivalent score of 4.1 reflects the group's expected mean or median score in October; 4.2 reflects the expected mean or median score in November, and so forth to 4.9, which reflects the group's expected mean or median score in June. Research has shown that the amount students progress is not equal from month to month within a year, or from year to year. However, the assumption of even progress will undoubtedly be used until a more realistic, yet systematic, method to describe progress is developed.

There are several important characteristics of grade equivalent scores that you should consider before interpreting them. One is that the observed mean or median score for each grade level in September is set at .0, such as 5.0. This implies that 50 percent of the students in the fifth-grade norm group are assigned a grade equivalent score below this level. A second characteristic is that, because norm-referenced tests are designed to yield a wide range of scores within each grade level, a wide range of grade equivalent scores are assigned to students within each grade. Thus, many students within a given grade will earn grade equivalent scores that are many grade levels lower or higher than their actual grade in school. One way to avoid misinterpreting a low or high grade equivalent score is to equate it to the percentile and stanine assigned to the same raw score. This will help remind you that a grade equivalent score that appears extreme might be within the average performance range for the norm group.

Consider some sample raw scores and their corresponding grade equivalent, percentile, and stanine scores for four subtests of the California Test of Basic Skills (1974). These norms are for the eighth grade and for tests administered in the fall of the year. The first column in Table 14.4 lists the subtests and the number of items each contains. The second column contains a range of selected raw scores for each subtest. The third, fourth, and fifth columns contain the corresponding grade equivalent, percentile, and stanine scores for each of the raw scores. Since the norm group took the test in the fall, the mean or median grade equivalent score should be around 8.0 and correspond to a percentile close to 50. Note that the third column contains two grade equivalent scores of 8.0 and that the corresponding percentiles for

TABLE 14.4 Selected Raw Scores and Their Corresponding Grade Equivalent Scores, Percentiles, and Stanines

Subtest	Raw Score	Grade Equivalent Score	National Percentile	National Stanine
Reading	5	3.3	5	2
Vocabulary	10	5.8	24	4
(40 items)	15	8.0	49	5
	20	9.8	70	6
	25	11.0	84	7
	30	12.7	93	8
	35	13.6	99	9
Reading	10	3.7	12	3
Comprehension	15	5.9	32	4
(45 items)	20	8.5	54	5
	25	10.2	71	6
	30	11.6	84	7
	35	13.6	93	8
Math	10	3.9	7	2
Computation	15	5.7	23	4
(48 items)	20	7.7	46	5
	25	9.4	65	6
	30	10.6	78	7
	35	12.1	86	7
Math	5	3.8	10	2
Concepts	10	8.0	49	5
(25 items)	15	10.3	80	7
	20	13.6	95	8
	25	13.6	99	9

Source: Synthesized from materials in *Examiner's Manual,* Level 4, Form S, pp. 46–47, 50–51 (Monterey, Calif.: CTB/McGraw-Hill, Inc., 1974).

both are 49. This means that 49 percent of the students in the eighth-grade norm group earned grade equivalent scores below 8.0.

Note the wide range of grade equivalent scores for each subtest. The grade equivalent scores for the reading vocabulary test range from 3.3 to 13.6. Using the corresponding percentile scores, you can see that a grade equivalent score of 3.3 reflects below-average performance for an eighth grader because it corresponds to a percentile of 5 and a stanine of 2. However, a grade equivalent score of 5.8, which might be misinterpreted as very low for an eighth grader, corresponds to a percentile of 24 and stanine of 4, reflecting average performance for eighth graders. A grade equivalent score of 9.8 is also within the average range for eighth graders because it corresponds to a percentile of 70 and a stanine of 6. A grade equivalent score of 11.0, which corresponds to a percentile of 84 and a stanine of 7, is just within the above-average range for eighth-grade students. This correspondence is the same between the grade equivalent scores and the percentile and stanine scores for each of the other three tests. Before you interpret a grade equivalent score as reflecting either above- or below-average achievement, check its corresponding percentile and stanine scores to verify your interpretation.

Educators who do not understand these characteristics of grade equivalent scores can make many mistakes in interpreting them. A statement such as, "Our goal is to have all students in Garfield School performing at or above grade level," is usually made by someone who does not understand grade equivalent scores. Reaching this goal is only possible in schools that have no below-average students enrolled. Such a statement as, "Although John is in the eighth grade, he is only working at a third-grade level," also demonstrates a misunderstanding of the grade equivalent score. No third graders took the eighth-grade form of the test. In addition, very few, if any, of the skills measured by the eighth-grade test would be found in a third-grade curriculum guide or instruction targeted for third-grade students. John's low grade equivalent score simply reflects low performance compared to that of the eighth-grade norm group.

A third characteristic to be aware of is that grade equivalent scores are more variable in some subjects than others. This feature is important to the score's main purpose, which is detecting the norm groups' performance patterns in a subject within and across grades. However, these scores should not be used to compare students' performances across subjects. The variability of the norm group's performance across subjects will lead you to conclude that differences exist when they may not.

To illustrate this point, consider the data in Table 14.5. These are raw scores and corresponding grade equivalent and percentile scores from the sixth-grade norms tables accompanying the California Achievement Test (1978). If you used the grade equivalent score to compare a student's performances on the language, reading, and mathematics subtests, you would undoubtedly conclude that the student performed best in language skills (12.1 and 10.7), less well in reading skills (9.3 and 10.1), and poorest in mathematics

(7.9 and 8.8). This conclusion would be incorrect, however, because all six of these grade equivalent scores correspond to a percentile of 91.

TABLE 14.5   Selected Raw Scores and Their Corresponding Grade Equivalent Scores and Percentiles

Test	Raw Score	Grade Equivalency	National Percentile
Reading			
Vocabulary	29	9.3	91
Comprehension	37	10.1	91
Language			
Mechanics	23	12.1	91
Expression	35	10.7	91
Mathematics			
Computation	35	7.9	91
Concepts and Application	31	8.8	91

Source: Synthesized from materials in *California Achievement Tests*, Level 15, Forms C and D, pp. 16–17, 30–31 (Monterey, Calif.: CTB/McGraw-Hill, 1978).

The differences among these grade equivalent scores simply reflect that the sixth-grade norm group was most variable in language, which resulted in a very wide range of grade equivalent scores. Their performance was less variable in reading, and least variable in mathematics, which resulted in narrower grade equivalent score ranges in these subjects.

Because parents are not familiar with the characteristics of grade equivalent scores and may misinterpret them, school districts and teachers should not use them to communicate students' achievement. If they are included in students' report forms, the easiest way to interpret them to parents is to equate them to their corresponding percentiles and stanines.

Interpreting Scale Scores

Another type of norm-referenced score is the *scale score*. These scores describe the relationships between means and standard deviations for successive grade levels, from kindergarten through twelfth grade. Using a series of overlapping test items and a complex score-equating system, raw scores earned by the fall and spring norm groups for each grade are matched to scores on a common scale. Different publishers use different numbers to report performance on their scales. Regardless of the numbers used, students in the lower grades are assigned lower scores on the scale, and those in higher grades are assigned higher scale scores. Unlike percentiles, scale scores are equal interval scores and can be used to compare (1) the progress groups make in each subject from grade to grade; (2) groups' performance variability across subjects within a grade and across grades within a subject; and (3) an individual's progress in each subject from fall to spring and from grade to grade.

Table 14.6 contains selected scale scores from the California Achievement Test: Technical Bulletin 1 (1979). The first column contains the grade levels for the fall norm groups. The next three columns contain students' scale score means and standard deviations for the reading comprehension, language mechanics, and mathematics computation tests. The scale used to report scores on the California Achievement Test ranges from 1 to 999. Related to students' progress across grades, notice that students in succeeding grades earn higher mean scale scores on all three tests. However, their progress from grade to grade within a subject is not equal. In reading comprehension, for example, the difference between mean scale scores for the first and second grades is greater ($362 - 284 = 78$) than the difference between the mean scale scores for the eleventh and twelfth grades ($622 - 609 = 13$). Related to students' variability in one subject across grades, notice that the standard deviations for students in the lower grades are smaller than those for students in higher grades in all three subjects. For example, in reading comprehension, first graders have a standard deviation of 43.5 whereas twelfth graders have one of 88.7. From these data, you can conclude that students' achievement progresses in a subject from grade to grade; that the rate of progress diminishes across grades; and that students' variability in each subject increases across grades.

TABLE 14.6   Selected Scale Score Means and Standard Deviations for Three Subtests of the California Achievement Test

Grade Level	Reading Comprehension		Language Mechanics		Mathematics Computation	
	$\overline{X}$	SD	$\overline{X}$	SD	$\overline{X}$	SD
1.2	284	43.5	—		238	29.1
2.2	362	50.7	402	46.9	294	34.8
3.2	401	55.5	444	52.9	337	37.1
4.2	441	60.2	481	55.2	394	41.6
5.2	472	66.1	506	60.9	436	50.7
6.2	498	68.5	525	65.7	469	53.3
7.2	521	73.1	537	72.2	495	66.1
8.2	548	77.2	561	77.3	552	79.0
9.2	568	79.9	576	80.1	579	84.6
10.2	587	84.0	591	83.2	597	87.7
11.2	609	86.5	608	83.7	613	91.1
12.2	622	88.7	619	85.5	621	94.2

Source: Synthesized from materials in *Technical Bulletin 1, California Achievement Tests,* pp. 93–97 (Monterey, Calif.: CTB/McGraw-Hill, Inc., 1979).

Students' variability across subjects can also be compared using scale scores. For example, notice that second graders are most variable in reading comprehension (SD = 50.7), less variable in language mechanics (SD = 46.9), and least variable in mathematics computation (SD = 34.8). Notice also that their variability across subjects is not consistent across grades. Contrary to the patterns in the lower grades, students' variability in the middle grades tends to be more even across subjects. During the high school years, the trends observed in the early elementary grades are reversed. Upper-level high school students are most variable in mathematics computation (94.2), less variable in reading comprehension (88.7), and least variable in language mechanics (85.5). Because of this variability, scale scores should not be used to compare one student's performance across subtests.

Besides detecting general trends in students' achievement across grades and subjects, scale scores can be used to evaluate an individual's progress in each subject during a year and across years. One important consideration in making these evaluations is that the amount of progress considered typical differs for below-average, average, and above-average students. To ensure that you make appropriate judgments for students at different achievement levels, you can create a small chart of scale scores based on the reported mean and standard deviation for each grade.

Using the data in Table 14.6 as an example, if you wanted to determine whether students in your class progressed normally in reading comprehension during the fifth grade, you would need to create a chart like the following one for fifth- and sixth-grade reading comprehension scale scores.

			(1)	(2)	(3)	(4)	(5)
Grade	$\overline{X}$	SD	$\overline{X} - 2SD$	$\overline{X} - 1SD$	$\overline{X}$	$\overline{X} + 1SD$	$\overline{X} + 2SD$
5.2	472	66.1	340	406	472	538	604
6.2	498	68.5	361	429	498	567	635

The first column identifies the grade level, and the next columns list the mean scale scores and standard deviations reported in the technical manual for each grade. These scores are used as anchors to calculate scale scores that are one and two standard deviations below and above the mean for the fifth and sixth grades. For example, a scale score of 340 for a fifth grader (column 1) is two standard deviations below the mean scale score for fifth grade (472 − 66 − 66 = 340). Likewise, a scale score of 635 (column 6) is two standard deviations above the mean for the sixth grade (498 + 68.5 + 68.5 = 635).

Once you have charted the scale scores, you can identify typical gains made by students at each performance level. For example, typical progress for a student who is two standard deviations below the mean (column 1) in the fifth grade is 21 points (361 − 340). Typical progress for an average student (column 3) is 26 points (498 − 472); and typical progress for a student who is two standard deviations above the mean (column 5) is 31 points (635 − 604). The difference between the scale scores at each performance level helps you set expectations for students at those levels.

To evaluate the progress made by each student in your class, you would locate the column containing the fifth-grade scale score closest to the one earned by your student in the fifth grade. The student's earned scale score in the sixth grade should then be compared to the sixth-grade scale score listed in the same column. For example, if your student's fifth-grade scale score is close to 538 (column 4) then this student's sixth-grade scale score should be close to 567 (column 4). If the student's sixth-grade score is comparable to the one in the chart, then the student has made normal progress in reading for a student one standard deviation above the mean. However, if the student's sixth-grade scale score is closer to 498 (column 3), then the student's progress can be considered atypically low. Likewise, if the student's sixth-grade score is closer to 635 (column 5), then the student's progress can be considered atypically high.

The technical manuals for most tests contain scale scores for both a fall and spring norm group for each grade level. In creating charts to evaluate your students' progress, be sure to select the norms for the time during the year when your students were tested.

Since scale scores are reported on students' records, parents might inquire about their meaning. You can interpret them quickly without referring to the reported means and standard deviations in the technical manual. Locate the corresponding percentiles and stanines for each score reported to decide whether the scale score reflects below-average, average, or above-average performance. For example, if the stanines and percentiles reflect below-average performance, then the corresponding scale score also reflects below-average performance.

Interpreting Anticipated Achievement Scores

Anticipated achievement scores are quite different from those previously described. These scores are calculated separately for each student tested and indicate the student's expected score for each test. These anticipated scores are compared to the obtained scores to determine whether the student's performance was as expected, atypically high, or atypically low.

The publisher establishes anticipated scores for each student by matching the student to a subset of students from the norm group with the same characteristics. Characteristics typically used to match students are age in months, year and month in school, and raw scores earned on an aptitude test administered at the same time as the achievement test. Sometimes gender is also used as a matching factor.

Once a matched set of students is selected from the norm group, their achievement test scores are ranked from highest to lowest and their mean score is calculated. The anticipated achievement score reported for each student is the mean score earned by the matched set of students from the norm group. Using a measure of the subgroup's variability, a confidence band is placed around the mean score to set boundaries above and below which scores can be considered atypical. The individual's obtained score is then compared to the matched group's score distribution. If the student's score falls within the confidence band, then the obtained score is considered typical. However, if the student's score falls outside the band, then the score is considered atypical or significantly different than anticipated. A plus sign is often used to indicate atypically high scores, and a minus sign is used to indicate atypically low scores.

Derived scores used to report anticipated achievement are the grade equivalent score, the scale score, and the normal curve equivalent score. The publisher clearly labels anticipated scores by placing the letters *AA* before the abbreviations for each type of score. *AAGE* is an anticipated grade equivalent score, *AASS* is an anticipated scale score, and *AANCE* is an anticipated normal curve equivalent score.

TEST RECORDS FOR INDIVIDUAL STUDENTS

Different publishers use different formats to report an individual's test performance. The report forms, sometimes called *profiles*, usually contain the names of subtests in the battery, the number of items on each subtest, the student's raw score on each subtest, and a variety of derived scores that match these raw scores to the performance of the norm group. The derived scores reported often include the scale score (SS), the grade equivalent score (GE), the national percentile (NP), the national stanine (NS), the normal curve equivalent score (NCE), and the anticipated achievement score (e.g., AAGE). The report form includes an anticipated achievement score only if both achievement and aptitude tests were administered. The form often includes a chart that illustrates the position of the student's percentile and stanine scores and the percentile bands.

Table 14.7 contains an individual's report form for the California Achievement Test (1978). Biographical information appears at the top. This section identifies the student, teacher, grade, school, city, state, the date of testing, and the particular test form used. In this section, it is important to note that Karen took the test in September of the sixth grade.

Section A lists the subtests and Karen's scores. The names of the scores corresponding to the initials are listed above the record. Consider Karen's scores on the reading vocabulary test. Her raw score is 18, which corresponds to a grade equivalent score (OGE) of 6.0 (the September median score for students in the sixth-grade norm group). This score reflects that Karen's performance is very close to the center of the norm group. Thus, the other derived scores reported for this subtest will also indicate that her performance is very close to the center of the norm group. Her percentile score (NP) is 48 and her stanine is 5. From this information, you can infer that her scale score (OSS) of 482 is very close to the mean scale score for sixth graders. Karen's

TABLE 14.7　The Individual Test Record for the California Achievement Tests

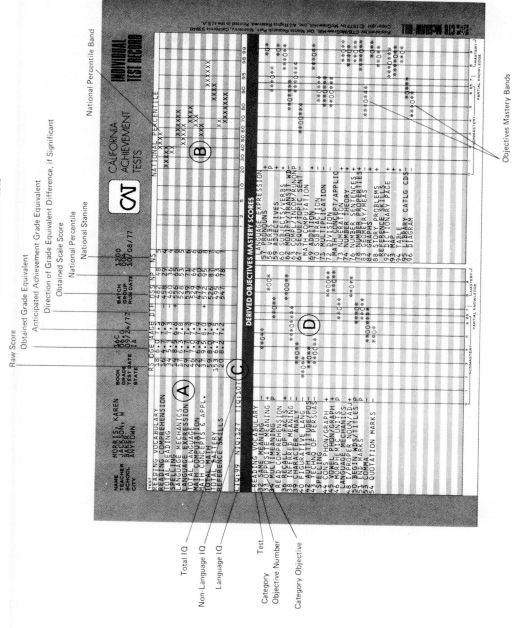

Source: From California Achievement Tests, Forms C and D, Test Coordinator's Handbook. Copyright 1977, 1978 by McGraw-Hill, Inc. Reproduced by permission of CTB/McGraw-Hill.

anticipated achievement score (AAGE) in reading is 7.1, which is higher than her obtained grade equivalent score of 6.0. Because no minus sign appears in the column beside the anticipated score, you can conclude that her observed score is not atypically, or significantly, lower than expected.

Now, consider Karen's performance on the reading comprehension test. Her grade equivalent score (OGE) is 4.7, yet her anticipated achievement score is 7.9. The minus sign in the DIF column indicates that her grade equivalent score is significantly lower than anticipated. Her percentile score of 29 and her stanine score of 4 place her in the average performance range for students in the sixth-grade norm group. From this information, you can infer that her scale score of 458 is below the mean for the sixth-grade group.

The next set of scores in the list, total reading, provide a summary of Karen's overall reading performance. Notice that her two raw scores on the reading tests (18 and 16) sum to make her raw score of 34 on the total reading test. The derived scores in this row reflect her overall reading performance compared to the norm group. Her raw score of 34 corresponds to a grade equivalent score of 5.3 and an anticipated score of 7.3. Notice that these scores are higher than her comprehension scores and lower than her vocabulary scores. With the subtest scores combined, her obtained achievement score is still significantly lower than anticipated. Overall in reading, however, her percentile of 36 and stanine of 4 reflect average performance for a sixth grader. To interpret her scores on the other subtests, use the same score comparison procedure.

Section C on the record contains Karen's scores on the aptitude portion of the test. This test included a language subtest and a nonlanguage subtest. Deviation IQ scores are used to report her performance on these tests. Remember that the mean IQ score is 100, and the standard deviation is either 15 or 16. Karen's nonlanguage IQ score of 127 is above average (one standard deviation above the mean would fall at either 115 or 116, and two standard deviations above the mean would be either 130 or 132). Thus, her nonlanguage reasoning skills are very good compared to children her age. Her language IQ score of 99 is very close to the mean score for children her age. Using these scores, you could generally infer that her language scores on the achievement tests should be close to the 50th percentile and that her math scores would be around one standard deviation above the mean, or the 84th percentile. Note in section A that her total math percentile score is 87, which is very close to what you would predict. Notice also that her language scores, a total reading percentile of 36 and a total language percentile of 64, are not entirely consistent with what you would predict.

The percentile bands for Karen's raw scores are plotted in section B of the record. The percentile scale is shown at the bottom of the graph. Notice that the scale is adjusted so that numbers in the center, between 30 and 70, are very close together whereas those above 70 and below 30 are printed farther apart. This tends to equalize the visual width of the bands plotted. However, using the percentile scores at the bottom of the chart, you can see that those corresponding to the upper and lower boundaries for each band encompass many more percentile points toward the center of the scale. For example, the percentile band for the math concepts and applications test appears wider (six Xs) than the percentile band for math computation (only three Xs). However, when you check the percentile scores at the bottom of the chart, you find that the opposite is true. The percentile band for math concepts and applications spans less than 10 percentile points, from about 91 to 98. On the other hand, the percentile band for math computation includes about 14 percentile points, from about 51 to 65.

This visual distortion, however, does not influence the interpretation of the bands. If the percentile bands for two subtests overlap, the observed difference in the percentile scores is considered insignificant. When they do not overlap, the differences can be considered meaningful. Comparing Karen's performance in reading vocabulary to her performance in reading comprehension, you can see that the bands are slightly overlapped. This means that the observed differences in the percentile scores may not be meaningful. Comparing her total reading, total language, and total math performance, you can see that her math score is significantly better than her language score and that her language score is significantly better than her reading score.

Section D of the record contains criterion-referenced or mastery scores. You should use caution in interpreting these scores because this test was constructed following the rules for a norm-referenced test rather than those for a criterion-referenced test. Thus, many of the skills measured are considered very difficult for typical sixth-grade students. The left-hand column lists the tests, an identifying number for each objective measured, and the content included in the objectives. Items on the reading vocabulary test measure three skill areas: words with the same meaning, words with opposite meaning, and words with multimeanings. Using these main objectives for each test, you can identify particular skills the student found difficult.

A student's mastery performance is reported using three symbols and a mastery band. The symbols −, P, and + indicate nonmastery, partial mastery, and mastery, respectively. Notice that these symbols are printed in the adjacent column beside each objective. Using these symbols, you can conclude that, within reading vocabulary, Karen did not master the same meaning objective, mastered the opposite meaning objective, and partially mastered the multimeaning objective.

In the remaining columns, a mastery band is plotted. As with percentile bands, these bands signify the degree of imprecision inherent in the measure. Notice the mastery scale from 1 to 10 at the bottom of the chart. Mastery scores between 0 and 6.5 are classified as nonmastery. Those between 6.5 and 8 are classified as partial mastery, and those above 8 are classified as mastery. These mastery scores are derived scores and not the number of items a student answered correctly for each objective. Publishers use a variety of factors in deriving mastery scores, such as the number of items answered correctly for the objective, the student's raw score on the remainder of the test, the correlation between the objective score and the overall score, and the reliability of objective scores and the overall test score. The mastery band includes a line of asterisks and zeros. The zeros reflect the best estimate of the student's mastery level, but the remainder of the band indicates that the estimate lacks precision.

Consider Karen's performance on the three objectives for the reading vocabulary test. The mastery band for the same meaning objective is within the nonmastery region; the band for the opposite meaning objective is within the mastery region; and the band for the multimeaning objective is in the partial mastery region. The norm-referenced vocabulary score in section A (OGE = 6.0; NP = 48) helps you keep this mastery information in perspective. Although Karen failed to master one objective and only partially mastered another, her performance was average compared to other sixth graders. However, her objective mastery scores do indicate that Karen needs additional instruction in words with the same meaning and in words with multiple meanings.

Next, review Karen's mastery of the objectives for the math computation test in the right-hand column. She mastered the addition objective but failed to master those for subtraction, multiplication, and division. Her norm-referenced score for this test (OGE = 6.4; NP = 60) shows that even though she failed to master three of the four test objectives, her performance can still be considered average for a sixth-grade student. Subsequent instruction for Karen in mathematics computation should focus on her subtraction, multiplication, and division skills.

This individual test record is comprehensive in that it includes several norm-referenced scores for each subtest, percentile bands, aptitude test scores, and mastery scores for objectives within tests. If you are comfortable interpreting the information provided in this example, you will have little difficulty interpreting the records provided by publishers of other norm-referenced tests that may be used in your school. The major difference in various records is their format.

CLASS RECORDS

The performance of a class is typically summarized for teachers using a class record form. The norm-referenced scores on these forms are the same as those reported on individual student's records. Although norm-referenced achievement tests focus on language and mathematics skills, teachers of all subjects can use the class record to describe the achievement characteristics of their groups. Knowing whether a class is homogeneous or heterogeneous in basic skills can aid both instructional planning and the assessment of any group's progress. Teachers of subjects other than language and mathematics typically use students' scores on the aptitude, total reading, total language, and total math tests to describe a group's achievement characteristics. Teachers of language and mathematics also use students' performances on the subtests to describe the achievement characteristics of their classes.

One good way to describe a group's achievement characteristics is to locate the highest and lowest scores earned by class members and the group's mean score on all tests of interest. If the highest and lowest scores reflect the same general level of performance, then the group can be considered homogeneous. However, if these extreme scores reflect different performance levels, then the class can be described as heterogeneous. The location of the group's average score compared to the two extreme scores provides information about the distribution of the group's scores.

Table 14.8 contains a sample class record sheet for the California Achievement Test (1978). Biographical information that identifies the group and test date is included at the top. Students' names are listed in the far left-hand column, and aptitude test information for each student is listed in the next three columns. The remaining columns list students' scores on the achievement tests. Although a regular class would contain more than six students, this record is used to demonstrate the comparison process.

The two extreme scores and mean scores for the aptitude, total reading, total language, and total math tests are summarized in the following chart:

Scores	Language Aptitude		Nonlanguage Aptitude		Total Reading Achievement		Total Language Achievement		Total Math Achievement	
	LIQ	LNP	NIQ	NNP	OGE	NP	OGE	NP	OGE	NP
Highest	114	75	127	96	8.0	78	9.7	87	8.0	87
Lowest	91	23	89	24	4.6	25	4.9	37	5.4	34
Class $\overline{X}$	94		99		5.3		6.0		6.8	
Norm group $\overline{X}$	(100)		(100)		6.0		6.0		6.0	

By comparing the IQ, percentile, and grade equivalent scores in this chart, the group's achievement characteristics can be described. Related to language aptitude, the group is homogeneous and contains average achievers since the lowest and highest percentile scores fall within the average performance range (NP 23 to 75). The group's average IQ score (94) is slightly below the mean (100). In nonlanguage aptitude, the group is heterogeneous since the percentile scores range between 96 (above average) and 24 (low average). The group's average nonlanguage IQ score (99) is equivalent to the norm group's score (100). The group is homogeneous and average in reading (NP 25 to 78), with a mean score below the midpoint for the norm group. The class is somewhat heterogeneous in both language (NP 37 to 87) and mathematics (NP 34 to 87). Although the group is somewhat heterogeneous, it contains no extremely low or high achievers in any of the three achievement areas. Teachers of language and mathematics skills can describe the group's performances on the subtests in the same manner.

Another, more detailed, class summary form is provided for teachers of language and mathematics. This form reports individual and group re-

TABLE 14.8 The Class Record Sheet for the California Achievement Tests

Source: From California Achievement Tests, Forms C and D, Test Coordinator's Handbook. Copyright 1977, 1978 by McGraw-Hill, Inc. Reproduced by permission of CTB/McGraw-Hill.

sponses to items within objectives. It can be used at the beginning of the school year to match the skills measured by the test to those prescribed in the curriculum guide. Students' performance level in each skill area can be noted and used to aid instructional planning.

Table 14.9 contains an example of this type of class record. It is the Right Response Record, which is provided with the California Achievement Test (1978). Biographical information about the class and the test appears in the upper left-hand corner. Students' names are listed in the diagonal columns on the right. The tests, content descriptions, main objectives within each content area, and items within each objective are listed in the left-hand column.

This information can be used to match the skills measured by the test to those included in your curriculum guide. For example, the reading comprehension test includes two main areas: literal comprehension and interpretative comprehension. Literal comprehension contains one objective, recall of facts. There are six items on the test used to measure students' skill in recalling facts. The interpretative comprehension section contains two objectives: inferred meaning (seven items) and character analysis (eight items).

For each objective, the average number of items answered correctly by the class (LOC) and the national norm group (NAT) are reported in the next two columns. Using these figures, you can compare the class average to the national average, objective by objective. For example, the norm group's average performance was slightly better than the class's performance on all three objectives for the reading comprehension test.

The next two columns report the percentage of students in the class (LOC) and percentage of students in the norm group (NAT) that answer each item within an objective correctly. These data are difficulty indices, or p values. Compared to the norm group, a smaller percentage of students in the class answered each item correctly for the objective on recalling facts. However the class's performance is comparable to that of the norm group since the two sets of scores are reasonably close. Another interesting comparison using these data is which skills in this objective the class found most difficult. They found recalling facts about people and events quite easy. However, they had more difficulty recalling facts about sequence, time, and things. This information can be noted in the curriculum guide, and instruction can be emphasized during the year to help students attend to these types of information in a passage.

The remaining columns report individual students' responses to each item. The numbers directly across from each objective indicate the number of items each student answered correctly for the objective. Below these objective totals, a plus sign indicates that the student answered the named item correctly, a minus sign indicates an incorrect answer, and a blank signals a failure to respond. For example, Maria Diaz answered correctly four of the six items included for recalling facts. She incorrectly answered the item for sequence and did not answer the item for time. You can use this information about individuals (1) to judge whether their response patterns were typical

TABLE 14.9 The Group Right Response Record for the California Achievement Tests

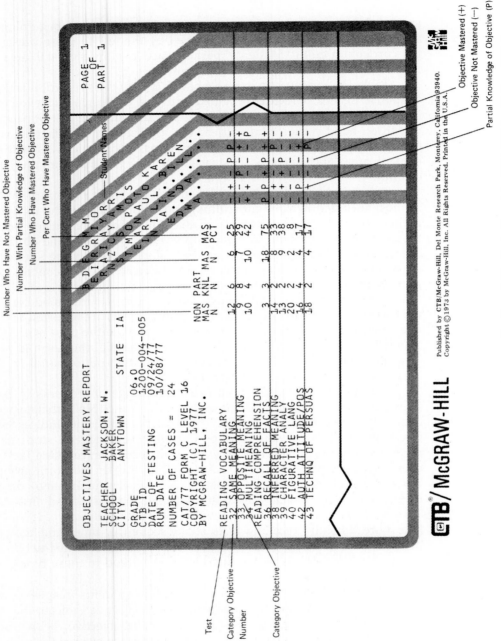

Source: California Achievement Tests, Forms C and D, Test Coordinator's Handbook. Copyright 1977, 1978 by McGraw-Hill, Inc.
Reproduced by permission of CTB/McGraw-Hill.

for them, (2) to locate particular skills that should be emphasized with each student, and (3) to group students who have similar needs for instruction.

SUMMARY

Due to the increasing emphasis on data-based decision making in schools, school personnel must be able to interpret and use information from standardized achievement and scholastic aptitude tests. The achievement tests, which may be either criterion-referenced or norm-referenced, measure students' knowledge and skills in school subjects. Scholastic aptitude tests measure students' general mental-processing skills.

School districts that intend to use test results for instructional planning, instructional evaluation, or grading students' progress generally select a criterion-referenced test that focuses on the school's curriculum. Districts that want to use test results to compare the performance of individuals or groups to a nationwide sample of students use norm-referenced achievement tests. Those that want to determine which students will probably succeed in a particular program use scholastic aptitude tests to predict students' achievement.

Scoring methods and scores used to report students' performance on the three types of tests differ. Performance on criterion-referenced tests is generally reported as nonmastery, partial knowl-

edge, and mastery. These levels can be based either on the number and percentage of items students answer correctly for each objective or on scores derived using a variety of factors besides the number of correct items. Professional judgment is used to set the cut-off scores for each of the three levels. Performance on norm-referenced tests is reported using derived scores that enable comparisons among students. These scores include percentiles, percentile bands, stanines, normal curve equivalent scores, normalized z and T scores, grade equivalent scores, and scale scores. An anticipated achievement score is also used when both aptitude and achievement tests are administered. Performance on aptitude tests is reported using a deviation IQ score and sometimes a percentile score. Table 14.10 summarizes the characteristics and interpretation of these scores.

Teachers of all subjects use aptitude scores and total scores from the achievement tests to describe the characteristics of their assigned classes. Teachers of language and mathematics use subtest scores and scores on each objective measured by the subtests to aid instructional planning.

TABLE 14.10   Scores Commonly Used to Report Students' Performances on Norm-Referenced Tests

Scores	Characteristics	Interpretation
Percentiles	Range from 1 to 99 Midpoint 50 $\overline{X} + 1SD = 84$ $\overline{X} - 1SD = 16$ There are unequal intervals between percentiles.	Percentiles reflect the percentage of students in the norm group surpassed at each raw score in the distribution.

Percentile Bands	These are confidence bands placed around each percentile using the test's standard error of measurement.
	    The width of percentile bands varies across the percentile scale. Those in the center of the distribution are wider than those toward the ends.
		A student's score on retesting could fall anywhere within the band.
		    Overlapping bands reflect no significant differences between observed percentile scores.

Stanines	Range from 1 to 9 Midpoint is 5	Stanines 1, 2, and 3 reflect below-average performance.

(continued on next page)

TABLE 14.10 *(Continued)*

Scores	Characteristics	Interpretation
	$\overline{X} + 1SD = 7$ $\overline{X} - 1SD = 3$ Stanines are band scores and encompass several raw scores and percentiles. Stanines in the center of the distribution encompass more percentiles than those toward the ends.	Stanines 4, 5, and 6 reflect average performance. Stanines 7, 8, and 9 reflect above-average performance.
Normalized z and T Scores	$z: \overline{X} = 0$ $SD = 1$ $\overline{X} + 1SD = 1$ $\overline{X} - 1SD = -1$ $T: \overline{X} = 50$ $SD = 10$ $\overline{X} + 1SD = 60$ $\overline{X} - 1SD = 40$	Scores of -1 or lower reflect below-average performance. Scores between $-.99$ and $.99$ reflect average performance. Scores of 1 or above reflect above-average performance. Scores of 40 and below reflect below-average performance. Scores of 41 through 59 reflect average performance. Scores of 60 and above reflect above-average performance.
Normal Curve Equivalents	Range from 1 to 99 $\overline{X} = 50$ $SD = 21.06$ $\overline{X} + 1SD = 71.06$ $\overline{X} - 1SD = 28.94$	Scores of 28.94 and lower reflect below-average performance. Scores between 29 and 70 reflect average performance. Scores of 71.06 and higher reflect above-average performance.
Deviation IQ Scores	$\overline{X} = 100$ $SD = 15$ or 16 $\overline{X} + 1SD = 115, 116$ $\overline{X} - 1SD = 85, 84$ These scores are used to report performance on scholastic aptitude tests.	Scores of 85, 84 and lower reflect below-average performance. Scores between 85, 86 and 114, 115 reflect average performance. Scores of 115, 116 and higher reflect above-average performance.
Grade Equivalent Scores	These are scores based on the median score earned by the norm group in two or three consecutive grades. These scores are decimal numbers; the first digit reflects a grade and the second reflects a month within a grade. All scores are derived from the two or three median scores using the processes of interpolation and extrapolation. Grade equivalent scores reflect the estimated median score earned by a group in a given grade and month.	A wide range of grade equivalent scores are assigned to students in each grade level. Match grade equivalent scores to their corresponding percentiles and stanines to determine whether they reflect below-average, average, or above-average performance for students in a particular grade. Do not use these scores to compare one student's performance across subtests. Do not use these scores to describe students' performance to parents and the community.
Scale Scores	These are scores on an arbitrarily set common scale used to measure students' variability in a subject and their progress across grades in a subject.	Scores 1 standard deviation below the mean and lower reflect below-average performance.

TABLE 14.10   (Continued)

Scores	Characteristics	Interpretation
	Mean scale scores and standard deviations vary for each subtest and grade level. These measures must be obtained from the test's technical manual for each grade and subject.	Scores within 1 standard deviation from the mean reflect average performance.
		Scores 1 standard deviation above the mean and higher reflect above-average performance.
		Students' progress in one subject should be compared using scale scores appropriate to each student's achievement level because students at different levels progress at different rates.
Anticipated Achievement Scores	These scores are the mean scores earned by a subset of students in the norm group who are matched to each student using aptitude scores and other characteristics. Confidence intervals are placed around these mean scores to differentiate between typical and atypically high or low observed scores.	Although anticipated and observed achievement scores are often different, the differences are considered insignificant unless a plus or minus sign is used to reflect atypically high or low performance.

PRACTICE EXERCISES

A. Matching Test Types and Purposes. Three types of tests are listed below. Indicate the type of test you would use to complete the tasks described in items 1 through 8: A. Criterion-referenced achievement test; B. Norm-referenced achievement test; C. Scholastic aptitude test;

  1. Compare the performance of students in your school district to the performance of a nationwide sample of students in basic skills.
  2. Plan lessons covering the punctuation of declarative, interrogative, exclamatory, and imperative sentences.
  3. Predict which students are likely to be most successful in an advanced mathematics program.
  4. Compare a student's performance across reading, language, and mathematics skills.
  5. Analyze the variability of students' performance in mathematics within and across grades.
  6. Diagnose problems a student or class has in performing district-prescribed instructional goals.
  7. Predict the students most likely to succeed in a special mathematics program for gifted students.
  8. Determine students' mastery of selected language usage skills.

B. Converting Raw Scores to Percentiles. Items 9 through 13 list the steps you would follow to convert raw scores to percentiles. Use the frequency distribution in Table 14.11 to make these conversions. Check your work using Table 14.11(F) in the Feedback section.

TABLE 14.11   Worksheet for Converting Raw Scores to Percentiles

(1) Raw Scores	(2) Frequency	(3) Cumulative Frequency below	(4) 1/2 Frequency within	(5) Proportion	(6) Percentile
40	1				
39	1				
38	2				
37	2				
36	3				
35	3				
34	2				
33	2				
32	2				
31	1				
30	1				

9. Beginning at the bottom of the table, calculate the cumulative frequency of raw scores below each raw score and record this number in column 3.
10. Divide the observed frequency for each raw score by 2 and record this number in column 4.
11. Sum the frequency below and one-half the frequency within (columns 3 and 4) for each score and record the total in column 5.
12. Divide the total in column 5 by the total number of students in the group to obtain the proportion of students whose scores fall below the midpoint for each raw score.
13. Multiply these proportions by 100 to obtain the percentile for each raw score and record this value in column 6.

C. Interpreting Percentile Scores. Judge whether each of the following statements about the characteristics of percentile scores and their interpretation is true.
14. There are equal intervals between percentile scores.
15. Percentiles reflect the percentage of items answered correctly.
16. Percentiles correspond to the standard normal distribution of scores.
17. Percentiles are created using the processes of interpolation and extrapolation.
18. There is an equal number of percentile points between the mean and one standard deviation above the mean and between one and two standard deviations above the mean.
19. There are larger intervals between the percentiles in the center of the distribution than between those toward the ends of the scale.
20. Percentiles range from 0 to 100.
21. Relatively small differences between percentiles toward the center of the scale are not meaningful.
22. Percentiles reflect the percentage of students surpassed at the midpoint for each raw score.
23. One standard deviation above the mean is equivalent to the 60th percentile.
24. Each increase of one raw score point can result in an increase of several percentile points.

D. Calculating and Plotting Percentile Bands. Use the raw score-to-percentile conversions made in Table 14.11 to complete this exercise. Table 14.12 contains three raw scores and their corresponding percentiles from Table 14.11. Follow the directions in items 25 through 27 to plot the percentile bands for these three scores. Check your work using Table 14.12(F) in the Feedback section.

TABLE 14.12   Worksheet for Calculating and Plotting Percentile Bands

SEM = 2

	−1 SEM	*Obtained* *Score*	+1 SEM	Percentiles 1 5 10 20 30 40 50 60 70 80 90 95 99
X		39		
%tile		93		
X		35		
%tile		48		
X		32		
%tile		15		

25. Using a standard error of measurement (SEM) of 2, calculate the raw score corresponding to +1 SEM and −1 SEM for each obtained score.
26. Locate the corresponding percentile scores in Table 14.11 for each extended raw score.
27. Using the chart on the right-hand side of Table 14.12, plot the percentile bands for each obtained percentile score. Mark the position of the obtained percentile score within the band.

E. Interpreting Percentile Bands. Judge whether each of the following statements about the characteristics of percentile bands and their interpretation is true. Place a check in the space preceding the true statements.

28. Percentile bands for percentiles throughout the scale are of equal width.
29. Percentile bands reflect that norm-referenced tests are imprecise measures of achievement.
30. The obtained percentile score usually falls in the center of the percentile band.
31. Percentile bands can be used to compare one student's performance on various subtests.
32. The performance of several students in the class can be compared on one test using percentile bands.
33. Tests that have a small standard error of measurement have wider percentile bands than tests that are less reliable.
34. Overlapping bands reflect meaningful differences in obtained percentile scores.
35. Percentile bands are confidence intervals that reflect the range of scores where a student's score is likely to fall on retesting.

F. Calculating Stanine Scores
36. What percentage of the norm group is assigned each stanine score?

Stanine Scores	1	2	3	4	5	6	7	8	9
Percentage									

37. If there were 1,000 students in the norm group, how many students would be assigned each stanine score?

Stanine Scores	1	2	3	4	5	6	7	8	9
Number of Students									

38. What is the cumulative percentage of students associated with the upper boundary of each stanine score?

Stanine Scores	1	2	3	4	5	6	7	8	9
Cumulative Percentages									

G. Interpreting Stanine Scores. Judge whether each of the following statements about the characteristics of stanine scores and their interpretation is true.
   39. An equal number of students is assigned each stanine.
   40. Each stanine encompasses a range of raw scores and percentile scores.
   41. An equal range of raw scores corresponds to each stanine.
   42. Stanines correspond to the standard normal curve.
   43. One standard deviation above the mean corresponds to a stanine score of seven.
   44. A stanine of three corresponds to one standard deviation below the mean.
   45. All nine stanines are one-half a standard deviation wide.
   46. A stanine score is more similar to a percentile band than to a percentile.
H. Selecting Scores from the Report Form. Select the score or scores that best answer the following questions.

Scores

A. Anticipated Achievement Scores
B. Deviation IQ Scores
C. Grade Equivalent Scores
D. Normal Curve Equivalent Scores
E. Normalized z and T Scores
F. Percentile Scores
G. Scale Scores
H. Stanine Scores

47. What two scores are used to compare the variability of students' achievement across grade levels?
48. What scores are used to determine whether a student's obtained score is atypical?
49. What score is used to report students' aptitude levels?
50. Of all the scores associated with achievement tests, which one is most likely to be misinterpreted?
51. Which score is created using the processes of interpolation and extrapolation?
52. Which achievement scores should not be used to compare a student's achievement on different subtests?

53. Which score should not be used to report students' performance to parents?

I. Interpreting Test Records. Use the California Achievement Test Individual Test Record in Table 14.13 to answer the following questions.

54. When did William take the CAT? (grade; month)
55. His scale score (SS) on the language mechanics test is 707. What level of performance does this score reflect?
    a. Above average
    b. Average
    c. Below average
56. How did you reach this conclusion?
57. On a retest, his language mechanics percentile score would probably fall within which range?
58. Which of William's scores could you use to compare his performance on the total reading, total language, and total mathematics tests?
59. On which of these tests did he perform best?
60. Is his performance in language superior to his performance in reading?
61. How do you know this?
62. William's grade equivalent score (GE) on the vocabulary test is 5.6, and his GE score on the language mechanics test is 7.4. On which test did he perform better?
63. His normal curve equivalent score (NCE) in math concepts and application is 27. Is this score lower than one standard deviation below the mean NCE score?
64. Use his stanine scores to describe his overall performance on the CAT.
    Use the California Achievement Test Class Record Sheet in Table 14.14 to complete the following exercise.
65. Use the group's obtained grade equivalency scores and national percentile scores on the spelling test to complete the following summary chart.

Spelling Test	OGE	NP
Highest Scores		
Lowest Scores		
Class Average		
Norm Group Average		

66. Using these scores, describe the group as being either heterogeneous or homogeneous in spelling and explain your rationale.

J. Enrichment

67. Make an appointment with a school guidance counselor to discuss the norm-referenced achievement and aptitude tests used by the district. Ask the following questions:
    a. How are tests selected?
    b. Which tests are used at each grade level?
    c. When are the tests administered?
    d. How do administrators and teachers use the test results?
68. If district policy permits, review samples of the following test materials:
    a. The administrator's guide for a test used at your grade level. Find a description of the objectives measured, the norm group, administration procedures, and sample report forms.
    b. Sample individual and group report records from the most recent test. The counselor may want to cover or block out students' names before you review these records.

TABLE 14.13   Individual Test Record for the California Achievement Tests

national stanine

grade equivalent

normal curve equivalent

scale score

local percentile

national percentile

range of confidence band

percentile and confidence band

objective performance index

level of mastery

opi and mastery band

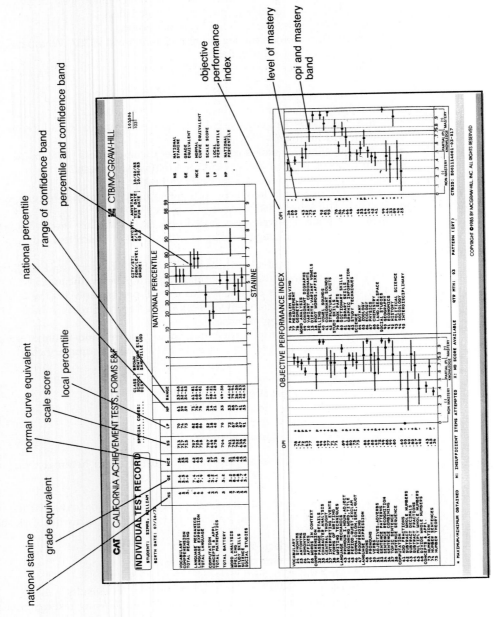

Source: From California Achievement Tests, Forms E and F, Test Coordinator's Handbook. Copyright 1986 by McGraw-Hill, Inc. Reproduced by permission of CTB/McGraw-Hill.

TABLE 14.14 Class Record Sheet for the California Achievement Tests

Source: From California Achievement Tests, Forms C and D, Test Coordinator's Handbook. Copyright 1977, 1978 by McGraw-Hill, Inc. Reproduced by permission of CTB/McGraw-Hill.

419

69. If you have kept your own test records or those of your students, analyze these reports and interpret the scores.

FEEDBACK

A. Matching Test Types and Purposes

Items	1	2	3	4	5	6	7	8
Answers	B	A	C	B	B	A	C	A

B. Converting Raw Scores to Percentiles. For items 9 to 13, see Table 14.11(F).

TABLE 14.11(F)   Raw Scores and Their Corresponding Percentiles

(1) Raw Scores	(2) Frequency	(3) Cumulative Frequency below	(4) 1/2 Frequency within	(5) Proportion	(6) Percentile
40	1	19	.5	19.5/20 = .98	98
39	1	18	.5	18.5/20 = .93	93
38	2	16	1	17/20 = .85	85
37	2	14	1	15/20 = .75	75
36	3	11	1.5	12.5/20 = .63	63
35	3	8	1.5	9.5/20 = .48	48
34	2	6	1	7/20 = .35	35
33	2	4	1	5/20 = .25	25
32	2	2	1	3/20 = .15	15
31	1	1	.5	1.5/20 = .08	8
30	1	0	.5	.5/20 = .03	3

C. Interpreting Percentile Scores. The following statements are correct: 16, 19, 21, 22, 24.
D. Calculating and Plotting Percentile Bands. For items 25 to 27, see Table 14.12(F).
E. Interpreting Percentile Bands. The following statements are correct: 29, 31, 32, 35.
F. Calculating Stanine Scores

Stanine Scores	1	2	3	4	5	6	7	8	9
36. Percentage	4	7	12	17	20	17	12	7	4
37. Number of Students	40	70	120	170	200	170	120	70	40
38. Cumulative Percentage	4	11	23	40	60	77	89	96	100

TABLE 14.12(F)   Percentiles and Their Corresponding Percentile Bands

SEM = 2

	−1 SEM	Obtained Score	+1 SEM	Percentiles 1 5 10 20 30 40 50 60 70 80 90 95 99
X	37	39	40	
%tile	75	93	98	
X	33	35	37	
%tile	25	48	75	
X	30	32	34	
%tile	3	15	35	

Note: The narrow range of raw scores in the example resulted in abnormally wide percentile bands. Because norm-referenced tests are designed to yield a wide range of scores, the percentile bands are narrower.

G. Interpreting Stanine Scores. The following statements are correct: 40, 42, 43, 44, 46.

H. Selecting Scores from the Report Form

Items	47	48	49	50	51	52	53
Scores	C	A	B	C	C	C	C
	G	B				G	

I. Interpreting Test Records

54. 5.1
55. b
56. By determining the performance level indicated by the corresponding percentile or stanine score.
57. It should fall between the 61st and 81st percentiles. This information was obtained by locating the percentiles that correspond to the outer edges of his percentile band for language mechanics.
58. Either percentile bands, stanines, or normal curve equivalent scores.
59. Language
60. Yes
61. Because the percentile bands for these tests do not overlap.
62. His performance is equivalent on the two tests. A GE score of 5.6 in vocabulary is equivalent to a stanine score of 6, and a GE score of 7.4 on the language mechanics test is equivalent to a stanine score of 6. The percentile bands for these two tests overlap.
63. Yes. For the NCE score, the mean is 50 and the standard deviation is 21.06. His score of 27 is lower than 50 − 21.06, or 28.94.
64. In comparison with the national norm group, William's performances in reading and language skills are average. His performance in mathematics, however, is below average.

65. Summary Chart

Spelling Test	OGE	NP
Highest Scores	8.5	65
Lowest Scores	5.1	37
Class Average	7.4	
Norm Group Average	6.0	

66. The percentile scores only range between 37 and 65; therefore, the group is homogeneous. Because rather large differences in percentile scores toward the center of the range are not meaningful, the group's performance can be described as very homogeneous. The mean grade equivalent score for the class is above that for the national norm group.

REFERENCES

CTB/McGraw-Hill. (1978). *California achievement tests: norms tables (level 15, forms C and D)*. Monterey, Calif.: Author, pp. 16–17, 30–31.

CTB/McGraw-Hill. (1978). *California achievement tests: test coordinator's handbook (levels 10–19, forms C and D)*. Monterey, Calif.: Author.

CTB/McGraw-Hill. (1979). *California achievement tests: technical bulletin 1*. Monterey, Calif.: Author, pp. 93–7.

CTB/McGraw-Hill. (1986). *California achievement tests (forms E and F): test coordinator's handbook*. Monterey, Calif.: Author, p. 94.

CTB/McGraw-Hill. (1974). *Comprehensive test of basic skills: examiner's manual (level 4, form S)*. Monterey, Calif.: Author, pp. 46–7, 50–1.

SUGGESTED READING

Crocker, L., and Algina, J. (1986). *Introduction to classical and modern test theory*. New York: CBS College Publishing, pp. 431–55.

Ebel, R. L., and Frisbie, D. A. (1986). *Essentials of educational measurement*. Englewood Cliffs, N.J.: Prentice-Hall, pp. 267–86, 288–99, 301–15.

Gronlund, N. E. (1985). *Measurement and evaluation in teaching*. New York: Macmillan Publishing Company, pp. 263–378.

Hills, J. R. (1981). *Measurement and evaluation in the classroom*. Columbus, Ohio: Charles E. Merrill Publishing Company, pp. 119–267.

Mehrens, W. A., and Lehmann, I. J. (1984). *Measurement and evaluation in education and psychology*. New York: CBS College Publishing, pp. 349–451.

Mehrens, W. A., and Lehmann, I. J. (1987). *Using standardized tests in education*. White Plains, N.Y.: Longman.

Nitko, A. J. (1983). *Educational tests and measurement*. New York: Harcourt, Brace, Jovanovich, pp. 355–84, 387–408, 467–85, 537–60.

Popham, W. J. (1981). *Modern educational measurement*. Englewood Cliffs, N.J.: Prentice-Hall, pp. 45–65, 126–54, 156–80, 181–98.

Appendixes

APPENDIX A

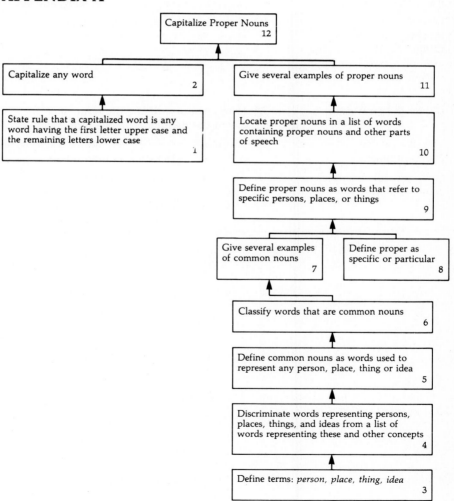

Capitalize Proper Nouns
12

Capitalize any word
2

State rule that a capitalized word is any word having the first letter upper case and the remaining letters lower case
1

Give several examples of proper nouns
11

Locate proper nouns in a list of words containing proper nouns and other parts of speech
10

Define proper nouns as words that refer to specific persons, places, or things
9

Give several examples of common nouns
7

Define proper as specific or particular
8

Classify words that are common nouns
6

Define common nouns as words used to represent any person, place, thing or idea
5

Discriminate words representing persons, places, things, and ideas from a list of words representing these and other concepts
4

Define terms: *person, place, thing, idea*
3

FIGURE 3.3
A Learning Hierarchy for the Instructional Goal: Capitalize Proper Nouns

APPENDIX B

TABLE 3.7   Behavioral Objectives for the Instructional Goal: Capitalize Proper Nouns (Figure 3.3)

Subordinate Skill	*Matching Behavioral Objectives*
1. State the rule for capitalizing words	1.1 From memory, state the rule for capitalizing words. 1.2 Select the rule for capitalizing words from a set of alternative rules.
2. Capitalize any word	2.1 Given a list of several words, select the letter in the words that should be capitalized. 2.2 Given some words that are properly capitalized and some that are improperly capitalized, select those that are properly capitalized.
3. Define the terms *person, place, thing,* and *idea*	3.1 From memory, define the terms *person, place, thing,* and *idea*. 3.2 Match the terms *person, place, thing,* and *idea* with their definitions.
4. Discriminate words that represent persons, places, things, and ideas from lists of words containing these and other concepts	4.1 Given a list of words that contains persons, places, things, and ideas, classify each word into the appropriate category.
5. Define the term *noun*	5.1 From memory, define the term *noun*. 5.2 Given the definition for the term *noun*, identify it as such.
6. Classify words that are common nouns	6.1 Given a list of words containing common nouns and other parts of speech, select the common nouns.
7. Give several examples of common nouns	7.1 List several words that refer to persons. 7.2 List several words that refer to places. 7.3 List several words that refer to things. 7.4 List several words that refer to ideas.

TABLE 3.7 (*continued*)

Subordinate Skill	Matching Behavioral Objectives
8. Define the term *proper* as specific or particular	8.1 From memory, define the term *proper*. 8.2 Given several definitions, select the one for the word *proper*. 8.3 Given the definition of the word *proper*, identify it as such.
9. Define proper nouns as words that refer to specific persons, places, or things.	9.1 From memory, define proper nouns. 9.2 Given several definitions, select the one for proper nouns. 9.3 Given the definition for a proper noun, identify it as such.
10. Classify words as proper nouns	10.1 Given a list of words containing both proper and common nouns, with some proper nouns not capitalized and some common nouns capitalized, select the proper nouns.
11. Give several examples of proper nouns	11.1 Given the category, *persons*, list several proper nouns that name persons. 11.2 Given the category, *places*, list several proper nouns that name places. 11.3 Given the category, *things*, list several proper nouns that name things.
12. Capitalize proper nouns (goal)	12.1 Given sentences that include proper nouns that are not capitalized and common nouns that are capitalized, locate the capitalization errors. 12.2 Write sentences that include proper nouns and capitalize the proper nouns.

APPENDIX C

TABLE 4.1 Table of Specifications for a Unit on Capitalizing Proper Nouns

| Major Skill Groups | Recall (Knowledge and Comprehension) | | *Learning* | |
	Subordinate Skills	Behavioral Objectives	Item Format[a]	Number of Items
Capitalize words (prerequisite skill)	1. State the rule for capitalizing words	1.1 From memory state the rule for capitalizing words.	W	1
		1.2 Select the rule for capitalizing words from a set of alternative rules.	S	1
Common nouns (prerequisite skill)	3. Define terms *person*, *place*, *thing*, and *idea*	3.1 From memory, define the terms *person*, *place*, *thing*, and *idea*.	W	4
		3.2 Match the terms *person*, *place*, *thing*, and *idea* with their definitions.	S	4
	5. Define the term *noun*	5.1 From memory, define the term *noun*.	W	1
		5.2 Given the definition for the term *noun*, identify it as such.	W/S	1
Proper nouns (enabling skills)	8. Define the term *proper* as specific or particular	8.1 From memory, define the term *proper*.	W	1
		8.2 Given several definitions, select the one for the word *proper*.	S	1
		8.3 Given the definition of the word *proper*, identify it as such.	W/S	1
	9. Define proper nouns as words that refer to specific persons, places, or things.	9.1 From memory, define proper nouns.	W	1
		9.2 Given several definitions, select the one for proper nouns.	S	1
		9.3 Given the definition for a proper noun, identify it as such.	W/S	1

[a] Item format codes: W = Write response from memory; S = Select response from among alternatives; W/S = Either write or select response.

Application

Subordinate Skills	Behavioral Objectives	Item Format	Number of Items
2. Capitalize any word	2.1 Given a list of several words, select the letter in the words that should be capitalized.	S	5
	2.2 Given some words that are properly capitalized and some that are improperly capitalized, select those that are properly capitalized.	S	5
4. Discriminate words that represent persons, places, things, and ideas from lists of words containing these and other concepts	4.1 Given a list of words that contains persons, places, things, and ideas, classify each word into the appropriate category.	S	12
6. Classify words that are common nouns	6.1 Given a list of words containing common nouns and other parts of speech, select the common nouns.	S	15
7. Give several examples of common nouns	7.1 List several words that refer to persons.	W	2
	7.2 List several words that refer to places.	W	2
	7.3 List several words that refer to things.	W	2
	7.4 List several words that refer to ideas.	W	2
10. Classify words as proper nouns	10.1 Given a list of words containing both proper and common nouns, with some proper nouns not capitalized and some common nouns capitalized, select the proper nouns.	S	16
11. Give several examples of proper nouns	11.1 Given the category, *persons*, list several proper nouns that name persons.	W	2
	11.2 Given the category, *places*, list several proper nouns that name places.	W	2
	11.3 Given the category, *things*, list several proper nouns that name things.	W	2
12. Capitalize proper nouns (goal)	12.1 Given sentences that include proper nouns that are not capitalized and common nouns that are capitalized, locate the capitalization errors.	S	5
	12.2 Write sentences that include proper nouns and capitalize the proper nouns.	W	3

TABLE 4.1A   Selected Objectives for Entry Behaviors Test, Pretest, Practice Tests, and Posttest

Entry Behaviors Test

Objectives (See Appendix D)	1.2	2.1	3.2	4.1	5.2	6.1	7.1	7.2	7.3	7.4	Total Items
Number of Items	1	5	4	12	1	15	2	2	2	2	46

Pretest

Objectives (See Appendix E)	8.2	9.2	10.1	11.1	11.2	11.3	12.1				
Number of Items	1	1	16	2	2	2	5				29

Practice Test One

Objectives (See Appendix F)	8.1	9.1	10.1								
Number of Items	1	1	16								18

Practice Test Two

Objectives (See Appendix F)	8.3	9.3	10.1	11.1	11.2	11.3					
Number of Items	1	1	16	2	2	2					24

Practice Test Three

Objectives (See Appendix F)	11.1	11.2	11.3	12.1	12.2						
Number of Items	2	2	2	5	5						16

Posttest

Objectives (See Appendix G)	8.2	9.2	10.1	11.1	11.2	11.3	12.1	12.2			
Number of Items	1	1	16	2	2	2	5	3			32

APPENDIX D

Entry	Objectives Passed _____	Capitalize Proper Nouns
Behaviors	Score _____	
Test	Name _____	Date _____
Objective		

1.2

1. To capitalize a word, which letters in the word would you capitalize?
   a. All the letters
   b. Only the first letter
   c. Only the first two letters
   d. Only the last letter

2.1

Directions: For each of the following words, circle the letter or letters that would be capitalized if you wanted to capitalize the word.

2. box
3. cat
4. hat
5. letters
6. candy

3.2

Directions: Match definitions and terms. List 1 contains definitions and List 2 contains terms. Draw a line from each definition to the term it defines. There are more terms than you will need.

List 1	*List 2*
7. A human being or people	a. common
8. An object	b. idea
9. A building, a park, a city, or a state	c. person
	d. place
10. A thought	e. thing

4.1

Directions: For each word, select whether it means an idea (I), a person (PR), a place (PL), or a thing (TH). If you think the word means an idea, circle the I. If you think it means a person, circle the PR. If you think it means a place, circle the PL. If you think it means a thing, circle the TH.

Words	Idea	Person	Place	Thing
11. boy	I	PR	PL	TH
12. book	I	PR	PL	TH
13. library	I	PR	PL	TH
14. holiday	I	PR	PL	TH
15. uncle	I	PR	PL	TH
16. pencil	I	PR	PL	TH
17. town	I	PR	PL	TH
18. religion	I	PR	PL	TH
19. doll	I	PR	PL	TH
20. teacher	I	PR	PL	TH
21. playground	I	PR	PL	TH
22. bike	I	PR	PL	TH

Objective

5.2	23. Words that refer to ideas, persons, places, or things are called _____ .

6.1   Which of the following words are nouns? Place an <u>N</u> before each word that is a noun.

____	24. happy	____	32. school
____	25. leg	____	33. puppy
____	26. singing	____	34. fast
____	27. mother	____	35. try
____	28. hurry	____	36. barn
____	29. fish	____	37. mailman
____	30. chair	____	38. running
____	31. skinny		

7.1   Name two words that refer to people.
39. _____   40. _____

7.2   Name two words that refer to places.
41. _____   42. _____

7.3   Name two words that refer to things.
43. _____   44. _____

7.4   Name two words that refer to ideas.
45. _____   46. _____

APPENDIX E

Pretest	Objectives Passed _____	Capitalize Proper Nouns
	Score _____	
	Name _____	Date _____
Objective		

8.2   _____ 1. Which of the following terms means the same as the term <u>proper</u> as it relates to nouns?
   a. any one
   b. general
   c. specific

9.2   _____ 2. Which of the following definitions is the one for <u>proper nouns</u>?
   a. A word that means any person, place, or thing
   b. A word that names a particular person, place or thing
   c. A word that names common nouns

10.1   *Directions:* From the following list of words, choose the ones that are <u>proper nouns</u>. Place a √ in front of the proper nouns. Be careful because some of the capital letters might fool you. Some proper nouns are <u>not</u> capitalized, and some common nouns are capitalized!

Words	*Words*
_____ 3. Corn	_____ 11. Nurse
_____ 4. Thomas Park	_____ 12. Memorial Library
_____ 5. Jack	_____ 13. Cherry Pie
_____ 6. School	_____ 14. parker house
_____ 7. bubble gum	_____ 15. baseball
_____ 8. bakery	_____ 16. mr. smith
_____ 9. Marty	_____ 17. turtle
_____ 10. snoopy (the dog)	_____ 18. snickers candy

11.1   Write two <u>proper nouns</u> that refer to <u>persons</u>.
19. _____   20. _____

11.2   Write two <u>proper nouns</u> that refer to <u>places</u>.
21. _____   22. _____

11.3   Write two <u>proper nouns</u> that refer to <u>things</u>.
23. _____   24. _____

12.1   *Directions:* Locate the <u>capitalization mistakes</u> in the following sentences. <u>Circle</u> any word that is capitalized and <u>should not be</u> and any word that <u>should be</u> capitalized but is not.
25. It was Raining on the day of the circus.
26. They played at jim's house until dark.
27. My puppy ate all the food and drank all the milk.
28. They went to the old mill restaurant for Annie's birthday.
29. The crossing guard, mr. jones, has a mickey mouse watch.

APPENDIX F

Practice   Objectives Passed _____   Capitalize Proper Nouns

Test 1   Score _____

                    Name _____   Date _____

Objectives

8.1   1. Define the term *proper* as it relates to <u>proper nouns</u>. _____

9.1   2. What is a <u>proper noun</u>? _____

10.1   *Directions:* From the following list of words, choose the ones that are <u>proper nouns</u>. Place a √ in front of the proper nouns. Be careful or some of the capital letters will fool you. Some proper nouns are <u>not</u> capitalized, and some common nouns are capitalized!

Words	*Words*
____ 3. pop corn	____ 11. pluto
____ 4. Horse	____ 12. Katie
____ 5. gerry allen	____ 13. food store
____ 6. pepsi cola	____ 14. boat
____ 7. garfield school	____ 15. Mr. Brown
____ 8. Jelly	____ 16. Terry's Market
____ 9. Kelly Ball Park	____ 17. city
____ 10. Mailman	____ 18. Girl

Practice   Objectives Passed _____   Capitalize Proper Nouns

Test 2   Score _____

                    Name _____   Date _____

Objectives

8.3   1. Another name for *specific* or *particular* is _____ .

9.3   2. A word that refers to a particular person, place, or thing is called a _____ .

10.1   *Directions:* From the following list of words, choose the ones that are <u>proper nouns</u>. Place a √ in front of the proper nouns. Be careful or some of the capital letters will fool you. Some proper nouns are <u>not</u> capitalized, and some common nouns are capitalized!

Words	*Words*
____ 3. cinderella	____ 11. peanut butter
____ 4. ron	____ 12. Donkey
____ 5. shoe store	____ 13. terry smith
____ 6. shoe	____ 14. planter's peanuts
____ 7. Miss Taylor	____ 15. memorial hospital
____ 8. Bill's Seafood Restaurant	____ 16. Soda Pop
____ 9. florida	____ 17. Lowrey Park
____ 10. Baby	____ 18. Fireman

Objective

11.1	Write two <u>proper nouns</u> that refer to <u>persons</u>.
	19. _____ 20. _____
11.2	Write two <u>proper nouns</u> that refer to <u>places</u>.
	21. _____ 22. _____
11.3	Write two <u>proper nouns</u> that refer to <u>things</u>.
	23. _____ 24. _____

Practice

Test 3

Objectives Passed _____   Capitalize Proper Nouns

Score _____

Name _____ Date _____

11.1   Write two <u>proper nouns</u> that refer to <u>persons</u>.
1. _____   2. _____

11.2   Write two <u>proper nouns</u> that refer to <u>places</u>.
3. _____   4. _____

11.3   Write two <u>proper nouns</u> that refer to <u>things</u>.
5. _____   6. _____

12.1   *Directions:*   Locate the capitalization <u>mistakes</u> in the following sentences. <u>Circle</u> any word that is capitalized and <u>should not be</u> and any word that <u>should be</u> capitalized but is not.
   7. Neither jane nor mickey could go to the Game.
   8. They ate all the cracker jacks in a hurry.
   9. Jerry rode his bicycle to the Library to borrow some books.
   10. Darcy usually does her homework before she plays the piano.
   11. We went to miller's planetarium to see the stars through the Telescope.

12.2   12. Write one sentence that has a proper noun that refers to a <u>person</u>. _____
_____

Directions: Write two sentences that have a <u>proper noun</u> related to <u>places</u>.
13. _____
14. _____

Directions: Write two sentences that have a <u>proper noun</u> related to things.
15. _____
16. _____

APPENDIX G

Posttest

Objectives Passed _____   Capitalize Proper Nouns

Score _____

Name _____   Date _____

Objective

8.2

___ 1. Which of the following words means the <u>same</u> as <u>proper</u>?
   a. common
   b. particular
   c. noun

9.2

___ 2. What is a <u>proper noun</u>?
   a. a word that modifies a noun
   b. a word that refers to any person, place, or thing
   c. a word that refers to a specific person, place, or thing

10.1

Directions: From the following list of words, choose the ones that are <u>proper nouns</u>. Place a √ in front of the <u>proper nouns</u>. Be careful because some of the capital letters may fool you. Some proper nouns are <u>not</u> capitalized, and some common nouns are capitalized!

Words	*Words*
___ 3. Light	___ 11. janitor
___ 4. London Zoo	___ 12. Brook's Toy Store
___ 5. tom	___ 13. Apple Cake
___ 6. Drug Store	___ 14. new york city
___ 7. mashed potatoes	___ 15. soccer
___ 8. fire station	___ 16. Mrs. Rust
___ 9. Andrew	___ 17. kitten
___ 10. superman	___ 18. jones's cough syrup

11.1

Write two proper nouns that refer to <u>persons</u>.
19. _____   20. _____

11.2

Write two <u>proper nouns</u> that refer to <u>places</u>.
21. _____   22. _____

11.3

Write two <u>proper nouns</u> that refer to <u>things</u>.
23. _____   24. _____

12.1

Directions: Locate the capitalization <u>mistakes</u> in the following sentences. <u>Circle</u> any word that is capitalized and <u>should not be</u> and any word that <u>should be</u> capitalized but is not.

25. The School bus had a flat tire Today.
26. It was about Seven O'clock when they returned.
27. On the way to the Park, jill saw many of her Friends.
28. John, the new Boy at orange park school, came from alaska.
29. On cold mornings, jerry likes to eat quaker oats.

12.2

30. Write a sentence that has a <u>proper noun</u> that refers to a <u>person</u>.
31. Write a sentence that has a <u>proper noun</u> that refers to a <u>place</u>.
32. Write a sentence that has a <u>proper noun</u> that refers to a <u>thing</u>.

APPENDIX H

TABLE 10.2   Item Summary Table for Posttest on Capitalization

Goals	First Word			Pronoun I			Proper Nouns						Proper Adjectives				Days and Months				Total Score
Items #:	7	11	14	3	9	17	1	5	13	16	8	19	2	6	10	18	4	12	15	20	
Correct Answers:	1	1	1	3	3	2	4	4	4	3	3	2	2	3	2	3	3	4	3	4	20
Rogers																					20
Jackson																					20
Ayres																					20
Augustine																					20
Deddens																					20
Talbot												3									19
McCoy												3									19
Jensen												3									19
Prince											3	3									18
Rust											2	3									18
R_U	10	10	10	10	10	10	10	10	8	10	10	5	10	10	10	10	10	10	10	10	
Wilson									3			3	1								17
Boyd									3			3		3							17
Merrill									2	2	1			3							16
Jones									1					3					2	2	16
Hart										1	2			3				1		2	15
Little								2			1			3					2	3	15
Moyle								2	3					3					4	1	15
Brown								2	3		1			3					2	2	14
Bentley								2	3	2	4		1	3			2				13
Rogers									3		2	2		3			1	3	2	3	12
R_L	10	10	10	10	10	10	10	6	2	6	4	8	10	8	1	10	8	9	4	4	
p	1.00	1.00	1.00	1.00	1.00	1.00	1.00	.80	.50	.80	.70	.65	1.00	.90	.55	1.00	.90	.95	.70	.70	
d	.00	.00	.00	.00	.00	.00	.00	.40	.60	.40	.60	−.30	.00	.20	.90	.00	.20	.10	.60	.60	
Item Number	7	11	14	3	9	17	1	5	13	16	8	19	2	6	10	18	4	12	15	20	

APPENDIX I

TABLE 10.5 A Summary Table for Organizing and Interpreting Difficulty and Discrimination Indices

Difficulty Classification			Easy			Moderately Easy				Fairly Difficult				Very Difficult
Maximum ∓*d*			.00	.10	.20	.30	.40	.50	.60	.70	.80	.90	1.00	.90–.00
Values of p			1.00	.95	.90	.85	.80	.75	.70	.65	.60	.55	.50	.45 ↓
Goals: Capitalize:		Items												*p/d*
First word of sentence		7	.00											
		11	.00											
		14	.00											
Pronoun I		3	.00											
		9	.00											
		17	.00											
Proper nouns	PR	1	.00											
	PL	15					.40							
	PL	13											.60	
	PL	16					.40							
	TH	8							.60					
	TH	19								− .30				
Proper adjectives		2	.00											
		6			.20									
		10										.90		
		18	.00											
Days and months		4			.20									
		12		.10										
		15							.60					
		20							.60					

TABLE 10.6   A Summary of Distractor Data for Selected Items on the Capitalization Posttest

Reason for Review	Goal	Item	Group	Responses				
				1	2	3	4	5
Items more difficult than anticipated	Capitalize proper adjectives	10	U		10*			
			L		1*	9		
	Capitalize days and months	15	U			10*		
			L	1	4	4*	1	
		20	U				10*	
			L	1	3	2	4*	
Items initially judged to be complex	Proper nouns	5	U				10*	
			L		4		6*	
		13	U		1	1	8*	
			L	1	1	6	2*	
		16	U			10*		
			L	1	3	6*		
		8	U			10*		
			L	3	2	4*	1	
Item discriminates negatively		19	U		5*	5		
			L		8*	2		

* Correct Answers

APPENDIX J

TABLE 11.1   A Frequency Distribution of Scores on the First Capitalization Test

	Raw Scores X	Tally	Frequency
Highest Possible Score	20	~~1111~~ 111	8
	19	11	2
	18	11	2
	17		0
	16	11	2
	15	111	3
	14	1	1
	13	1	1
	12	1	1
	•		
	•		
Lowest Possible Score	0		

FIGURE 11.3   A Frequency Polygon for Students' Scores on the First Capitalization Test

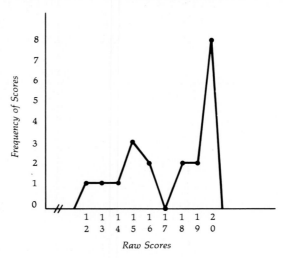

TABLE 11.2 Calculating the Mean Using a Frequency Table

1. Multiply each score by its frequency and sum the products.

Raw Scores X		Frequency f		Product fX
20	×	8	=	160
19	×	2	=	38
18	×	2	=	36
17	×	0	=	0
16	×	2	=	32
15	×	3	=	45
14	×	1	=	14
13	×	1	=	13
12	×	1	=	12
		$\sum X =$		350

2. Divide $\sum X$ by the number of students (20).

$$\overline{X} = \frac{350}{20} = 17.5$$

TABLE 11.3 Calculation of the Standard Deviation for the First Capitalization Test

$(X - \overline{X})$	x	x^2	
20 − 17.5 =	2.5	6.25	*Formula*
20 − 17.5 =	2.5	6.25	
20 − 17.5 =	2.5	6.25	
20 − 17.5 =	2.5	6.25	$SD = \sqrt{\dfrac{\sum(X - \overline{X})^2}{N}}$
20 − 17.5 =	2.5	6.25	
20 − 17.5 =	2.5	6.25	
20 − 17.5 =	2.5	6.25	
20 − 17.5 =	2.5	6.25	$= \sqrt{\dfrac{141}{20}}$
19 − 17.5 =	1.5	2.25	
19 − 17.5 =	1.5	2.25	$= \sqrt{7.05}$
18 − 17.5 =	.5	.25	
18 − 17.5 =	.5	.25	$= 2.66$
16 − 17.5 =	−1.5	2.25	
16 − 17.5 =	−1.5	2.25	
15 − 17.5 =	−2.5	6.25	
15 − 17.5 =	−2.5	6.25	
15 − 17.5 =	−2.5	6.25	
14 − 17.5 =	−3.5	12.25	
13 − 17.5 =	−4.5	20.25	
12 − 17.5 =	−5.5	30.25	
$\sum x^2 = 141$			

TABLE 11.4   A Summary of the Predicted and Observed Measures of Group Performance on the First Capitalization Test

Performance Indicator	Estimation Based on Relatively Easy Tasks and a Heterogeneous Group	Observation	Discrepancy
Location of highest earned score	The highest possible score	The highest possible score	None
Location of the lowest earned score	Slightly more than half the number of items correct	12 or 60% of the items correct	None
Location of the mean score	Close to the high end of the distribution	17 or 85% correct	None
Location of the median score	Higher than the mean score	18.5	None
Location of the mode	Around the mean and median	Around the mean and median	None
Range	Between one-third and one-half of the total number of items. $$\frac{20}{3} = 6.66$$ $$\frac{20}{2} = 10$$	8	None
Standard deviation	Somewhere around one-third of the range: $$\frac{8}{3} = 2.66$$	2.66	None
Distribution shape	Negatively skewed	Negatively skewed	None

APPENDIX K

TABLE 12.1   Mastery Analysis of Students' Performances on the First Capitalization Posttest

Goals	First Word			Pronoun I			Proper Nouns						Proper Adjectives				Days and Months				Total Score	Goals Mastered
Items #	7	11	14	3	9	17	1	5	13	16	8	19	2	6	10	18	4	12	15	20		
Correct Answers	1	1	1	3	3	2	4	4	4	3	3	2	2	3	2	3	3	4	3	4	20	
Rogers, T.																					20	5
Jackson																					20	5
Ayres																					20	5
Augustine																					20	5
Deddens																					20	5
Talbot												3									19	5
McCoy												3									19	5
Jensen												3									19	5
Prince									3			3									18	4
Rust									2			3									18	4
Wilson									3			3	1								17	4
Boyd									3			3		3							17	4
Merrill									2	2	1			3							16	4
Jones									1					3					2	2	16	4
Hart										1	2			3					1	2	15	3
Little								2			1			3					2	3	15	3
Moyle								2	3					3					4	1	15	3
Brown								2	3		1			3					2	2	14	3
Bentley								2	3	2	4		1	3			2				13	3
Rogers, B.									3	2	2			3			1	3	2	3	12	3
Number who mastered goal	20			20			9						19				14					
Percentage who mastered goal	100			100			45						95				70					

FIGURE 12.3 Prescribed Instructional Activities for Capitalization Based on Mastery Analysis

| | Activities | | |
| | Additional Instruction and Practice | | |
Enrichment	Proper Nouns	Proper Adjectives	Days and Months
Augustine	Bentley	Bentley	
Ayres	Boyd		
	Brown		
Deddens	Hart		
Jackson	Little		Brown
Jensen	Merrill		Hart
McCoy	Moyle		Little
	Prince		Jones
Rogers, T.	Rogers, B.		Moyle
	Rust		
Talbot	Wilson		Rogers, B.

FIGURE 12.4 Evaluation of Instruction Based on Percentage of Students Mastering Each Capitalization Goal

Goal	Total Number of Students Mastering Goal	Percentage of Students Mastering Goal
Capitalize		
1. First word	20	100
2. Pronoun *I*	20	100
3. Proper nouns	11	45
4. Proper adjectives	19	95
5. Days and Months	14	70

TABLE 12.2　A Student Progress Chart for the First Capitalization Posttest

Students	First Word	Pronoun "I"	Proper Nouns	Proper Adjectives	Days and Months
Augustine	X	X	X	X	X
Ayres	X	X	X	X	X
Bentley	X	X			X
Boyd	X	X		X	X
Brown	X	X		X	
Deddens	X	X	X	X	X
Hart	X	X		X	
Jackson	X	X	X	X	X
Jensen	X	X	X	X	X
Jones	X	X	X	X	
Little	X	X		X	
McCoy	X	X	X	X	X
Merrill	X	X		X	X
Moyle	X	X		X	
Prince	X	X		X	X
Rogers, B.	X	X		X	
Rogers, T.	X	X	X	X	X
Rust	X	X		X	X
Talbot	X	X	X	X	X
Wilson	X	X		X	X

Index